ANCIENT RECORDS OF EGYPT

VOLUME 1

The First through the Seventeenth Dynasties

ANCIENT RECORDS OF EGYPT

VOLUME 1

*The First through the
Seventeenth Dynasties*

Translated and Edited by

JAMES HENRY BREASTED

Introduction by

PETER A. PICCIONE

UNIVERSITY OF ILLINOIS PRESS

Urbana and Chicago

FRONTISPIECE: James Henry Breasted, copying a hieroglyphic text
in the Temple of Buhen, Egypt; Egyptian Expedition of the University
of Chicago, Oriental Exploration Fund, Egyptian Section;
photographed by Friedrich Koch, 1906.
Courtesy of The Oriental Institute of
the University of Chicago.

First Illinois paperback, 2001
Introduction © 2001 by Peter A. Piccione
All rights reserved
Manufactured in the United States of America
P 5 4 3 2 1
⊗ This book is printed on acid-free paper.

Library of Congress Cataloging-in-Publication Data
Ancient records of Egypt / translated and edited by
James Henry Breasted ; introduction and supplementary
bibliographies by Peter A. Piccione.
p.   cm.
Originally published: Chicago : University of Chicago Press, 1906.
Includes bibliographical references and indexes.
Contents: v. 1. The first through the seventeenth dynasties —
v. 2. The eighteenth dynasty — v. 3. The nineteenth dynasty —
v. 4. The twentieth through the twenty-sixth dynasties —
v. 5. Supplementary bibliographies and indices.
ISBN 0-252-06990-0 (vol. 1 : pbk. : alk. paper) — ISBN 0-252-06974-9
(vol. 2 : pbk. : alk. paper) —ISBN 0-252-06975-7 (vol. 3 : pbk. : alk.
paper) —ISBN 0-252-06976-5 (vol. 4 : pbk. : alk. paper) —
ISBN 0-252-06991-9 (vol. 5 : pbk. : alk. paper)
1. Egypt—History—To 332 B.C.—Sources.
I. Breasted, James Henry, 1865–1935.
DT83.A658   2001
932—dc21   00-053216

University of Illinois Press
1325 South Oak Street
Champaign, IL 61820-6903
www.press.uillinois.edu

TABLE OF CONTENTS

VOLUME I

VOLUME II

LIST OF FIGURES

VOLUME III

LIST OF FIGURES

VOLUME IV

LIST OF FIGURES

INTRODUCTION TO THE ILLINOIS PAPERBACK

Peter A. Piccione

The years 2000 and 2001 mark the transition to the third millennium of modern human history. By comparison, the field of Egyptology is less than two centuries old. Jean-François Champollion completed the decipherment of Egyptian hieroglyphs in 1824. Since then we have seen, generation by generation, Egyptologists the likes of Mariette, Lepsius, Petrie, Breasted, Černý, Habachi, and all of their respective contemporaries who have contributed their researches and understanding to the study of ancient Egypt. Recent years have seen the torch of inquiry pass to a new generation of scholars, ever broadening the frontiers of our knowledge of ancient Egyptian civilization, its culture, languages, history, and archaeology. And yet, even as scholarship continues to improve and new standards of research evolve, Egyptologists are always aware that they stand academically on the shoulders of their predecessors, accumulating new knowledge and insights and building upon and refining earlier interpretations, as well as rejecting them where appropriate. Generally, even when they discard older Egyptologists' notions or translations as obsolete, they still regard those scholars and their work with great respect. Indeed, that work might represent the highest standard of scholarship for its time. Furthermore, to know that something is not true of a historical process is almost as valuable as knowing what is true. In that regard, no honest study of the past is ever in vain, and it will always have some meaning and value for later scholars.

Of course, no scholar writes with the intent that his or her work will eventually become obsolete. It is also true that all scholars want their findings, interpretations, and translations to stand the test of time—for as much of it as possible to be as true in the future as it appears to be in the present. As for bygone Egyptologists, the longer their work, at least in part, remains cogent or unsurpassed by modern scholarship, the more highly regarded they remain by current scholars. In this sense, many past Egyptologists have been more fortunate than others, because a high percentage of their work is still valid or useful for building new historical inferences. Here we include the likes of Borchardt, Gardiner, Lefebvre, Petrie, Piankoff, and many others. These Egyptologists include, for the most part, archaeologists and the publishers of texts and documents, although perhaps only few strictly interpretive historians and analysts. The fact is publications of purely archaeological data or inscriptions have a longer scholastic lifetime than do wholly interpretive and synthetical studies, which can be heavily dependent on the current state of historical and linguistic knowledge, which is always in flux. Egyptologists could increase the longevity of their publications by confining their scholarship to archaeology and epigraphy or by basing their interpretive studies solidly on the widest amount of archaeological data or the greatest breadth possible of primary texts and documents.

In general, the research and publications of Professor James Henry Breasted fall into the latter category. Dr. Breasted was among the brightest of that third generation of Egyptologists who began their studies at the end of the nineteenth century and labored mostly in the first third of the twentieth century. Born in Illinois in 1865, James Breasted was educated at Yale University. Thereafter, he studied at the University of Berlin, where he received his doctorate in 1894 in Oriental Studies. As an Orientalist, Breasted was erudite in the history, languages, religion, art, and archaeology of most of the major cultures of the ancient Near East, including Egypt, Palestine, Syria, Phoenicia, Mesopotamia, Persia, and Anatolia. However, his particular specialization was ancient Egypt. In 1895, he joined the faculty of the University of Chicago, which at that time was the only university in the United States to offer studies in ancient Egyptian civilization. In 1901 he was appointed director of the Haskell Oriental Museum at the university. In 1905, he was promoted to the first academic chair of Egyptology in America, and today he is recognized as the father of ancient Near Eastern studies in the United States, as distinct from biblical history and Bible studies. It was James Breasted who coined the term "Fertile Crescent" to refer to the arc of habitable land in western Asia where civilization first evolved. In 1935, at the age of seventy, he died from pneumonia which he contracted on a voyage home from Egypt.

The period in which Breasted worked was a formative one in scientific and academic research, including Egyptology and Near Eastern studies. The ini-

tial decipherment of Egyptian writing and the first opening of Egyptian civilization in the nineteenth century led to more systematic understanding of
Egyptian languages and texts by the early twentieth century. Scholars were
learning to be more circumspect in their historical and linguistic analyses,
as well as more sophisticated in their interpretations of history and culture.
Even before the turn of the century, William Flinders Petrie was already in-
venting a rigorous empirical method in archaeological excavation and publication. The era of Egyptology's third generation was an exciting time, as a
large number of new archaeological sites were being excavated and identified.
Famous biblical cities were being unearthed, so that for the first time scholars possessed contemporary Egyptian sources of information that were independent of biblical accounts and free of Hebrew/Israelite interpretations.
Zoan had become Tanis; Pithom was Pi-Atum; and On was Iunu (Heliopolis). Egyptologists were discovering or publishing even greater numbers of
hieroglyphic and hieratic inscriptions, leading philologists to write more
advanced grammars of Egyptian languages and even to begin compiling a
great dictionary of ancient Egyptian. In Breasted's era, Egyptology had out-
grown its infancy and entered its adolescence. Scholars were marveling at
the newly discovered splendors of the Egyptian past, and yet because they
had only selective access to historical data and texts, they tended to be over-
ly romantic about the Egyptians' achievements, for example, by incorrectly
ascribing to them the first development of religious monotheism, the invention of rational medicine, et cetera.

Breasted was swept up in the scientific discourse of the day, which included
such subjects as evolution, anthropology, paleontology, geology, physics, and
astronomy. His own personal experience with science was a direct one, since
even before he attended Yale University, he had completed an earlier course
in pharmacy and had even worked a brief time as a pharmacist. Later, as an
Egyptologist, among his closest confidants was the famous astronomer
George Ellery Hale. In Europe, Egyptology and Assyriology had originally
developed as adjuncts to classical studies, while in the United States they were
primarily an outgrowth of biblical studies. Even Breasted himself had begun
his ancient studies as a Bible student. However, his appreciation of contemporary scientific dialogue ultimately led him to develop a new vision for
American Egyptology and Near Eastern studies, in which their methodologies would be based more on empirical scientific method than on a traditional

classical or biblical approach. His early letters and writings are full of this vision. Just as paleontology and anthropology were scientific disciplines for researching the origins and evolution of the human species, so Near Eastern studies and archaeology would become scientifically based disciplines for unraveling the origins and evolution of human civilization.

Although, compared to the Europeans, Americans had come late to Egyptology and Near Eastern studies, Breasted realized that developing the scientific methodologies of this new approach could be America's lasting contribution to these fields. In time Breasted came to realize the need to establish a new institute for the comprehensive study of the ancient Near East modeled along the lines of scientific inquiry. Sometimes he even referred to this institute as a "research laboratory."[1] Ultimately, he managed to convince some of the most rational of people, namely, the corporate industrial and commercial leaders of the United States, including John D. Rockefeller Jr. (Standard Oil), Martin Ryerson (Inland Steel), and Julius Rosenwald (Sears and Roebuck). By 1919, with their help, he founded the Oriental Institute of the University of Chicago. Here was an international center for broad-ranging interdisciplinary research in the civilizations and languages of the ancient Near East. By 1923, through the nomination of George Ellery Hale, Breasted became the first historian and archaeologist elected to the U.S. National Academy of Sciences. This achievement was a significant milestone, indicating that the science academy had finally recognized and accepted historical archaeology and Breasted's approach to the past as a science and not merely an aspect of antiquarianism. His admission ultimately paved the way for many other famous archaeologists into the academy, including Robert McCormack Adams, William F. Albright, Robert Braidwood, Patty Jo Watson, and others.

Breasted maintained a scientific approach in his own writings and research, not only in such landmark seminal studies as *The Edwin Smith Surgical Papyrus* (1930) but even in the writing of general history. As a philologist and historian, he recognized very early the need to assemble a compendium specifically of all the ancient Egyptian historical texts that were known at the time. The texts would date from the inception of Egyptian history in the fourth millennium B.C. to the end of its independence after the Persian conquest in 525 B.C. Only by assembling and translating a complete corpus of such texts could he provide himself with the historical data he would need on which to base a new and comprehensive history of ancient Egypt. At the same time, this corpus would serve as a major tool for teaching ancient Egyptian history and culture in the university classroom.

Immediately after completing his doctorate, Breasted embarked on the collecting and translating of Egyptian historical texts wherever they happened to be, either in situ among the monuments and ruins of Egypt and Nubia or in the museums of Europe and the United States. In this activity, he also ultimately served as a collector and copyist for the great Berlin Egyptian Dictionary project (later to be published as the *Wörterbuch der ägyptischen Sprache* [1926–31]). Under an endowment of the German kaiser, the four royal academies of Germany (those of Berlin, Göttingen, Leipzig, and Munich) had joined to prepare a new dictionary of the languages of ancient Egypt. In scope, this dictionary was to be fully comprehensive, since ideally, every word from every known Egyptian hieroglyphic and hieratic text was to be copied, collected, catalogued, and analyzed for its meaning. To accomplish these ends, the German academicians culled through all the publications of Egyptian inscriptions. They also commissioned a number of Egyptologists, including Breasted, to copy unpublished texts from monuments, papyri, and objects located in western museums or found throughout Egypt. For Breasted, the task of copying consumed years of intermittent labor—whenever he could steal time from teaching and his other regular duties.

Given the immense numbers of Egyptian inscriptions, it might seem ludicrous to us to consider trying to publish all the known historical texts. However, the number of inscriptions known to Egyptologists by the early twentieth century was small compared to what we have today. Literally thousands of new Egyptian documents and inscriptions have been discovered or unearthed since Breasted's generation, and they consist of all manner of historical texts, letters, legal and economic documents, literary texts, mathematical and medical treatises, architectural plans and drawings, religious inscriptions, et cetera, in every writing medium possible.

By 1905, Breasted completed editing his compendium of Egyptian historical texts, and between 1906 and 1907, he published it as the *Ancient Records of Egypt: Historical Documents from the Earliest Times to the Persian Conquest.* However, as great and as useful as this collection was, it was only the second of two related publications that appeared within a year of each other. Previously in 1905, Breasted had published *A History of Egypt,* which was his new and comprehensive study of Egyptian political and social history. In addition to being remarkably well written, the strength of this work was that it was exhaustively researched, and its argumentation was firmly grounded on the full body of Egyptian historical texts, as they were known then, which Breasted had translated according to the highest grammatical standards of the day. As such, *A History of Egypt* was the first of its kind. It had a great appeal to the general public, while it was also useful to professional Egyptologists. Breasted's rigorous methodology gave his history a longevity unsurpassed by any other general Egyptian history book. Indeed, the first cracks in the historical narrative did not begin to appear until more than thirty years after its publication. Even so, much of the book was still considered professionally useful for at least another twenty years (into the 1950s). Its popular reputation was so great that as late as the 1960s and 1970s, it remained the first serious reading on ancient Egypt for most fledgling ancient historians and amateur Egyptologists. To this day, no other general history of Egypt has had a useful lifetime as extensive as Breasted's *History of Egypt*. Sixty-five years after his death, Breasted's scholarship, although dated, is still highly regarded, and as late as 1995, *Who Was Who in Egyptology* cited it as "probably the best general history of Pharaonic Egypt ever published."[2] Even today, *A History of Egypt* is still useful in many ways.

A History of Egypt and the *Ancient Records of Egypt* mark a milestone in the history of Egyptology, so precise and well-considered was Breasted's methodology. He intended the *Ancient Records* and *A History of Egypt* to be a related pair, each serving the purposes of the other. Since the narrative of the history was completely founded on the ancient documents, one could read the inscriptions in the *Ancient Records* to supplement and further explicate the narrative, while at the same time one might consult excerpts from *A History of Egypt* to provide context for specific inscriptions in the *Ancient Records*.

Late in the writing of the *Ancient Records,* Breasted was convinced that the scope of the project should be broadened to include the texts of other cultures of the ancient Near East. Thus, as the last volumes of the *Ancient Records of Egypt* were being completed, the University of Chicago announced the formation of an *Ancient Records* series, edited by William Rainey Harper, of which the five volumes of Egyptian texts would be only the first set. The second set would include Mesopotamian records from Assyria and Babylonia, while the third set would contain Semitic texts from Palestine, Phoenicia, and Syria. Each set was to be compiled and edited by a different scholar. Breasted also planned to augment his five volumes of the Egyptian histori-cal records with seven new volumes of records of other types (economic, religious, etc.).[3] However, before the project could get off the ground, it was slowed by the untimely death of Harper, compounded by the advent of World War I and then the reorganization of Breasted's department and staff to found the Oriental Institute. It was not until 1926 that the two-volume *Ancient Records of Assyria and Babylonia* appeared, edited by Daniel D. Luckenbill. Unfortunately, these were the last volumes ever to be published in the *Ancient Records* series.

* * *

Breasted spent ten years copying, collecting, and translating texts for the *Ancient Records of Egypt*. Finally, in 1904, he closed the manuscript to further additions and began the final editing of the publication. Thereafter, the great work was published in five volumes, each volume appearing separately in print from 1906 to 1907. Volumes 1 to 4 contain the historical documents them-selves, arranged in chronological order through the length of Egyptian histo-ry up to the Persian conquest of the sixth century B.C. Volume 5 consists of various indices and word-lists that make the corpus accessible for reference and research. The specific contents of the volumes are divided as follows:

> Volume 1: Dynasties 1 to 17 (c. 3050–1570 B.C.)
> Volume 2: Dynasty 18 (c. 1570–1293 B.C.)
> Volume 3: Dynasty 19 (c. 1293–1185 B.C.)
> Volume 4: Dynasties 20 to 26 (c. 1185–525 B.C.)
> Volume 5: Indices and corrections

The texts of each volume are arranged chronologically in order of era or king's reign. Within each reign, they are further subdivided by theme or content. In his treatment of each inscription, Breasted methodically begins with a short description of the text, including general commentary about its historicity and significance. Then follows the translation itself. Throughout, he provides footnotes with more detailed remarks on the text's history, grammatical is-sues, and orthography. Moreover, he divides both the commentary and the translations into numbered sections to facilitate organization and citation. By this thoughtful arrangement of translation and commentary, Breasted keeps his work accessible to the layman while still satisfying the needs of the specialist. Researchers and historians would find in the footnotes the detailed information they require about provenance, grammar, and lexicography, and the general reader could concentrate only on the translations. This method of dividing the text has been employed ever since Breasted's day by all editors of Near Eastern texts who have sought to direct their publications jointly to the general public and the professional.

When it was published, the *Ancient Records of Egypt* was lauded for its direction, comprehensiveness, and consistency. As for direction, Breasted intended the work not only for the professional Egyptologist but also as a popular resource for the general historian untrained in Egyptian languages and for the interested lay reader. Previously, Egyptological translations were published, for the most part, by Egyptologists for Egyptologists in highly specialized publications. They employed professional jargon and a highly literal style of translation that was often difficult for the nonspecialist (what some Egyptologists might jokingly refer to as "translationese"). On the other hand, Breasted prepared his renderings in a simple, idiomatic English. As he notes in his preface, he consciously avoided any paraphrasing in his translations, a practice that he laments was, otherwise, too common in his day. Rather, he states that his effort is to render the Egyptian as literally as possible without wrenching English idiom.[4] Here he was quite successful, even by the standards of today, and book reviewers at that time regularly touted the clear, unpedantic quality of his translations as one of the hallmarks of the *Ancient Records.*

As for comprehensiveness and consistency, prior to the publication of the *Ancient Records,* there was no comparable collection of translations of Egyptian texts in any language. As Breasted notes in his preface to volume I, "no attempt has ever been made to collect and present *all* the sources of Egyptian history in a modern language" (italics added).[5] While earlier Near Eastern scholars had collaborated to pool their translations into single publications,[6] they had never included the entire corpus of any written genre, nor did the various scholars regularize their translations to make them consistent with each other. For these reasons, styles of translations differed from text to text in the same compendia, and the same words might even be translated differently. In his volumes, Breasted worked to overcome such limitations by being as inclusive as possible in his choice of documents, as well as being consistent in all his translations.

Although many of the inscriptions in the volumes had been copied and published previously by other scholars, Breasted chose to recopy or collate many of them to make corrections and additions. Even where earlier he published texts himself, he still translated these again for his corpus. Another strength of the *Ancient Records* was that the corpus included many texts that had not been published before. These texts Breasted originally copied himself in Egypt and the Sudan and in the museums of Europe, or he received hand copies and squeezes from colleagues. He also culled a large number of inscriptions from the files of the Berlin Dictionary project. The addition of these new inscriptions made Breasted's corpus especially valuable as a historical resource.

At the time of publication, the *Ancient Records of Egypt* represented the pinnacle of Egyptological achievement and the highest standard of philological research. It was the most complete translation in any language of historical texts according to the most modern understanding of Egyptian grammar. It even employed a modification of the new Berlin system of transliteration, which was the most highly evolved of the contemporary systems for rendering Egyptian hieroglyphs into Roman letters and which ultimately became the international standard.

Near Eastern scholars and the reading public were quick to recognize the *Ancient Records of Egypt* as a great achievement, and in general they received it with enthusiasm. All the reviewers, American and otherwise, were consistent in praising the publication for its readability and comprehensiveness, as well as its epigraphic trustworthiness and philological authority. No one doubted the accuracy of Breasted's hieroglyphic copies nor the quality of his translations. What is interesting, however, was the reaction of certain English and French colleagues. The issues where they found fault sometimes reflected as much upon their own sense of nationalism and rancor against German Egyptology and the Berlin school as on purely Egyptological issues. So French Egyptologist George Foucart, although praising the volumes overall, complained that Breasted ignored the work of French Egyptologists and that he neglected to include certain important French studies in his bibliography, which—on the whole—he took as a slight against the French school of Egyptology.[7] However, a dispassionate perusal of Breasted's footnotes and citations reveals that Foucart's complaints are unjustified, since there are many references to the works of French Egyptologists. Breasted later responded to these charges himself in the preface to volume 5 (p. xxii), where he noted that the work of certain French Egyptologists was omitted necessarily because it became available only after October 1904, when his manuscript was closed to further additions.

Similarly, while British reviews generally praised the work, some of these also could not refrain from casting their comments within nationalistic frames of reference. So, for example, one unidentified reviewer wrote:

> Some twenty-five years ago the Berlin School . . . gave birth to the theory that Egyptian was a Semitic language; . . . but unfortunately the professors of the Berlin School, instead of answering in detail the objections which their French, Italian, and English colleagues were not slow to bring against it, seem to have resolved to treat it henceforth as proved, and to ignore as far as may be the work of every Egyptologist who is not prepared at once to pronounce their shibboleth. This Bismarckian method of compelling the adoption of their own conclusions by hook or by crook has aroused much heartburning, and Dr. Breasted, who throughout his Egyptological career has shown himself more German than the Germans, has thought fit to adopt it. . . . Exactly one-half of the corrigenda which Dr. Breasted announces in his fifth volume are caused by the uncouth and barbarous system of transliteration which forms the trademark of Berlin Egyptology.[8]

Breasted, of course, was trained in Germany, and he always maintained close relations with his colleagues and teachers there, except during the years when the United States was a combatant in World War I (1917–19). His adoption and popularization of the Berlin transliteration system did cause some resentment among those French and English Egyptologists who still had stubbornly clung to their older, less precise, and increasingly obsolete system. However, only a short time after the publication of the *Ancient Records,* the Berlin system did become the standard international system of transliteration in Egyptology, and it remains so today.

Ninety-four years after its initial publication, we must ask, how useful does the *Ancient Records of Egypt* remain both for modern academic purposes and for general reading and referencing? To what extent is the work obsolete, and how much of it has been surpassed by scholarship since its publication in 1906–7? In many regards, the work has been overtaken in the quality of translation and in the quantity of texts published subsequently. Despite that, however, it still has great value as a publication, and it remains remarkably useful, especially to the general reader and the interested lay reader. Admittedly, for the professional Egyptologist, its utility is diminished, but it is still safe to say that most Egyptologists who can afford to own a set of the *Ancient Records,* especially historians and bibliophiles, probably do so, or they would wish to own it. The reason is its size and comprehensive scope. However, the forces of progress are constantly working against it.

In the first decade of the twentieth century, Egyptological scholarship was growing, and a critical mass of publications was beginning to answer enough questions so that scholars were coming to appreciate just how much they did not know of ancient Egypt. With every generation since Breasted's death in 1935, the number of publications and the amount of research in Egyptology has increased geometrically, so that today it almost seems to have reached a surfeit. The number of authors and productive scholars in the field has continued to expand. Only in the last generation (since the 1970s), are Egyptologists beginning to feel that so much material is being published they can no longer encompass it all as easily as they could previously. As a result, they are focusing their researches more narrowly and specializing their interests more discretely.

Many of the new publications include new texts and inscriptions of all types that add to our historical knowledge. Consequently, these new texts are undermining the value of the *Ancient Records* as an exhaustive anthology. The new publications also include innovative grammatical studies that continue to improve our understanding of Egyptian languages. Here, too, these are affecting the accuracy of the *Ancient Records'* translations.

In his preface to volume 1, Breasted notes that by 1905, a complete revolution in the knowledge of Egyptian grammar had occurred during the previous twenty-five years, and that up to that time, those advances had not been applied to historical inscriptions, as a whole. A far-thinking man, he would not find it ironic that his own translations also would succumb ultimately to continuing improvements in Egyptian grammar. In 1927, Sir Alan H. Gardiner published his *Egyptian Grammar,* which caused an upheaval in Egyptian philology. Thereafter, he revised that study successively in 1950 and 1957. However, even before Gardiner completed his second edition, Hans J. Polotsky had begun a new quiet revolution in grammatical knowledge that ultimately overwhelmed Gardiner's neat reconstruction of the Egyptian verbal system. Polotsky's seminal studies, published from 1944 to 1990, refined our understanding of Egyptian clause structure, tenses, syntax, and aspect. Now, for the third time in a century, Egyptian philology is being rocked by new revolutionary interpretations. The innovative post-Polotskian grammars of Antonio Loprieno and James P. Allen, as well as the work of Mark Collier and others, herald a new "verbalist" and linguistic approach to the study of Egyptian that is both wonderful and disconcerting. To paraphrase the popular advertisement, "it's not your grandfather's Egyptology."

New knowledge about history and historical processes, geography, and the discovery of new inscriptions have combined, so that today we often understand more than what Breasted's translations tell us. For example, his treatment of the inscriptions from the tomb of Governor Pepinakht, called Heqaib (vol. 1, §§355–60), does not even hint at Heqaib's great social and religious significance at the end of the Old Kingdom and in the First Intermediate Period. That fact only became known after the 1930s, when Egyptologists uncovered a royal sanctuary dedicated to his deified spirit. This discovery led archaeologists to reexcavate his tomb in the 1950s, where they discovered an addition to the structure and more inscriptions.

In certain inscriptions, Breasted worked with copies that were filled with many lacunae, that is, gaps in the texts due to breaks in the writing surface (e.g., torn papyri, broken walls, etc.). Necessarily, he had to leave gaps in his translations. If he could deduce their content, he might restore what was broken (by enclosing the text in brackets and half-brackets). As frequently happens in Egyptology, after his anthology was published, more complete copies of some of these texts came to light, superseding his translations. An extreme example of this is his excerpt of the "Tale of Sinuhe" (vol. 1, §§486–97), which he translated from the one copy known at that time. However, today most of the tale is recovered due to the discovery of additional copies and fragments.

Another factor that helps to date the translations is Breasted's archaic treatment of personal names and toponyms. Although he uses the Berlin system to transliterate these names, he employs an antiquated system of rendering them into English. So, he transcribes z where we now understand dj (e.g., Senezemib for Senedjemib); th where we now employ tj (e.g., Methethi for Metjetji); enekh for ankh (e.g., Enekhnes-Merire for Ankhenesmeryre). Still, even this aspect of the publication is not hopeless, since many other personal names are still in present use or are close to the current standard.

Curiously, despite the immense changes and discoveries that have occurred in Egyptology, Breasted's translations, although dated, are not obsolete. In most cases, even though the translations have been overtaken, Breasted's overall interpretations of the individual documents remain valid. Certainly, many of them have since been further refined, but very few of his textual interpretations have been completely repudiated.

On the other hand, his interpretations of history and historical processes are a different issue. Founded as they were on the limited texts known at the time, they can be unreliable to varying degrees. One gross example is his hoary account of the reigns of Hatshepsut and Thutmose III (vol. 2, §§128–30), which was based on the then-current belief that Thutmose I, Thutmose II, Hatshepsut, and Thutmose III were all contemporaries vying and machinating against each other for the throne of Egypt.

So here we give readers fair warning. While in most cases Breasted's interpretations of individual documents are still measurably reliable, his historical narratives and his analyses of Egyptian chronology can no longer be relied upon to any great extent. Readers are warned to seek elsewhere more modern treatments of ancient Egyptian history (see the introduction to volume 5 for a listing of modern histories), and to use the *Ancient Records* only as an anthology of interesting and informative texts.

The *Ancient Records of Egypt* can point the way to new translations and modern treatments. It can identify issues that are still important and cogent to Egyptology, for example, the translation of the Boundary Stelae of Sesostris III (vol. 1, §§651–60) segues into the new scholarship and understandings about Nubia and the kingdom of Kush in the second millennium B.C. Breasted's translations are still serviceable; they are useful and informative for the casual reader. They can be used reliably by the general reader and student as a comprehensive introduction to Egyptian historical inscriptions. They are good for understanding general content and for learning about major historical issues. However, on the whole, they are inappropriate for a close analysis and study of the texts. After surveying the inscriptions in the anthology, serious students and scholars would be served best by seeking out more modern translations and other interpretations (again see the introduction to volume 5 for updated bibliographies of many texts).

Where the *Ancient Records of Egypt* clearly has not been superseded is in regard to its scope. Breasted's more than ten thousand manuscript pages remain the largest corpus of Egyptian translations ever published by any one

scholar. The closest that any single author has come to matching this achievement is perhaps Miriam Lichtheim's three-volume study, *Ancient Egyptian
Literature* (see the introduction to volume 5) with its 656 printed pages devoted to a broad range of Egyptian inscriptions (literary, religious, historical). However, even then, she might translate only excerpts of texts, where
Breasted presents entire compositions; for example, regarding the texts of the
Vizier Rekhmire (vol. 2, §§663–711), her translation covers only the "Instructions" (§§665–70) but not the as-important detailed descriptions of the vizier's activities and responsibilities.

The sheer scope of the *Ancient Records* has also reinforced its longevity
in another manner. Despite the plethora of Egyptological publications and
translations that have appeared since 1907, the *Ancient Records* still contain
certain texts and inscriptions that have not been retranslated into English since
that time. In this regard, the anthology remains particularly useful to the
English-reading public as the sole source of these translations, although Egyptologists will rely upon their own personal translations or those in other
modern languages.

Finally, where the *Ancient Records of Egypt* has not been superseded, even
for the specialist, is in its capacity to reveal legacy in Egyptology, not merely in the fact that it is an important work that should be preserved. The further away that we get from the origins of Egyptology, the more we can lose
touch with early important analyses and arguments, so that we take for granted
facts and historical processes, forgetting who deduced them and how they
were analyzed. A particular value of the *Ancient Records* is that it often provides us with the sources and inscriptions that underlie our most basic understanding of ancient Egyptian history and society.

Making the *Ancient Records of Egypt* available again not only introduces
the work of an Egyptological pioneer to a new generation of readers, it also
brings Egyptology full circle back to its roots, allowing us to take stock of
how far this field has progressed and hopefully providing some insight into
where it may grow in the future.

NOTES

1. E.g., James H. Breasted, "Editor's Foreword," in *Ancient Records of Assyria and
Babylonia,* vol. 1: *Historical Records of Assyria from the Earliest Times to Sargon,*
ed. Daniel D. Luckenbill (Chicago: University of Chicago Press, 1926), viii.

2. Warren R. Dawson and Eric P. Uphill, *Who Was Who in Egyptology: A Biographical Index of Egyptologists,* 3d ed., rev. by Morris Bierbrier (London: Egypt Exploration Society, 1995), 62.

3. Breasted, "Editor's Foreword," vii–ix.

4. *Ancient Records of Egypt,* vol. 1, x–xi.

5. Ibid., vii.

6. E.g., *Records of the Past: Being English Translations of the Assyrian and Egyptian Monuments. Published under the Sanction of the Society of Biblical Archæology,* ed. Samuel Birch, 12 vols. (London: S. Bagster and Sons, 1874–81); *Records of the Past: Being English Translations of the Assyrian and Egyptian Monuments,* n.s., ed. A. H. Sayce, 6 vols. (London: S. Bagster and Sons, 1888–92).

7. *Journal des Savants* (June 1906): 335–36; (Aug. 1907): 445–48.

8. [Anon.], *The Atheneum* (July 18, 1907). It is true that throughout Breasted's career, his colleagues did identify him closely with German Egyptologists and German Egyptology in general. Among most of them, this was never an issue. However, later during the hysteria associated with World War I, a few apparently went so far as to question his political loyalties and to cast unjustified aspersions against him. This issue was partially laid to rest when his son, Charles, joined the U.S. army in 1917 with the intent of serving on the European front (see C. Breasted, *Pioneer to the Past: The Story of James H. Breasted* [New York: Charles Scribner's Sons, 1943], 227, 234–35).

PREFACE

In no particular have modern historical studies made greater progress than in the reproduction and publication of documentary sources from which our knowledge of the most varied peoples and periods is drawn. In American history whole libraries of such sources have appeared or are promised. These are chiefly in English, although the other languages of Europe are of course often largely represented. The employment of such sources from the early epochs of the world's history involves either a knowledge of ancient languages on the part of the user, or a complete rendition of the documents into English. No attempt has ever been made to collect and present all the sources of Egyptian history in a modern language. A most laudable beginning in this direction, and one that has done great service, was the *Records of the Past;* but that series never attempted to be complete, and no amount of editing could make consistent with themselves the uncorrelated translations of the large number of contributors to that series.

The author is only too well aware of the difficulties involved in such a project. In mere bulk alone it has been a considerable enterprise, in view of the preliminary tasks made necessary by the state of the published texts. These I have indicated briefly in the chapter on the sources herein (Vol. I, §§ 27–32). Under these circumstances, the author's first obligation has been to go behind the publications to the original documents themselves, wherever necessary. The method pursued has also been indicated herein (Vol. I, §§ 33–37). The task has consumed years, and demanded protracted sojourn among the great collections of Europe. In this work a related enterprise has been of the greatest assistance. A mission to the museums of Europe to collect and copy their Egyptian monuments for a commission of the four Royal Academies of Germany (Berlin, Leipzig, Göttingen, and Munich), in order to make these documents available for an exhaustive *Egyptian Dictionary* endowed by the German Emperor, enabled the author to copy from the originals practically all the historical monuments of Egypt in Europe. The other sources of material, and particularly the papers of the *Dictionary* just mentioned, have enabled the author to base the translations in these volumes directly, or practically so, upon the originals themselves in almost all cases.

Unfortunately, the possession of these materials is but the beginning of the difficulties which beset such an enterprise. In the preface to the first edition of his English *Dictionary*, Noah Webster complains of the difficulties caused by the new meanings taken on by English words as they are modified by the new environment which envelops them in America. If such changes are involved in the voyage across the Atlantic, and the lapse of a few generations, how much wider and deeper is the gulf due to the total difference between the semitropical northern Nile valley of millenniums ago, and the English-speaking world of this twentieth century! The psychology of early man is something with which we have as yet scarcely begun to operate. His whole world and his whole manner of thinking are sharply differentiated from our own. His organization, socially, industrially, commercially, politically; his tools, his house, his conveniences, constantly involve institutions, adjustments, and appliances totally unknown to this modern age and this western world. In the translation of the New Testament for the tribes of Alaska, I am told, there has been great difficulty in the rendition of the term " Good Shepherd," for the reason that many of these people never saw a sheep and never heard of a shepherd. Similarly, how shall one rehabilitate this ancient world of the Nile-dweller, and put his documents into intelligible English, when the ideas to be rendered are often unknown to the average modern and western reader, and, needless to say, there are no corresponding terms in the English language ?

Another constant source of difficulty has been the lack of those indispensable helps, the legion of concordances, glossaries, handbooks, and compilations for ready refer- ence, which the worker in Greek or Hebrew has constantly at his hand. In spite of the colossal industry of Brugsch, we are still without a dictionary of Egyptian to which one can turn with any hope of finding other examples of a rare word. Hardly any Old Kingdom documents at all were employed by Brugsch in the compilation of his dictionary, and, grateful as we are for what he was able to furnish us, we must still await the great Berlin *Dictionary* before we shall possess an exhaustive compendium of the language. I was able to employ the alphabetically arranged materials of the *Dictionary* here and there, but the compilation was not sufficiently far advanced at the conclusion of my work to be of much service. Wherever I have drawn examples from it, they are carefully acknowledged in the footnotes. A good many distinctions in the meanings of words have become evident to me in the course of the work upon the documents. Wherever such have become clear late in the progress of the work, it was impossible to go through the translations and revise the entire manuscript for the sake of such words alone. I have tried to control these cases as far as possible in the proofs, but I am confident that some such

changes have been overlooked as the accumulation of alter-
ations demanded in the proofreading was quite beyond
my powers of observation in so large a mass of materials.
Thus, for example, the common word *sr* is usually translated "prince," and this is undoubtedly sometimes the
meaning of the word; but it very frequently means "official," a fact which I did not observe until far along in the
progress of the work.

Some danger of confusion also arises from the fact that
titles indicative of rank or office suffer great change in
meaning in the lapse of several thousand years. Thus the
ḥ²ty or "count" of the feudal and pre-feudal ages becomes
a mere magistrate or town-mayor in the Empire, although
in sporadic cases the word still retains its old meaning.
The translation of titles has perhaps been the greatest
source of difficulty in the entire course of the work. Many
of the offices found cannot be determined with precision.
We have as yet no history of titles—one of the most needed
works in the entire range of Egyptian studies. Under these
circumstances, it has been impossible always to define with
precision the range and scope of a given office. Even when
these were determinable, the corresponding term was often
wanting in English, and could not be devised without the
use of a whole phrase. In some cases awkward combina-
tions have been necessary in the renderings of titles. Thus
the compound "king's-son" was adopted because it is
occasionally followed in the original by a pronoun referring
to "king," which made the rendering "royal son" impossible. For this reason a series of such compounds has been
employed: "king's-son," "king's-daughter," "king's-wife,"
"king's-mother," "king's-scribe," and the like. It is hoped
to render all such matters clear in the index.

In general, the effort has been to render as literally as

possible without wrenching English idiom. In this latter particular I probably have not always succeeded; but I have deliberately preferred this evil to a glib rendering which reads well and may be a long distance from the sense of the original. We have had so much of so-called "paraphrasing," which does not even remotely resemble the purport of the original, that I have felt justified in gratifying a righteous horror of such romancing, even at the cost of idiomatic English. The reader has a right to expect that the subjective fancies of the translator have been rigidly excluded, and a right to demand that he may put implicit dependence both upon the individual words and the general sense of the renderings. At the same time, the author would distinctly disclaim any desire to give to these translations the authority of monographs. The extent of the materials, and the amount of time expended in the collection, collation, and correction of the original texts before doing anything toward a formal version, have made it impossible to devote to the translation of each document as much time as one would deem necessary for the production of a monograph upon it. While the most conscientious attention has been given to the versions, and they have sometimes been revised three times (always once), yet it is undoubtedly the case that, in the course of rendering such a mass of materials, errors have crept in. Notice of any that may be observed by my fellow-workers in this field will be gratefully received, and utilized should a future edition of these volumes ever appear.

For the benefit of the general reader, it should be noted that a complete revolution in our knowledge of the Egyptian grammar has taken place in the last twenty-five years. The exhaustive study of syntax and of verbal forms which has been in progress for generations in the classic languages,

or even in the Semitic group, has been going on for only a
little over a quarter of a century in Egyptian. This is no
reflection on the work of the first two generations of Egyptologists, for such work was impossible in their day.   In
this quarter-century, immense progress has been made
and certain definite results have been attained. It cannot
be said that these results have yet been applied to the understanding of the historical documents of Egypt as a whole.
One of the main purposes of this work has been the attainment of this end.   Indeed, its chief object may be indicated
in this connection as: first, the attainment of copies which
in correctness adequately reproduce the original document;
and, second, an English version which shall embody our
modern knowledge of the language. Every effort has
been made to realize these two aims, and only in such degree
as they may have been attained will these volumes form a
contribution to knowledge.

In the selection of documents there has sometimes been
difficulty in deciding what should and what should not be
included by the term "historical document." All purely
religious compositions, as well as all exclusively literary
documents (belles-lettres), all science, like mathematics and
medicine, and in most cases all business documents, have
been excluded. In the Old Kingdom, however, the last
have been included, in view of the limited materials surviving from that distant age. It is hoped that these other
classes of documents will appear in further volumes of this
series. In all cases, however, where the other classes of
documents were of vital historical importance—that is,
bore directly on events and conditions closely touching the
career of the Egyptian state—they have been included
here. These volumes, therefore, include the entire series of
written documents from which we draw our knowledge

of the career of the Nile valley peoples as a nation, until
the beginning of permanent foreign domination at the
advent of the Persians in 525 B. C.

Besides furnishing an English version of these documents, the scope of this work also includes the proper
introduction of the reader to their intelligent study; hence
the versions are accompanied by notes and introductions.
These are threefold in character. Firstly, in a footnote
appended to the title of each document, the reader will
find a brief description of it, indicating whether it is of
stone or papyrus, a stela, a relief, an obelisk, or whatever
it may be, with statement of its size and material whenever
the data were obtainable. The state of preservation is
noted, and then all the publications in which the text of
the monument has appeared. In a word, this footnote
contains the *lower* criticism of the document. No attempt
has been made to add to the bibliography the various
treatments and discussions of the monument which have
at various times appeared. The bulk of these essays are
long since obsolete, and the time has certainly come when
we can detach our usable bibliography from this incum-
bering inheritance, without at the same time failing to
recognize with gratitude the great service which it once
rendered to the science. Furthermore, it has seemed a duty
to indicate to the reader in this footnote, the comparative
value of the more important publications of the text. If an
edition of the text has proved inaccurate and untrustworthy,
it is but right that it should be known as such. In a purely
objective and impersonal manner, therefore, such materials
have been characterized in these introductory footnotes.

Secondly, each monument is supplied with a usually
short introduction, setting forth the historical significance
of the document, its character, and where necessary, a

résumé of its content. It therefore contains in brief compass the *higher* criticism of the document. Much of the historical background, and literary value of the more important documents will be found set forth more fully in the author's *History of Egypt*,[a] which is based upon the documentary sources in these volumes. As a further aid in gaining a comprehensive idea of the content, the version of each document itself has been divided into logical paragraphs, each with a subtitle. It is intended that by this plan a given passage of the document may be referred to by number, thus furnishing a very brief system of reference to all the monuments, by means of the volume number (Roman) followed by the paragraph number (Arabic).

Thirdly, the version of each monument is accompanied by running footnotes explaining obscure matters in the text as far as possible. It has been impossible to make these any fuller, although the author is quite aware that many details requiring explanation have been left without comment. It has been his especial endeavor to adduce in the footnotes, or at least call attention to, all related matter, whether in this series of translations or elsewhere among the monuments of Egypt. It has often been more convenient to introduce a very brief or fragmentary inscription of a few words in a footnote attached to a related passage in some larger document, than to give such flotsam and jetsam independent heads as separate documents. It is expected to render these all easily discoverable in the index. The maps necessary to an understanding of the geography of the monuments will also appear with the index.

I have attempted to solve the unwelcome problem of the transliteration of Egyptian words and names by giving

---

[a]*A History of Egypt*, large 8vo, 640 pp., 200 illustrations, Charles Scribner's Sons, New York, 1905.

the proper names where necessary in two forms: first, a vocalized form for the layman; and, second, a purely consonantal transliteration placed after it in parentheses. As the layman for whom the first is intended knows nothing of Egyptian orthography, it is not important that he shall be able to recognize in the forms the consonants of the original. This vocalized form should, however, as nearly as possible reproduce the consonants upon which it is based, without introducing elements unintelligible to the layman. Hence I have ignored ꜣ and ꜥ, *y* becomes *i* or *y*, and *w* is indicated by *u* or *w*. The consonantal transliteration adopted is the most nearly satisfactory system yet evolved, viz., that of the Berlin school, with some slight modifications. It is as follows:

ꜣ = Semitic א	n = Semitic נ	š = Semitic שׁ
y = " י	r = " ר or ל	ḳ = " ק
w = " ו	h = " ה	k = " כ
ꜥ = " ע	ḥ = " ח, ح	g = " ג
b = " ב	ḫ = " ח, خ	t = " ת
p = " פ	ẖ = " ח, خ	ṭ = " ט
f = our f	s = " sᵃ	d = " ד
m = Semitic מ	š = " שׂ	ḏ = " צ

In the so-called "syllabic orthography" employed by the Egyptians in writing foreign words, only the first consonant of each biconsonantal sign has any significance. The second has no phonetic value in such words.

This is not the place to discuss the closer equivalences of these consonants. It is probable the ꜣ (Eagle) diverges

---

ᵃThe nature of the difference between this and the following *š* is entirely obscure. From the Middle Kingdom on, they represent the same sound. Herein the distinction has been consistently indicated only in the Old Kingdom.

slightly from the pure *aleph* of the Semitic languages, while the initial *y* has frequently become an *aleph*. It has not seemed wise to burden a work of this character with such distinctions, and the *y* appearing in these volumes at the beginning of a word merely indicates that the initial consonant of the original word is "reed-leaf" without predicating anything as to whether its sound is ˚ or א.

To the numerous colleagues in Europe who have been so ready with assistance whenever called upon, I would here publicly express the deepest obligation. For untrammeled access to their collections, and never-failing co-operation, my sincere acknowledgments are due to the authorities of the museums at Berlin, London (British Museum, University College, Petrie Collections), Paris (Louvre, Bibliothèque Nationale, Musée Guimet), Vienna (Hofmuseum), Leyden, Munich, Rome (Vatican, and Capitoline), Florence (Museo Archæologico), Bologna, Naples, Turin, Pisa, Geneva, Lyons, Liverpool, and some others. It is with the greatest pleasure that I recall the years of work in the Berlin Museum to which these volumes have called me. It would be impossible, were I to attempt it, to enumerate the daily kindnesses or tell of the constant co-operation which I have enjoyed there. For daily access to the materials of the academic *Dictionary*, already mentioned, I would express to Professor Erman, and the gentlemen of the *Dictionary* staff, my hearty thanks. For never-failing personal counsel and aid my thanks are also due to Erman, Schaefer, and Sethe; while Steindorff, Borchardt, Spiegelberg, Gardiner, Bissing, Weigall, Newberry, Petrie, and Legrain have placed valuable copies, collations, photographs, or reports at my disposal. The unremitting labors of Maspero and Wiedemann have given us indispensable bibliographies of the historical documents, and these have been of great service to me—a service for which I would express to them my sincere thanks. I did not, however, depend solely upon these works, but made an independent bibliography from the beginning—a plan which not infrequently turned up invaluable old sources not before employed.

To my friend, President William R. Harper, for his interest in this enterprise, and his unfailing support in arranging for my repeated absence in Europe for the prosecution of these studies, I owe a debt of gratitude. Likewise to the Board of Trustees of the University of Chicago, for the same privileges, it is an agreeable duty to express my appreciation here.

Finally my thanks are due the staff of the University of Chicago Press for unremitting attention to the difficult typographical work of these volumes—an attention to which the appearance of the work is of itself sufficient evidence. I should add that circumstances entirely beyond my control have obliged me to read the proofs of the volumes very rapidly, and it is probable that they contain more typographical errors due to this fact than I could wish. For great assistance in reading the proofs I am indebted to my brother-in-law Dr. R. S. Padan, and for like aid to my wife and her sister, Miss Imogen Hart.

JAMES HENRY BREASTED.

WILLIAMS BAY, WIS.,
September 22, 1905.

EXPLANATION OF TYPOGRAPHICAL SIGNS AND SPECIAL CHARACTERS

1. The introductions to the documents are in twelve-point type, like these lines.

2. All of the translations are in ten-point type, like this line.

3. In the footnotes and introductions all quotations from the documents in the original words of the translation are in *italics*, inclosed in quotation marks. *Italics* are not employed in the text of the volumes for any other purpose except for titles.

4. The lines of the original document are indicated in the translation by superior numbers.

5. The loss of a word in the original is indicated by —, two words by — —, three words by — — —, four words by — — — —, five words by — — — — —, and more than five by ————. A word in the original is estimated at a "square" as known to Egyptologists, and the estimate can be but a very rough one.

6. When any of the dashes, like those of No. 5, are inclosed in half-brackets, the dashes so inclosed indicate not lost, but uncertain words. Thus ⌐—⌐ represents one uncertain word, ⌐— —⌐ two uncertain words, and ⌐————⌐ more than five uncertain words.

7. When a word or group of words are inclosed in half-brackets, the words so inclosed are uncertain in meaning; that is, the translation is not above question.

8. Roman numerals I, II, III, and IV, not preceded by the title of any book or journal, refer to these four volumes of Historical Documents. The Arabic numerals following such Romans refer to the numbered paragraphs of these volumes. All paragraph marks (§ and §§, without a Roman) refer to paragraphs of the same volume.

9. For signs used in transliteration, see Vol. I, p. **xvii.**

THE DOCUMENTARY SOURCES OF
EGYPTIAN HISTORY

THE DOCUMENTARY SOURCES OF EGYPTIAN HISTORY

1. The general course and the gradual development of Egyptian civilization are in some respects roughly traceable in its surviving material documents, in the products of the artist and the craftsman, which we are accustomed to assign to the domain of the archæologist. With these invaluable material documents the present volumes of course do not deal. They purpose to present only those written documents from which the career of the Nile valley peoples may be drawn at the present day. A rapid survey of the materials herein presented may enable the non-Egyptologist to gain some preliminary conception of their general character.

2. Comparatively speaking, but very little of the rich and productive civilization which flourished for at least five millenniums before Christ on the banks of the lower Nile, has survived in written documents for our enlightenment. Accident has preserved but here and there the merest scrap of the vast mass of written records which the incessant political, legal, administrative, religious, industrial, commercial, and literary activities filling the life of this ancient people, were constantly putting forth. We may make one exception: the religious literature, doubtless the least instructive, as a whole, of all their literary documents, has survived in an incalculable mass of temple inscriptions and papyri, which have never even been adequately published, much less exhaustively studied.

3. It is with those documents in which the national career as a whole can be traced that we have here to deal. From the pre-dynastic age onward the kings kept a series of

annals, recording in each year the great deeds and achievements of the Pharaoh which he thought worthy of perpetuation.   Of such annals only two fragments have survived:
the Palermo Stone, part of a record extending from the
earliest times down into the Fifth Dynasty; and the annals
of Thutmose III's wars, of which a few extracts were
excerpted by a priestly scribe and recorded on the walls of
the Karnak temple.   Had we the annals of the Pharaohs in
complete form, we might perhaps write almost as full a
history of Egypt as it is possible to do for the Middle Ages
of European history.   Without these, we are dependent
upon a miscellaneous mass of documents of the most varied
character and value, which chance and circumstance have
preserved from destruction these thousands of years.   In
general, such documents show more literary character and
picturesqueness than the Assyro-Babylonian records; but
the latter dry and formal annals possess greater historical
value, and exhibit a preciseness which indues them with a
rare availability as sources.   The Egyptian records which
chance has preserved to us are, as a whole, so vague and
indefinite in their references to peoples, localities, persons,
and the character of events, that they are often tantalizing
in what they do not tell us.   Thus in records of whole campaigns of Thutmose III in Syria the hostile Syrian king is
designated merely as *"that foe"* (lit. *"fallen one"*), and we are
uncertain whether the king of Kadesh, of Mitanni, of Aleppo,
or of some other realm is meant.   The real excerpts from
Thutmose III's Annals (II, 391 ff.), however, show that such
records contained an elaboration of detail not less precise
and historically available than the cuneiform annals.   So
much the more must we deplore their loss.

4. How hazardous was the life of such a document may
be well illustrated by the great building inscription, upon a

huge stone stela, erected by Sesostris I nearly two thousand years before Christ, in his new temple at Heliopolis. The great block itself has since perished utterly; but the practice-copy made by a scribe, who was whiling away an idle hour in the sunny temple court, has survived, and the fragile roll of leather (§§ 498 ff.) upon which he was thus exercising his pen, has transmitted to us what the massive stone could not preserve.

5. That we possess any documents at all from the Old Kingdom (2980–2400 B. C.) is chiefly due to the massive masonry tombs of that age, in which they were recorded. The exceptions are inscriptions on foreign soil, and a few scanty fragments of papyrus containing accounts and letters. The vast quantity of such papyrus documents which once existed is evidenced by the constant appearance of the scribe with his rolls, his pens, and his ink palette, in the tomb reliefs. Such hints from the numerous reliefs in the tombs of this age are the source of our knowledge of the material culture of the time. The chief inscriptions which accompany them consist almost exclusively of the name and many titles of the owner of the tomb. Now and again the legal enactment by which the tomb was endowed and maintained is recorded on the wall. Such wills and conveyances are, of course, invaluable cultural documents.

6. Gradually the nobles were inclined to add a few biographical details to the series of bare titles. The first of such scanty biographies appears at the end of the Third Dynasty (§§ 170 ff.), after which there is a growing fondness for recording at least the chief honors received by the deceased from the Pharaoh, especially the furnishing and equipment of his tomb at the king's expense. The daily intercourse of the deceased with the king, the privileges which he enjoyed in connection with the royal person, or now and then the copy

of a letter from the king to his favorite—all these serve to make such biographies of inestimable value in completing our picture of the culture of the time. In the Sixth Dynasty these biographies become real narratives of the career of the departed noble, or at least of his most notable achievements in the service of the Pharaoh. The most important documents of this character are the biographies of Uni (§§ 291 ff.), and the nobles of Elephantine (§§ 325 ff., 355 ff., 362 ff.), one of whom has included therein a personal letter from the king (§§ 350 ff.).

7. As the aggressiveness of the Pharaohs increased, their foreign enterprises found record on the rocks in a number of distant regions (outside of Egypt proper), where they still exist. In the Peninsula of Sinai they appear in the First Dynasty (began 3400 B. C.); by the Fifth Dynasty (ended by 2580 B. C.) the officials who led such expeditions commenced to add their own records below the mere relief depicting the triumphant king, a scene to which heretofore only the name of the king was appended. From the Fourth Dynasty such memorials begin to appear in the alabaster quarries of Hatnub, behind Amarna; and from the reign of Isesi, in the Fifth Dynasty, they become more and more numerous in the quarries of Hammamat in the eastern desert, on the road from Coptos to the Red Sea. Practically all that we know, for example, of the power and deeds of the Eleventh Dynasty (2160–2000 B. C.) is drawn from records in these quarries.

8. They soon become so regular that their stoppage is almost certain evidence of an interruption in the orderly course of government in the Nile valley. Similar inscriptions on the rocks at the first cataract (§§ 316 ff.) begin in the time of Mernere, of the Sixth Dynasty (2625–2475 B. C.). The earliest inscription (§§ 472, 473) above the cataract in

Nubia itself dates from the reign of Amenemhet I, the first king of the Twelfth Dynasty (2000–1788 B. C.). Under the Empire such records on foreign soil appear also in Syria and Palestine (III, 297). Quarry inscriptions within the borders of Egypt do not begin until the Middle Kingdom, when we find them in the limestone quarries of Ayan (Turra-Ma'sara) just south of Cairo (§§ 739, 740); at the sandstone quarries of Silsileh they first appear under the Empire.

9. From the Middle Kingdom (2160–1788 B. C.) on, the memorial stelæ at Abydos are exceedingly valuable.[a] Officials on various commissions, whose business carried them to the holy city, improved the opportunity to erect memorial stones craving the favor of Osiris, the great god of the dead, for themselves and their relatives. Now and again such an officer narrates the circumstances which called him to Abydos; thus Ikhernofret, the treasurer of Sesostris III, records on his stela (§§ 661–70) not only the occasion of his visit, but also a copy of the royal letter which contained the command dispatching him thither.

10. In this age the tomb biographies become extremely valuable, because of their tendency to fulness and family details—a tendency already visible in the Tenth Dynasty tombs at Siut (§§ 391 ff.). But unfortunately only the tombs of Middle Egypt, chiefly at Benihasan (§§ 619 ff.), are preserved. Royal monuments with inscribed records become more plentiful, especially in Nubia, where the boundary stelæ of Sesostris III (§§ 651–60) are especially noteworthy; and in the quarries of Hammamat and the mines of Sinai. Papyri of any kind in the Middle Kingdom are still none too plentiful. Literary papyri are well represented by

---

[a]The great Old Kingdom inscription of Uni at Abydos hardly belongs to the class of memorial stelæ here designated. The inscription of Zau (§§ 344–49), of the Sixth Dynasty, however, should probably be included in this class; but it is unique in its time.

several magnificent manuscripts.   Of business and administrative documents, like letters, bills, accounts and tax lists,
we have examples in the Kahun Papyri, of which the second
find, now at Berlin, is still unpublished.   But papyrus documents of strictly historical import, such as we can include
here, are still rare in this age.

11. Under the Empire (1580–1150 B. C.) the available
documents both in quantity and quality for the first time
approach the minimum which in European history would
be regarded as adequate to a moderately full presentation
of the career of the nation.   Scores of important questions,
however, still remain unanswered, in whatever direction we
turn.   Nevertheless, a rough framework of the govern-
mental organization, the constitution of society, the most
important achievements of the kings, and to a limited extent
the spirit of the imperial age, may be discerned and sketched,
in the main outlines, with clearness and fair precision, even
though it is only here and there that the sources enable us
to fill in the detail.

12. It is especially royal monuments which are more
plentiful in the Empire, as compared with earlier times.
The first and most important class of such documents is
found in the temples—a source which in the earlier periods
has totally perished.   It was customary already at the
beginning of the dynasties for the king to commemorate his
victories in the temples.   This custom led in the Empire to
extensive and magnificent records on the temple walls, on
a scale not before attempted.   Such documents were less
records than triumphal memorials, and as historical sources
they are therefore very insufficient.   They dealt with events
with which all were familiar at the time of their erection,
and hence specific references to the said events are rare,
or, if present at all, are couched in such vague and

general terms that little can be drawn from them at the present day.

13. They consist chiefly in extensive reliefs on the temple walls, depicting the victorious Pharaoh in battle, capturing prisoners, or presenting prisoners and spoil to Amon. They are accompanied by descriptive and explanatory inscriptions, which unfortunately consist, for the most part, in conventional phrases in laudation of the Pharaoh as a mighty ruler. As the temples of the Eighteenth Dynasty have to a large extent perished, the priceless records of that imperial family have perished with them. We have three great series of reliefs: one representing the birth of Queen Hatshepsut (II, 187 ff.), and a duplicate depicting the birth of Amenhotep III (II, 841 ff.), while the third pictures the voyage of Hatshepsut to the land of Punt (II, 246 ff.). More valuable are the extracts from the annals of Thutmose III on the walls of the Karnak temple (II, 391 ff.), already mentioned, and a similar record of his son Amenhotep II on a large stela at Karnak (II, 780 ff.). The temple records of the Nineteenth and Twentieth Dynasties are much more plentiful; but they are almost exclusively of the unprecise character above described. Besides the great record of Merneptah's Libyan war, (III, 569–617), which is a much better source, they are chiefly memorials of the wars of Seti I (III, 80–156), of his son, Ramses II (III, 294–391, 448–91), and of Ramses III, of the Twentieth Dynasty (IV, 1–145).

14. Another class of temple records is the building inscriptions. Apart from their value as records of building enterprises, they contain valuable references to the history of the builder. In a number of cases the early career of the builder and the manner in which he came to the throne are prefixed as an introduction to the record of the building itself. This is observable as far back as the building

inscription of Sesostris I, in the Twelfth Dynasty (§§ 498 ff.);
in the Eighteenth Dynasty (1580–1350 B. C.) we gain
invaluable hints of the early life of Thutmose III from his
great building inscription in the Karnak temple (II, 131 ff.).
Such building records not infrequently also contain priceless
references to the wars and campaigns of the Pharaoh, whence
he may have obtained the wealth for the edifice in question.
Notable examples of this class are the stela of Thutmose III
in the Ptah temple at Karnak (II, 609 ff.), and the great
summary of the buildings of Amenhotep III left by him on
a stela in his mortuary temple at Thebes (II, 878 ff.).

15. Records of restorations are not less valuable. The
restoration record of Hatshepsut at Benihasan (II, 296 ff.)
throws a significant sidelight on the reasons necessitating
such restoration of the temples, after their neglect by the
Hyksos; while the short remarks of Harmhab and Seti I,
recording their restorations after the revolution of Ikhnaton,
are invaluable indications of the widespread activity of the
latter (II, 878).   Again, we gain a hint of the anarchy following this revolution, from the record of Harmhab's restoration of the mummy of Thutmose IV, after its violation by
tomb-robbers (III, 32 A ff.).

16. Stelæ dedicating the finished temple to the god were
set up in the holy of holies, at the place where the king stood
in the performance of the royal ritual.   Some of these were
of enormous size, that of Amenhotep III in his temple
behind the Memnon colossi being no less than thirty feet
high, and hewn of a single block (II, 904 ff.).   The content
of these dedication stelæ does not differ essentially from
that of the building inscriptions; they likewise contain
references to the wars of the kings erecting them.   The
most important of these now surviving are the two in duplicate erected by Amenhotep II at Amada and Elephantine

(II, 791 ff.). The temple obelisks also occasionally bear inscriptions of historical importance, and among these the inscriptions of Hatshepsut (II, 304 ff.), of Thutmose III (II, 623 ff.), and of Thutmose IV (II, 830 ff.) furnish very useful data.

17. All these temple records, being for the glory of the Pharaoh, are couched in language very poetic and highly colored, although the poetic form is not always discernible. Among them, however, are found poems in praise of the sovereign, exhibiting strictly poetic structure, with rigid division into strophes. Some of these contain references and allusions which, in view of the scantiness of our materials, may be employed historically. Such hymns probably existed from the earliest days of the dynasties, but the earliest example preserved is dedicated to the praise of Sesostris III, of the Twelfth Dynasty.[a] In the Empire the most notable example celebrates the fame of Thutmose III (II, 655 ff.). It is the earliest of such poems possessing real historical importance.

18. Royal records not of this class of temple memorials are not numerous. Of actual state documents we possess very few. The viceroy of Kush recorded on stone the decree in which Thutmose I announced his coronation, and of this rescript we possess two copies (II, 54 ff.). At the opening of the Nineteenth Dynasty (1350–1205 B. C.) we have the royal decree instituting the administrative reforms of Harmhab; it is possibly in its original form (III, 45–67). Another great example of a state document is the famous treaty between Ramses II and the Hittite king Khetasar (III, 367–91). The remarkable report of the unfortunate envoy to Syria, Wenamon, may also be a few pages from the

---

[a] Its historical references are too vague and general to warrant its insertion in this series.

royal archives at Thebes (IV, 557 ff.). A few letters from the king personally (e. g., §§ 350 ff., 664, 665) and some legal records (IV, 499–557) complete the list of state documents. The remaining royal documents are of a miscellaneous character, like the unique memorial scarabs of Amenhotep III (II, 860 ff.), or the huge stelæ erected as landmarks by Ikhnaton for the purpose of demarking the limits of his new capital at Amarna (II, 949 ff.). Finally, the greatest of all royal documents is the enormous Papyrus Harris, recording the good deeds of Ramses III (1198–1167 B. C.) to gods and men, compiled for his tomb, as a title to consideration at the hands of the gods in the future life (IV, 151–412).

19. The private monuments of the Empire are also more numerous than before and contribute greatly to our knowledge of it. The tombs of the Pharaoh's grandees have now become more personal monuments than ever before. These men, who were guiding Egypt on her imperial career, delighted to perpetuate in their tombs some record of the brilliant part which they were playing in these great events. The generals and administrative officials who under the Pharaoh governed the Empire, now sleep in rock-hewn tombs at Thebes, the chambers of which still bear magnificently painted scenes from their active and adventurous lives. Here we behold the reception of tribute from the remotest limits of the Empire, borne on the shoulders of Palestinians, Syrians, or northern islanders, the whole being accompanied by explanatory inscriptions. The various duties and activities of the greatest officials of the government are here depicted, and from these scenes and the appended inscriptions we can draw fuller data respecting the Empire and its organization than from any other source.

20. These tomb chapels, besides the Amarna Letters,

are also the only surviving contemporary source for the civilization of Syria and Palestine in the second millennium before Christ. The most important of such tombs is that of Rekhmire, the vizier of Thutmose III (II, 663–762). The biographies of the generals preserved in these tomb chapels are not infrequently our only source for entire wars of the Pharaoh, of which we should not otherwise have known anything at all—not even that they took place. Besides these tomb inscriptions, the nobles also recorded their biographies, or at least some of their achievements, on the statues accorded them by the Pharaoh in the Karnak temple. Examples of such records are the statue of Senmut (II, 345 ff.), or that of Beknekhonsu (III, 561 ff.). After the Eighteenth Dynasty the Empire abounds in papyri: letters, bills, receipts, administrative and legal documents, memoranda, numerous literary compositions, scientific treatises like those on medicine, mathematics, or astronomy, religious documents, and innumerable ostraca, or potsherds and flakes of limestone bearing receipts, letters, memoranda, or literary fragments. These, for the most part, fall outside of the scope of the present volumes and will appear in later series of these *Ancient Records*.

21. Such are the main sources for the history of the Empire; there are, of course, numerous unimportant miscellaneous monuments which we have not mentioned; nor do we recall all the classes of documents already referred to in the older epochs, like the inscriptions abroad, which now become very plentiful. Indeed, the rocks of the first cataract under the Empire became a veritable visitors' register of the officials and functionaries who, passing on some commission in Nubia, left a record of the errand, or merely name and titles, engraved on the rocks above the reach of the inundation (e. g., II, 675 ff.). Inscriptions of the

emperors are found in Nubia as far south as the island of Tombos, and mere cartouches with titles up to the fourth cataract.

22. With the decline of Thebes in the Decadence (1150–663 B. C.), and the transference of the seat of power to the North, the great mass of records of the royal houses was produced, and their monuments were erected, in the Delta, where almost the whole has perished forever, with the destruction of the exposed Delta cities, overwhelmed by invasion after invasion from abroad, and gradually engulfed by the rising soil as deposited from century to century by the inundation. The fortunes of the northern dynasties can therefore be traced only in the scanty monuments of Thebes, in which the Pharaohs no longer built largely, and at Memphis, where we have a series of dated stelæ recording Apis burials in the Serapeum. These are of great value from the Twenty-second to the Twenty-sixth Dynasty. At Thebes the records of the restoration of royal mummies extend from the last generation of the Twentieth into the Twenty-second Dynasty (IV, 592 ff., 636 ff., 661 ff., 664 ff., 688 ff., 690 ff., 699 f.); and a series of dated Nile levels on the quay at Karnak continues from the Twenty-second to the Twenty-sixth Dynasty (IV, 693 ff.). We have at Thebes also a few temple records from the priest-kings of the Twenty-first Dynasty (1090–945 B. C.), a series of decrees of Amon (IV, 614 ff., 650 ff., 669 ff.), and some not very important building records of the high priests of Amon, during the same period. The same is true in the Twenty-second Dynasty (945–755 B. C.), through the brief Twenty-third and Twenty-fourth Dynasties (755–712 B. C.), and the Ethiopian period (Twenty-fifth Dynasty, 712–663 B. C.). At this point, fortunately, the scanty monuments of the Delta are supplemented by the historical stelæ erected by

the Ethiopians at Gebel Barkal (Napata). Among these, the narrative of his conquest of Egypt by Piankhi is one of the most remarkable documents of ancient Egypt (IV, 796–883).

23. The paucity of documents, so painfully evident during the Decadence, is even worse under the Restoration (Twenty-sixth Dynasty, 663–525 B. C.). Besides the great adoption stela of Psamtik I at Thebes (IV, 935 ff.), a few Serapeum stelæ, important for the chronology, a small number of statue inscriptions of noblemen of the time, and some miscellaneous stelæ of little importance, we possess almost nothing from the Restoration. Unhappily, the papyri, which are so plentiful during the Nineteenth, Twentieth, and Twenty-first Dynasties, are few and unimportant throughout the remainder of the Decadence and the whole of the Restoration. Fortunately, Herodotus, and the Greek historians after him, enter at this point with invaluable accounts of the history and civilization of the Restoration epoch; but these foreign sources do not fall within the province of these volumes.

24. Besides these contemporary native sources, we possess also a series of later native versions of important events in the history of the nation. These documents are either merely folk-tales, of course differing strikingly in form from the more formal contemporary records; or they are products of the later priesthoods, which, in the form of a tale, give an account of some earlier event, which they so interpret or so distort as to bring reputation, or even material gain, to their sanctuaries. Of the folk-tales we have three of importance: Papyrus Westcar, relating the prodigies attending the birth of the first three Fifth Dynasty kings; Papyrus Sallier I, narrating the cause of the war with the Hyksos; and Papyrus Harris 500, in which is told the story of the capture of

Joppa by one of Thutmose III's generals, named Thutiy.
As tales these documents have no place in this series, although
each is based on some actual historical incident, which may
be obscurely discerned in the narrative.   The priestly tales
are likewise three in number: the Sehel inscription, recount-
ing the gift of the Dodekaschoinos at the first cataract to
Khnum by King Zoser of the Third Dynasty; the Sphinx
Stela (II, 810 ff.), recording the accession of Thutmose IV
to the kingship, because as prince he cleared the Sphinx of
sand; and finally the Bentresh Stela, containing a tale in
honor of one of the Theban Khonsus, by showing that he
was carried to a distant Asiatic kingdom in order to heal
its king's daughter, in the days of Ramses II (III, 429–47).
The last two stories seemed of sufficient importance to be
included here.   It was with tales in common circulation
like these that Herodotus' informants regaled him, and the
narrative portions of Manetho's history were largely made
up of just such stories, of which further examples from
Ptolemaic times have survived in Demotic dress.

25. It will be seen that the great mass of the documents
available are found in Upper Egypt, and but a scanty few
in the Delta.   This unfortunate fact makes all our knowledge one-sided, and the history of the Delta, the civilization
of which must have risen at a very remote date, remains for
the most part unknown to us.   Our loss is here like that in
Greek history, in which we know almost nothing of the
great civilization in the powerful cities of Asia Minor, from
which the culture of the early states in Greece drew so much.

26. The documents thus briefly surveyed have reached
us, with very few exceptions, in a state of sad mutilation.
This mutilation and gradual destruction are a ceaseless
process, which, if not as rapid as formerly, nevertheless
proceeds without cessation at the present day.   In Egypt,

the exposed monuments, like the great geographical list of Sheshonk I, are perishing with appalling rapidity, and many of them without ever having been properly copied or published. Even the portable stone monuments at present in the museums of Europe suffer more or less; and I have seen valuable stelæ so attacked by the moist air of northern Europe that whole layers might be blown from the inscribed surface by a whiff of the breath. Such an inscription is doomed to disappear in a few years. Papyri when mounted between hermetically sealed glass plates survive indefinitely.

27. These monuments, as employed in Egyptological science, are, for the most part, not accessible in the originals, but are consulted chiefly in publications. Such publications, to omit earlier and cruder attempts, began as far back as the colossal report issued in huge folios by the members of Napoleon I's expedition. Notable and useful as this great work was, its copies of the inscriptions are now quite unusable. To copy an inscription of any kind with accuracy is not easy. So close and fine an observer of material documents as Ruskin, could copy a short Latin inscription with surprising inaccuracy. In his incomparable *Mornings in Florence*[a] he reproduces the brief inscription on the marble slab covering the tomb which he so admired in the church of Santa Croce; and in his copy of these eight short lines, which I compared with the original, he misspells one word, and omits two entire words ("et magister") of the mediæval Latin.

28. This experience of the great art critic is not infrequently that of the schooled and careful paleographer as well. The best-known of the Politarch inscriptions appeared in eight different publications,[b] each of which diverges in

---

[a]Third edition, 1889, 16.
[b]See Burton, *American Journal of Theology*, II, 600–604.

some more or less important respect from all the rest, before a correct copy was obtained. The Greek and Latin inscriptions on the bronze crab from the base of the New York obelisk were long incorrectly read, and the mistake in the date led Mommsen to a false theory of the early Roman prefects of Egypt.[a] In working on a mutilated inscription, the best of copyists will now and again overlook traces which his successors may discover and utilize, while now and then he will "nap," and be guilty of some egregious blunder of omission or misreading in a clear and perfectly preserved passage. Under these circumstances, an inexperienced or careless copyist will commit the most incredible blunders, and every line of his copy will contain many such. In the early days of Egyptology, when a reading knowledge of hieroglyphic was still impossible, it required a copyist of exceptional ability to produce a copy which can be used at the present day.

29. This difficulty was sorely felt by accurate and discerning scholars as far back as the days of Chabas, who in 1872 remarked, concerning the inscriptions of Ramses III: "Ces deux publications [Rosellini and Burton] sont très imparfaites; et les signes inexactement reproduits ajoutent à la difficulté causée par les lacunes."[b] The introduction of hieroglyphic type, while very useful in some respects, has also proved disastrous to accuracy, and the persistence of the old loose methods was bemoaned by Brugsch in the introduction to the last volume of his *Thesaurus* thirteen years ago. Brugsch already showed surprising appreciation of the necessity of modern methods in such work. He wrote:

The indispensable demands upon the publisher of known or unknown texts may be comprehended in a few words. In the first place, it is not a task to be undertaken by laymen and mere amateurs . . . . but

[a]See II, 632, note.
[b]*Études sur l'antiquité historique*, 227 f.

only by the schooled specialist, who is thoroughly familiar with the language and writing of the ancient Egyptians, and with the researches and results in all departments of Egyptological investigation. How largely such a conviction is still lacking is proved . . . . by a number of publications by Egyptological tyros [*Halbwisser*] and laymen, who do not yet seem to have learned that Egyptology has ceased to be the pursuit of amateurs, and has become a very serious study, demanding a man's entire strength and entire time.[a]

30. Not long after this, Griffith called attention to the hurried, inaccurate, and insufficient methods still often observable, so that numerous publications could only be regarded as provisional.[b] Two years later he referred to such work in these words: "Too often almost every third sign in the printed texts has had to be corrected according to probabilities by the would-be reader."[c] This condition of things has gone so far that we have had publications issued at government expense, containing texts in vertical columns copied with the lines numbered backward, and even translated in this inverted order of the lines.[d] It is safe to say that such a condition of things cannot be found in any other branch of paleographical science.

31. This is not the place to discuss the proper methods to be observed in the publication of ancient documents, but there is no doubt that better methods are constantly gaining ground. From decade to decade the publication of inscriptions has steadily improved, but it is only within the last ten or fifteen years that Egyptian documents on stone have in some cases appeared in a form which satisfies the demands of modern paleographic accuracy. With the exception of

---

[a]*Thesaurus*, VI, vi.

[b]*Egypt Exploration Fund Archæological Report*, 1893–94, 10, 11.

[c]*Ibid.*, 1895–96, 21.

[d]In the old publications plenty of examples of such inversion exist, especially in Mariette's books; nor are instances lacking in which modern scholars have employed such texts without discovering the inversion.

such perfectly preserved rolls as the great Papyrus Harris, which was long ago accurately published, the same remark is in general true of the papyri also.

32. The result of all this is that many of the most important documents of ancient Egypt are at present accessible to the Egyptologist only in publications so incorrect that in many cases they are absolutely unusable. It will be evident, therefore, that he who wishes to know exactly what the original documents of ancient Egypt state cannot work exclusively in his library, but must go behind the publications and turn back to the originals themselves, in Egypt and the museums of Europe.

33. For the purposes of these volumes it was therefore absolutely indispensable in most cases to go back of the publications. The author, therefore, made and repeatedly revised his own copies of practically all the historical monuments in Europe, before the originals themselves. In the few cases where the original was not accessible, good squeezes and photographs supplied the deficiency, or professional colleagues furnished from the originals specially collated readings of doubtful passages. Of the monuments in Egypt the author copied a great many at all the more important sites, especially Thebes and Amarna, where he made a complete copy of all the historical inscriptions; and in the museum at Cairo (formerly Gizeh). Of monuments in Egypt not included in the author's copies, squeezes were in most cases found in the enormous collection made by Lepsius, and now in the Berlin Museum. Where none of these sources furnished the desired monument, the author had access to the extensive collations made for the Berlin Egyptian Dictionary; and where these failed, he was able, in all important cases, to secure large-scale photographs of the originals. The final remainder of monuments for which the

author was dependent upon the publications alone is very
small, and in most such cases the publication was one made
on modern methods and almost as good as the original
itself.

34. Nevertheless, it must not be supposed that the old
publications, however inaccurate, can be ignored.   Some
monuments have perished entirely since publication, and
almost all have lost more or less important portions of the text.
In the case of all the longer and more important texts, often
reproduced in the old folios, the author took the best copy as
a basis and collated with it all the other publications, noting
in parallel columns all the variant readings.   By this labori-
ous means, some readings were secured which have since
disappeared from the original, and all that is now available,
whether in publications or in the original, was thus incorporated in the final composite copy, from which the translation was made.   In a few cases the author was spared this
labor by the industry of a modern editor of the document,
as in the publication of the Benihasan tombs or those of
Siut; but ordinarily the modern editor has not given himself
this trouble, as in the last publication of Der el-Bahri.

35. The dangers involved in such neglect are evident.
Thus so careful a scholar as Chabas discussed the so-called
"eclipse inscription" (IV, 756 ff.) of Takelot II, using only
the publication of Lepsius; whereupon Goodwin[a] called
his attention to the fact that the very conscientious plate of
Lepsius had nevertheless introduced confusion into the text
by the accidental misplacement of a piece of the paper
squeeze from which his copy was made, thus inverting the
proper order of two sections of the very obscure text.   Had
Chabas also employed Young's otherwise obsolete copy of
the original, this embarrassing error would not have occurred.

---

[a]*Zeitschrift für ägyptische Sprache*, 1868, 25 ff.

36. Chabas[a] himself convicted Lenormant of a similar error in discussing Ramses II's victory over the Hittites at Kadesh. Lenormant[b] employed only the Abusimbel version of the report of the battle, not noticing that the ancient Egyptian scribe had omitted an entire line of the document, as is shown by the Ramesseum version. This omitted line happens to be of vital importance to a proper understanding of the battle, and the failure to observe its omission is fatal to any discussion of the conflict. The same error, nevertheless, has since been repeated in at least one notable modern treatise on the same battle.[c] Further examples might be adduced in illustration of the danger incurred in making a study of any inscription as found in a single publication of the text.

37. The translations in the following volumes, we repeat, are therefore based upon all the available material for the reconstruction of each document, whether in the original or in old publications made at a time when the original was possibly in a better state of preservation. In no other way can all the available material be obtained, and scholars who would compare the renderings herein with the original documents themselves will in many cases be able to do so only by reconstructing the text in the same way.

---

[a]*Revue archéologique*, XV[2] (1858–59), 573 ff., 701 f.

[b]*Correspondant*, VII (February, 1858), second article.

[c]See my *Battle of Kadesh*, **4, 5.**

CHRONOLOGY

CHRONOLOGY

38. The state of our modern chronology of early Egyptian history is so confused that a brief presentation of the system herein employed seemed indispensable, although space will not permit even partial discussion of the materials upon which it is based. The following presentation,[a] moreover, will attempt nothing more than an explanation of the elementary factors of the problem, as even these are unknown to some who have nevertheless arbitrarily rejected their invaluable data.

39. The Egyptians, as far back as the fifth millennium before Christ, had discovered approximately the length of the year. They, like all other peoples, had suffered from the vexatious fact that the lunar month is not an even divisor of the year. Instead of attempting to adjust this obstinate incommensurability by constant and complicated intercalations, they showed amazing appreciation of the practical demands which a calendar should satisfy, and boldly abandoned the lunar month as the basis of the calendar. Believing the year to be 365 days long, they divided it into twelve months of thirty days each, and an intercalated period of five days at the end of the year. The creation of this convenient and practical, though artificial, calendar was an achievement unparalleled in any other ancient civilization. It was as useful to men of science as to civil life in general, and for this reason it was in later times

---

[a]Since this brief discussion was written, the admirable essay of Meyer (*"Aegyptische Chronologie," Abhandlungen der Königlichen Preussischen Akademie*, 1904) has appeared, from which the author has frequently added valuable observations to the above presentation. The literature of the subject is large, but Meyer's invaluable treatise furnishes a compendium of the whole obscure and difficult field.

adopted by the Greek astronomers as the basis of all their computations.

40. The Egyptian began his year at the advent of the inundation, and this event, by a happy accident, approximately coincided with the reappearance of Sirius (Sothis) at sunrise on the eastern horizon, after he had been for some length of time invisible. This occurred each year on July 19[a] (Julian). The interval between such heliacal risings of Sothis was thus fortunately approximately a solar year.[b] The feast of the Rising of Sothis on July 19 was therefore the New Year's feast of the Egyptians. The year was also arbitrarily divided into three seasons, each containing four months of thirty days each. These were: the season of verdure, or the inundation; the season of winter or sowing; and the season of summer or harvest. When this remarkably rational calendar was introduced, it of course coincided with the seasons as determined for the people by the sun and the inundation. But the Sothic year was almost exactly, and in 3231 B. C.[c] was exactly, a quarter of a day longer than the new calendar year of 365 days. Every four years, therefore, the calendar reached the end of the year and began the next year one day too soon, so that the rising of Sirius fell on the second day of the new year. As this process continued, and each calendar New Year's Day arrived earlier and earlier, it finally passed gradually around the whole year and again fell on the astronomical New Year's Day. This process consumed four times as many years as

---

[a]It took place on July 19 (Julian) as the normal date, in the latitude of Memphis, for many thousands of years B. C., until far down in the last thousand years B. C., when the Sothic year had sufficiently lengthened to shift the heliacal rising of Sothis to July 20. (See Meyer, *op. cit.*, 1904, 17 ff.)

[b]Neither the solar nor the Sothic year is constant in length, and at present they are slowly diverging.

[c]Meyer, *op. cit.*, 14.

there were days in the calendar year; that is, 1,460 years; or we may say: 1,461 calendar years =1,460 Sothic (Julian) years.

Without knowing it, the Egyptian was thus dealing with three different years: [a]

1. His calendar year of 365 days, by which most of the business of civil life was transacted and all documents were dated.

2. The Sothic (or Julian) year of $365\frac{1}{4}$ days, on the first of which the people celebrated the feast of the Rising of Sothis.

3. The solar (or Gregorian) year of a little less than $365\frac{1}{4}$ days (which was therefore slowly diverging from the Sothic year).

41. The Egyptian, as we have intimated, never learned that the Sothic (Julian) and the solar years were not identical; the divergence[b] was so slow, and so slight, that it was entirely imperceptible to the masses, or possibly even to the learned, of the time. On the contrary, the difference between his calendar and the feast of the heliacal Rising of Sothis (that is, 1 and 2) must have been early observed. Nevertheless, the actual shift within an average lifetime was not so great as to occasion inconvenience. Thus each generation accepted the place of the calendar in the seasons as they found it, and without remark considered it as a matter of course that the beginning of the inundation, or the advent of summer heat, fell on about such and such a day of a certain month. Both these events had occurred

---

[a]See Meyer, *op. cit.*, 16.

[b]In 4231 B. C. the summer solstice fell on July 28 (Julian); but as it was always eighteen hours and forty minutes earlier than the Sothic rising each century, it had advanced thirty-one days, to June 27, by 231 B. C. In the thirty-first century (3001–3100) B. C. it coincided with the Sothic rising on July 19 (Julian). (See Meyer, *op. cit.*, 14 f.)

at about that time since their earliest remembrance. A peasant of fifty or sixty—that is, at the end of an average life—hardly remarked that the seasons were now ten or twelve days later in the calendar than when he was a lad of ten. Unfortunately, references to the place of the seasons, or of astronomical events, in the calendar are rare; nevertheless, there are enough of such references to trace the gradual revolution of the calendar on the seasons.

42. In the Sixth Dynasty, Uni, a nobleman who had been sent to Assuan to procure granite from the quarries there, narrates that he succeeded in landing his cargo at the king's pyramid, although it was in the eleventh month, when, he adds (as everyone knew), there was no water for such transportation. The time of advancing low water, terminating heavy transportation of this sort, normally in the eighth to the ninth month of the calendar, thus fell two months later in Uni's time (§ 323).[a] In the Middle Kingdom a hitherto misunderstood inscription (§§ 735 ff.) narrates how an unfortunate official, dispatched to the mines of Sinai, arrived there in the third month of (calendar) winter, when he and his men suffered greatly from the summer heat! This shows a divergence of seven or eight months; as we should expect, in the centuries which have elapsed since the Old Kingdom the calendar had shifted several months. A letter[b] from a priest in the 120th year of the Twelfth Dynasty, notifying his subordinates that the feast of the Rising of Sothis would occur on the fifteenth of the eighth month,[c] shows us the exact amount of the shift at that

---

[a][Later: Practically the same interpretation of the inscription has now appeared in Meyer's essay (*Aegyptische Chronologie*).]

[b]Among papyri found at Kahun, now at Berlin (Borchardt, *Zeitschrift für ägyptische Sprache*, 37, 99 ff.).

[c]Temple entries from the same papyri, recording the offerings made at the Sothis feast, are dated the next day.

time; for the feast thus fell exactly 225 days (seven months and fifteen days) after New Year's Day in the calendar.

43. The divergence steadily increased, and in the early part of the Eighteenth Dynasty, in the ninth year of Amenhotep I, it was exactly 308 days.[a] A Sothic date somewhere between 47 and 101 years later, in the reign of Thutmose III, shows that it had then increased to 327 days (II, 410, note). It is, furthermore, roughly indicated by the dates of his campaigns in Syria (II, 409 ff.), which, as we know, always occurred from April to October. His son Amenhotep II's campaigns carry the divergence a little farther, and some 150 years later its continuance is shown by the dates of Ramses II's campaigns (III, 307). For nearly six centuries after this we have no indication of the place of the calendar,[b] but in the third year of Shabataka, about 700 B. C., the first day of high Nile is recorded at Thebes as occurring on the fifth of the ninth month of the calendar (IV, 887). The calendar had thus completed its revolution around the seasons, and had also shifted nearly 180 days in another revolution, since the reign of Thutmose III. The shift of the calendar can thus be traced for some 2,000 years, as determined by six different dates of astronomical or seasonal events, and a series of other significant occurrences, in terms of the calendar.[c]

---

[a]Calendar of Papyrus Ebers.

[b]The date of the high water in the reign of Osorkon II, in the Twenty-second Dynasty (IV, 742 ff.), will be of assistance when the correct date is known; but as given by Daressy (*Recueil*, 18, 181) it has certainly been incorrectly transliterated from the hieratic. The calendar of Ramses III (largely copied from an almost completely lost original of Ramses II), which places the Rising of Sothis on New Year's Day, is of course a normal calendar intended to avoid constant readjusting of its long list of dates from time to time. Such a calendar of feasts could be perpetually used without alteration, by merely allowing in each date for the then amount of the divergence.

[c]The conjecture (*eo ipso* very improbable) that the calendar was at irregular intervals readjusted to the astronomical year, is completely disproved by the procession exhibited by the above series.

44. These data are of significance and value in two respects. In the first place, they demonstrate the very early advance of the Egyptians in the discernment and calculation of astronomical and calendrical phenomena. For we know from the use of the Egyptian year by classic astronomers and mathematicians that the calendar coincided with the Sothic year, and that a new Sothic cycle began, some time in the period 140/41 to 143/44 A. D.[a] It must therefore also have coincided with the Sothic year 1,460 years earlier; that is, in 1320 B. C.; and still earlier, in 2780 B. C.[b] Now, it is impossible that this calendar was first introduced so late as the twenty-eighth century, in the midst of the highest culture of the Old Kingdom. Moreover, the five intercalary days at the end of the year, proving the use of the shifting year of 365 days, are mentioned in the pyramid texts, which are far older than the Old Kingdom.

45. The calendar, therefore, existed before the Old Kingdom; but if this be true, we must seek its invention at a time when its three seasons coincided roughly with those of nature, as they must have done at its introduction. This carries us 1,460 years back of their coincidence in the Old Kingdom; that is, the calendar was introduced in the middle of the forty-third century B. C. (4241 B. C.). This is the oldest fixed date in history. This fact demonstrates not only a remarkable degree of scientific knowledge in that remote age, but also stable political conditions, and a wide recognition of central authority, which could gradually introduce such an innovation. The date employed was that for the rising of Sothis in the latitude of Memphis or the southern Delta, and this fact is a significant indication of the high culture prevailing in the north at this time.[c]

---

[a]Censorinus, 21, 10, and Meyer, *op. cit.*, 28.

[b]For convenience, ignoring the uncertainty of four years.

[c]See Meyer, *op. cit.*, 38 ff.

46. In a second respect the calendar is of inestimable value to us in establishing the chronology of Egyptian history. Where the heliacal rising of Sothis is recorded in terms of the calendar, it is a matter of the simplest arithmetic[a] to determine, within a margin of four years, in what year B. C. the rising occurred. As we have seen, three such dates are preserved to us, two of which each give the year of the king's reign, and from these the entire Twelfth Dynasty, and the reign of Amenhotep I in the Eighteenth Dynasty, are established within four years in terms B. C. They show that the Twelfth Dynasty began in 2000 B. C., and the reign of Amenhotep I in 1557 B. C., thus determining the accession of the Eighteenth Dynasty as 1580 B. C.[b] The third Sothic rising, in the reign of Thutmose III, is not dated in a particular year of the reign, so that it furnishes only a rough approximation of the date of his reign, proving that the year 1470 B. C. fell within his reign. This approximation may be rendered precise by a computation based upon the feasts of the New Moon, which Thutmose III is recorded to have celebrated in his twenty-third and twenty-fourth years (II, 430). These new-moon dates[c] establish the date of Thutmose III's reign as May 3, 1501, to March 17, 1447 B. C.[d] The two other early dates are chiefly of

---

[a]Thus: The rising of Sothis at the beginning occurs on the first day of the calendar year. From a given calendar date of its rising the amount of the shift of the calendar can be computed in an instant. In the 120th year of the Twelfth Dynasty Sothis arose 225 days after New Year's Day. As the shift occurred at the rate of one day in four years, the 225 days' shift had taken place in 900 years since the calendar coincided with nature; that is, since 2780 B. C. The 120th year of the Twelfth Dynasty was thus 1880 B. C., and the dynasty began in 2000 B. C. (or between 2000 and 1996 B. C.).

[b]Meyer, *op. cit.*, 46 ff.

[c]The phases of the moon occupy the same position in the calendar every nineteen years. The date of Thutmose III's reign being roughly determined by the Sothic rising, the new-moon dates can then be employed to place this reign more precisely. Without the Sothic date the new-moon dates would be of no use, as they merely present conditions recurring every nineteen years.

[d]Meyer, *loc. cit.*

significance in demonstrating the fact of the shift of the calendar in the Old and Middle Kingdoms, but are not precise enough to determine with exactness the date B. C.

47. Besides the above astronomical method, minimum dates as far back as the beginning of the Eighteenth Dynasty can be determined by dead reckoning back from a fixed starting-point. The result thus obtained, without reference to the astronomically determined dates, can then be compared with these, for the sake of testing both. The dates by dead reckoning are obtained by simply adding together the totals of reigns and dynasties, and with these reckoning back from the accession of the Persians in 525 B. C. In this process I have employed only the testimony of the contemporary monuments.[a]

48. Our first task is to determine the length of the dynasties preceding the invasion of the Persians; that is, the Eighteenth to the Twenty-sixth Dynasty. The method is first to seek the highest known date in each reign of a dynasty, and thus to determine the minimum length of the dynasty. In the use of royal dates given in years of the reign only, there is danger both of over- and of under-reckoning. Thus Ramses III reigned thirty-one years and forty days; but a date from his thirty-second year might lead one to think he had reigned thirty-two years, which is nearly a year in excess of the truth. As the newly crowned successor to the throne began to number his years from the death of his predecessor, it will be seen that the remainder of what would have been Ramses III's complete thirty-second year is included in the reign of his successor.[b] If counted in both reigns, it is therefore counted twice. It has therefore

---

[a]Wherever he can be controlled, Manetho is generally wrong in his figures, and any chronology based on his data is hopelessly astray.

[b]This is supposing that, as in the Eighteenth Dynasty, the years of a king began with the day of his accession, and not on the New Year's Day preceding his accession, as in the Middle Kingdom and the Twenty-sixth Dynasty.

been thought necessary to deduct one year for every transfer of the crown.[a] This method, however, is extreme, as
we shall show. In the first place, it applies only when the
maximum date preserved is actually the respective king's
last year. Again, it does not always apply even then.
Thutmose III reigned fifty-four years lacking thirty-four
days. The reign of his successor, therefore, included only
the last thirty-four days of what would have been Thutmose III's complete fifty-fourth year. To deduct a year
at this transfer of the crown is as extreme as to count the
thirty-second year of Ramses III's reign. It is evident
that the last year of a king's reign is as likely to be nearly
complete as it is to be scarcely begun; hence the only fair
method of reduction for double counting at the transfers of
the crown is to count the number of transfers in an entire
dynasty, and for each transfer to deduct a half-year; that is,
a mean between the two extremes of deducting a whole
year for each transfer, or of deducting nothing. In the
course of a whole dynasty the errors both ways will probably
compensate each other.[b]

49. In the following table I have made no deduction for
transfer of the crown either to or from a king from whose
reign we have no dates, but in all such reigns (marked x)
such deduction has been included in the estimate of the
reign. It is needless to add that in cases of coregency such
deduction is unnecessary. In estimating the x, or unknown
years in a given reign, the historical facts of the reign, if any,
have been duly considered, though there has not always

---

[a]Mahler, *Zeitschrift für ägyptische Sprache*, 32, 104 f.; Lehmann, *Zwei Hauptprobleme*, 56.

[b]This method can apply with certainty only in the Eighteenth Dynasty, in which the king's year begins with his accession. I have supposed, however, that this system of numbering continued until the end of the Ethiopian period. In the Twelfth and Twenty-sixth Dynasties such allowance must be differently computed.

been space to note the said facts. That this is absolutely necessary will be evident. Thus Sheshonk I took out the stone from the Silsileh quarry for his Karnak building in his twenty-first year. The vast forecourt of the Karnak temple of Amon, or the enormous front pylon, was then built by him. Yet his highest date is that of the said quarry operations in the twenty-first year. It is clear, therefore, that he must have ruled several years more, and no fair chronological reckoning can disregard these years.

50. Observing the above precautions, we obtain as a minimum for the Empire and following dynasties, down to the accession of the Persians, the following figures:[a]

Eighteenth Dynasty	230 years
Nineteenth Dynasty	145 "
Interim	5 "
Twentieth Dynasty	110 "
Twenty-first Dynasty	145 "
Twenty-second Dynasty	200 "
Twenty-third Dynasty	23 "
Twenty-fourth Dynasty	6 "
Twenty-fifth Dynasty	50 "
Twenty-sixth Dynasty	138 "
Total	1,052 "

As the accession of the Persians occurred in 525 B. C., the beginning of the Eighteenth Dynasty will have been 1,052 years earlier, or about 1577 B. C.[b]

51. Our second task is now to compare with this result the dates in the Eighteenth Dynasty obtained by astronomi-

---

[a]A detailed table by reigns will be found §§ 58–75; and for the Twenty-first, Twenty-second, and Twenty-sixth Dynasties still further details will be found in IV, 604–7, 693–98, 959, 974, 984, 1026, 1027.

[b]This result of a dead reckoning from minimum dates cannot be brought down any later. Mr. Cecil Torr's attempt (*Memphis and Mycenæ*) to establish a much later date for the beginning of the Eighteenth Dynasty by the same process was extreme in method, and rested upon incomplete material.

cal means, which place the accession of Ahmose I within the
four years from 1580 on.[a]   It will be seen that the result of
the astronomical calculation is remarkably corroborated by
the dead reckoning with minimum dynastic totals.   It should
be noted, however, that the above date for the beginning of
the Eighteenth Dynasty, based upon the Sothic date in the
ninth year of Amenhotep I, is corroborated, not only by the
above dead reckoning, but also by the Sothic and new-moon
dates in the reign of Thutmose III, a calculation from which
places this king's reign at just the right remove from that
of Amenhotep I, as determined by the Sothic date (see § 46).

52. The existing contemporary monuments do not suffice
to determine by dead reckoning the length of the obscure
period which preceded the Eighteenth Dynasty, including
the Hyksos.   It should be noted, however, that these monuments do not indicate a long[b] period.   They are few and
scanty.   There is nothing to show that the long list of kings
which the Turin Papyrus places in this period were not
partially contemporaneous.   The same document gives no
indication in its enumeration of the kings of the Twelfth
Dynasty that they were partially contemporary; and it is
only in the sum-total of the dynasty that parallel years are
deducted.   The same was evidently done for this long
series of kings between the Twelfth and Eighteenth Dynasties.   Two hundred years is ample for the whole period,
including the Hyksos.[c]   The Sothic date from the Twelfth

---

[a]There is no choice between these limits; but as a round number is convenient,
I have taken 1580, which brings the end of the Eighteenth Dynasty to 1350 B. C.

[b]The figures given in Manetho's scanty notes are not worthy of the slightest
credence.

[c]Under the Moslems 77 viceroys held the throne of Egypt in 118 years, from
750 to 868 A. D.   In Europe some 80 Roman emperors after Commodus ruled
in a period of 90 years (193–283 A. D.; see Meyer, op. cit.).   The 118 kings
enumerated in this confused age by the Turin Papyrus may have ruled no more
than 150 years; 100 years is ample for the Hyksos, of which 50 years may be
contemporary with the native dynasts.

Dynasty, placing its fall in 1788 B. C., determines the maximum length of the period as 208 years.[a] The Eleventh Dynasty, as shown herein (§§ 415–18), lasted at least 160 years, so that the second dark age, between the Old and Middle Kingdoms, terminated about 2160 B. C.

53. The data for determining the length of the dark period preceding the Middle Kingdom are scanty. Its beginning, in Manetho's so-called Seventh Dynasty, is hopelessly obscure, but fortunately the time during which this Seventh Dynasty ruled, as well as the length of the Eighth Dynasty also, is included by the Turin Papyrus in a summation of the time which elapsed from the rise of the Sixth Dynasty to the fall of Memphis (180 years),[b] and also in a grand total of the length of the whole period from the accession of Menes to the close of Memphite supremacy, which terminated with the fall of the Eighth Dynasty. The Heracleopolitan rule, which falls between the end of Memphite and the beginning of Theban domination, is therefore the uncertain factor. Manetho divides the Heracleopolitans into two dynasties, the Ninth and the Tenth. The Turin Papyrus had a dynasty of eighteen kings immediately preceding the Eleventh, and these must be the Heracleopolitans, as is shown by the occurrence of Manetho's second Akhthoes, near the beginning of the series. We have no means of determining how long these eighteen Heracleopolitans ruled, for Manetho's data (with nineteen kings

---

[a]The proposal to push back the said Sothic date by a whole Sothic cycle, thus lengthening the above period between the Twelfth and Eighteenth Dynasties by 1,460 years, is hardly worthy of a serious answer. It involves the assumption that nearly fifteen hundred years of history have been enacted in the Nile valley without leaving a trace behind! It is like imagining that in European history we could insert at will a period equal to that from the fall of Rome to the present!

[b]That this summation includes the Eighth Dynasty is shown by the fact that the Heracleopolitans (the Ninth and Tenth Dynasties) immediately follow. So also Meyer, *op. cit.*, 171 ff.

in each of his Heracleopolitan dynasties), like most of his figures, are not to be accepted, unless clearly supported by the contemporary monuments. These eighteen Heracleopolitans vouched for by the Turin Papyrus, if given sixteen years each (a sum below the customary average, in a long period of time[a] under orderly conditions of government), reigned, in round numbers, 285 years. It will be evident that this estimate is extremely uncertain. The period is the only undetermined epoch in the dynastic chronology, and it introduces a margin of uncertainty of several generations in all dates back of the Eleventh Dynasty.

54. The Turin Papyrus gives the length of the Sixth Dynasty (with which it merges the Eighth, ignoring the Seventh[b]) as 181 years. The length of the Fourth and Fifth together is determined by the Turin Papyrus and the contemporary monuments as follows: The royal favorite Mertityôtes, after having been in the harem of Snefru and Khufu successively, was still living under Khafre (§§ 188 ff.). Prince Sekhemkere lived under Khafre, Menkure, Shepseskaf, Userkaf, and Sahure.[c] With Snefru counted in the Third Dynasty, and Userkaf and Sahure (together nineteen years[d]) falling in the Fifth, the length of the Fourth cannot have been more than 150 years, as measured by part of two successive human lives. A third lifetime connects the latter part of the Fourth and the first part of the Fifth. Thus Ptahshepses, the son-in-law of

---

[a]The Fourth and Fifth Dynasties (including Snefru at the beginning of the Fourth) show an average of 16.6 years for each ruler (Meyer, *op. cit.*, 151); that is, 18 kings ruled 300 years. Again, at the beginning of the dynastic age 18 kings (First and Second Dynasties) ruled 420 years—an average of over 23 years each. The first 53 kings of the Turin Papyrus (from the First to the Eighth Dynasty) ruled 995 years—an average of nearly 19 years. But among these, it should not be forgotten, there are 15 reigns of less than 10 years each, footing up to only 70 years.

[b]See § 53.

[c]Lepsius, *Denkmäler*, II, 42; Rougé, *Six premières dynasties*, 77.

[d]See Meyer's reconstruction of the Turin Papyrus (*op. cit.* plate opposite p. 145).

King Shepseskaf, was born under Menkure and lived into the reign of Nuserre, the sixth king of the Fifth Dynasty (§§ 254 ff.). Now, granting him a long life, he could not have lived more than 40 or 50 years in the Fifth Dynasty. The Turin Papyrus has preserved the length of the reigns at the end of the Fifth Dynasty from Nuserre on, making a total, including him, of about 100 years. If Ptahshepses survived 10 years under Nuserre, the length of the dynasty was at most 130 years, more probably 125 years. The lengths of seven out of the nine reigns are preserved in the Turin Papyrus, and make a total of 122 years + x.

55. The overlapping of these three lifetimes is very significant:

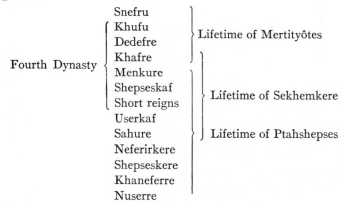

Three lifetimes somewhat overlapping, a matter of 200 years at most, run parallel, as stated above, with the end of the Third Dynasty, the whole Fourth, and the first half of the Fifth. The Fourth and Fifth Dynasties thus lasted together not more than 300 years.

56. Now, the Turin Papyrus has preserved the length of the reigns in the Third Dynasty, and they foot up to about 80 years (including Snefru). The Palermo Stone insures at least 500 years for the first three dynasties, leaving about

420 years for the first two dynasties. This gives us a total of 950–75 years for the entire period from the beginning of the dynasties to the final fall of Memphis. Now, it is practically certain that the total of 955 years on a fragment of the Turin Papyrus is a summary of the same period,[a] belonging at the end of the Memphite kings. Deducting the length of the Memphite dynasties (535 years) from this total of 955 years, we have left 420 years for the preceding Thinite period (First and Second Dynasties), just as shown by the Palermo Stone. We thus reach the date 3400 B. C. for the beginning of the dynasties, and 3400 to 2980 B. C. as the Thinite age, the first two dynasties. It is highly improbable that future discovery will shift these dates more than a century in either direction.

57. To recapitulate, in the following table it should be remembered that the dates in the Twelfth Dynasty are astronomically computed and correct within three years. The early part of the Eighteenth is closely correct (all dates astronomically established are starred), and the latter part probably within a decade of error. The margin of error is doubtless somewhat greater between the close of the Eighteenth and the accession of the Twenty-sixth Dynasty, where the dates are again accurate. Back of the Middle Kingdom, the unknown length of the dark age (from the Seventh to the Tenth Dynasty) produces the wide limits of uncertainty affecting all the preceding dynasties (from the First to the Tenth), the end of which period fell about 2160 B. C. It is back of 2160 B. C., therefore, that our chronology of Egyptian history becomes unstable and exhibits a margin of uncertainty of at most two centuries; that is, a century either way.

---

[a]Frag. No. 44. It was already placed here by Seyffarth; a study of the possibilities shows clearly that this position is correct. [Later: This is also the opinion of Meyer (*op. cit.*).]

CHRONOLOGICAL TABLE

58. Introduction of Calendar . . . . 4241 B. C.
Accession of Menes and Beginning of
    Dynasties . . . . . . 3400 "
First and Second Dynasties . . . 3400–2980 "
    (Eighteen kings, 420 years)

Third Dynasty

Zoser to Snefru . . . . 80 years 2980–2900 B. C.

Fourth Dynasty[a]

59. Khufu . . . . . . 23 years
Dedefre . . . . . 8 "
Khafre . . . . . x "
Menkure . . . . . x "
. . . . [b] . . . . . x "
. . . . [c] . . . . 18 "
Shepseskaf . . . . . 4 "
. . . . [d] . . . . 2 "
    Total . . . . . 150 years 2900–2750 B. C.

Fifth Dynasty[e]

60. Userkaf . . . . . 7 years
Sahure . . . . . 12 "
Neferirkere . . . . x "
Shepseskere[f] . . . . 7 "
Khaneferre[g] . . . . x "
Nuserre . . . . . 30[h] " $(+x)$
Menkuhor . . . . 8 "
Dedkere-Isesi . . . . 28 "
Unis . . . . . 30 "
    Total . . . . . 122 years $+x$
    Minimum . . . . 125 " 2750–2625 B. C.

---

[a]As reconstructed by Meyer from the Turin Papyrus, the Sakkara and Abydos lists, and Manetho. The years are from the papyrus.

[b]Lost in Turin Papyrus; Manetho's Ratoises.

[c]Lost in Turin Papyrus; Manetho's Bikheris. The years may be 28.

[d]Lost in Turin Papyrus; Manetho's Thamphthis.

[e]As restored by Meyer (*op. cit.*, 145 ff.).

[f] Same as Neferefre of the Abydos list.

[g]Only in Sakkara list, but spacing shows room for him in the Turin Papyrus.

[h]Numeral in Turin Papyrus is either 10, 20, or 30 (+ units?), and, as Nuserre celebrated his thirty-years' jubilee, doubtless 30 is correct.

SIXTH DYNASTY

61. Teti II . . . . . x years
   Userkere[a] . . . . . x "
   Pepi I . . . . . 20 "
   Mernere I . . . . . 4 "
   Pepi II . . . . . 90[b] " $(+x)$
   Mernere II[c] . . . . 1 "
       Total . . . . 115 years $+x$
       Minimum . . . . 150 "   2625–2475 B. C.

SEVENTH AND EIGHTH DYNASTIES[d]

62. Total . . . . . . 30 years   2475–2445 B. C.

NINTH AND TENTH DYNASTIES

   18 Heracleopolitans, estimated . 285 years   2445–2160 B. C.

ELEVENTH DYNASTY[e]

63. Horus Wahenekh-Intef I . . 50 years $+x$
   Horus Nakhtneb-Tepnefer-Intef II x "
   Nibhotep-Mentuhotep I . . x "
   Vassal Intef III (Shaṭṭ er-Regâl) . x "
   Nibkhrure-Mentuhotep II . . 46 " $+x$
   Senekhkere-Mentuhotep III . . 28 " $+x$
   Nibtowere-Mentuhotep IV . . 2 " $+x$
       Total . . . . . 126 years $+x$
       Known total . . . 160[f] "   2160[g]–2000 B. C.

---

[a]Only in the Abydos list; Meyer suggests that he is the same as Ity of whom we have a quarry inscription at Hammamat (§ 386).

[b]Probably 94, as given also by Manetho.

[c]From the Abydos list, instead of Nitokris formerly assigned here on a misplaced fragment of the Turin Papyrus. (See Meyer, *op. cit.*, 164.)

[d]The Seventh Dynasty of Manetho (70 Memphites ruling 70 days) cannot be found in the lists or on contemporary monuments. The ephemeral Eighth Dynasty is given 7 kings in the Turin Papyrus, of whom the reigns of 4 are preserved (2 years, 4 years, 2 years, 1 year). The Eighth Dynasty is passed over in the Sakkara list, but is given 17 kings in the Abydos list.

[e]See reconstruction, §§ 415–18; also my essay, *Abhandlungen der Königlichen Preussischen Akademie*, 1904 (in Meyer's essay, *Aegyptische Chronologie*, 156–61); and also my remarks in the *American Journal of Semitic Languages*, XXI, April.

[f]From Turin Papyrus; the units are lost.

[g]From here on approximately accurate chronology.

TWELFTH DYNASTY[a]

64.

Amenemhet I . . .	30 years	2000*–1970* B. C.	
Sesostris I	45 "	1980*–1935* "	
Amenemhet II . . .	35 "	1938*–1903* "	
Sesostris II	19 "	1906*–1887* "	
Sesostris III	38 "	1887*–1849* "	
Amenemhet III . . .	48 "	1849*–1801* "	
Amenemhet IV . . .	9 "	1801*–1792* "	
Sebeknefrure	4 "	1792*–1788* "	
Total	228 years		
Allowance for coregencies .	15 "		
Final total . . .	213[b] years	2000*–1788* B. C.	

THIRTEENTH TO SEVENTEENTH DYNASTIES
(Including the Hyksos)

65. 208[c] years . . . . . . 1788*–1580 B. C.

EIGHTEENTH DYNASTY

66.

Ahmose	$22^d + x$ years	1580–1557* B. C.	
Amenhotep I . $10^e + x$ ⎱	56[f] "	1557*–1501* "	
Thutmose I . . $30^g + x$ ⎰			
Thutmose III . . . 54^h	"	1501*–1447* "	

(Including Thutmose II and Hatshepsut)

---

[a]A fuller statement of this dynasty, especially of the Sothic date and of the coregencies, will be found in §§ 460 ff.

[b]This total is given by the Turin Papyrus (§ 461) as exactly 213 years, 1 month, and 17 days.

[c]See § 52.   [d]II, 27.

[e]*Recueil*, IX, 94. Accession is astronomically established (Meyer, *op. cit.*, 46 ff.).

[f]Determined by the two limits: the accession of Amenhotep I in 1557 and that of Thutmose III in 1501, both these dates being astronomically fixed.

[g]He celebrated his thirty-years' jubilee, and, as he was never crown prince, he must have ruled at least 30 years. He reached old age (II, 64).

[h]Really a little less (see II, 592). The date of this reign is astronomically established by means of a Sothic date and two calendar dates of the new moon in Thutmose III's Annals (II, 430). Mahler computes his accession as 1504 (*Zeitschrift für ägyptische Sprache*, 1888, 97); Lehmann noticed that such a calculation must be based on the actual appearance of the new moon, and not on a calculation of when it astronomically occurred. Lehmann thus dated the accession of Thutmose III in 1515 (*Zwei Hauptprobleme*, 154–58). Meyer accepted Lehmann's method, but showed a slight error in L.'s figures, thus finally placing the date of Thutmose III's accession in 1501 B. C. (Meyer, *op. cit.*, 50). The exact limits are May 3, 1501, to March 17, 1447 B. C.

Amenhotep II . . .	26^a+x years	$1447^*–1420$	B. C.
Thutmose IV . . .	8^b+x "	$1420–1411$	"
Amenhotep III . .	36^c "	$1411–1375$	"
Amenhotep IV . 17^d+x			
(or Ikhnaton, $1375–1358$)			
Sakere . . . x	25^e "	$1375–1350$	"
Tutenekhamon . . $6+x$			
Eye . . . 3^f+x			

Total	$227+4x$ years		
Allowance for double counting (3 transfers and 1 coregency, 1 year) . .	3 "		
Final total . .	$224+4x$ years		
Minimum . . .	*230 years*	*1580–1350*	*B. C.*

NINETEENTH DYNASTY

67. Harmhab	34^g+x years	$1350–1315$	B. C.
Ramses I	2^h "	$1315–1314$	"
Seti I	21^i+x "	$1313–1292$	"

---

aPetrie, *Six Temples*, Plate V; about one year coregent with Thutmose III (II, 184).

bII, 825.

cLepsius, *Denkmäler*, III, 71 *c–d;* and *Amarna Letters*, 20.

dPetrie, *Amarna*, Plates XXII ff., pp. 32 ff.

eIn the reign of Ramses II, in the records of a legal suit, reference is made to legal proceedings in year 59 of Harmhab. As it is evident that Harmhab was not a young man at his accession, it is exceedingly improbable that he reigned nearly 60 years. The highest known date on any monument of his reign is year 21. It is therefore probable that in the early Nineteenth Dynasty, when the chronology for the government files of the immediately preceding reigns was being made up, the series of Ikhnaton and his successors was added to the reign of Harmhab, and the names of the kings at any time implicated in the Aton heresy were swept from the records. We thus have at least 59 years from year 1 of Ikhnaton to the end of Harmhab's reign, of which at least 25 must be credited to Ikhnaton and his successors (*Zeitschrift für ägyptische Sprache*, 39, 10, l. 8).

fII, 1043.

gSee preceding note on Ikhnaton and successors. Estimating 25 years for Ikhnaton and successors, we have $34+x$ years for Harmhab.

hTotal length; maximum of $2\frac{1}{2}$ years (III, 74).

i See III, 131.

Ramses II	67^a years	1292 1225 B. C.
Merneptah	10^b+x "	1225–1215 "
Amenmeses . . .	x "	1215 "
Siptah	6^c+x "	1215–1209 "
Seti II	2^d+x "	1209–1205 "
Total	$142+6x$ years	
Allowance for 4 transfers (= 2 years) and 1 coregency	3 "	
Final total . . .	$139+6x$ years	
Minimum . .	*145 years*	*1350–1205 B. C.*

INTERIM

68. Anarchy and reign of Syrian
usurper[e] . . . .   5 years   1205–1200 B. C.

TWENTIETH DYNASTY[f]

69. Setnakht	$1^g(+x)$ years	1200–1198 B. C.
Ramses III . . .	31^h "	1198–1167 "
Ramses IV	6^i "	1167–1161 "
Ramses V	4^j+x "	1161–1157 "

---

[a]Total length (IV, 471). The attempts to determine the accession of Ramses II astronomically have been unsuccessful.

[b]Papyrus Sallier I, 3, 4; 8, 8; see Erman, *Westcar*, II, 37. I am unable to find any confirmation of Brugsch's remark (*Reiseberichte*, 194) that Merneptah's highest date was not less than 25 nor more than 33. In Lepsius, *Denkmäler*, Text, III, 2, plan of "Temple A" at a place marked *h* is the remark, "Datum des Merneptah," which perhaps refers to Brugsch's remark, but Lepsius has no reference to the date in his text.

[c]See III, 650.

[d]Champollion, *Notices descriptives*, II, 258, and Griffith, *Kahun Papyri*, II, Plate 39, and p. 95. He built a temple at Karnak, and another at Eshmunên (*Proceedings of the Society of Biblical Archæology*, 24, 86).

[e]Papyrus Harris, 75, 2–4 (IV, 398), States that the anarchy lasted "*many years;*" then followed the rule of the Syrian. Five years for all this is a minimum.

[f]I accept in this reconstruction the results of Sethe (*Untersuchungen*, I, 59–63).

[g]Papyrus Sallier, I, 6.

[h]Exactly 31 years and 40 days (IV, 153).

[i]Papyrus Turin; Pleyte and Rossi, Plates 51–60; Spiegelberg, *Zeitschrift für ägyptische Sprache*, 1891, 73 ff., on Plate 54, ll. 12, 13; Maspero, *Momies royales*, 663.

[j]Ostracon in Turin, Maspero, *Recueil*, II, 116, 117.

Ramses VI	. .	x years		
Ramses VII	.	x "	15^a years	1157–1142 B. C.
Ramses VIII .	.	x "		
Ramses IX	. . . .	19^b "	1142–1123 "
Ramses X	. . . .	1^c+x "	1123–1121 "
Ramses XI	. . . . .	x "	1121–1118 "
Ramses XII .	. . . .	27^d+x "	1118–1090 "
Total .	. . .	$104+5x$ years	
Allowance for 1 transfer and 1 coregency .	.	$1\frac{1}{2}$ "	
Final total .	. . .	$102\frac{1}{2}+5x$ years	
Minimum	. . .	*110 years*	1200–1090 B. C.

TWENTY-FIRST DYNASTY[e]

70. Nesubenebded	. . .			
Hrihor	. . . . .	x years	1090–1085 B. C.
Pesibkhenno I	. . .	$17+x$ "	1085–1067 "
Paynozem I	. . . .	$40+x$ "	1067–1026 "
Amenemopet	. . .	$49+x$ "	1026–976 "
Siamon .	. . . .	$16+x$ "	976–958 "
Pesibkhenno II	. . .	$12+x$ "	958–945 "
Total	. . . .	$134+6x$ "	
Minimum	. . .	*145 years*	1090–945 B. C.

TWENTY-SECOND DYNASTY[f]

71. Sheshonk I	. . . .	$21\ (+x)$ years	945–924 B. C.
Osorkon I .	. . .	$36\ (+x)$ "	924–895 "
Takelot I	. . . .	$23^g\ (+x)$ "	895–874 "

---

[a]For this period we have no dates, but it is limited by the following facts: (1) the term of Setau as high priest at El Kab (IV, 415); (2) the succession of the high-priests of Amon; Amenhotep, known as high priest under Ramses IX at least from year 10 (IV, 487) to year 17 (Papyrus Amherst, ed. Newberry, No. VII, p. 1, l. 5), was the son of Ramsesnakht, high-priest known under Ramses IV, year 3. The term of Setau will not permit lengthening the uncertain interim beyond 15 years; nor is it likely to have been less in view of the succession of high-priests.

[b]IV, 535.   [c]IV, 535. This year is a coregency with Ramses IX.

[d]Mariette, *Abydos*, II, 62 = *Catalogue général d'Abydos*, No. 1173, pp. 442 f.

[e]A fuller statement of this dynasty will be found in IV, 604 ff.

[f]A fuller statement of this dynasty will be found in IV, 693 f.

[g]See IV, 693, and Daressy (*Recueil*, XV, 174–75), who is undoubtedly correct in recognizing Takelot I on a stela of year 23.

Osorkon II	30 $(+x)$ years	874–853 B.C.
Sheshonk II	∞ died about	877 "
(Died during coregency with Osorkon II)		
Takelot II	$25+x$ years	860–834 "
(7 years coregent with Osorkon II)		
Sheshonk III	52 "	834–784 "
Pemou	$6+x$ "	784–782 "
Sheshonk IV	$37+x$ "	782–745 "
Total	$230+6x^a$ years	
Allowance for transfers and coregencies . .	30 "	
Final total . . .	$200+6x$ years	
Minimum	*200 years*	*945–745 B.C.*

Twenty-third Dynasty[b]

72.	Pedibast	23^c+x years	745–722 B.C.
	Osorkon III	$14+x$ "	
	Takelot III[d]	x "	————
	Total	$37+3x$ years	
	Minimum	27^e *years*	*745–718 B.C.*

Twenty-fourth Dynasty

73.	Bekneranef	6^f years	718^g–712 B.C.
	Minimum	*6 years*	*718–712 B.C.*

---

[a]The x at the end of Osorkon II's reign falls outside of this total, as his son's reign is counted from his own year 23.

[b]This dynasty will be found fully discussed, with table, in the introduction to the Piankhi Stela (IV, 811 ff.).

[c]IV, 794, 4.

[d]Only known as coregent with Osorkon III. The years between Osorkon III and Bekneranef may be filled up by Takelot III or by the two kings, Psammus and Zet, placed by Africanus after Osorkon III.

[e]Africanus gives a total of 89 years, and Syncellus 44, to this dynasty. The 27 is merely the amount necessary to fill up the gap between the end of the Twenty-second Dynasty and Bekneranef.

[f]IV, 884.

[g]From here on, the date B. C. is obtained by dead reckoning back from the accession of the Twenty-sixth Dynasty in 663 B. C.

TWENTY-FIFTH DYNASTY

74. Shabaka	12^a years	712–700 B. C.
Shabataka	12^b "	700*–688 "
Taharka (Tirhaka) . . .	26^c "	688–663 "
Total	50 years	
Minimum	*50 years*	*712–663 B. C.*

TWENTY-SIXTH DYNASTY

75. Psamtik I	54^d years	663–609 B. C.
Necho	16^e "	609–593 "
Psamtik II	5^f "	593–588 "
Apries (Hophra) . . .	19^g "	588–569 "
Ahmose II (Amasis) . . .	44^h "	569–525 "
Psamtik III	a few months 525 "	
Total	138 years	
Known total, 138 years and a few		
months		*663–525 B. C.*

---

^{a}Lepsius, *Denkmäler*, V, 1, *e*. ^{e}See IV, 984–5.

^{b}IV, 885. ^{f}*Ibid.*

^{c}A little over 26 years (IV, 959). ^{g}IV, 984 ff.

^{d}IV, 974 ff.

^{h}IV, 1026–7. This date is found in a contemporary inscription in Hammamat (Lepsius, *Denkmäler*, III, 275*b*); as Herodotus also gives 44 as the length of this reign, there is evidently no doubt that we have in it the highest date of the reign.

ADDENDUM ON CHRONOLOGY (§ 42)

A letter from Eduard Meyer calls my attention to a fragmentary relief in the tomb of Thutnakht (*El Bersheh,* II, Pls. 8 and 9) which shows that the flax harvest in the middle of the twentieth century B. C. took place between the twenty-third and twenty-seventh of the fourth month. This harvest at the present day in the province of Minieh occurs during the early part of April. Thus the 113th–117th days of the calendar, which normally fell between November 9 and 13 (Julian), then fell in early April, showing a shift of the calendar of over 200 days, and corresponding completely with the shift of 225 days indicated by the Kahun Sothic date (§§ 42, 46). The date of the Twelfth Dynasty is thus confirmed beyond a doubt.

THE PALERMO STONE
FIRST TO THE FIFTH DYNASTIES

THE PALERMO STONE[a]

76. The content of this document, remarkable as it is, is perhaps not more valuable than the revelation it furnishes of the existence of royal annals of an official character, regularly kept by the kings of Egypt in the Old Kingdom and extending back into the time of the two kingdoms of the North and South. They reveal a great and powerful kingdom from the beginning of the dynasties, enjoying ordered government under a highly developed and aggressive state, and exhibiting a high degree of culture and civilization such as we could not have anticipated in this remote age.

77. While a translation of the document, owing to its unique and archaic character, is accompanied by many uncertainties, yet the whole is of an importance which justifies a sufficient presentation of the content to make clear the character, scope, and arrangement of these oldest annals of Egypt.[b] The voluminous commentary necessary for the explanation of many obscure references and allusions is unavoidably omitted here; but the obscurity of these par-

---

[a]A fragment of "Diorite anfibolica," 6.5 cm. thick, 0.435 m. high, and 0.25 m. wide; since 1877 in the Museum of Palermo, and commonly known as the "Palermo Stone." It was published by Pellegrini (*Archivio storico Siciliano*, nuova serie, anno XX, 297–316, and 3 plates); by Schaefer, who first recognized its real character (*Ein Bruchstück altaegyptischer Königsannalen* [Anhang zu den *Abhandlungen der Königlichen Preussischen Akademie*, 1902], with 2 plates); and by Naville (*La pierre de Palerme*, Rec. XXV, 1–20, with 2 plates). Besides the interpretations of the above scholars, see Maspero (*Revue critique*, 1899, I, 1, and 1901, I, 383), who was the first to recognize the character of the year-names; also Spiegelberg, *Zeitschrift für ägyptische Sprache*, XXXV, 10.

[b]The following translation is largely an editing of the rendering of Schaefer and Sethe; but, although space and time for commentary fail me, I have made some changes and additions, like the expedition of Snefru to Syria.

ticular points does not affect the significance of the whole
document, which will be clear to everyone.

78. The fragment herewith presented was broken out of
the middle of a large slab some seven feet long and over
two feet high, as it stood on the long edge.   It was inscribed
on both sides with a series of royal annals, beginning with
the predynastic kings of the period before the union of the
North and the South, and continuing into the dynastic age
to the middle of the Fifth Dynasty.   The arrangement of
these records can be best understood from the figure (—).
The upper line of the front contains at present nine names
of predynastic kings of Lower Egypt (the Delta).[a]   If the
line was full, there were possibly some 120 predynastic kings
here enumerated, each rectangle of line 1 (front) containing
one name, with no indication of how long each king reigned.[b]
In the Fifth Dynasty, therefore, the predynastic kings, the
last of whom had reigned some seven centuries before the
preparation of this table, were already merely a series of
names.   Other reasons for the mere citation of the bare
names are, however, quite conceivable, such as lack of
interest in the predynastic kings on the part of the scribe.

79. But, while the length of the predynastic reigns remains totally uncertain, the date of the beginning of the
dynastic period is certainly established by this monument
within narrower limits than ever before; and the period
from the accession of Menes to the beginning of the Fourth
Dynasty is determined within reasonable margins for the
first time.   The dynastic kings are probably arranged as

---

[a]Meyer has identified the place of these kings of Lower Egypt in the Turin
Papyrus, where no corresponding kings of Upper Egypt were included, and in
Manetho (*Aegyptische Chronologie*, 199 ff., 203 f.).   They follow the gods
and precede the "Worshipers of Horus," the immediate predecessors of the
dynasties.

[b]Meyer believes that this row must have begun with the gods (*ibid.*, 203).

follows: [a]the First Dynasty occupied ll. 2 and 3, following directly upon the predynastic kings; ll. 4 and 5 contained the Second Dynasty; there is some uncertainty about the disposition of reigns in l. 6, but as the first line of the back contained the end of the Fourth Dynasty, the last two lines[b] (7 and 8) of the front must have contained the bulk of the Fourth, which in all probability throws the Third Dynasty back to l. 6,[c] including possibly the end of l. 5. The larger part of the back was occupied with the three reigns of the Fifth Dynasty, which filled up ll. 2-5, and perhaps continued (in two lines) into the reign of Nuserre.

80. The arrangement of each reign (except l. 1, front) was so that in the narrow horizontal space above each line the name of the king was placed, while below it the years of his reign were distributed in successive rectangles, one year in each rectangle. As the space occupied by the years of each reign far exceeded the length of the king's name, the latter was placed over the middle, thus:

KING'S NAME								
Year	Year	Year	Year	Year	Year	Year	Year	Year

81. The vertical line on the right of each rectangle has the form of the hieroglyphic sign for *"year."* Each year-rectangle contains the chief events which occurred in that year, one of which furnished the official name for that year. Thus we have the *"Year of the Battle and Smiting*

---

[a]The Turin Papyrus of kings shows no clear dynastic division for this period, and hence such division rests solely on the lists of Manetho. But Sethe has shown (*Untersuchungen*, III) that such division is practically certain in our monument, and Meyer indicates that it is probable in the Turin Papyrus.

[b]Or three lines may have followed l. 6.

[c]See § 86.

of the Northerners," dating a jar of King Besh (*Bš*) in Phila-
delphia; or the "*Year of Smiting the Troglodytes*" in our
fragment (front, l. 6, § 104). This was parallel with the
same usage in early Babylonia, as has been long known.
As time passed, it became more and more common to name
the year after the corresponding fiscal enumeration, thus:
"*Year of the Second Occurrence of the Numbering of all
Large and Small Cattle of the North and the South*"
(§ 339), or "*Year of the Seventh Occurrence of the Numbering
of Gold and Lands*" (front, l. 5, § 135). This was often
abbreviated to "*Year of the x'th Occurrence of the Numbering,*" or still more to "*Year of the x'th Occurrence.*"

82. All other events were then gradually abandoned as
designations of the years, and by the Fifth Dynasty the fiscal
numberings were almost exclusively used. These occurred
every two years, in uninterrupted sequence, irrespective of
the changes in reign, and hence it was necessary to call a
year when no numbering took place, the "*Year after the
x'th Occurrence (of the Numbering).*" Finally, when the
numberings became annual, each year received the name of
a new numbering, and this was the system of dating in
Egypt from the Sixth Dynasty on. It amounted to numbering the years themselves, and gradually became nothing
else. The Palermo stone thus furnishes us the origin of the
Egyptian system of dating.

83. In addition to the chief events of the year, each year-
rectangle contained, at the bottom in the middle, a datum
giving a number of cubits, palms, and fingers, which have
been thought to be the height of the inundation[a] for each
year; but this is very uncertain.

---

[a]Measured from some fixed point only a few cubits below high water; but
the fine subdivisions in the measurements (down to fractions of a finger-breadth)
are against the theory.

84. In ll. 2-5 (front), containing the First and Second Dynasties, the events of each year are for the most part celebrations of religious feasts and the like, and in the latter part the *"numberings"* appear. With the Third Dynasty (l. 6) the events known to the chronicler become more numerous, increasing and making irregular in size the year-rectangles. They become still larger in the Fourth and Fifth. Small as are the rectangles of the First and Second Dynasties, they are in each line of the same size, and this offers the basis for a rough estimate of the number of years in these dynasties, if we can gain even a distant approximation of the total length of the stone.

85. An examination of the back shows that from one-tenth to one-eighth of the total length of the lines is preserved on the fragment. This insures roughly five hundred years for the length of the first three dynasties, of which only about eighty would belong to the Third Dynasty.[a]

86. In this computation the stone offers little for determining the length of the Third Dynasty. This is, however, shown by the Turin Papyrus to have been only fifty-five years before Snefru; or, with Snefru, seventy-nine years, x months; or, in round numbers, eighty years. That Snefru belonged to the Third Dynasty is favored by the arrangement of the stone, although the Manethonian tradi-

---

[a]The first attempt at restoring the length of the stone was made by Sethe, who obtained the following results:

　　　　First Dynasty (ll. 2–3)...................253 years
　　　　Second Dynasty (ll. 4–5)................302 years
　　　　Third Dynasty (l. 6).........maximum, 100–110 years

These pioneer results have been modified by Meyer (*Aegyptische Chronologie*) to the following:

　　　　First Dynasty (ll. 2–3)...................210 years
　　　　Second Dynasty (ll. 4–5)................243 years

The possible difference is thus about a century. Meyer's results are certainly a minimum, and Sethe's a maximum, but the principle employed by Meyer would now doubtless be accepted by Sethe.

tion perhaps placed him at the head of the Fourth Dynasty. It should be remembered that this difficulty with the Third Dynasty is not peculiar to any theory of restoration of the stone. We cannot, on any scheme of restoration, push the Third Dynasty back into l. 5 (front), for the birth of Khasekhemui, a king of the latter part of the Second Dynasty, is recorded in l. 5 (No. 4). Nor can we assume that Snefru is here reckoned with the Fourth Dynasty, which would leave only the first half of l. 6 for the whole Third Dynasty. Finally, as Snefru is reckoned with the Third Dynasty, and we know that he was its last king (for he was the predecessor of Khufu), all his predecessors in the dynasty, as well as at least six years of his own reign, must have been included in the first half of l. 6. If all the rectangles of the first half of l. 6 were as small as those of l. 2, this would leave perhaps fifty years for his predecessors in the dynasty. The supposition that more lines are lost at the bottom would not at all affect the Third Dynasty. Again, any great prolongation of the lines is forbidden by the back.

87. The stone offers little aid as to the length of the Fourth Dynasty, as most of that dynasty is lost at the bottom of the front, but it furnishes valuable hints as to the close of the Fourth and the first half of the Fifth Dynasty. The short reigns at the close of the Fourth are fragmentarily indicated in l. 1, and the lengths of the short reigns of the first three kings of the Fifth Dynasty roughly corroborate those indicated in the Turin Papyrus.

88. It will be seen that the monument is invaluable as a source for the chronology of the earliest dynasties. Accepting 2900 B. C. as the date for the accession of the Fourth Dynasty, the Palermo Stone furnishes us an assured minimum of 3400 B. C. as the beginning of the dynastic period and the accession of Menes. This date is only affected by

the uncertainty attending all our dates back of the Heracleopolitan rule. Future discovery may reduce the date of Menes by at most a century.

89. The content of these annals is also of great importance, but, as they are themselves only a summary, we cannot epitomize them here. Such facts as the dispatch of a fleet of forty vessels to bring cedar from Lebanon under Snefru are, of course, invaluable.

I.   PREDYNASTIC KINGS

Kings of Upper Egypt (?) or the Gods (?)

90. [1]————————

Kings of Lower Egypt

—-pu (——*pw*); Seka (*Šk^ɔ*); Khayu (*Ḥ^ɔ-yw*); Teyew (*Tyw*); Thesh (*Tš*); Nerheb[1] (*N-rhb*[1]); Wazenez (*W^{ɔ}ḏ-^{c}nḏ*); Mekh (*Mḫ*); —a (—^{ɔ}); ————————[a]

II.   FIRST DYNASTY

KING T[b] (NAME LOST)

x years

91. [2]————————

Year *x+1*

Worship of Horus.[c]
Birth of Anubis.[c]

Year *x+2*

92. 6 months and 7 days.[d]

KING U[e] (NAME LOST)

Year *1*

93. Fourth month, thirteenth day.[f]

---

[a]At least four more names followed.

[b]Either Menes or his successor, Atothis.   [c]Name of a feast.

[d]This is the fraction of the king's last year which was interrupted by his death and left incomplete.

[e]Either Atothis or his successor.

[f]This is the date of the king's accession, and the following name is the regular designation of a king's first year.

Union of the Two Lands.
Circuit of the Wall.[a]
6 cubits.[b]

Year 2

94. Worship of Horus.
Feast of Desher (*Dšr*).

Year 3

95. Birth of the two children of the King of Lower Egypt.
4 cubits, 1 palm.

Year 4

96. Worship of Horus.
⌜— — —⌝

Year 5

97. ⌜Design⌝ of the House (called): "Mighty-of-the-Gods" (*Šḥm-nṯrw*).
Feast of Sokar.
5 cubits, 5 palms, 1 finger.

Year 6

98. Worship of Horus.
Birth of the goddess Yamet (*Yˀm·t*).
5 cubits, 1 palm.

Year 7

99. Appearance[c] of the King of Upper Egypt.
Birth of Min.
5 cubits

Year 8

100. Worship of Horus.
Birth of Anubis.
6 cubits, 1 palm.

Year 9

101. First occurrence of the Feast of Zet (*Ḏt*).
4 cubits, 1 span.

---

[a]Name of a feast.

[b]See explanation, § 83.

[c]Or "*coronation*" (*ḫˁ*); it is a feast probably in commemoration of the king's coronation.

Year 10

102. ——————ᵃ

LOST KINGS

3.————

KING V

King's Name

103. —————ᵇ [ᵣborn of Meᵣ]ret-[ᵣNeitᵣ].

Year x+1

Station (in)ᶜ the temple of Saw (*Sꜣw*) in Heka— (*Ḥkꜣ—*).
3 cubits, 1 palm, 2 fingers.

Year x+2

104. Smiting of the Troglodytes (*Yntyw*).
4 cubits, 1 span.

Year x+3

105. Appearance of the King of Upper Egypt.
Appearance of the King of Lower Egypt.
Sed jubilee.
8 cubits, 3 fingers.

Year x+4

106. (ᵣNumbering ofᵣ)ᵈ all people of the nomes of the west, north,
and east.
3 cubits, 1 span.

Year x+5

107. Second occurrence of the Feast of Zet (*Ḏt*).
5 cubits, 2 palms.

ᵃAt least sixteen years more of this reign are lost, as the king's name was
placed in the middle over the horizontal line of years. Our fragment does not
reach to the middle; hence over ten years more are lost at the other end, besides
six which stood under the name. This makes a minimum total of twenty-six
years for this king; but the restoration of the stone shows that he (Atothis) probably
reigned some fifty years.

ᵇWe should probably restore the name of King Miebis; see Sethe, *Untersuchungen*, III, 47.

ᶜThe omission of such prepositions is common in these archaic texts.

ᵈOr is the plant sign (*ḥꜣ*) an incorrectly made plant of the South? This would
give us all the cardinal points.

Year x+6

108. ⌈Design⌉ of the House (called): "Thrones-of-the-Gods."
Feast of Sokar.
5 cubits, 1 palm, 2 fingers.

Year x+7

109. Stretching of the Cord (for) the House (called): "Thrones-of-the-Gods," (by) the priest of (the goddess) Seshat (*Šš⸮t*, Sefkhet).
Great Door.
4 cubits, 2 palms.

Year x+8

110. Opening of the Lake of the House (called): "Thrones-of-the-Gods."
Shooting of the Hippopotamus.
2 cubits.

Year x+9

111. Station (at) the lake of the temple of Harsaphes (*Ḥry-š·f*) in Heracleopolis.
5 cubits.

Year x+10

112. Voyage (to) Sahseteni (⌈Š⸮ḥ⌉-*štny*).
Smiting of Werka (*Wr-k⸮*).
4 cubits, 1 span.

Year x+11

113. Birth of Sed (*Šd*).
6 cubits, 1 palm, 2 fingers.

Year x+12

114. Appearance of the King of Lower Egypt.
First occurrence of "Running-of-Apis."[a]
2 cubits, 1 span.

Year x+13

115. Birth of Seshat (*Šš⸮·t*) and Mefdet (*M⸮ĵd·t*).
3 cubits, 5 palms, 2 fingers.

---

[a]Some unfamiliar Apis ceremony. Schaefer calls attention to Manetho's statement that the Apis-cult began under King Kaiechos.

Year x+14[a]

116. [Appearance] of the King of Upper Egypt.
Birth of —.

———

III.   SECOND DYNASTY

KING NETERIMU

Lost Reigns

117. 4——— —

King's Name

Horus: Neterimu (*N ṯry-mw*[b]) son of —

Year 1

118. ———

Year 2

———

[First occurrence of the numbering.]

Year 3

———

Year 4

———

[Second occurrence of the numbering.]
[First occurrence of the Feast of Sokar.][c]

Year 5

———

Year 6[d]

Worship of Horus.
[Third occurrence of the numbering.]

Year 7

119. Appearance of the King of Upper Egypt.

———

[a]There must have been fourteen years on the other side of the royal name.
Of these twenty-eight, two fall under the royal name.   There were at least two
or three more under it, making a minimum of thirty or thirty-one years for this
king.

[b]On the reading of the name see Sethe, *Untersuchungen*, III, 40.

[c]This feast occurred at intervals of six years; see years 10 and 16.

[d]This may be the fifth year, as the first numbering may have taken place in
the first year.

Stretching of the Cord (for) the House (called) Hor-Ren (*Ḥr-rn*).
3 cubits, 4 palms, 2 fingers.

Year 8

120. Worship of Horus.
Fourth occurrence of the numbering.
4 cubits, 2 fingers.

Year 9

121. Appearance of the King of Upper Egypt.
Appearance of the King of Lower Egypt.
Running of Apis.
4 cubits, 1 palm, 2 fingers.

Year 10

122. Worship of Horus.
Fifth occurrence of the numbering.
4 cubits, 4 palms.

Year 11

123. Appearance of the King of Lower Egypt.
Second occurrence of the Feast of Sokar.
3 cubits, 4 palms, 2 fingers.

Year 12

124. Worship of Horus.
Sixth occurrence of the numbering.
4 cubits, 3 fingers.

Year 13

125. First occurrence of the Feast: "Worship-of-Horus-of-Heaven"
(*Dwꜣ-Ḥr-pt*).
Hacking up of the city: Shem-Rè (*Šm-Rꜥ*).
Hacking up of the city: "House-of-the-North."
4 cubits, 3 fingers.

Year 14

126. Worship of Horus.
Seventh occurrence of the numbering.
1 cubit.

Year 15

127. Appearance of the King of Lower Egypt.

Second occurrence of "Running-of-Apis."
3 cubits, 4 palms, 3 fingers.

Year 16

128. Worship of Horus.
Eighth occurrence of the numbering.
3 cubits, 5 palms, 2 fingers.

Year 17

129. Appearance of the King of Lower Egypt.
Third occurrence of the Feast of Sokar.
2 cubits, 2 fingers.

Year 18

130. Worship of Horus.
Ninth occurrence of the numbering.
2 cubits, 2 fingers.

Year 19

131. Appearance of the King of Lower Egypt.
⌐—⌐ the Feast of Zet (*Dt*).
⌐— —⌐.ª
3 cubits.

Year 20

132. Worship of Horus.
Tenth occurrence of [the numbering].

Year 21ᵇ

LOST KINGS

s.————

KING W (NAME LOST)
Year 12ᶜ

133. Worship of Horus.
Sixth occurrence of the numbering.
2 cubits, 4 palms, 1½ fingers.

ªSchaefer: "Opfer (?) . . . . Göttin *N ḫbt* . . . . *Dt*-Fest."

ᵇOf these twenty-one years, sixteen were before the royal name; sixteen more, therefore, followed it; five are under it, making a total of at least thirty-seven.

ᶜOr possibly year 11, according to the beginning of the numbering in year 1 or year 2.

Year 13

134. Appearance of the King of Upper Egypt.
Appearance of the King of Lower Egypt.
(The temple called): "The-Goddess-Abides" was built (of) stone.
2 cubits, 3 palms, 1 finger.

Year 14

135. Worship of Horus.
Seventh occurrence of the numbering of gold and lands.
3⅔ cubits.

Year 15

136. Birth of Khasekhemui (*Ḥˁ-sḫmwy*).
1 cubit, 6 palms, 2½ fingers.

Year 16

137. Worship of Horus.
Eighth occurrence of the numbering of gold and lands.
4 cubits, 2 palms, 2⅔ fingers.

Year 17

138. Fourth occurrence of bringing the wall of Dewazefa (*Dwꜣ-ḏfꜣ*).
Shipbuilding.
4 cubits, 2 palms.

Year 18

139. 2 months, 23 days.[a]

KING X (NAME LOST)

Year 1

140. Appearance of the King of Upper Egypt.
Appearance of the King of Lower Egypt.
Union of the Two Lands.
Circuit of the Wall.
4 cubits, 2 palms, 2⅔ fingers.

Year 2

141. Appearance of the King of Upper Egypt.

---

[a]The total length of this reign was thus either sixteen or seventeen years, two months, and twenty-three days.

Appearance of the King of Lower Egypt.
⌜Introduction⌝ of the King into the double Senut^a-house.
4 cubits, 1⅔ palms.

Year 3

142. Worship of Horus.
Birth of Min.
2 cubits, 3 palms, 2¾ fingers.

Year 4

143. Appearance of the King of Upper Egypt.
Appearance of the King of Lower Egypt.
Stretching of the Cord (for) the House (called): "Shelter-of-the-Gods" (*Ḳbḥ-nṯrw*).
3 cubits, 3 palms, 2 fingers.

Year^b 5

144. Worship of Horus.

———

3 cubits, — —, — —.

IV.   THIRD DYNASTY

LOST REIGNS

6_____

KING SNEFRU

145.

Year x + 1^c

———

[Birth of] the two children of the King of Lower Egypt.
[Sixth occurrence of the numbering.]

———

Year x+2

146. Building of 100-cubit^d dewatowe-ships (*Dwꜣ-tꜣwy*) of meru (*mr*) wood, and of 60 sixteen^e-barges of the king.

———

^aThe senut (*šnwt*) are flag-staves on a temple front
^bAt least eleven years more may be added to this reign.
^cAs the numberings are irregular in this reign, it is not safe to compute the year from the two given.
^dThis refers to the length, which was thus some 167 feet.
^eThis numeral refers to a dimension or to the number of oars in each barge, or something similar. Schaefer relevantly recalls the "*eights*" (ships) of Uni (§ 322, l. 41).

Hacking up the land of the Negro.

Bringing of 7,000 living prisoners, and 200,000 large and small cattle.

Building of the wall of the Southland and Northland (ˈcalledˈ) "Houses-of-Snefru."

Bringing of 40 ships filled (with) cedar wood.[a]

2 cubits, 2 fingers.

Year x+3

147. Making 35 houses.[b]

⌐—⌐ of 122 cattle.

Building of a 100-cubit dewatowe-ship (*Dwꜣ-tꜣwy*) of cedar wood, and 2 100-cubit ships of meru wood.

Seventh occurrence of the numbering.

5 cubits, 1 palm, 1 finger.

Year x+4

148. Erection of:

"Exalted-is-the-White-Crown-of-Snefru-upon-the-Southern-Gate."[c]

"Exalted-is-the-Red-Crown-of-Snefru-upon-the-Northern-Gate."[c]

Making the doors of the king's palace of cedar wood.

Eighth occurrence of the numbering.

2 cubits, 2 palms, $2\frac{3}{4}$ fingers.

Year[d] x+5

149. ――――――

――――――

[a]This is an expedition by sea to Lebanon. The omission of the prepositions (here *m*, "*with*") is common in this inscription, having been copied without change by the Fifth Dynasty scribe, from the ancient original of Snefru's time, in which, as commonly in the archaic inscriptions, the prepositions were lacking.

[b]Some particular kind of building is meant.

[c]These are the names of two gates or parts of the palace of Snefru: one for the South and one for the North. We have thus the double name of a double palace, which, like the organs of the government, was double, to correspond with the old kingdoms of South and North. These two gates are still preserved in the palace of the Empire as seen in the Amarna tombs. The palace front was always referred to as the "*double façade*" or "*double gate*" (*Rwty*); hence also the dual determinative of *pr-ꜥꜣ*. The state temples also were double; each had a "*double façade*," and the hypostyle was divided into north and south by the central aisle. The division of the palace audience hall will have been the same. That the two names in § 148 do not refer to two separate buildings is shown by the record of the making of the doors in the next remark, as in the year 7 of Miebis.

[d]After the year-sign, the sign for king and, below, the cubit-sign are visible.

V.   FOURTH DYNASTY

LOST REIGNS

7.————

KING Y

King's Name

————————a

LOST REIGNS

1b————————

KING MENKURE (?)c

Year x

— [months], 24 days.d

KING SHEPSESKAF

Year 1

150. *a)* Month 4 (+x), eleventh day.e

b) Appearance of the King [of Upper Egypt].

Appearance of the King of Lower Egypt.

Union of the Two Lands.

Circuit of the Wall.

Seshed (*Ššd*) Feast.f

Birth of Upwawet.

The king worships the gods who united the Two Lands.

151. *c)* ———— selection of the place of the pyramid (called):
"Shelter-of-Shepseskaf."

152. *d)* ———— 20 ⌜—⌝ of the South and North every day.

e) ———— 1,624g—; ———— 600 —.

4 cubits, 3 palms, 2½ fingers.

————————

aThe determinative after the name of his mother and the tip of one sign before it are all that remains of his reign.

bBeginning of the back.

cPossibly one of the three ephemeral kings placed by the Sakkara list and Manetho at the close of the Fourth Dynasty. See Meyer, *Aegyptische Chronologie*, 195.

dMeyer (*ibid.*) would see in the vacant space left by the scribe before this note an evidence of the illegitimacy of this king; it would seem, however, that a number of the exigencies of space might have produced such a vacancy.

eThe date of his accession.

fConfer the coronation of Hatshepsut, II, 240.

gThese numerals, like those in ll. 2–4, are the numbers of the stat of land in the temple endowments of that year.

VI.   FIFTH DYNASTY

KING USERKAF

Years 1–3

153. ⸺

Year 4

Third occurrence of the finding of —.

Year 5[a]

154. The King of Upper and Lower Egypt Userkaf; he made (it) as his monument for:

155. The spirits of Heliopolis: 20 offerings of bread and beer at every ⸢—⸣ and every ⸢—⸣ feast; 36 stat of land ⸢— —⸣ in the domain of Userkaf.

156. 1. The gods of the sun-temple (called): Sepre (*Sp-R^c*):
24 stat of land in the domain of Userkaf;
2 oxen, 2 geese every day.

2. Re: 44 stat of land in the nomes of the Northland;

3. Hathor: 44 stat of land in the nomes of the Northland.

4. The gods of the House of ⸢—⸣ of Horus: 54 stat of land; erection of the shrine of his temple (in) Buto of the nome of Xois;

5. Sepa (*Sp^3*): 2 stat of land; building of his temple.

6. Nekhbet in the sanctuary (*nṭry*) of the South: 10 offerings of bread and beer every day.

7. Buto in Pernu (*Pr-nw*): 10 offerings of bread and beer every day.

8. The gods of the sanctuary (*nṭry*) of the South: 48 offerings of bread and beer every day.

157. Year of the third occurrence of the numbering of large cattle.
4 cubits, 2½ fingers.

Year 6

158. [The King of Upper and Lower Egypt, Userkaf; he made (it) as his monument for]:

⸺[b]: 1,700 stat ⸢— —⸣ in the North; ⸺

---

[a]This may be year 6, according as the numbering began in year 1 or 2; but the restoration of the stone rather favors year 5.

[b]Some god's name.

KING SAHURE

3————

Year 5[a]

159. *a*) The King of [Upper] and Lower Egypt, Sahure; he made (it) as his monument for:

　1. — in Heliopolis; ———— 200 ⌈—⌉, ———— divine barque ———— ⌈—⌉.

　2. Nekhbet, mistress of Perwer (*Pr-wr*): 800 daily offerings of bread and beer;

　3. Buto, mistress of Perneser (*Pr-nsr*): 4,800 daily offerings of bread and beer;

　4. Re in the Senut-house (*Šnwt*): 138 daily offerings of bread and beer;

　5. Re in the Sanctuary (*nṯry*) of the South: 40 daily offerings of bread and beer;

　6. Re in Tep-het (*Tp-ḥt*): 74 daily offerings of bread and beer;

　7. Hathor in the sun-temple, Sekhet-Re (*Šḫt-Rꜥ*): 4 daily offerings of bread and beer;

　8. Re of the sun-temple, Sekhet-Re: ⌈2,000⌉ ⌈—⌉ stat of land in the nome of ⌈Xois⌉;

　9. Mes (*Mš*): 2 stat of land in the nome of Busiris;

　10. Sem (*Šm*): 2 stat of land in the nome of Busiris;

　11. Khent-yawetef (*Ḫnt-yꜣwtf*): 2 ⌈— —⌉ stat of land in the Memphite nome;

　12. Hathor in Ro-she (*Rꜣ-š*) of Sahure: 2 ⌈— —⌉ stat of land in the East;

　13. Hathor in (the temple of) the pyramid, "The-Soul-of-Sahure-Shines": 1 stat of land in the Libyan nome;

　14. The White Bull: 13 ⌈— —⌉ stat of land in the eastern Khent nome (XIV).

　15. *b*) Third occurrence of the finding of ⌈— —⌉
Year of the second numbering.
2 cubits, 2¼ fingers.

Year 6

160. The King of Upper and Lower Egypt [Sahure; he made it as his monument for]:

————

[a]It is the second numbering, and may be year 4.

The Divine Ennead,

Year 13[a]

161. [4][The king of Upper and Lower Egypt, Sahure; he made it as] his monument for:

1. ————
2. Re ⌜—⌝: — [stat] of land in the North and South;
3. Hathor: — [stat] of land in the North and South;
4. —: — [stat] of land in the North and South;
5. —: ———— all things.
6. There were brought from:
7. The Malachite-country, — — ⌜6,000⌝ —.
8. Punt, 80,000 measures of myrrh, ⌜6,000⌝ — of electrum, 2,600 ⌜—⌝ staves, ⌜— —⌝.

Year after the ⌜seventh⌝[b] numbering.

Year 14

162. ⌜9⌝ months, ⌜6⌝ days.

KING NEFERIRKERE

King's Name

163. Horus: *Wśr-ḫᶜw;*[c] King of Upper and Lower Egypt; Favorite of the Two Goddesses: *Ḥᶜw-m-sḥmw* ————.

Year 1

164. Second month, seventh day.
Birth of the Gods.
Union of the Two Lands.
Circuit of the Wall.

---

[a]The "*numbering*" is uncertain, being either 6 or 7. The year may be anywhere from 11 to 15, according as the first numbering was in the year 1 or year 2, or the numbering be the sixth or seventh. Meyer's results make 13 the most probable here.

[b]The number is unfortunately not quite certain, but the margin of uncertainty is not great. The Turin Papyrus gives Sahure twelve years, and Manetho gives him thirteen, both of which numbers might be practically correct, as one might take account of the nine months of the last year, and count the thirteenth year as complete.

[c]"*Rich in Diadems.*"

165. The King of Upper and Lower Egypt, Neferirkere (*Nfr-yr-k³-Rꜥ*); he made (it) as [his] monument [for]:

1. The Divine Ennead in ⌐—¬ of the Senut-house (*Šnwt*): ⌐—¬ stat of land in the city (called): "Neferirkere-Beloved-of-the-Divine-Ennead," under[a] the House of Neferirkere in ⌐—¬;

2. The Spirits of Heliopolis and the Gods of Khereha (*Ḥr-ꜥḥ³*): ⌐—¬ stat of land in the city (called): "Neferirkere-Beloved-of-the-Spirits-of-Heliopolis;" 251 (+x) stat of land in the eastern Khent nome (XIV) — under the two high-priests of Heliopolis, the prophets and ⌐officials¬ of his house ⌐————¬

3. Re: an altar;

4. Hathor: an altar; ⌐————¬; ⌐210¬ divine offerings, 203 offerings of bread and beer; there was made ⌐— —¬ peasant serfs ⌐—¬.

5. There was fashioned ⌐—¬ of electrum, (⌐for¬) Ihi (*Yḥy*), a statue, followed to the house of Hathor, [mistress] of the sycomore, in Meret-Snefru;

6. Re of Tep-het (*Tp-ḥt*); there was done for him the like————

———

3 cubits, — — ,— —.

5.———

Year 9[b]

166. [The King of Upper and Lower Egypt, Neferirkere; he made it as his monument for]:

1. ————

2. ⌐————¬

3. Re in the sun-temple: "Favorite-Seat-of-Re;" there was made for him a feast of the Circuit-[of-the-Wall] ————.

King Setneh (*Stnḥ*):[c] — stat of land.

Year of the fifth occurrence [of the numbering].

Year 10

167. 1. Appearance of the King of Upper Egypt.

Appearance of the King of Lower Egypt.

———

ᵃUnder charge of?

ᵇOr possibly 10; Meyer's results make 9 more probable.

ᶜAn ancient king, also mentioned in the tomb of Methen; he was perhaps a king of Upper Egypt.

2. Erection of the wall of the sun-barque at the south side [of the sun-temple: "Favorite-Seat-of-Re"].[a]

3. The King of Upper and Lower Egypt, Neferirkere; he made (it) as [his] monument [for]:

4. Re in the sun-temple: "Favorite-Seat-of-Re": ⌜8 —⌝ loaves: for the evening sun-barque —; and for the morning sun-barque —.

5. The Souls of Heliopolis: — — — of electrum;

6. Ptah, "South-of his-Wall": — stat ————.

7. Buto of the South: — — — of electrum.

8. ————

---

[a]This is a sun-barque like that found at Abusir beside the sun-temple of Nuserre by the excavations of the Berlin Museum.

THE THIRD DYNASTY

REIGN OF SNEFRU

SINAI INSCRIPTIONS[a]

168. Although the Pharaohs had operated in the copper region of Sinai as far back as the First Dynasty, Snefru was later regarded as the great founder of the Egyptian mining there. He became a patron god of the region (§ 722), he gave his name to the roads and stations of the eastern Delta (§ 493, l. 9), and officials boasting of their achievements there claimed that nothing like them had been done since the time of Snefru (§ 731).

Being the only existing inscriptional record of achievement by Snefru, this document is of especial importance. The relief to which the inscriptions belong is as important as they. It represents the king in the etef-crown, with upraised war-club about to smite a Bedwi, whom he has forced to kneel, holding him by the hair of his head.[b] This, of course, symbolizes Snefru's victory over the Bedwin of this region, during his mining operations here.

169. The inscriptions contain only titles and names of Snefru; they are:

King of Upper and Lower Egypt; Favorite of the Two Goddesses: Lord of Truth; Golden Horus: Snefru. Snefru, Great God, who is given Satisfaction, Stability, Life, Health, all Joy forever.

---

[a]Engraved on the rock-walls of the Wadi Maghara in the Peninsula of Sinai. Text: Lepsius, *Denkmäler*, II, 2 a; Laborde, *Voyage de l'Arabie Petrée*, Pl. 5, No. 4; Laval, *Voyage dans la Péninsule Arabique*, Inscriptions hiéroglyphiques, Pl. 3, No. 1; Brugsch, *Thesaurus*, VI, 1492 (inscriptions only); Sethe, *Urkunden*, I, 7, 8; Morgan, *Recherches*, I, 233; Weill, *Sinai*, 103.

[b]This form of relief is as old as the early First Dynasty. Such a scene had already been left here by King Semerkhet, of the early dynastic age (Weill, *Revue archéologique*, II [1903], 231); and an ivory tablet shows King Usephais, of the First Dynasty, smiting a Bedwi native in the same way (Macgregor Collection, Spiegelberg, *Zeitschrift für ägyptische Sprache*, XXXV, 8).

Horus: Lord of Truth.[a]
Smiter of Barbarians.

A second, similar relief of Snefru in the Wadi Maghara is near the above.[b]

BIOGRAPHY OF METHEN[c]

170. This is the earliest biography which we possess, and it clearly betrays its primitive character. It is impossible to determine with certainty the succession of the parts distributed on the different walls, and the language is so bald, abbreviated, and obscure that some of the narrative remains unintelligible. Apart from the fact that it is our earliest document of the kind, and the only one from the Third Dynasty, the biography is especially valuable because it deals with the geography and government of the North, narrating Methen's activity in the Delta, of the administration of which at this early period we otherwise know almost nothing. The narrative tells of his gradual rise, from a beginning as scribe and overseer of a provision magazine, until he governs a considerable number of towns and districts in the Delta. He also obtained in Upper Egypt the rule of the eastern part of the Fayum and the Anubis nome (Seventeenth). He was liberally rewarded with gifts of lands, became master of the hunt, and tells us the size of his house, with some account of the grounds; all of which, from an age so remote, is of especial interest. He died in the reign of Snefru; all his affiliations were with the families preceding Snefru, and he was naturally buried beside the terraced pyramid of Zoser, of the earlier part of the Third Dynasty.

---

[a]In the palace façade, the so-called "banner."   [b]Weill, *Sinai*, 104.

[c]From his mastaba-chamber, found by Lepsius at Sakkara, and now in Berlin (Nos. 1105, 1106); published by Lepsius in *Denkmäler*, II, 3–7, 120, *a–e;* Schaefer, *Aegyptische Inschriften aus dem Königlichen Museum zu Berlin*, I, 68, 73–87; Sethe, *Urkunden*, I, 1–7.

Death of Methen's Father

171. ¹There were presented to him the things of his father,ª the judge and scribe Anubisemonekh; there was no grain or anything of the house, (ᶜbutᴵ) there were peopleᵇ and small cattle.

Methen's Career

172. ²He was made chief scribe of the provision magazine, and overseer of the things of the provision magazine. ³He was made ᶜ————ᴵ ⁴becoming local governor of Xois (Ox-nome), and inferior field-judge of Xois. ⁵He was appointed ᶜ—ᴵᶜ-judge, he was made overseer of all flax of the king, ⁶he was made ruler of Southern Perked (*Pr-ḳd*), and ᶜdeputyᴵ, ⁷he was made local governor of the people of Dep, ⁸palace-ruler of Miper (ᶜ*Myᴵ-pr*) and Persepa (*Pr-sp*ᵓ), and local governor of the Saitic nome, ⁹ruler of the stronghold of Sent (*Snt*). ᶜdeputyᴵ of nomes, ¹ºruler of Pershesthet (*Pr-šsṭt*), ruler of the towns of the palace, of the Southern Lake.ᵈ ¹¹Sheret-Methen (*Šrt-Mṭn*) was founded, ᶜand the domain whichᵉᴵ his father Anubisemonekh presented to him.

Honors and Gifts

173. ¹ᶜAdministratorᴵ, nomarch, and overseer of commissions in the Anubis nome,ᶠ overseer of ᶜ—ᴵ of ²the Mendesian nome, ᶜ— —ᴵ 4 ᶜstatᴵᵍ of land, (with) people and everything . . . . ³. . . . . ⁴There were founded for him the 12 towns of Shet-Methen (*Št-Mṭn*) in the Saitic nome, in the Xoite nome, and the Sekhemite nome. . . . . . , ⁵There were conveyed to him as a reward 200 stat of lands by numerous royal ᶜ—ᴵ; ⁶a ᶜmortuaryᴵ offering of 100 loaves every day from the mor-

---

ªSupply a *t*, which clearly has been lost or omitted.

ᵇSee the same expression, § 175, l. 18. These are the serfs attached to the land and conveyed with it.

ᶜ*Nḫt-ḫrw*, lit. "*strong-voiced*," an administrative position having to do with lands.

ᵈThe Southern Lake occurs also next to Nomes XX and XXI (combined) of Upper Egypt in a Tehneh tomb, *Annales* III, 76.

ᵉOr "*when his father A. gave (it) to him.*"

ᶠSeventeenth nome of Upper Egypt.

ᵍOn the doubtful character of the measure here, see Griffith, *Proceedings of the Society of Biblical Archæology*, XIV, 412.

tuary temple of the mother of the king's children, Nemathap (N-mʾᶜ·t-$ḥ$ʾp); ⁷a house 200 cubits long and 200 cubits wide, built and equipped; fine trees were set out, a very large lake was made therein, figs and vines were set out. ⁸It was recorded therein according to the king's writings; their names were according to the decree (sr) of the king's writings. ⁹Very plentiful trees and vines were set out, a great quantity of wine was made therein. ¹⁰A vineyardª was made for him: 2,000 stat of land within the wall; trees were set out, (ᶜinᵓ) ᵇImeres (Yy-mrs), Sheret-Methen ($Šr$-$Mṭn$), Yat-Sebek (Yʾt-Sbk), Shet-Methen ($Št$-$Mṭn$).

Methen's Offices

174. ¹Rulerᶜ of Southern Perked (Pr-$ḳd$);

²Rulerᵈ of Perwersah (Pr-wr-sʾ$ḫ$);

³Ruler and local governor of the stronghold, Hesen ($Ḥsn$); in the Harpoon nome;

⁴Palace-ruler and local governor in Sekhemu ($Sḫmw$) of Xois (Ox-nome).

⁵Palace-ruler and local governor in Dep (Buto);ᵉ

⁶Palace-ruler and local governor in Miper (ᶜMyᵓ-pr), of the Saite nome;ᶠ

⁷Palace-ruler and local governor in Two Hounds, of the Mendesian nome;

⁸Palace-ruler in Heswer ($Ḥs$-wr); ruler of fields in the west of the Saitic nome;ᵍ

⁹Palace-ruler of the Cow stronghold;ʰ local governor in the desert, and master of the hunt;

¹⁰Ruler of fields, ᶜdeputyᵓ and local governor in the Sekhemite nome;ⁱ

¹¹Nomarch, ᶜadministratorᵓ, and deputy in the eastern Fayum;

¹²Field-judge, palace-ruler of the west of the Saitic nome, leader of ᶜ—ᵓ.

ªThe first vineyard seems to have been in the garden around his house; the second is a large vineyard by itself.

ᵇThe connection of these four towns is not evident.

ᶜ$Ḥḳ$ʾ.   ᵈVar., "*Palace-ruler.*"

ᵉVar., "*Local governor of Dep, local governor of the people of Dep.*"

ᶠHe was also "*Palace-ruler and local governor in Mesezut (Msḏwt), of the Saitic nome.*"

ᵍVar., "*Palace-ruler of fields, and local governor in the Saitic nome.*"

ʰVar., "*Local governor of the Cow stronghold;*" this was one of the oases.

ⁱSecond nome of Lower Egypt.

Gifts of Land

175. [13]There were conveyed to him, as a reward, 200 stat of land by the numerous royal ⌐—⌐.

[14]There were conveyed to him 50 stat of land by (his) mother Nebsent (*Nb-snt*); [15]she made a will thereof to (her)[a] children; [16]it was placed in their possession by the king's writings (in) every place.

[17]Ruler of ⌐—⌐ of the Sekhemite nome. There were given to him 12 stat of land, with[b] his children; [18]there were people and small cattle.[c]

---

[a]Not "*my children*," see l. 7, where "*the people of Dep*" is written in the same way.

[b]That is: "and to his children likewise."

[c]With the land; see §171.

THE FOURTH DYNASTY

REIGN OF KHUFU

SINAI INSCRIPTIONS[a]

I

176. The relief is like that of Snefru,[b] except that the god Thoth is here added in the place of the Horus-name, and the king wears the double crown. Similarly also the inscriptions consist only of titles of the king. They are:

Khnum-Khufu,[c] Great God, Smiter of the Troglodytes ————.
All protection and life are with him.

II[d]

Consists only of titles of Khufu.

INVENTORY STELA[e]

177. The references to the Sphinx, and the so-called temple beside it in the time of Khufu, have made this monument from the first an object of great interest.

---

[a]Cut into the rock-walls of the Wadi Maghara. Text and relief: Laborde, *Voyage de l'Arabie*, Pl. 5, No. 2; Laval, *Voyage dans la Péninsule Arabique*, Insc. hiér., I, No. 2; II, No. 1; Lepsius, *Denkmäler*, II, 2, *b, c*; *Ordnance Survey*, III, 5; Brugsch, *Thesaurus*, VI, 1493 (inscriptions only); Sethe, *Urkunden*, I, 8; Weill, *Sinai*, 105.

[b]See §§ 168, 169.

[c]The full form of Khufu's name; it means: "*Khnum protects me.*" For the omission of the god's name cf. the similar usage in Hebrew, e. g., Nathan and Nathaniel. See Müller, *Recueil*, IX, 176.

[d]Immediately on the right of 1, and published with it.

[e]Discovered by Mariette during his excavations of the Sphinx and vicinity (September, 1853, to 1858), in the little temple of Isis built by Pesebkhenno, east of the great pyramid; now in Cairo. Text: Mariette, *Album*, Pl. 27; *Monuments divers*, 53; Maspero, *Dawn of Civilisation*, 413; Rougé, *Recherches sur les monuments qu'on peut attribuer aux VI premières dynasties*, 46; Birch, *Egyptian Texts*, 5, 6; Bunsen, *Egypt's Place*, 2d ed., V, 719–21. See also Mariette, *Le Sérapéum de Memphis*, 90, 100; Meyer, *Geschichte des alten Aegyptens*, 207, 208; and Brugsch, *Thesaurus*, V, 1231.

These references would be of the highest importance if the monument were contemporaneous with Khufu; but the orthographic evidences of its late date are entirely conclusive, and the reference to the temple of a goddess whose cult arose as late as that of Isis, as well as the title of Isis, viz., *"mistress of the pyramid,"* prove conclusively that the present stela is not a copy of an older document.[a] The fact that the priests of Pesebkhenno's time regarded the building beside the Sphinx, as the temple of *"Osiris of Rosta"* (R°-st°) is, however, of great interest, but does not determine for us the original character of that structure.[b]

178. [c]He made (it) for his mother, Isis, Divine Mother; Hathor, Mistress of ⌜Nun⌝.[d] The investigation[e] was placed on a stela. He gave to her an offering anew, and he built her temple of stone again. He found these gods in her place.[f]

179. The inscription in the lowermost section of the sunken panel is also of importance in connection with § 180.

---

[a]Maspero, *Dawn of Civilisation*, 364, n. 8.

[b]It is well to recall that in the Empire the true character of the Sphinx had been forgotten or misunderstood. The same might equally well have happened in the case of the building alongside it. [Later: It is now known that the building is a monumental portal, the entrance to the causeway leading up to the second pyramid.]

[c]Top and left side; introduction same as top and right side (§ 180).

[d]Text has the three *nw* signs used in writing *Nun*.

[e]Of her titles to the land? It is probably this remark which led Maspero to conclude that this stela is a copy of an older document. The word translated *"investigation"* (*sp·t* for *s·yp·t*) occurs also in Dümichen, *Bauurkunde des Dendera-tempels*, 16, in the same connection; cf. Brugsch, *Hieroglyphisch-demotisches Wörterbuch*, 1206, and a better example in Brugsch, *Thesaurus*, V, 1223, top line (time of Ramses II).

[f]A reference to the statues of the gods enumerated in the sunken panel. The stela is really an inventory of such statues; see § 180.

The district of the Sphinx of Harmakhis ($\underline{H}r$-m-y° $\underline{h}w \cdot t$) is on the south of the house of Isis, Mistress of the Pyramid; on the north of[a] Osiris, Lord of Rosta (R°-st°).   The writings ⌐of the goddess[b] of⌐ Harmakhis, were brought, in order to investigate.[c]

— may he grow; may he live forever and ever, ⌐looking⌐ toward the east.

180. The sunken panel occupying the greater part of the stela contains only reliefs[d] representing the statues of gods, belonging to the temple, and texts giving their names, the materials of which they were made, and their dimensions. The following texts occupy the raised margin and the edge:

[e]Live the Horus: Mezer ($M\underline{d}[r]$), King of Upper and Lower Egypt: Khufu, who is given life.   He found the house of Isis, Mistress of the Pyramid,[f] beside the house of the Sphinx of [g][Harmakhis] on the northwest of the house of Osiris,[h] Lord of Rosta (R°-$st^{\circ}w$).   He built his pyramid beside the temple of this goddess, and he built a pyramid for the king's-daughter[i] Henutsen ($\underline{H}nwt$-sn) beside this temple.[j]

---

[a]One expects "house of."   [b]Isis ?

[c]The connection between this sentence and the preceding is probably that the limits of "*The district of the Sphinx*" were investigated as found recorded in "*the writings* (viz., the records) *of the goddess.*"   (It is possibly this statement also which leads Maspero to believe the document is a copy of an older one.)   The same word (*syp*) is used in reference to the investigation of old titles, e. g., in Khnumhotep's tomb, Benihasan (§ 625, l. 44.).

[d]But see § 179.   [e]Top and right side.

[f]This is also her title in the sunken panel.

[g]The genitive *n* shows that "*Harmakhis*" as found in the same phrase in the sunken panel, has been omitted.

[h]That this would identify the so-called "temple of the Sphinx" as the temple of "*Osiris of Rosta*" was early noticed by Mariette (cf. *Le Sérapéum*, p. 99); but the fact seems to have been unnoticed, and does not find mention in any of the archæologies.   The mere statement that the king "*found*" the Isis temple is unusual; one expects *m ws:* "*in ruins*" as so very often, and this is confirmed by the statement of the left side: "*He built her temple again.*"

[i]According to Herodotus, the middle of the three small pyramids east of the Great Pyramid, belonged to Khufu's daughter (Herodotus, II, 126).   Henutsen is mentioned in a contemporary tomb at Gizeh (Brugsch, *Thesaurus*, V, 1231).

[j]According to this statement, the little Isis-temple east of the Great Pyramid was standing on the Gizeh plateau before any of the pyramids were built!   If Maspero accepts this statement, he should add this Isis-temple to the buildings which he believes were the predecessors of the pyramids on the Gizeh plateau (Maspero, *Dawn of Civilisation*, 365, n. 2).

EXAMPLES OF DEDICATION INSCRIPTIONS BY SONS

181. Many of the larger mastabas of the Old Kingdom contain long inscriptions by the sons of the deceased nobles relating their pious solicitude for the tombs of their departed fathers. In some cases the tomb was even built by the son after the father's death. All these longer inscriptions will be found herein; the following are only the more important shorter ones. They are all from the Fourth and Fifth Dynasties.

182. ªBy his eldest son, the chief mortuary priest and scribe, Ptah: "I came that I might do this for him, when he was buried in the beautiful west, according to that which he spake about it, while he was [alive] upon his two feet."

183. ᵇOne whose son shall do this for him, when he is in the west,ᶜ Ikhi (*Yḫy*), he saith: "I did this for my father, when he journeyed to the west upon the beautiful ways, whereon the revered (dead) journey."

184. ᵈBy his son, the overseer of the pyramid, "Great-is-Khafre," the king's-confidant, Thethi (*Ṯty*), who made (this) for his father and his mother, when they were both buried in the western highland.

185. ᵉRevered by the great god, king's-confidante, Henutsen. It was her eldest son, the field-judge, who made (it) for her, to make mortuary offerings to her therein.

ªFrom the tomb of Thenti (*Ṯnty*) at Gizeh; published by Lepsius, *Denkmäler*, II, 34, *d;* Mariette, *Mastabas*, 538; Sethe, *Urkunden*, I, 8 (from drawing No. 282, Berlin Museum).

ᵇFrom a false door seen in the hands of a dealer; published by Sethe, *Urkunden*, I, 9, from Berlin squeeze, No. 1675.

ᶜA reminder to the son of the pious son, by recalling what the latter did for his father.

ᵈMastaba at Gizeh; now in British Museum, No. 80; published by Lepsius, *Auswahl der wichtigsten Urkunden*, 8D; Sethe, *Urkunden*, I, 15 (collated with Berlin squeeze, No. 661).

ᵉCairo, No. 1691; published by Rougé, *Inscriptions hiéroglyphiques*, 5; Sethe, *Urkunden*, I, 34 (copy by Erman).

186. [a]By the Pharaoh's[b] treasurer of the god, Zezemonekh, who made this[c] for his wife Nubhotep.   He buried her in this beautiful tomb.

[a]The Pharaoh's[b] treasurer of the god Zezemonekh.   I made this[c] for my eldest son, the treasurer of the god, Theshen (Ts-$ḥn$), while he was a child.

187. [d]Sole companion of love, leader of the palace-hall, overseer of the baths of the palace, overseer of the bounty of the king's field of offerings, revered by his lord every day, governor of the Cow stronghold, Kam.   (This tomb is) what his eldest son, his revered, the judge and inferior scribe Hotep, made for him, that he (the son) might be revered by him (the father) when he (the son) journeyed to his (own) ka (viz., died).

---

[a]From the tomb of Zezemonekh, priest of Kings Userkaf and Sahure; Cairo, Nos. 1415, 1417; published by Mariette, *Mastabas*, 201 (K 1417), 200 (K 1415); Sethe, *Urkunden*, I, 33 (collated by Erman).

[b]Or simply "*palace-treasurer, etc.*"

[c]A false door.

[d]Mariette, *Mastabas*, 160; Sethe, *Urkunden*, I, 33 f.

REIGN OF KHAFRE

STELA OF MERTITYÔTES[a]

188. This document is especially useful as indicating the place of Snefru with relation to the first kings of the Fourth Dynasty, and was long ago so employed by E. de Rougé.

189. [b]Kings-wife, his beloved, devoted to Horus,[c] Mertityôtes (*Mrtt-yt· š*).

[d]King's-wife, his beloved, Mertityôtes; beloved of the Favorite of the Two Goddesses; [e]she who says anything whatsoever and it is done for her.[e]

Great in the [f]favor of Snefr[u] (*Snfr-*) — — —; great in the favor of Khuf[u] (*Ḫf[w]*), devoted to Horus,[c] honored under Khafre (*Ḫ ᶜ f-R ᶜ*), Merti[tyôt]es.

WILL OF PRINCE NEKURE, SON OF KING KHAFRE[g]

190. A new date of Khafre is the contribution furnished by Sethe's collation of this inscription. The twelfth "*numbering*" as the numberings took place at this time twice a year, indicates the twenty-fourth year of Khafre. This surprisingly confirms the Turin Papyrus, which gives twenty-

---

[a]Limestone false door of the usual type noted in the *Appendice* (p. 565) of Mariette's *Mastabas*, but without text. According to the headline of the page, the tomb stands on the "Plaine de Gizeh;" the false door has never been removed. The text is published by Rougé, *Inscriptions hiéroglyphiques*, I, 62; Rougé, *Recherches sur les monuments qu'on peut attribuer aux VI premières dynasties*, 36 f.

[b]At the top.   [c]The king.   [d]Right side.

[e]An obscure title of the queens of Egypt, extending from the Old Kingdom down into the Empire. Sethe, *Zeitschrift für ägyptische Sprache*, 36, 143 f.; cf. also Naville, *ibid.*, 142.

[f]Left side.

[g]In his tomb at Gizeh; published by Lepsius, *Denkmäler*, II, 15, *a;* Sethe, *Urkunden*, I, 16, 17 (collated with Berlin drawing, No. 253, and Berlin squeezes, Nos. 35 and 38).

four years as the length of Khafre's reign.   The king's son, Nekure, was then old enough to feel the necessity of making a will.   It is the only document of the kind from the Old Kingdom, which has survived in such excellent preservation.

191. The fortune which Prince Nekure bequeathed to his heirs consisted of fourteen towns, and two estates in the pyramid-city of his father.   The latter doubtless consisted of his "town-house" and gardens.   These he had left to a daughter, but she had evidently died, and on the reversion of the legacy to himself he left it to his wife.   The fourteen towns he distributed among five heirs, of whom one was his wife, and three were his children, while the name of one is lost.   Eleven of the fourteen towns are named after Khafre, and there is no reason to doubt that the other three were also so named, but they are now unreadable.   Besides these fourteen towns, Prince Nekure had at least twelve[a] towns in the mortuary endowment of his tomb, of which nine were named after Khafre.   It is impossible to determine whether these had belonged to the prince's estate, or whether they were given by the reigning king at the prince's death.

Date

192. [1]Year of the twelfth [occurrence] of the numbering of large and sm[all] cattle.

Introduction

193. [2]King's son, Nekure (R^c-n-$k^{\backslash}w$) — — he makes the (following) [「command「],[b] (while) living upon his two feet without ailing in any respect.[c]

---

[a]See Lepsius, *Denkmäler*, II, 15, *b*.   There could not have been more than fourteen towns, as no more than two are broken out.

[b]The determinative of a document is visible at the end of the lacuna; "*command, edict*" ($w\underline{d}\cdot t$-$md\cdot t$) is usual after "*make*" or "*made*" in this connection.

[c]"*Being of sound mind.*"   This line (2) is engraved horizontally over the following columns, and is evidently the prescript or title of the will.   There are eight of the subjoined columns, each column being headed by the name of an heir, below which is entered the legacy bequeathed him.   Each legacy is a town or towns; the district or nome is given first and then the town-name, or names, each of which is compounded with that of Khafre, the king.

First Legacy

194. [3]I have given to the king's-confidant, Nekennebti (*N-kɔ-n-nbty*), (in) —,[a] (the towns[b] of) "Khafre- —," and "Khafre- —."

Second Legacy

195. [4c]His son, the king's-confidant, Nekure (in) the eastern back-land, (the towns of) ["⸢Khafre-⸣ —," "⸢Khafre⸣- —" and "⸢Khafre⸣- —"].[d]

Third Legacy

196. [5]His daughter, the king's-confidant, Hetephires, (in) the eastern district, (the town of) "Khafre- —;" (in) the eastern back-land, (the town of) "Khafre- —."

Fourth Legacy

197. [6][His son] the king's-confidant, Kennebtiwer (*Kɔ-n-nbty-wr*) (in) —, (the town of) "Great-is-[the-Fame]-of-Khafre;" (in) the Mendesian nome, (the towns of) "Khafre- —," and "Khafre- —."

Fifth Legacy

198. [7]— — — — —, (in) the Mendesian nome, (the towns of) "Khafre- —" and "Khafre- —."

Sixth Legacy

199. [8]His beloved wife, the king's-confidante, Nekennebti (*N-kɔ-n-nbty*), (in) the nome of the Cerastes-Mountain, (the town of) "Beautiful-is-Khafre;" (in) the nome of [e]Upper (the town of) "⸢Brilliant⸣-is-Khafre" (*Ḥɔj-Rɔ-[ḫ]ɔ*); (in the pyramid-town) "Great-is-Khafre," the estate of his daughter, — and —.[f]

---

[a]A nome-name is lost.   [b]Two towns at least.

[c]The formula "*I have given*" is omitted after its occurrence once for all in l. 3; hence "*his son*" instead of "*my son.*"

[d]Three towns, from the size of the lacuna.

[e]Twentieth nome of Upper Egypt.

[f]Two small subcolumns, each containing a designation of some piece of property, but they are no longer legible; it is doubtless the estate, or part of the estate, of a deceased daughter, which, after its reversion to him, he now leaves to his wife. Hence her occurrence twice in the will.

THE TESTAMENTARY ENACTMENT OF AN UNKNOWN OFFICIAL, ESTABLISHING THE ENDOWMENT OF HIS TOMB BY THE PYRAMID OF KHAFRE[a]

200. As a revelation of the legal organization of this remote age, this document, like the similar instrument of Senuonekh[b] (§§ 231 ff.), is of great interest. Economically it is of importance to note that the king gives whole towns as mortuary endowment, to keep the tomb of the deceased constantly supplied with offerings.

Introduction

201. [1]————[c] while he was alive upon his two feet, even the sole companion, lord of Nekhen, member of the king's court every day . . . . local governor of "Praise-of-Horus-First-of-Heaven,"[d] [2]———— these mortuary priests forever[e] ————[f].

Endowment is Entailed

202. [3]— — — — This is the [dec]ree which I made concerning it: I have not empowered — — any of [my brothers], [4]my sisters, or my daughter's children, inferior mortuary priests, or assistant mortuary priests, [⌈to take lands⌉,] [5]people, or anything which I have conveyed to them, for making mortuary offerings to me therewith, whether their man-servant [or their maid-servant], [6]their brothers or their sisters, save to make mortuary offerings [to me therewith, in the cemetery in] [7]my eternal tomb which is at the pyramid, "Great-is-Khafre;" according to the portion of lands, people, and [everything, which I have conveyed to them, for making mortuary offerings to me] [8]therewith.

---

[a]Stela in Cairo (No. 1432); published by Brugsch, *Thesaurus*, V, 1210 ff.; Sethe, *Urkunden*, I, 11–15 (collated with Berlin squeeze, No. 1597).

[b]Whence the restorations below are drawn.

[c]The lost introduction will be found in the preceding will (§ 193).

[d]Name of a vineyard estate founded by Zoser of the Third Dynasty; see Sethe, in Garstang's *Bet-Khallâf*, 21. I have omitted before this title a repetition of titles already mentioned.

[e]Probably so rather than "*endowment;*" for "*these mortuary priests of the endowment*" is expressed by *ḥn-kꜣ ḏt (y)pn* (Sethe, *Urkunden*, I, 36, l. 1).

[f]Probably a lacuna of more than one line.

Line of Entailment

203. I have not empowered any mortuary priest of the endowment, to give the lands, people or [anything which I have conveyed to them, for making mortuary offerings to me] ⁹therewith, in payment to any person; or to give as property to any person, except that [they] shall give [it to their children], ¹⁰entitled to the division of it with any mortuary priest among these mortuary priests.ᵃ

Violation of Endowment

204. Whatsoever mortuary priest of the endowment shall violate, — — — — ¹¹of my mortuary offerings, which the king gave to honor me, the portion in his possession shall be taken from him — — — — —.ᵇ

Endowment not Involved in Suits of Priests

205. ¹²Whatsoever mortuary priest of the endowment shall institute legal proceedings against his fellow, and he shall make a writ of his ⌜claim⌝ against the mortuary priest, by which [⌜he⌝ (the defendant ?) ⌜forfeits⌝ the portion] ¹³in his possession; the lands, people and everything shall be taken from him,ᶜ which I gave to him for making mortuary offerings to me therewith — — — — — ¹⁴therewith. It shall be conveyed back to him because of not instituting proceedings before the officials, [concerning the lands, people and everything, which I conveyed] ¹⁵to the mortuary priests of the endowment, for making mortuary offerings to me therewith, in my eternal tomb, which is in the cemetery at [the pyramid: "Great-is-Khafre"].

Transfer of Priests to Other Service

206. ¹⁶Whatsoever mortuary priest of the endowment shall go forth to other service, in the presence of the officials, — — — — — ¹⁷the

---

ᵃNot all their children were entitled to a share in the division, but only those who became mortuary priests; hence the document distinguishes particularly those "*entitled to (lit. belonging to) the division of it (the property) with any given (ymn) mortuary priest of these mortuary priests*" (viz., those endowed by this document). The paragraph occurs again in the enactment of Senuonekh (§ 233).

ᵇSethe suggests for the lacuna; "*for or by the (priestly) order, to which he belongs*," as in l. 17.

ᶜOf course, read *nḥm mᶜf* as in l. 11. See the similar clause in the decree of Senuonekh, § 235.

officials, he shall go forth to other service and the portion in his possession shall revert to the (priestly) order to which he belonged. — — — — — [18]of lands, people and everything, which I conveyed [to] them, for making mortuary offerings to me therewith, in my tomb which is in [the cemetery at the pyramid: "Great-is-Khafre"]; [19]he shall go forth with his meat.

Land Given by King

207. As for this field, which the king gave to me, to honor me — — — — — [20]for making mortuary offerings to me therewith in the cemetery.

Alienation of Endowment

208. As for whatsoever shall be paid out, of that which I gave to them, [I will enter into judgment with them in the place] [21]wherein judgment is had. The portion which remains afterward, shall belong, by tenths, to these (priestly) orders to [whom] I have conveyed this — — — — — [the portion] [22]which remains, for making mortuary offerings to me therewith, in the cemetery in my eternal tomb, which is at [the pyramid: "Great]-is-Khafre."

Towns of the Endowment

209. [As for the towns] [23]of the (mortuary) endowment, which the king gave to me, to honor me, which are maintained for my mortuary offerings, according to the list — — — — — [24]forever, wherewith mortuary offerings are made to me, in my eternal tomb which is in the cemetery at the pyramid: "Great-is-Khafre," — [lands, people,] [25]and everything which I conveyed to them.

As for the towns of the (mortuary) endowment of the purification, wherewith purification is made ————.[a]

---

[a]At least three lines are lost at the end.

REIGN OF MENKURE

DEBHEN'S INSCRIPTION, RECOUNTING KING MENKURE'S ERECTION OF A TOMB FOR HIM[a]

210. The unfinished condition of this interesting inscription renders it extremely fragmentary. But mutilated as it is, it tells us plainly enough of the king's visit to the Gizeh cemetery to inspect the work on his family pyramids, and of his detailing fifty men to build a tomb for Debhen. Later the king orders his own people, who are bringing limestone for a temple, to bring also the necessary false doors, etc., for Debhen's tomb from the quarry at Troja.

The Royal Command

211. [1b]————. [2]He saith:

As for this tomb, it was the king of Upper and Lower Egypt, Menkure, [living forever], who caused that it be [ʳmadeⁱ], when [his majesty] was [upon] the road beside the pyramid, Hir[c] (*Ḥr*), [3]in order to inspect the work ʳonⁱ the pyramid: "Divine-is-Menkure."

— — — [ʳthere cameⁱ] the [naval] commander and the two high priests of Memphis, and the [work]men,[d] [4]standing upon it,[e] to inspect

---

[a]From his tomb (No. 90 on Lepsius' plan) at Gizeh; published by Lepsius, *Denkmäler*, II, 37, *b;* Sethe, *Urkunden*, I, 18–21 (collated with Berlin drawing, No. 284). The inscription was left unfinished by the sculptor. The artist had drawn all the hieroglyphs in ink, but they were only partially cut, and the uncut portions of the lines disappeared.

[b]This line contained his titles, as the sole remaining sign shows.

[c]Name of pyramid usually supposed to be that of Menkure. It is, however, evidently one of the smaller three beside his own pyramid, the name of which here follows. "*Hir*" will have belonged to one of his family. That the two pyramids were close together is evident from the text. The king stands on the road by the Hir-pyramid to inspect the other. This disposes of the idea that the former was in Abu Roash (Petrie, *History of Egypt*, I, 56).

[d]Only the plural determinative of "*men*" is visible.

[e]The pyramid.

94

the work ⌜on⌝ [the pyramid, "Divine-is-Menkure"].   — 50 men were assigned to do the work on it[a] every day, besides ⌜exacting⌝ of them, [5]that which the ⌜—⌝ desired.   His majesty commanded that [no man should be taken[b]] for any forced labor, except to do the work on it,[a] to his satisfaction.

Building of the Tomb

212. [6]His majesty commanded to ⌜clear⌝ the place of ⌜rubbish⌝ — — —this tomb. His majesty commanded to ⌜hack⌝ — — — — —[7]in order to ⌜clear⌝ the ⌜rubbish⌝ — — — — —.   [His majesty commanded] that the two treasurers of the god should come; [said his majesty to them] — — [8]————— given to them ————— [9]————— men, whom his majesty judged, that he should go around the work ⌜exacted⌝ [10]————— in his — that there be brought stone from Troja (R°-$^\circ w$) to clothe[c] with limestone the temple there,[d] [11]together with two false doors, and a front for this tomb, by the naval commander and the two high priests of Ptah, together with the king's master-builder, who came [12]————— [that there] be [brought] for me a statue ⌜much greater than⌝ life [13]————— every — every day. It is today ⌜—⌝ upon its highland, together with the pure house.   [14]————— together with two statues of the assistant, of which one was — — — — — [the other was] — — — — — [15]————— feast of Apis in the temple [16]————— [He did] this, in [order] that I might be his revered one by his lord [17]————— for my [father] and my mother, for whom I have maintained [18]————— green cosmetic, eye-paint — ⌜—⌝ — — [19]outside of the place.   Then [⌜I be⌝]sought [[⌜from my lord⌝]] ⌜— —⌝ in the Northland, of the cattle in this place ⌜—⌝.   There was issued [20]a command of the king to the chief of [⌜all works of the king to take⌝] people to make it, a tomb of — cubits in its length, [21]by 50 ⌜cubits⌝ in ⌜its width,⌝ by — cubits [⌜in its height⌝] — — according to ⌜that which⌝ this my father did, while he was living.   Then the king caused [22]—————.[e]

---

[a]Debhen's tomb.   [b]Read *yn·t.*

[c]Verb *ᶜyn,* meaning "*to build or clothe with limestone of Ayan (ᶜyn).*"

[d]The expedition to the quarry which brought stone for the temple, brought also the false doors, etc., for Debhen's tomb. The temple meant is probably the pyramid-temple of Menkure.

[e]The remainder of the inscription was never executed.

THE FIFTH DYNASTY

REIGN OF USERKAF

TESTAMENTARY ENACTMENT OF NEKONEKH[a]

213. Besides being the most elaborate document of the
kind preserved to us, there are important historical facts
contained in these inscriptions. They chiefly concern the
disposal of two parcels of land of sixty stat each, given by
King Menkure: the one as endowment of the temple of
the local Hathor of Royenet (Tehneh); the other as a wakf
or endowment of the tomb of Khenuka, a nobleman of
Menkure's time. Both endowments were administered by
one priesthood, who served at the same time as priests of
Hathor and as mortuary priests of Khenuka. At the
beginning of the Fifth Dynasty, its first king had honored
one of his favorites, a steward of the palace named Nekonekh, by conveying to his single person the offices of priest
of Hathor at Tehneh and of mortuary priest of Khenuka.
In so doing—though, of course, nothing is said about it in
these inscriptions—Userkaf, as the first king of the Fifth
Dynasty was plainly dispossessing some supporter of the
old dynasty, and strengthening his own house by winning
the allegiance of another noble family.

214. Nekonekh, having the right to bequeath the two
land-endowments to whom he will, now makes a will, stating
the origin of both endowments in Menkure's time, and his
own title to them by appointment from Userkaf, and
decreeing that they shall now be distributed among his

---

[a]From his tomb in Tehneh, excavated and copied by G. Fraser in 1890; published by him in 1902 in *Annales*, III, 122–30, and Pls. II–V (see also Maspero,
ibid., 131–38); again from Fraser, with useful restorations and corrections by
Sethe, *Urkunden*, I, 24–32.

children, acting corporately as his successor in both offices. Each child is annually to serve one month as priest of Hathor, and another month as mortuary priest of Khenuka. For this purpose twelve children were required, and, as Nekonekh had thirteen, he gave to eleven a month each, and divided the remaining month between two. The income from the land was also divided, each of the eleven children receiving the income from five stat for the Hathor temple, and five stat for Khenuka, while the remaining two each received half of this. The twelve months of the year were thus all provided for, the sixty stat belonging to each endowment were completely disposed of, and the thirteen children all made legatees. It is of importance to notice that the mortuary endowment, established in the latter half of the Fourth Dynasty, is still respected and continued in the Fifth Dynasty.

215. Nekonekh's will disposing of his own estate is also among the inscriptions in the tomb (§§ 223–25), though very fragmentary. Another document establishes and adjusts his own mortuary priesthood (§§ 226, 227), and in conclusion he and his wife, probably after decease, receive mortuary statues from two of their children (§§ 228–30).

I.   THE PRIESTHOOD OF HATHOR

Introduction

216. [1]Steward[a] of the Palace, governor of the New Towns, superior prophet of Hathor, mistress of Royenet, king's-confidant, Nekonekh (*N-k*ꜣ-ꜥ*nḫ*); [5]his wife [Hezethekenu (*Ḥḏt-ḥknw*)], revered by [Hathor].

[8]He makes a decree to his children, to be priests of Hathor, mistress of Royenet.

---

[a]The lines are too short at the beginning to number them all.

List of the Priests of Hathor

217. ⁹These are the prophets whom I have made, of my children, of the endowment,ᵃ to be priests of Hathor. Now, it was King Menkure who conveyed two piecesᵇ of land, to these prophets to be priest therewith.

¹⁰King's-confidant, steward of the Palace, Nekonekh; his wife, the king's-confidante, Hezethekenu; her children.

ᵃRead *ḏt;* the *n* is misread from the hieratic, as commonly in this word; e. g., Sebni, l. 4 (Sethe, *Urkunden*, I, 136). Maspero's correction, *wḏtny*, producing a feminine relative form, is ungrammatical, for it follows a masculine noun. The endowment meant is probably that of Khenuka, which the same children administered.

ᵇThis was probably not a unit of measure, for the document afterward assigns 120 stat, 60 for the Hathor temple, and 60 for the mortuary service of Khenuka; and these 120 stat are obviously the itemization of the two pieces of land above mentioned (the 5 stat of l. 21 are not to be counted).

218.

[11]King's-confidante, Hezethekenu, re-vered (woman)[b]	Five intercalary days		Land
	1st month	First Season[a]	5 stat
[12]Scribe of the King's records, Hen-hathor (man)	2d month		5 stat
[13]Shepseshathor, ⌈priest⌉ (man)	3d month		5 stat
[14]Nessuhathoryakhet (man)	4th month		5 stat
[15]Shepseshathor, ⌈priest⌉ (man)	1st month	Second Season	5 stat
[16]Webkuhathor ([$W^c b$-$k^ɔ w$-] $Ḥtḥr$)(man)	2d month		5 stat
[17]Kisuthathor ($K^ɔ$-$yšwt$-$Ḥtḥr$) (man)	3d month		5 stat
[18]Khebuhathor ($Ḥ^c$-$b^ɔ w$-$Ḥtḥr$) (man)	4th month		5 stat
[19]Khentisuthathor ($Ḥnt$-$yšwt$-$Ḥtḥr$) (disappeared)	—	Third Season	5 stat
[20]Royenet ($R^ɔ$-$yn^. t$) (disappeared)	—		5 stat
[21]Left vacant (disappeared)	—		5 stat[c] *sic!*
[22]— meat, his tenth of all that is paid [into] the temple, beside the rations of bread and beer. Prophet, Henhathor (man with libation vase)	3d month		5 stat
[23]Mortuary Priest	Mer — (man)	4th month	5 stat
[24]Mortuary Priest	⌈Keksire ($K^ɔ k$-$s^ɔ Re$)⌉ (man)		

[a]Written ᐦ *ḫ·t* and determining the reading of this season. [Later: See Sethe, *Zeitschrift für ägyptische Sprache*, 41, 89.]

[b]In the original, the names are arranged in perpendicular columns, and a figure of the person named is depicted below each name. I have added the sex of the person in each case. The first column is therefore the priests, the second (double) column is the time of service for each priest, and the third is the amount of land from which each draws the necessary income.

[c]This is an error of the scribe as the other table shows, for in it the entire line, date and all are vacant.

The Decree

219. [25]It was the majesty of Userkaf who commanded that I should be priest[a] of Hathor, mistress of Royenet; whatsoever was paid into the temple, it was I who was priest over everything that came[b]into the temple. [26]Now, it is these my children who shall act as priests of Hathor, mistress of Royenet, as I myself did, while I journey to the beautiful west, as one revered, — — in charge of these my children.

II.   THE MORTUARY PRIESTHOOD OF KHENUKA

List of Priests of Khenuka

220. [27]Now, it is these people[c] who make the mortuary offerings to the king's-confidant, Khenuka (*Ḥnw-kʾ*), his father, his mother his children, and all his ⌐house⌐.

---

[a]The text is perfectly clear and correct; emendation is entirely unnecessary.

[b]Read *wdb* (as Sethe has done) after the inscription of Persen (*Urkunden,* I, 37).

[c]The priests of Hathor just mentioned.

221.

ᵃFive intercalary days		
²⁸1st month		———
²⁹2d month	First Season	Prophet, Henhathor
³⁰3d month		Royenet ($R^{?}$-[$yn \cdot t$])
³¹4th month		Khentisuthathor
³²1st month		Khebuhathor
³³2d month	Second Season	Kisuthathor
³⁴3d month		Webkuhathor
³⁵4th month		Shepseshathor, ⌜priest⌝
³⁶1st month		Nessuhathoryakhet
³⁷2d month	Third Season	Shepseshathor, ⌜priest⌝
³⁸Vacant		Left vacant
³⁹3d month		Scribe of the king's records, Henhathor
⁴⁰4th month		King's-confidante, Hezethekenu

ᵃThis table corresponds exactly with the preceding, and as it contains no column for the land, it is probable that the land column of the first table was intended to serve for both instead of repeating it. Thus both parcels of land mentioned in l. 9 were used: one for Hathor, and one for Khenuka.

The Decree

222. [41]Now, it is these my children who make the mortuary offerings to the king's-confidant, Khenuka, his father, his mother, and all his ⌜house⌝, at the feast of Wag, the feast of Thoth, and every feast-day.

III.   NEKONEKH'S WILL

223. The document is largely lost; the fragments beside the statues are possibly not parts of it, but are relevant, as showing Nekonekh's own enactments regarding these persons.

Introduction

224. The steward of the Palace, king's-confidant, Nekonekh, revered; the king's-confidante, Hezethekenu; — said — — — [to] his children, while he was upon his two feet, alive before the king — — — —.

By Two Statues of Henhathor

225. — the scribe of the king's records, Henhathor (*Ḥn-Ḥtḥr*) is my heir upon my seat, and lord of all my possessions.

— her[a] eldest son, honored of his father, scribe of the king's records, Henhathor.

— property; they shall deliver to this my heir, as they did [⌜to⌝] myself.

— ⌜given⌝ to her ⌜for⌝ the ration of bread and beer as property, ⌜while⌝ upon my seat, — — as property. May they deliver the [ration of] bread and beer to this my heir, as they did [⌜to⌝] myself.

IV.   NEKONEKH'S MORTUARY PRIESTHOOD

Scene

226. The deceased Nekonekh sits before a table of food-offerings, while his eight mortuary priests approach from behind in pairs, each pair being designated as under the authority of one of Nekonekh's sons.[b]

---

[a]This figure is doubtless beside the mother, the other beside the father. Fraser's description is not explicit in this particular.

[b]Only one pair is perfectly preserved, and one is entirely lost, but the remains indicate that all four pairs were alike.

The Decree

227. [These mortuary priests[a]] are under the authority of these my children. I have not empowered [any] person[b] to take them for any forced labor, save to make mortuary offerings which are divided in this house — — — these mortuary priests. As for these my children, who shall do any work with these mortuary priests, and as for any man who shall violate (this will), I will enter into judgment with him.

V.   NEKONEKH'S MORTUARY STATUE

228. A man and woman, the latter the daughter of Nekonekh, had three statues made, representing Nekonekh and themselves. The inscriptions are these:

Dedication

229. His daughter and his son, who made this for him, according to his honor with him.

Over the Three Figures

230. The revered by Hathor, king's-confidante, Ikhnoubet (*Y⁾ ḥ-nb· t*);

Inferior scribe of the king's records, king's-confidant, Nonekhsesi (*N-ᶜnḥ-ššy*).

Nekonekh, revered by the great god.

TESTAMENTARY ENACTMENT OF SENUONEKH, REGULATING HIS MORTUARY PRIESTHOOD[c]

231. Senuonekh was a priest of Userkaf and Sahure. This decree from his tomb closely resembles and, in some parts, is identical with the decree of Khafre's unknown official (§§ 200–209), but it is better preserved, and also clearer in the wording.

---

[a]Sethe's very probable restoration.

[b]The connection renders Sethe's restoration certain.

[c]From his tomb; published by Mariette, *Mastabas*, 318; Sethe, *Urkunden*, I, 36 f.

Installation of Priests and Descendants

232. [1]These mortuary priests of the endowment, and their children and further the children of their children whom they shall bear forever, are ————

Entailment of Endowment

233. [2]I have not empowered them [to give] (it)[a] in payment as property to any person; but they shall give (it) to their children, entitled to the division of [it with any mortuary priest of these mortuary priests].[b]

Transfer of a Priest

234. [3]As for any mortuary priest among them who shall ⌜default⌝, or who shall be taken for other service, everything which I have given to him shall revert to the mortuary priests who are in his (priestly) order.   I have not em[powered] — — — — —

Endowment not Involved in Suits

235. [4]As[c] for any mortuary priest among them who shall institute legal proceedings against his fellow, everything which I have given to him shall be taken away, and shall then be given to the mortuary priest against whom he instituted legal proceedings.   I have not empowered ————.

---

[a]The mortuary endowment.

[b]With this compare the similar precautionary clause of the unknown official of Khafre (§ 203, ll. 8, 9), and see also explanatory note, *ibid.*

[c]See similar clause in decree of an unknown official under Khafre (§ 205).

REIGN OF SAHURE

SINAI INSCRIPTIONS[a]

Relief

236. King in the crown of Upper Egypt, smites kneeling Bedwi as in §§ 168, 169.[b]

The texts, as in §§ 168, 169, and 176, contain only names and titles of the king:

Horus: Lord of Diadems; King of Upper and Lower Egypt: Sahure ($S^{ɔ} ḥw-R^{c}$); who is given life forever.

Smiter of all countries.

The Great God smites the Asiatics (*mnṯw*) of all countries.

TOMB STELA OF NENEKHSEKHMET[c]

237. The stela is a well-executed false door of Turra limestone, contrasting strikingly with the poor material and mediocre workmanship of the modest tomb to which it belonged. The cause of this contrast is indicated in the inscription, viz., that the stela was a gift from the king.

The Request

238. The chief physician, Nenekhsekhmet (*Shmt-n-ᶜnh*) spoke before his majesty: "May thy person, beloved of Re, command that there be given to me a false door of stone for this my tomb of the cemetery."

---

[a]Cut into the rocks of the Wadi Maghara in the Peninsula of Sinai. Text and relief: Lepsius, *Denkmäler*, II, 39, *a;* Laval, *Voyage dans la Péninsule Arabique*, insc. hiér., Pl. 2, No. 2; Laborde, *Voyage de l'Arabie*, 5, No. 3; Brugsch, *Thesaurus*, VI, 1494 (inscriptions only); Sethe, *Urkunden*, I, 32; Weill, *Sinai*, 106.

[b]Two gods stand behind the king.

[c]From a mastaba at Sakkara, excavated by Mariette; text: Mariette, *Monuments divers*, 12, 203, 204; Sethe, *Urkunden*, I, 38–40. Erman's manuscript copy collated with original; Maspero, *Proceedings of the Society of Biblical Archæology*, XI, 309. Translated by Maspero (*ibid.*), with discussion of architectural terms; treated by Erman, *Aegypten*, 431.

King's Compliance

239. His majesty caused that there be brought for him two false doors[a] from Troja (*R⸱-⸱w*) of stone, that they be laid in the audience-hall[b] of the house (called): "Sahure-Shines-with-Crowns," and that the two high priests of Memphis and the artisans of the ⌜—⌝ be assigned to them, that the work on them might be done in the presence of the king himself. The stone-work[c] went on every day; there was an inspection of that which was done on them in the court daily. His majesty had ⌜color⌝ put on them, and had them painted in blue.

Presentation of the Gift

240. His majesty[d] said to the chief physician Nenekhsekhmet: "As these my nostrils enjoy health, as the gods love me, mayest thou depart into the cemetery at an advanced old age as one revered." I praised the king greatly and lauded every god for Sahure's sake, for he knows the desire of the entire suite. When anything goes forth from the mouth of his majesty, it immediately comes to pass. For the god has given to him knowledge of things that are in the body,[e] because he is more august than any god. If ye love Re, ye shall praise every god for Sahure's sake, who did this for me. I was his revered one; never did I do anything evil toward any person.

TOMB INSCRIPTION OF PERSEN[f]

241. This inscription is over a scene showing people in the act of bringing mortuary offerings of food for Persen's tomb. According to the inscription, these offerings are

---

[a]Erman suggests that a double false door is meant. The same reference to a double false door is found in the tomb of Debhen (*Dbḥn*). This is the same word (*rwty*) used later for a temple façade, which would explain the dual.

[b]*Ḏ⸱dw*, see § 501, l. 2.

[c]Read *št*, which I have rendered "*quarry-service*" in the Empire (II, 935, l. 6). In the Old Kingdom it retains its literal meaning, "*stone-cutting*." There was an "*overseer of stone-cutting*," or quarry service, in the Old Kingdom (§ 343).

[d]The following is the presentation of the false doors by the king.

[e]Of anyone else, "*body*" or "*belly*" being the seat of the mind, as we use "heart."

[f]Limestone slab in Berlin (15004); published by Mariette, *Mastabas*, 300; Schaefer, *Aegyptische Inschriften aus dem Königlichen Museum zu Berlin*, I, 22.

drawn from the income of the queen mother, Neferhotepes, coming to her from the temple of Ptah.

The bringing of the mortuary offerings to Pharaoh's overseer, Persen, being the payment of heth(*ḥt*)-loaves, pesen(*psn*)-loaves, and sefet(*sft*)-oil, which comes from the temple of Ptah-South-of-His-Wall, for the king's-mother, Neferhotepes, every day, as a perpetual offering, which he gave for making mortuary offerings therewith in the time of Sahure.

REIGN OF NEFERIRKERE

TOMB INSCRIPTIONS OF THE VIZIER, CHIEF JUDGE, AND CHIEF ARCHITECT WESHPTAH[a]

242. It is much to be regretted that this unusually interesting inscription has suffered so sadly at the hands of time. Weshptah was the greatest man at the court of Neferirkere, being vizier, chief judge, and chief architect. His son Mernuterseteni was called upon to build his father's tomb, and thus narrates how this happened. The king, his family and the court were one day inspecting a new building in course of construction under Weshptah's superintendence as chief architect. All admire the work, and the king turns to praise his faithful minister, when he notices that Weshptah does not hear the words of royal favor. The king's exclamation alarms the courtiers, the stricken minister is quickly carried to the court, and the priests and chief physicians are hurriedly summoned. The king has a case of medical rolls brought; but all is in vain; the physicians declare his condition hopeless. The king is smitten with sorrow, and retires to his chamber, where he prays to Re. He then makes all arrangements for Weshptah's burial, ordering an ebony coffin made and having the body anointed in his own presence. Weshptah's eldest son, Mernuterseteni, was then empowered to build the tomb, the king furnishing and endowing it. The son therefore erected it by the pyramid of Sahure, and, as we have said, recorded the whole story on its walls.

---

aFrom his tomb at Abusir; blocks in Cairo (Nos. 1569, 1570, 1673, 1702); published by Sethe, *Urkunden*, I, 40–45 (from a copy by Erman).

Erection of the Tomb by His Son

243. ¹[It was] his eldest [son], first under the king, ⸢advocate of the people⸣, Mernuterseteni (*Štny-mr-ntr*), who made (it)ᵃ for him, while he was in his tomb of the cemetery.

King Visits a New Building

244. ²—————— Neferirkere (*Nfr-yr-k³-Rᶜ*) came to see the beauty ofᵇ —————— when he came forth upon them ⁴——————. His majesty [caused] that it be ⸢—⸣ ⁵—————— the royal children [s]aw ⁶——— and they ⸢wondered⸣ very greatly beyond ⁷[everything]. Then, lo, his majesty praised him because of it.ᶜ

Weshptah's Sudden Illness

245. His majesty saw him, however, that [he] heard not. ⁸——— ⸢—⸣.ᵈ When the royal children and companions, who were of the court, heard, great fearᵉ was in their hearts.

He is Conveyed to Court, and Dies

246. ¹————— ⸢⸢He was conveyed to⸣⸣ the court, and his majesty had the royal children, companions, ritual priests, and chief physicians come ²——————. His majesty [had] brought for him a case of writingsᶠ — ³——————. They said before his majesty that he was lostᵍ ⁴——————. ⸢⸢The heart of his majesty⸣ was⸣ exceedingly ⸢sad⸣ beyond everything; his majesty said that he would do everything according to his heart's desire, and returned to the privy chamber.

King Furnishes Him Sepulture

247. ⁵—————— he prayed to Re ⁶—————— ⸢put⸣ into writing on his tomb ⁷——————. ⸢⸢His majesty commanded that there be

---

ᵃThis inscription.

ᵇEvidently some new building in course of erection by Weshptah should here follow, as Sethe has surmised.

ᶜThe fine tomb.

ᵈA speech of the king is lost in the lacuna, as is shown by a pronoun of the second person singular still discernible.

ᵉLit. "*fear beyond everything.*"

ᶠ This is, of course, a medical papyrus, like the great Papyrus Ebers. This confirms the claim of this papyrus that some of its recipes were made and used already in the Old Kingdom.

ᵍMortally sick.

made for him a] coffin of] ebony wood, sealed.   Never [⌐was it done to one like him before]] ————— laid therein.   9————— these — of the northern 10—————.   His majesty had him anointed by the side of his majesty.

His Eldest Son Builds the Tomb

248. 1[It was] his eldest son, etc.,[a] ————— 2————— there was [⌐made1] for him a flight of steps 3—————plenty.   When 4————— that he [⌐might be consigned1]] therein to the earth 5————— he had him come 6————— all — from the court 7————— one caused that it be put into writing upon 8[his tomb][b] ————— [⌐His majesty praised him[c]1] on account of it, and he praised the god for him (thanked him) exceedingly.

King Endows His Tomb

249. From the scanty fragments of a fourth inscription[d] of the same length, it is evident that the king established a mortuary endowment for Weshptah's tomb *"which was by the pyramid: The-Soul-of-Sahure-Shines."*

---

[a]As above § 243, l. 1.   [c]The son.
[b]See l. 6, § 247.   [d]Sethe, *Urkunden*, I, 44, 45. **D.**

REIGN OF NUSERRE

SINAI INSCRIPTION[a]

Relief

250. King in crown of Upper Egypt smiting a Bedwi as in § 168. The texts, as in the similar Sinai tablets, contain only names and titles of the king.

Great God, Lord of the Two Lands, King of Upper and Lower Egypt, Favorite of the Two Goddesses: Favorite ($Y\check{s}\cdot t\text{-}yb$);[b] Golden Horus: Nuter ($N\underline{t}r$); Nuserre ($N\text{-}w\check{s}r\text{-}R^c$)[c] [d]; . . . . Smiter of all countries.

Horus: Favorite of the Two Lands ($Y\check{s}\cdot t\text{-}yb\text{-}t^{\ni}wy$), Nuserre, who is given life forever; smiter of the Asiatics of every country.

TOMB INSCRIPTIONS OF HOTEPHIRYAKHET[e]

251. Hotephiryakhet was a priest of Neferirkere and of the sun-temple of Nuserre at Abusir. The motive which he proposes to future visitors in his tomb, to induce

---

[a]Cut on the rocks of the Wadi Maghara in the Peninsula of Sinai. Text: Lepsius, *Denkmäler*, II, 152, *a*; Brugsch, *Thesaurus*, VI, 1495 (inscriptions only); Sethe, *Urkunden*, I, 53, 54; Weill, *Sinai*, 107.

[b]Elsewhere $Y\check{s}\cdot t\text{-}yb\text{-}t^{\ni}wy$, meaning "*Favorite of the Two Lands.*"

[c]This name is to be read $N\text{-}wsr\text{-}R^c$. It is of the same formation as the name of Amenemhet III: $N\text{-}m^{\ni c}t\text{-}R^c$ for which we have the Greek Λαμαρης. It is a common formation in proper names, e. g., $N\text{-}k^{\ni}w\text{-}Re$, $N\text{-}k^{\ni}w\text{-}Ptḥ$, $N\text{-}^c nḥ\text{-}Sḥm\cdot t$, etc., in all of which the divine name, written first, is to be read last.

[d]There is uncertainty in the arrangement of signs here; the title "*Son of Re,*" inserted at this point, is later followed by the name "*Yn*" (Cf. Rougé, *Recherches sur les monuments qu'on peut attribuer aux VI premières dynasties*, 88, 89), and the cartouche containing it perhaps stood under the title in the space now broken away. Likewise the following "*Buto*" must belong to something lost below. The order of the fivefold titulary of the Middle Kingdom has not yet developed.

[e]Mariette, *Mastabas*, 342; Sethe, *Urkunden*, I, 49–51.

them to make mortuary offerings to him, is of especial interest. He offers to commend them to the god, just as Seti I
later intercedes with the gods for Ramses II, his son (III,
253), and as Ramses III also did for his son (IV, 246 *et
passim*).

252. ¹Judge, attached to Nekhen, Hotephiryakhet (*y³ ḥw· t-ḥtp-
ḥr*); he saith:

"I have made this tomb as a just possession, and never have I
taken a thing belonging to any person. ²Whosoever shall make offering to me therein, I will do (it) for them; I will commend them to the
god for it very greatly; I will do this for them, ³for bread, for beer,
for clothing, for ointment, and for grain, in great quantity. Never
have I done aught ⁴of violence toward any person. As the god
loves a true matter, I was in honor with the king.

253. ¹Judge, eldest of the hall, Hotephiryakhet; he saith:

"I have made this my tomb upon the western arm in a pure place.
There was no ²tomb of any person therein, in order that the possessions
of him, who has gone to his ka, might be protected. As for any people
who shall enter into ³this tomb as their mortuary property or shall
do an evil thing to it, judgment shall be had with them for it, ⁴by the
great god. I have made this tomb as my shelter; I was honored
by the king, who brought for me a sarcophagus."

INSCRIPTION OF PTAHSHEPSES[a]

254. This document is especially important for the concluding history of the Fourth Dynasty, and the chronology
of the first half of the Fifth. Ptahshepses was born under
Menkure, of the Fourth Dynasty, and was still living under
Nuserre, the fifth king of the Fifth Dynasty;[b] thus deter-

---

[a]From a false door in his mastaba, discovered at Sakkara by Mariette, published by Mariette, *Mastabas*, 112, 113; Rougé, *Recherches sur les monuments qu'on
peut attribuer aux VI premières dynasties*, 66–73; Rougé, *Inscriptions hiéroglyphiques*, 79–80; Sethe, *Urkunden*, I, 51–53.

[b]He was priest in Nuserre's sun-temple (Mariette, *Mastabas*).

mining that the period from the last years of Menkure to the first of Nuserre was not longer than a man's lifetime. Unfortunately, the upper ends of the eight vertical lines containing the inscription are broken off at the top. The first two lines are occupied by two reigns, showing that Ptahshepses is narrating his life by reigns. Now, ll. 4, 5, 6, and 7 all begin alike at the point where the loss at the top ends. It is perfectly clear, therefore, that they each contain a reign.[a] Line 3 is different and has "*his majesty*" so close to the top that it can hardly refer to a new king, but probably continues the reign of Shepseskaf from l. 2. As we know that Ptahshepses lived into the reign of Nuserre, we must insert this king at the top of the last line. Omitting the brief reign of Shepseskaf's successor, and the probably equally brief reign of Khaneferre in the Fifth Dynasty,[b] the kings enumerated by Ptahshepses were not improbably as in following section.

---

[a]Confer the same wording in the reigns of Menkure and Shepseskaf.

[b]Ptahshepses has omitted two reigns between Menkure and Shepseskaf, hence the other omissions assumed are not wholly arbitrary.

255.

FOURTH DYNASTY			FIFTH DYNASTY				
1	2	3	4	5	6	7	8
Menkure (preserved)	Shepseskaf (preserved)	"his majesty," or Shepseskaf continued	Userkaf (name lost)	Sahure (name lost)	Neferirkere (name lost)	Neferefre (name lost)	Nuserre (from Ptahshepses's titles)
Birth and childhood	Youth	Marriage	Manhood	Manhood	Manhood	Manhood	Old age

Reign of Menkure

256. [1]— — —[a] [in] the time of Menkure (Mn-kᵓw-Rᶜ); whom he educated among the king's-children, in the palace of the king, in the privy chamber, in the royal harem; who was more honored before the king than any child (hrd); Ptahshepses (Pth-$špss$).

Reign of Shepseskaf

257. [2]— — — [in] the time of Shepseskaf ($Špss$-kᵓf); whom he edu- cated among the king's-children, in the palace of the king, in the privy chamber, in the royal harem; who was more honored before the king

---

[a]Probably: "I was born in the time of M."

than any youth (*yd*), Ptahshepses ³— — — —. His majesty gave to him the king's eldest daughter, Matkha (*M ᵓ ᶜ · t-ḥ ᶜ*) as his wife, for his majesty desired that she should be with him more than (with) anyone; Ptahshepses.

Reign of Userkaf

258. ⁴[Attachedᵃ to Userkaf, high priest of Memphis,] more honored by the king than any servant. He descended into every ship of the court; he entered upon the ways of the southern palaceᵇ at all the Feasts-of-the-Coronation;ᶜ Ptahshepses.

Reign of Sahure

259. ⁵[Attachedᵃ to Sahure, more honored by the king thanᵃ] any servant, as privy councilor of every work which his majesty desired to do; who pleased the heart of his lord every day; Ptahshepses.

Reign of Neferirkere

260. ⁶[Attachedᵃ to Neferirkere, more honored by the king than] any servant; when his majesty praised him for a thing, his majesty permitted that he should kiss his foot, and his majesty did not permit that he should kiss the ground; Ptahshepses.

Reign of Neferefre

261. ⁷[Attached to Neferefre, more honored by the king than] any servant; he descended into the sacred barge at all Feasts-of-the-Appearance;ᵈ beloved of his lord; Ptahshepses.ᵉ

Reign of Nuserre

262. ⁸——————— attachedᶠ to the heart of his lord, beloved of his lord, revered of Ptah, doing that which the god desires of him, pleasing ing every artificer under the king; Ptahshepses.

ᵃFollowing Sethe, after Mariette, *Mastabas*, 375.

ᵇCf. the parallel in tomb of Sebu (Rougé, *Inscriptions hiéroglyphiques*, 95) which renders the reading certain here.

ᶜThe appearances in public of the king at anniversaries of his coronation.

ᵈThe appearance of the gods in festal procession on the river.

ᵉThe remaining three lines contain chiefly conventional phrases and titles.

ᶠPtahshepses is now an old man; hence the change in form.

REIGN OF MENKUHOR

SINAI INSCRIPTION[a]

263. The relief, if there was any, has cracked off. The text is as follows:

Horus: Menkhu (Mn-$ḥ^cw$); King of Upper and Lower Egypt: Menkuhor (Mn $k^ɔw$-$Ḥr$), who is given life, stability [like Re, forever]. Commission of [the king],[b] which —[c] executed.

The inscription is the earliest in Sinai in which the leader of the expedition has ventured to insert a commemoration of himself beside that of the king. Such a record of the leader and his followers now becomes customary.

---

[a]Cut in the rocks of Wadi Maghara on the Peninsula of Sinai; text: Lepsius, *Denkmäler*, II, 39, *e;* Brugsch, *Thesaurus*, VI, 1493 (inscriptions only); Sethe, *Urkunden*, I, 54; Weill, *Sinai*, 109.

[b]Cf. Lepsius, *Denkmäler*, II, 39, *d,* where the same phrase occurs uninjured (§ 264).

[c]The lacuna contained the name of the official who executed the commission.

REIGN OF DEDKERE-ISESI

SINAI INSCRIPTIONS

I[a]

264. The relief, if any existed, has disappeared. At the top appears the titulary of the king, as follows:

Horus: Dedkhu (Dd-h $^c w$), Son of Re, who lives forever. ————— Dedkere (Dd-k $^>$-R ^{c}), beloved of Buto and the souls of [Pe], [who is given] life, health, [all] joy [forever].

Commission of the king, which —[b] executed.

II[c]

265. There was apparently no relief; the text is both uncertain and owing to the crudity of the signs is very difficult. It furnishes an excellent example of the old method of dating by the fiscal census.

266. Year after the fourth occurrence of the numbering of all large and small cattle,[d] when the god caused[e] that costly stone be found in the secret mine ⌜—⌝ a ⌜stela⌝ with writing of the god himself;[f] (under)

---

[a]Cut into the rocks of Wadi Maghara, Sinai; text: Lepsius, *Denkmäler*, II, 39, *d;* Brugsch, *Thesaurus*, VI, 1494 (inscriptions only); Sethe, *Urkunden*, I, 55; Weill, *Sinai*, 118.

[b]Name of official has fallen out; "hw — hk —" is still preserved.

[c]Also in the Wadi Maghara; published by Birch, *Zeitschrift für ägyptische Sprache*, 1869, 26 f.; Brugsch, *Thesaurus*, VI, 1494, No. 20 (incomplete); Sethe, *Urkunden*, I, 55, 56 (from a collation of a squeeze in the British Museum by R. Weill).

[d]Compare § 340 (Lepsius, *Denkmäler*, II, 116, *a*); we have here dates according to the fiscus.

[e]Infinitive in a date? Read *dy·t ntr.*

[f]I take it that the whole of this is a date, followed by the name of the king, and then the event below. A "*writing of the god himself*" is the customary designation of any ancient document. Some stela of their ancestors led them to the desired vein.

Horus: Dedkhu (Dd-h^cw); king of Upper and Lower Egypt, Favorite of the Two Goddesses: Dedkhu; Golden Horus: Ded (Dd); Dedkere (Dd-k^2-R^c) Isesi, living forever.

Royal commission sent with the ship-captain, Nenekh-Khentikhet (N-^cnh-$Hnty$-ht)[a] to the terrace,[b] the name of which is "Malachite."[c]

A list of the members of the expedition followed.[d]

III[e]

267. The king is shown smiting a Bedwi; beside him the words:

Smiter of all countries.
[The Great God][f] smites the [Asiatics].[f]

IV[g]

Same scene repeated; inscription:

Smiter of all countries.

Perhaps belonging to these scenes is the date:[h]

Year of the ninth occurrence of the numbering of large cattle

---

TOMB INSCRIPTIONS OF SENEZEMIB, CHIEF JUDGE, VIZIER, AND CHIEF ARCHITECT[i]

268. The most powerful man at Isesi's court here narrates his favors with the king, in the course of which he includes verbatim two letters from his lord, one of which his

---

[a]A name of the same form as Nenekhsekhmet (N-^cnh-$Shm^.t$).

[b]Confirming my note (*New Chapter*, p. 29, n. b).

[c]$Fk^2 \cdot t$ as in the Pyramid Texts; see also the duplicate of Pepi II (§ 342).

[d]Weill, *Sinai*, 110, and possibly also 114.

[e]Also in Wadi Maghara; published by Brugsch, *Thesaurus*, VI, 1494, 21; Sethe, *Urkunden*, I, 56; Weill, *Sinai*, 119.

[f]So Sethe.   [g]Wadi Maghara; Brugsch, *Thesaurus*, VI, 1494, 19.

[h]Sethe, *ibid.;* Weill, *Sinai*, 118.

[i]From his mastaba-tomb by the pyramid of Khufu at Gizeh; published by Lepsius, *Denkmäler*, II, 76, *c–f* (cf. Text, I, 55, 56); Sethe, *Urkunden*, I, 59–67 (collated with drawings in Berlin Museum, Nos. 366, 367).

majesty wrote with his own hand.   A lake of 1,200 cubits' length is planned for by the architect, and the king expresses his delight with the plan.   Unfortunately, the fragmentary state of the inscription renders the narrative very obscure.

269. The closing inscriptions were the work of Senezemib's son, who after his father's death recorded in the tomb the mortuary endowment of his father, and the presentation of the sarcophagus by the king.

Senezemib's Fidelity and Honors

270. [a][1][ʳI was one who pleased the king[1] as mas]ter of secret things of his majesty, as favorite of his majesty in everything, [2]— — —   As for any work which his majesty commanded to do, I did (it) according to the desire of his majesty's heart toward it [3]——————— his majesty, while he was in the place[b] of writings.   When it came to pass [4]——————— his majesty caused that I be anointed with fat [5][by the side of his majesty][c] ——————— [Neve]r [was done] the like by the side of the king for anyone [6]———————.   [His majesty] himself wrote with his (own) fingers,[d] in order to praise me [7][ʳbecause I did every work which his majesty commanded to do[1]] well and excellently according to the desire of his majesty's heart toward it.

Letter by the King's Own Hand

271. [8]Royal command (to)[e] the chief judge, vizier, chief scribe of the king's writings, [9]chief of all works of [the king, Senezemib].

[10]My majesty has seen this thy letter, which thou hast sent to inform me that [11]——————— for (the building called:) "Beloved-of-Isesi," which is built — for the palace of — —, ʳbeing truly[1] Senezemib — — — — — [12]in rejoicing the heart[f] of Isesi . . . . ; [ʳfor thou

---

[a]Lepsius, *Denkmäler*, II, 76, *d*, Sethe, A.   A horizontal line may have preceded this, and contained Senezemib's name and titles.

[b]The king thus visited the public archives in company with the vizier, Senezemib.

[c]The restoration is certain; see Weshptah (§ 247, l. 10).

[d]Dual; this is the letter given below, ll. 8–16.

[e]Omitted also in the second letter and in the letter of Harkhuf (§ 351).

[f]Senezemib's name means "*Rejoicing the heart*," and the king is punning on his official's name.

canst¹] ¹³speak that which Isesi loves, better than any men who are in this [whole land] — — — ¹⁴. When indeed — — — every vessel ——————— ¹⁵it rejoices the heart of Isesiᵃ — true ——————— ¹⁶most excellent ———————.

King Isesi Counsels with Senezemibᵇ

272. ¹———————. "Thou shalt make a lake according as he saith in — ²——————— his lord —. [My majesty] greatly desires to hear this thy word ³——————— my majesty — everything — — —." Said the chief of all works of ⁴[the king, Senezemib]ᶜ ———————.

Second Letter from the King

273. ⁷Royal command (to)ᵈ the chief judge, vizier, chief of all works of the king, ⁸chief scribe of the king's writings, Senezemib.

⁹My majesty has seen the plan of this command ——————— ¹⁰for the palace of Isesi (called): Nehbetᵉ ——————— ¹¹— [length] 1,200 cubits, [width] 221ᶠ cubits, according to that which was commanded to [thee] — ⌜—⌝ — — — —. ¹²Now, the god hath made thee the favorite of Isesi [more than any men] ¹³who are in this whole land —. I will do every great thingᵍ ———————.

Endowment of Tomb

274. In the next sectionʰ Senezemib's son, Senezemib, called Mehi (*Mḥy*) says that "*a command was issued*" to "⌜*gather the princes*⌝" and other people. The command evidently concerned the endowment of his father's tomb, called "*this his tomb which I made for him in only one year and*

ᵃSenezemib's name means "*Rejoicing the heart*," and the king is punning on his official's name.

ᵇLepsius, *Denkmäler*, II, 76 f.; Sethe, B.

ᶜHere followed the reply of Senezemib in three lines, but it has almost entirely disappeared; the words "*whom Re loves*" still visible, show that he is addressing the king.

ᵈSee § 271, and note.   ᶠMay be a few units more.

ᵉSethe suggests a garden of the palace.   ᵍFragments of two more lines.

ʰLepsius, *Denkmäler*, 76, *c;* Sethe, C.

⌜three⌝ *months, while he was in* ⌜— — —⌝ *in the eternal house*[a] *which is at the pyramid: 'Isesi* ⁴*-is-[Beautiful']."*

The son then adds: *There was brought grain from the accounting of the divine offerings, from the North and the South,* with a reference, after a break in the text, to the continuance of the offerings *"until today as new. Then his majesty caused decrees to be sealed* ⌜*with*⌝ *the seal of writings,"* of course for the perpetuation of the mortuary offerings. A long lacuna doubtless contained other benefactions, after which we find, *" he appointed mortuary priests [of the endowment], and I had it put into writing."* The record of it was placed in the tomb where *"it was* ⌜*engraved*⌝ *by the artists."* The mortuary priests were *"divided into phyles,"* and the son then asked the king to give the equipment and furniture of the tomb, referring to the well-known quarry of Troja, whence came so much of the stone used in the Old Kingdom cemeteries.

Sarcophagus

275. Another inscription,[b] now very fragmentary, narrates the bringing of the sarcophagus, etc., for which the son had asked. After a statement of the king's command, we find the usual officials *"on a ferry-boat. Everything was done by these sailors, according to that which had been [commanded]*⁹ *concerning it in the court.* ¹⁰————. *This sarcophagus, together with [its lid], arrived at the pyramid: 'Horizon-of-Khufu,'"* where the tomb of Senezemib was located. The officers who conducted the work were praised by the king, and *"this sarcophagus"* was conveyed to its *" place."*

---

[a]A temporary resting-place, while the tomb was being built.
[b]Lepsius, *Denkmäler*, II, 76, *e;* Sethe, D.

Relief

276. This inscription is accompanied by a relief, showing the transport of the sarcophagus across the river. Over the relief are the words:

The great ⌈tow⌉-boat, the name of which is "Mighty-is-Isesi."

Three men on the bow are designated as: *Overseer of ten;* [*naval*] *commander; overseer of* ⌈—⌉ (*sb⸰*); while one in the stern is called "*captain.*" The sarcophagus and lid are shown, accompanied by the words "*sarcophagus*" and "*lid.*"

Son's Inscription

277. The son Senezemib, called Mehi, left in his father's tomb a short inscription[a] stating that he placed the above records on the walls of his father's tomb. Only the ends of the three lines remain, but the son closes the record of his pious work with a reminder to his own son by referring to himself as one "*whose son shall do the like for him.*"

MORTUARY INSCRIPTION OF NEZEMIB[b]

278. A short mortuary prayer, interesting for its quaint claim that the deceased was never beaten! Nezemib (*Nḏm-yb*) was probably a private citizen of the middle class, from whom very few monuments have descended to us.

279. O ye living who are (yet) upon earth, who pass by this tomb; let water be poured out for me, for I was a master of secret things. Let a mortuary offering of that which is with you come forth for me, for I was one beloved of the people. Never was I beaten in the presence of any official since my birth; never did I take the property of any man by violence; (but) I was a doer of that which pleased all men.

---

[a]Lepsius, *Denkmäler*, II, 78, *b;* Sethe, *Urkunden*, I, 67.

[b]Cairo, 1732; published by Mariette, *Mastabas*, 417; Brugsch, *Thesaurus*, V, 1212; Sethe, *Urkunden*, I, 75.

TOMB INSCRIPTION OF THE NOMARCH HENKU[a]

280. This nomarch, with his brother, was ruler of the Cerastes-Mountain nome, the twelfth nome of Upper Egypt, opposite the Lycopolite, or thirteenth, nome. He flourished late in the Fifth or early in the Sixth Dynasty, and his descendants enjoyed the favor of the Sixth Dynasty Pharaohs (§§ 344 ff.). So little is known of the nomarchs of the Old Kingdom that the meager data of this inscription are of importance. Especially noteworthy are the statements regarding the settlement of people from other nomes in his nome. Besides being much mutilated, the inscription is frequently very obscure. I have only rendered the more important passages and those which are most intelligible.[b]

281. [1]O all ye people of the Cerastes-Mountain; O ye great lords of other nomes, who shall pass by this tomb, I, Henku (*Hnkw*), tell good things:

. . . . [11]. . . .

I gave bread to all the hungry of the Cerastes-Mountain; [12]I clothed him who was naked therein. I filled its shores [13]with large cattle, and its ⌜lowlands⌝ with small cattle. [14]I satisfied the wolves[c] of the mountain and the fowl of heaven with ⌜flesh⌝ [15]of small cattle . . . . . . [16]I was lord and overseer of southern grain in this nome . . . . [18]I settled the ⌜feeble⌝ towns in this nome with the people of other nomes;

---

[a]In a cliff-tomb at Der el-Gebrâwi; published by Davies, *Deir-el-Gebrâwi*, II, Pls. 24, 25; Sethe (from Davies), *Urkunden*, I, 76–79.

[b]See Davies' excellent remarks on Henku, *ibid.*, 42.

[c]This general beneficence toward man and beast includes here the animals sacred in Henku's locality. Across the river the jackal was the sacred animal, while in Henku's own nome the hawk was sacred. It is no accident that these are just the two animals which Henku fed, for the word translated "*wolf*," should be more general, designating all wild animals of the canine family and the like. We have here then the first symptoms from which the belief in the sacredness of whole classes of animals (as opposed to one member only) afterward grew up. The same thing in a later stage is observable in the Saite time. On a stela in Miramar a man says: "*I gave bread to the hungry, water [to] the thirsty, clothing to the naked; I gave food to the ibis, the hawk, the cat, and the jackal*" (Bergmann, *Hieroglyphische Inschriften*, Pl. VI, ll. 9, 10).

[19]those who had been peasant-serfs therein, I made their offices as officials (*šr*).   [20]I never oppressed one in possession of his property, so that he complained of me because of it to the god of my city; (but) I spake, and told that which was good; [21]never was there one fearing because of one stronger than he, so that he complained because of it to the god.

I arose then [22]to be ruler (*ḥḳ꜄*) in the Cerastes-Mountain, together with my brother, the revered, the sole companion, ritual priest, Re-am (*R꜄ᶜ-ꞓ꜄-mꜣ*), [23]I was a benefactor to it (the nome) in the folds of the cattle, in the settlements of the fowlers.   I settled its every district [24]with men and cattle — — small cattle indeed.   I speak no lie, [25]for I was [26]one beloved of his father [27]praised of his mother, [28]excellent in character to his brother, [29]and amiable to [his sister]. . . . .[a]

---

[a]Seven short lines are omitted.

THE SIXTH DYNASTY

REIGN OF TETI

INSCRIPTIONS OF SABU, ALSO CALLED IBEBI[a]

282. Sabu, called also Ibebi, was a favorite official at the courts of Unis, the last king of the Fifth, and Teti, the first king of the Sixth Dynasty. Under both he held the important office of high priest of Ptah at Memphis, and to this oft-repeated title he adds also his other offices, mingled with a long series of self-laudatory epithets and phrases. Of these the inscriptions chiefly consist, but he gives us also a few interesting statements which throw light on the career of such a noble at court. The inscriptions are rendered below with all repetitions, as an unaltered example of such records in the Old Kingdom. In some phrases Sabu's inscription is identical with that of Ptahshepses (§§ 254 ff.).

Career under Unis[b]

283. Attached to (King) Unis, high priest of Ptah, more honored by the king than any servant. He[c] descended[d] into every barge; a member of the court, [when he entered] the ways of [the southern palace] at feasts,[c] Sabu (*S*ꜣ*bw*), whose beautiful name was Ibebi (*Ybby*).

284. [e]Honored by the king, doing his pleasure, one whom his lord

---

[a]From his mastaba-tomb at Sakkara; the publications will be found with each section below.

[b]Mariette, *Mastabas*, 375 D; Sethe, *Urkunden*, I, 81 A, at the entrance on the right.

[c]Compare Ptahshepses, § 258, l. 4.

[d]*Ḥ*ꜣ*f* is evidently past tense here, as Unis was deceased when the inscription was made.

[e]Mariette, *Mastabas*, 375 C; Sethe, *Urkunden*, I, 81 B; at the entrance on the left.

loves, high priest of Ptah, attached to the Double House, feast-day attendant, prophet of Ptah, prophet of Sokar, Sabu, etc.[a]

Career under Teti

285. [b][1]Today in the presence of the Son of Re: Teti, living forever, high priest of Ptah, more honored by the king than any servant, as master of secret things of every work which his majesty desired should be done; pleasing the heart of his lord every day, high priest of Ptah, Sabu. [2]High priest of Ptah, cup-bearer of the king, master of secret things of the king in his every place, honored by the king, high priest of Ptah, attached to the Double House, feast-day attendant, pleasing every artificer, honored by every sovereign, a member of his court, attached to the heart of his lord, the favorite of his lord's heart, beloved of his lord, revered of Ptah, doing that which the god desired of him every day in the king's presence.

286. [c]Today in the presence of the Son of Re: Teti, living forever; high priest of Ptah, more honored in the king's presence than any servant. He descends[d] into any barge; a member of the court when he enters upon the ways of the southern palace at the "Feasts-of-the-Coronation," high priest of Ptah, feast-day attendant, Sabu. When his majesty favored me, his majesty caused that I enter into the privy chamber, that I might set for him the people[e] into every place; where I found the way.[f] Never was done the like to any servant like me, by any sovereign, because his majesty loved me more than any servant of his; because I did that which he praised every day, because I was honored in his heart. I was useful in his majesty's presence, I found a way in every secret matter of the court, I was honored in his majesty's presence.

---

[a]As above, § 283.

[b]False door now in Cairo Museum, No. 1565, right side; published by Mariette, *Mastabas*, 413, 414; Sethe, *Urkunden*, I, 82, 83 (from copy by Erman).

[c]Same false door, left side; published by Rougé, *Inscriptions hiéroglyphiques*, 95; Mariette, *Mastabas*, 412–414; Sethe, *Urkunden*, I, 83, 84 (from copy by Erman).

[d]As Teti was still living at the time the inscription was made, the verbs are evidently present tense; but in Ptahshepses (§ 258, l. 4) they are past.

[e]The people (*ʿnḫw*) of the court, to whom he assigned their places.

[f]As he pleased? The sense is doubtful, as there are several possible renderings of the construction.

INSCRIPTION OF SABU, ALSO CALLED THETY[a]

287. This Sabu was the successor of Sabu, called also Ibebi (§§ 282 ff.), as High Priest of Ptah.[b] His inscription is of importance as showing that before his time there were always two high priests of Ptah.

288. ————. Today in the presence of his majesty. His majesty appointed me [ʳas High Priest of Memphis aloneˈ]ᶜ ————. [The temple] of "Ptah-South-of-His-Wall" in its every place was under my charge, although there never was [ʳa single High Priest of Ptah beforeˈ]ᵃ ———— Sokar in Shetyt (*Štt*), all the sacred possessions and all duties which two high priests of Ptah did. ———— although never was the like done by any high priest of Ptah in the time of [any king] ———— of the house of the crown-possessions as an honor from his majesty. His majesty appointed me ———— under my charge, although their offices were like (those of) [their] fathers ———— under my charge, which was done in the whole land; the heart of his majesty being mightier than anything that is done therein.

INSCRIPTION OF AN UNKNOWN BUILDER[d]

289. The unknown, a mere fragment of whose tomb inscription here follows, was perhaps the builder of the pyramid-temple of Teti, for he relates a royal commission to conduct the work on a ka-temple (*ḥt-kˀ*) for which the materials came from the Troja quarry, opposite the Sakkara cemetery where Teti's pyramid stands.

ᵃFragment of a false door in Cairo Museum, Nos. 1709, 1756; published by Mariette, *Mastabas*, 390; Sethe, *Urkunden*, I, 84, 85 (from copy by Erman).

ᵇStill another Sabu, a third of the name, was called "*Sabu the black*" (*Sˀbw km* Mariette, *Mastabas*, C 23), perhaps to distinguish him from the other two, for he was also high priest of Ptah.

ᶜSo restored by Sethe; and, in view of the following context, the restoration is very probable.

ᵈFragment in Cairo, No. 1433, published by Sethe, *Urkunden*, I, 86, 87 (from copy by Erman).

290. I did so that his majesty praised me on account of it ⌈— —⌉ ————. [His majesty caused that I enter] into the privy chamber, and that I become a member of the sovereign's court ————— . . . . Today in the presence of (king) Teti, my lord —————. His majesty sent me to conduct the works in the ka-temple made — — and in (the quarry) of Troja ————— I made a false door there, conducting [the work] ————— . . . . . His majesty caused that I come downstream ——————— . . . .

INSCRIPTION OF UNI[a]

291. This is the longest narrative inscription and the most important historical document from the Old Kingdom. Uni's career is narrated from its beginning under King Teti, through the entire reign of Pepi I, to its termination under Mernere. Besides the general instructiveness of the life of a great lord of the court in the Old Kingdom, Uni's narrative tells us of the only important wars of the Old Kingdom of which we are informed.

The biography falls into three parts:

I.   Career under Teti (l. 1), §§ 292–94.
II. Career under Pepi I (ll. 2–32), §§ 306–15.
III. Career under Mernere (ll. 32–50) §§ 319–24.

---

[a]From his mastaba-tomb, discovered by Mariette at Abydos. It occupies a single block of limestone 1m, 10 high and 2m. 70 wide, which formed one of the walls of the exterior chapel of the mastaba (*Catalogue général d'Abydos*, 84, No. 522). It is now in Cairo. Published by de Rougé, *Mémoires de l'Académie des Inscriptions et belles-lettres*, XXV, (Paris, 1866); Rougé, *Recherches sur les monuments qu'on peut attribuer aux VI premières dynasties*, VII–VIII; Mariette, *Abydos*, II, 44; Erman, *Zeitschrift für ägyptische Sprache*, 1882, 1–27 (text collated with copies by Brugsch and Golénischeff); a collation of Erman with the original by Piehl, *ibid.*, 1888, 111 f.; Brugsch, *Thesaurus*, VI, 1470–77; Grébaut, *Musée*, Pl. 27, 28 (photo.); Sethe, *Urkunden*, I, 98–110. Grébaut's photograph and Sethe's copy from the Berlin squeeze (No. 1541) are the only correct texts. Beside Sethe, I had also a copy collated with the original by Erman and Borchardt.

I. CAREER UNDER KING TETI

292. Under this king Uni passed his childhood and entered upon his official career at the bottom of the ladder as an under-custodian of a royal domain.

Introduction

293. [Count, governor of the South], chamber-attendant, attached to Nekhen, lord of Nekheb, sole companion, revered before Osiris, First of the Westerners, Uni (*Wny*). He says:

Beginning of Career

294. [1][I was a child][a] who fastened on the girdle under the majesty of Teti (*Tty*); my office was that of supervisor of ⌐—⌐ and I filled[b] the office of inferior custodian of the domain of Pharaoh.[c]

[Continued §§ 306 ff.]

---

[a]Restored from the stela of Simontu (§ 597, l. 5); that we are to read *"girdle"* here, and not "crown" (Maspero, *Dawn*, 417), is shown by a pyramid passage (Pepi I, l. 428); see Erman; also Piehl, *Sphinx*, II, 134. Hence, the current description of the garland-wearing children is without support from the inscriptions.

[b]Lit.: *"made,"* as often elsewhere.

[c]Perhaps a word lost at end of line here.

REIGN OF PEPI I

HAMMAMAT INSCRIPTIONS[a]

295. It is a question whether these inscriptions are the record of three expeditions or of one. If only one party left these records, it is probable that the jealousies between the bureau service and the practical craftsmen can be discerned in them.[b] They are further interesting, because the master pyramid-builder accompanied the expedition, the object of which must therefore have been the securing of the hard and costly stone for the finer portions of Pepi I's pyramid and its temple at Sakkara.[c]

I. THE KING'S INSCRIPTIONS

296. The royal memorial of this expedition occurs twice: in the first[d] the king's figure appears twice, back to back, enthroned in the jubilee-hall, accompanied by his titulary and the words: "*First occurrence of the Sed Jubilee.*" The second[e] shows the king with staff and war-club standing before the ithyphallic Min; above is his titulary, and in front: "*Beloved of the lord of Coptos (Min).*" Behind the king: "*First occurrence of the Sed Jubilee.*"

---

[a]Engraved on the rocks of the Hammamat quarry; on this place, see Erman, *Life in Ancient Egypt,* 472. They are published by Lepsius, *Denkmäler,* II, 115, a, b, c, e, g, i, k; Sethe, *Urkunden,* I, 93–96.

[b]See Schaefer, *Zeitschrift für ägyptische Sprache,* XL, 75–77.

[c]See Schaefer, *loc. cit.*

[d]Lepsius, *Denkmäler,* II, 115, a; Sethe, *Urkunden,* I, 96 A.

[e]Lepsius, *Denkmäler,* II, 115, e; Sethe, *Urkunden,* I, 96 B. Three other inscriptions on vessels made for the jubilee celebration, and merely bearing the king's name and the words, "*First occurrence of the Sed Jubilee,*" will be found in Sethe, *Urkunden,* I, 97 C, D, E.

II.   THE EXPEDITION'S INSCRIPTION[a]

297. This is the inscription recording the expedition as a whole, led by the chief architect and the two treasurers of the god.

298. Year[b] after the eighteenth occurrence (of the numbering), third month of the third season (twelfth month), day 27 of the king of Upper and Lower Egypt, Merire (Pepi I), who lives forever; first occurrence of the Sed Jubilee. Royal commission which the chief of all works of the king, the sole companion, master-builder of the king, attached to the Double House, Merire-meriptah-onekh; his son, the ritual priest, Merire-meriptah-onekh; and the treasurers of the god, Ikhi (*Yḫy*) and Ihu (*Yḥw*), carried out.

The names of five "*assistant artisans*" and of three "*king's-confidants and master-builders*" are then recorded below.

III.   CHIEF ARCHITECT'S INSCRIPTION[c]

299. This record places all the bureau officers first and the two treasurers of the god last.

Year after — — —.

Royal commission which the chief of all works of the king, sole companion, master-builder of the king, attached to the Double House, Merire-meriptah-onekh, carried out.

---

[a]Lepsius, *Denkmäler*, II, 115, *g;* Sethe, *Urkunden*, I, 93 (collated with drawing by Lepsius' expedition.)

[b]The date of the Sinai inscription, which is also coincident with the Sed Jubilee, is eleven days later. The discrepancy is easily explained by the fact that these expeditions were both sent out to secure materials for monuments in the year of this festival; the dates given were not intended to indicate its exact day. If the numberings took place every two years, then the first Sed festival occurred in the thirty-sixth or thirty-seventh year, which we know is impossible. Meyer supposes that the numberings had now become more frequent (*Aegyptische Chronologie,* 169–70), which is probable. See also Sethe, *Untersuchungen,* III.

[c]Lepsius, *Denkmäler*, II, 115, *k;* Sethe, *Urkunden*, I, 94.

Overseer of the administration of divine offerings, attached to the Double House, first under the king, judge, inferior scribe, Sesi (*Ssy*).

Scribe of the king's records, Khenu (*Ḥnw*).

Judge, attached to Nekhen, Khui (*Ḥwy*).

Treasurer of the god, Ihu.

Treasurer of the god, Ikhi.

IV. INSCRIPTION OF THE TREASURER OF THE GOD, IKHI[a]

300. One of the two treasurers of the god, perhaps incensed at being placed at the foot of the list in the preceding inscription, has in this inscription recorded himself alone as the leader of the expedition, omitting the chief architect and the bureau officials entirely, and even his colleague, Ihu.

At the extreme right, framed between two scepters and the sign for heaven at the top, is the titulary of Pepi I, accompanied by the words: "*First occurrence of the Sed Jubilee.*"   At the left of this appears the inscription:

301. Royal commission which the treasurer of the god, Ikhi (*Yḫy*), carried out.

His son, the ship-captain Ikhi.

Below appear the names of five "*assistant artisans of the palace*" and the "*master pyramid-builder, Thethi.*"[b]

SINAI INSCRIPTION[c]

302. 1. The titulary of the king in one line at the top is: "*King of Upper and Lower Egypt, Favorite of the Two Goddesses; Merikhet (Mry-ḫt); Merire (Mry-Rᶜ), Pepi I,*

---

[a]Lepsius, *Denkmäler*, II, 115, *c;* Sethe, *Urkunden*, I, 94, 95.

[b]Another inscription (Lepsius, *Denkmäler*, II, 115, *b*) contains only the names of the sons of some of the officials.

[c]Engraved on the rocks at Wadi Maghara; text: Lepsius, *Denkmäler*, II, 116, *a;* Brugsch, *Thesaurus*, VI, 1496, No. 26; Sethe, *Urkunden*, I, 91–92 (from squeeze); Morgan, *Recherches*, I, 235; Weill, *Sinai*, 121.

given all life forever."   It surmounts two reliefs: that on
the right contains the Horus-name of the king: *"Meri-towe
(mryy-t'wi, 'Beloved of the Two Lands'),"* and the figure of
the king striding as at a ceremonial, preceded by the words:
"First occurrence of the Sed Jubilee." Establishment[a] *of the
field* ⌜— —⌝. The relief on the left shows Pepi I smiting
the Asiatics in the manner conventional since prehistoric
times.

303. 2. Below the reliefs is the inscription of the officers
of the expedition, as follows:

> Year after the eighteenth occurrence (of the numbering), fourth
> month of the third season (twelfth month), day 6.   Commission
> which the commander of the army Ibdu (*Ybdw*),[b] son of the
> commander of the troops Merire-onekh, carried out.

Then follows a list of fifteen subordinate officials and
members of the expedition; such a list, better preserved
will be found in § 343.

INSCRIPTION IN THE HATNUB QUARRY[c]

304. In the year of the twenty-fifth numbering, Pepi I
sent an expedition to the alabaster quarries of Hatnub, back
of Tell el-Amarna, under charge of the nomarch of the
Hare nome (XV) of Upper Egypt.   Attached to the king's
name is the phrase *"First occurrence of the Sed Jubilee,"* and
on any theory of the Sed Jubilee this date is in glaring con-
tradiction of Pepi I's Sed Jubilee in the year of the eighteenth

---

[a]*(W)d "put"* or *"place;"* perhaps an endowment of land is indicated.

[b]Or *"Ibdu's son . . . . Merire-onekh."*

[c]Blackden-Fraser, *Hieratic Graffiti*, Pl. 15, 1; Sethe, *Urkunden*, I, 95, 96,
after Blackden-Fraser, but with useful corrections of evident errors; whence also
the restorations.

numbering. Is it used here at Hatnub only as an epitheton ornans, in recollection of the feast?

305. Horus: Beloved of the Two Lands (*mryy-t⁰wy*); king of Upper and Lower Egypt: Merire (Pepi I), given life forever. First occurrence of the S[ed Jubilee]. Year of the twenty-fifth occurrence (of the numbering), first (month) of the first season, [day] —.

[ʳRoyal commission whichᴵ] the sole companion, chief [of the six courts of justice], — — —, first under the king, master of se[cret things] — — —, marshal of the two thrones, governor of the palace, ʳrealᴵ governor of the South, great lord of the Hare nome, Khuu's (*Ḥᶜww*) son, Nenekhseskhnum (*Ḥnm-n-ᶜnḫ-ss*), [ʳexecutedᴵ].

INSCRIPTION OF UNI

[Continued from § 294]

II.   CAREER UNDER PEPI I

306. Pepi I promoted the obscure under-custodian of the royal domains, to be a judge of the Nekhen court; at the same time giving him rank among the courtiers and an income as inferior prophet of the pyramid-temple. As judge he soon gained the confidence of his superiors. The king granted him the equipment for his tomb, which was brought from the Troja quarry for him, and then promoted him to a superior custodianship of the royal domain. He rapidly gained royal favor, and when it became necessary to prosecute one of the king's wives, probably for conspiracy, he was chosen to hear the case with only one colleague. He was then called upon to organize an army for a campaign against the Bedwin north of Sinai, and five times he was sent to quell revolts in this region. He finally pushed up into southern Palestine, which is the first Egyptian invasion of that country known in history.

Appointment as Judge

307. ²— — — — [I was] eldest of the ⌐—¹ chamber under the majesty of Pepi (*Ppy*). His majesty appointed me to the rank of companion and inferior prophet of his pyramid-city. While my office was — ³his [majesty made me] judge attached to Nekhen (*Nḥn*). He loved me[a] more than any servant of his. I "heard,"[b] being alone with (only) the chief judge and vizier,[c] in every private matter ⁴— in the name of the king, of the royal harem and of the six courts of justice;[d] because the king loved me[a] more than any official of his, more than any noble of his, more than any servant of his.

Equipment of His Tomb by the King

308. ⁵Then I [be]sought — the majesty of the king[e] that there be brought for me a limestone sarcophagus from Troja (*R²-²w*).[f] The king had the treasurer of the god ferry over, together with a troop ⁶⌐of¹ sailors under his hand, in order to bring for me this sarcophagus from Troja; and he arrived with it, in a large ship belonging to the court, together with [its] lid, ⁷the false door; the ⌐setting¹, two ⌐—¹, and one offering-tablet.[g] Never was the like done for any servant, for I was excellent to the heart of his majesty, ⁸for I was pleasant to the heart of his majesty, for his majesty loved me.

Appointment as Superior Custodian

309. While I was judge, attached to Nekhen, his majesty appointed me as sole companion and superior custodian of the domain of Pharaoh, and ⌐—¹ʰ of the four superior custodians of the domain of Pharaoh, who were there. I did so that his majesty praised me, when preparing

---

[a]Lit.: "*his heart was filled with me.*"

[b]Meaning: heard cases in court as judge.

[c]One person; this vizier, whose name is not mentioned, was perhaps Zau (§§ 344 ff.).

[d]Lit.: "*six great houses.*"

[e]Lit.: "*the majesty of the lord.*"

[f]Quarries opposite Memphis, five or six miles south of Cairo.

[g]Cf. note on l. 40, § 322. *Gmḥw* is connected by Lemm with *gmḥ·t* "*wick*," and thought to be an oil basin (*Zeitschrift für ägyptische Sprache*, 1887, 115).

[h]*Nš* with a strange determinative; see Gardiner, *Inscription of Mes*, p. 25, n. 2.

court,[a] when preparing the king's journey (or) when making stations.
I did throughout [10]so that his majesty praised me for it above everything.

Prosecution of the Queen

310. [b]When legal procedure was instituted in private[b] in the harem
against the queen,[c] Imtes (*Ymts*)[d] his majesty caused me to enter, in
order to hear (the case) alone. No [11]chief judge and vizier at all, no
prince at all was there, but only I alone, because I was excellent, because
I was pleasant to the heart of his majesty; because his majesty loved
me. I alone was the one who put (it) in writing, [12]together with a single
judge attached to Nekhen; while my office was (only) that of superior
custodian of the domain of Pharaoh. Never before had one like me
heard the secret of the royal harem, except that the king caused [13]me
to hear (it), because I was more excellent to the heart of his majesty
than any official of his, than any noble of his, than any servant of his.

War against the Bedwin

311. His majesty[e] made war on[e] the Asiatic Sand-dwellers
([c] *m-ḥryw-š* [c]) and [14]his majesty made an army of many ten thousands:
in the entire South, southward to Elephantine,[f] and northward to Aphroditopolis; in the Northland on both sides[g] entire [15]in the ⌜stronghold⌝,[h]
and in the midst of the ⌜strongholds⌝, among the Irthet (*yrṯt*) negroes,
the Mazoi (*Mḏꜣ*) negroes, the Yam (*Ymꜣm*) negroes, [16]among the
Wawat (*Wꜣwꜣ·t*) negroes, among the Kau (*Kꜣꜣw*) negroes, and in the
land of Temeh (*Ṯmḥ*).[i]

---

[a]There is a contrast here between his duties at the fixed court and making
preparations for the king's journeys. The third reference is perhaps to the duty
of assigning court stations to noblemen according to rank.

[b]Lit.: "*When the matter was contested.*" Cf. similar phrase, note l. 14 and
note l. 29.

[c]Lit.: "*great king's-wife.*"   [d]Acc. to Sethe, *ymꜣ* (Verbum I).

[e]Lit.: "*repulsed the matter of the A*" (*ḥsf yḥ·t*), which Erman holds to be an
idiom for "*punish*" (*Gespräch*, 72).

[f]See § 320, l. 33 and note.   [g]See Griffith, *Kahun Papyri*, II, 21.

[h]Some particular stronghold is apparently meant; Erman suggests "the old
fortress in the eastern part of the Delta," but this is a conjecture.

[i]This list of Nubian lands has been treated by Brugsch, *Zeitschrift für ägyptische Sprache*, 1882, 30–36; Cf. also Lepsius, *Nubische Grammatik*, lxxxvii ff.
The discovery of the Harkhuf inscription has thrown light on the location of **Yam**,
showing that the journey thither and return occupied seven months.

Uni Leads the Campaign

312. His majesty sent me at the head of this army [17]while the counts, while the wearers of the royal seal, while the sole companions of the palace, while the nomarchs and commanders of strongholds belonging to the South and the Northland; the companions, the caravan-conductors, [18]the superior prophets belonging to the South and the Northland, the overseers of the crown-possessions, were (each) at the head of a troop of the South or the Northland, of the strongholds and cities which they commanded, and of the negroes of these countries. [19]I was the one who made for them the plan while my office was (only) that of superior custodian of the domain of Pharaoh of ⌈— — —⌉. Not one thereof ⌈—⌉[a] with his neighbor; [20]not one thereof plundered ⌈dough⌉ (or) sandals from the wayfarer; not one thereof took bread from any city; [21]not one thereof took any goat from any people. I despatched them from the Northern Isle, the Gate of Ihotep (y-ḥtp), the bend[b] of Horus, Nibmat[c] (Ḥr-nb-mꜣꜤt, Snefru).[d] While I was of this rank [22]— — — everything, I ⌈inspected⌉[e] the number of these troops, (although) never had any servant inspected.[e]

Return of the Army

313. This army returned[f] [23]in safety, (after) it had hacked up the land of the Sand-dwellers; this army returned in safety, (after) it had destroyed the land of the Sand-dwellers; [24]this army returned in safety, (after) it had overturned its strongholds; this army returned in safety, (after) it had cut down [25]its figs and its vines; this army returned in

---

[a]Verb.   [b]A river bend, or a district.

[c]See Sethe, *Zeitschrift für ägyptische Sprache*, XXX, 62.

[d]Are these three places in apposition or are they three different localities? Erman (*Zeitschrift für ägyptische Sprache*, 1891, 120, n. 1) thinks we should, as in some other analogous cases, consider the two following names as partitive appositions denoting two places located in the "*northern isle*." The latter is, I think, the same as the "*Isle of Snefru*," reached by Sinuhe on his flight through the same region (§ 493, l. 9). In view of the "*bend of Snefru*" above, this is at least very probable. The name is of course due to the activity of Snefru in this frontier region necessitated by his opening the mines in the Sinai peninsula.

[e]*wbꜣ*. It occurs also in Harkhuf inscriptions, § 334, where the meaning is modified to "*explore*."

[f]This verb is regularly used of the return from Asiatic campaigns in the Empire, and must have the same meaning here.

safety, (after) it had thrown fire in all its [ʳtroupsˈ]; this army returned
²⁶in safety, (after) it had slain troops therein, in many ten thousands;
this army returned in safety (after) [it had carried away[a]] ²⁷therefrom a
great multitude as living captives. His majesty praised me on account
of it above everything.

Revolts of the Bedwin

314. His majesty sent me to despatch [this army] ²⁸five times, in
order to traverse the land of the Sand-dwellers at each of their rebellions,
with these troops. I did so that [his] majesty praised me [on account
of it].

Campaign in Southern Palestine

315. ²⁹When it was said there were revolters because of a matter
among these barbarians in the land of Gazelle-nose,[b] I crossed over
³⁰in troop-ships with these troops, and I voyaged to[c] the back of the
height of the ridge[d] on ³¹the north of the Sand-dwellers. When this
army had been ʳbroughtˈ in the highway, I came and smote them all
³²and every revolter among them was slain.[e]

[Continued §§ 319 ff.]

---

[a]There was probably a first object before *ymf*, with which *"multitude"* was
in apposition.

[b]*m šrt* ʳ—ˈ. The reading *"Tiba"* for this name, given by Maspero (*Zeitschrift für ägyptische Sprache*, 1883, 64) is not supported by the careful collation
of Erman and Borchardt, nor by Piehl (*ibid.*, 26, 112); nor by Sethe.

[c]The same use of *m* as in Harkhuf, ll. 6 and 8, *et passim* in that text.

[d]The Palestinian highlands; Maspero in placing this region between Gaza and
the Serbonis Lake seems to have overlooked the word *"ridge;"* there are no
highlands in the locality defined by him. Uni must have landed a little
farther north and reached the highlands of southern Palestine. See also Müller,
Asien und Europa, 33.

[e]The end of Uni's career under Pepi I is marked by a line of separation on the
stone.

REIGN OF MERNERE

INSCRIPTIONS AT THE FIRST CATARACT

316. These important inscriptions, which record a visit of Mernere to the region immediately above the first cataract, are supported in their statement that the Nubian chiefs came to do him obeisance, by the biography of Uni (ll. 46–47, § 324), whom Mernere sent to excavate a channel through the cataract. The same negro tribes who furnished the wood for Uni's quarry-boats, here do reverence to his king. This visit and his construction of the canal, are important evidences of Mernere's activity on the Nubian frontier, thus preparing the way for the conquest of lower Nubia in the Twelfth Dynasty.

Northern Inscription[a]

317. The king stands leaning upon his staff, with the lion's tail as his only symbol of royalty. Behind him is the god Khnum, and before him the chiefs of Nubia.[b] Over his head are the usual name and titles:[c] *"King of Upper and Lower Egypt, Mernere;"* behind him the words:[d] *"Beloved of Khnum, Lord of the Cataract;"* below him the date: *"Year 5, second month of the third season[e] (tenth month), day 28."*

---

[a]Roughly cut on a block of granite south of the first cataract "on the eastern bank of the Nile, facing the southern extremity of the island of El-Hesseh;" (not "on" the island as stated, *Egypt Exploration Fund Archæological Report*, 1903–1904, 12); text by Sayce, *Recueil*, XV, 147; manuscript copy by Borchardt; Sethe, *Urkunden*, I, 110.

[b]There must be a row of Nubian chiefs before him (not noticed by Sayce) as in § 318.

[c]The treasurer's seal at the beginning is probably an error in the reading.

[d]Belonging to the lacking Khnum figure, for undoubtedly there is a figure of Khnum at the left of this column, not noticed by the copyists.

[e]Sayce has $\supset \d{h} \cdot t$.

Before the king is a column of text, as follows:[a]

The coming of the king[b] himself, standing[c] behind the hill-country, while the chiefs of[d] Mazoi (*Mḏ*ꜣ),[e] Irthet (*Yrṯt*), and Wawat (*W*ꜣ*w*ꜣ·*t*), did obeisance[f] and gave great[g] praise.

Southern Inscription[h]

318. This is practically a duplicate of the preceding, but there is no date; one of the Nubian chiefs is still visible standing before the king, and the accompanying record is slightly fuller, thus:

The coming of the king himself, appearing behind the hill-country, ⸢that he might⸣ see that which is in the hill-country, while the chiefs of, etc. (as above).[i]

INSCRIPTION OF UNI

[Continued from § 315]

III.   CAREER UNDER MERNERE

319. By Mernere Uni is at length appointed to exalted office, for this king made him governor of the South.   As such he was entrusted by the king with the expedition to the granite quarries at the first cataract to secure the neces-

---

[a]This text contains apparently only the beginning of this column; for the rest we fortunately possess a duplicate in Petrie, *Season in Egypt*, XIII, 338. See § 318.

[b]*"King"* is from Petrie, *Season in Egypt*.   [c]Read ꜥ*ḥ*ꜥ.

[d]So far Petrie, *Season in Egypt*, is parallel and must be corrected to *sṯ ḥkꜣw nw;* the copyists could read no farther, as the line is badly preserved.

[e]The final *t* is of course misread from the determinative.   Later: Verified by Borchardt's copy.

[f] *sn-t*ꜣ *"smelled the earth;"* Sayce has misread the *t*ꜣ-sign as *n*.

[g]Adverb *wr·t.*

[h]On the rocks, "road valley near Philae," Petrie, *Season in Egypt*, XIII, 338 =Lepsius, *Denkmäler*, II, 116, *b*=de Morgan, *Catalogue des monuments*, I, 17, No. 78. Sethe, *Urkunden*, I, 111 (from the publications); de Morgan's text is simply a copy of Lepsius, *Denkmäler*, with all the mistakes; the best copy is Petrie, *Season in Egypt*.

[i]But only the m of *"mazoi"* and part of the word *"praise"* can be read.

sary stone for the royal pyramid. Likewise he led another expedition to the quarry of Hatnub, back of Amarna, to procure an alabaster altar of vast size for the pyramid-temple. He then canalized the first cataract, excavating five channels, probably the first ever made there. This is in accordance with the interest in Nubia, displayed by Mernere, who visited the cataract in person and received the homage of the lower Nubian chiefs (§§ 316 ff.). Finally, under Mernere, short as his reign was, Uni seems to have died.

Appointment as Governor of the South

320. When I was ⌜master of the footstool⌝ of the palace and sandal-bearer, the king of Upper and Lower Egypt, Mernere (*Mr-n-R⁽*), my lord, who lives forever, made me count (*ḥʾty-⁽*), and governor of the South, 33southward to Elephantine, and northward to Aphroditopolis;[a] for I was excellent to the heart of his majesty, for I was pleasant to the heart of his majesty, for his majesty loved me.

34When I was ⌜master of the footstool⌝ and sandal-bearer, his majesty praised me for the watchfulness[b] and vigilance, which I showed in the place of audience, above his every official, above [his every] noble, 35above his every servant. Never before was this office conferred upon any servant. I acted as governor of the South to his satisfaction.[c] Not one therein ⌜—⌝[d] with [his] neighbor. 36I accomplished all tasks; I numbered everything that is counted[e] to (the credit of) the court in this South twice; all the corvée that is counted to (the credit of) the court in this South twice. I performed the ⌜— — 37— —⌝[f] in this

---

[a]The northern and southern limits of Upper Egypt. See Griffith, *Ptahhotep*, II, p. 25.

[b]Read *ḥr rśw* (with determinative of staff and hide) these determinatives make it certain that we have the word *rś* "*watch*" as in Harkhuf (Letter l. 14, also with the hide).

[c]Lit.: "*for him . . . . to satisfaction.*"   [d]Same verb as in l. 19.

[e]For the same use of "*count to*" see Rekhmire, II, 717.

[f]This obscure sentence is plainly parallel with the preceding, thus:

1. *ypy yḫt nb ypt n ḥnw m rś pn.*

2. *yry srt yrt ḳd m rś pn;* this suggests the rendering: "*I exercised the princeship that is exercised* ⌜—⌝ *in this South.*" *Sr·t* would then be a feminine abstract from *sr* "*prince;*" but *ḳd* remains a problem. Possibly *my* has been omitted before it.

South; never before was the like done in this South. I did throughout so that his majesty praised me for it.

Expedition to the Southern Quarries

321. His majesty sent me [38]to Ibhet[a] (*Ybh ꜣ·t*), to bring the sarcophagus (named): "Chest-of-the-Living," together with its lid and the costly, splendid pyramidion for the pyramid (called): "Mernere-Shines-and-is-Beautiful," of the queen.[b]

322. [39]His majesty sent me to Elephantine[c] to bring a false door of granite,[d] together with its offering-tablet, doors and ⌈settings⌉ of granite; [40]to bring doorways and offering-tablets[e] of granite, belonging to the upper chamber of the pyramid (called): "Mernere-Shines-and-is-Beautiful," of the queen.[b]   Then I sailed down-stream [41]to the pyramid (called): "Mernere-Shines-and-is-Beautiful," with 6 cargo-boats, 3 ⌈tow⌉-boats and 3 ⌈—⌉-boats to only one warship.   Never had Ibhet

---

[a]This unknown quarry must be in the vicinity of Assuan, where black granite is found; the material of the sarcophagus (not given here) as discovered in Mernere's pyramid at Sakkara in January, 1881, by Mariette (just a few days before his death) is a fine black granite.   (See Maspero, *Recueil*, IX, 178, and *Proceedings of the Society of Biblical Archæology*, XI, 312).   Brugsch however says: "aus rothgesprenkeltem Granit" (*Zeitschrift für ägyptische Sprache*, 1881, 4, and Brugsch, *Thesaurus*, VI, 1478).   Maspero is corroborated by Petrie (*History of Egypt*, I, 97).   The lid mentioned in our text is pushed back, but still lying on the sarcophagus, within which Mariette's native assistant, Mustapha, found the body of the king Mernere, now in Cairo Museum.—The "*pyramidion*" or final capstone of the pyramid was of finer material than the other masonry; it is no longer preserved, but tomb paintings often show this final block colored black by the artist.   Cf. Maspero, *Proceedings of the Society of Biblical Archæology*, XI, 312.

[b]The exact place and meaning of the last three words are uncertain; possibly they refer to a burial place of the queen in connection with the pyramid.

[c]This voyage was made in connection with the preceding, as Ibhet could not have been far from Elephantine (see l. 42).

[d]Lit.: "*Granite, a false door.*"

[e]These terms have been compared with the pyramid as existent today by Maspero (*Proceedings of the Society of Biblical Archæology*, XI, 304–17).   The meaning of *rw·t* "*false door*" and *st* "*offering-tablet*" had already been established by Erman (*Zeitschrift für ägyptische Sprache*, 1882, 22 and *Festschrift für Georg Ebers*, 431); the ʿw or "*doors*" Maspero thinks are the three portcullises found in the entrance passage; and the *rwy·t*, he thinks are the granite settings in the side walls in which the portcullises played.   His identification of the "*upper chamber*" with the exterior chapel is obvious (so also Erman).

and ⁴²Elephantineᵃ been visitedᵇ in the time of any kings with only one warship. Whatsoever his majesty commanded me I carried outᶜ completely according to all that his majesty commanded me.

Expedition to the Alabaster Quarry at Hatnub

323. His majesty sent me to ⁴³Hatnub (*Ḥt-nb*) to bring a huge offering-table of hard stoneᵈ of Hatnub. I brought down this offering-table for him in only 17 days, it having been quarriedᵉ in Hatnub, and I had it proceed down-stream in thisᶠ cargo-boat. ⁴⁴I hewed for him a cargo-boat of acacia wood of 60 cubits in its length, and 30 cubits in its breadth, builtᵍ in only 17 days, in the third month of the third season (eleventh month). Although there was no ⁴⁵water on the ⌜—⌝ʰ, I landed in safety at the pyramid (called): "Mernere-Shines-and-is-Beautiful;" and the whole was carried out by my hand, according to the mandate which the majesty of my lord had commanded me.

Second Expedition to Southern Quarries

324. His majesty sent [me]ⁱ to dig five canalsʲ ⁴⁶in the South and to make 3 cargo-boats and 4 ⌜tow⌝-boats of acacia wood of Wawat

---

ᵃShowing both were visited on one trip.

ᵇLit.: "*been made or done;*" this rare idiom "*to do a place*" meaning "*to visit it*" occurs also in Harkhuf (Letter l. 9); and Khui (§ 361); see Breasted, *Proceedings of the Society of Biblical Archæology*, May, 1901, 237–39.

ᶜ*Ḥpr* transitive.

ᵈ*Rwd·t* "*enduring or hard stone*" (not *šs*, alabaster, which is masculine) is applied to the stone of Hatnub in the Middle Kingdom also; (see § 696, l. 2).

ᵉThis word *wḥꜣ* is used of cutting grain, papyrus, plucking grapes, separating blocks from the quarry, and the like. It is used (in pseudo-participle) exactly as here, in the Hammamat inscription of the official Sesostris (Lepsius, *Denkmäler*, II, 138, e): *twt . . . . wḥꜣ m rnp·t tn*, "*a statue . . . . quarried in this year;*" and often in the quarry inscriptions. The meaning "suppression" given it in *Proceedings of the Society of Biblical Archæology*, XI, 315, does not exist.

ᶠThe boat of which the description follows.

ᵍLit.: "*bind*" (*sp*), taken from the binding of reed boats, cf. Breasted, *Proceedings of the Society of Biblical Archæology*, May, 1901, 238 f., note. It occurs also in Pepinakht, l. 12 (§ 360).

ʰThis uncertain word (*ṯsw*) = perhaps "*flats*," a pure guess. Maspero guesses "dos de sable." The word also occurs in Ikhernofret's stela (§ 669, l. 21). Petrie has made our passage the basis for reckoning the date of the period (*Season*, 19–21); but see § 42 above.

ⁱOmitted in text.

ʲThese must be for passing the cataracts; cf. the canal of Sesostris III (§§ 642 ff.).

($W\,{}^{\jmath}w\,{}^{\jmath}\cdot t$). Then the negro chiefs of Irthet ($Yrtt$), Wawat, Yam ($Y\,{}^{\jmath}m$) and Mazoi ($M\underline{d}\,{}^{\jmath}$)[a] [47]drew timber therefor, and I did the whole in only one year. They were launched and laden with very large granite blocks for the pyramid (called): "Mernere-Shines-and-is-Beautiful." I then ⌐—⌐b [48]for the palace in all these 5 canals, because I honored, because I ⌐—⌐, because I praised the fame of the king of Upper and Lower Egypt, Mernere, who lives forever, more than all gods, and because I carried out everything [49]according to the mandate which his ka commanded me.

I was one beloved of his father, and praised of his mother; first-born [50]— pleasant to his brothers, the count, the real governor of the South, revered by Osiris, Uni (Wny).

INSCRIPTIONS OF HARKHUF[c]

325. The important inscriptions of this tomb inform us more fully than any other source, of the commercial relations of the Old Kingdom with the Negro peoples of the extreme

---

[a]The same chiefs do obeisance to King Mernere at Assuan in the year 5. See §§ 316 ff.

[b]$sn\underline{d}s$.

[c]The tombs of the Assuan nobles were first noticed (1885) and excavations in them were begun by Mustafa, British consular agent at Assuan. They were then excavated by Gen. Sir F. W. Grenfell (1885), assisted by Budge in 1886. See Budge, *Proceedings of the Society of Biblical Archæology*, X, 4–40, and Bouriant, *Recueil*, X, 181–98 (supplemented by Scheil, *Recueil*, XIV, 94–96), who published the shorter texts, discovered before the end of 1886. The entire series of inscribed tombs discovered up to date has been published with plans by de Morgan (*Catalogue des monuments*, 141–201). They are seventeen in number, and unfortunately de Morgan's copyists have collated so carelessly that the more difficult texts are worthless. Only three of the tombs have furnished texts of length or great historical importance: that of Sebni (§§ 362 ff.), of Pepi-nakht (§§ 355 ff.), and Harkhuf. Curiously enough, the fellahin on the island of Elephantine discovered a mass of correspondence on papyrus belonging to the same noblemen who are interred in the cliffs opposite. These papyri of the Old Kingdom are in a very fragmentary condition, but will be published by the Berlin Museum, where they now are. One letter has already been translated by Erman in *Aus den Papyrus der Königlichen Museen*, Berlin, 1899, 91, 92.

The inscriptions of Harkhuf were first noticed by Schiaparelli and published by him in *Memorie della Reale Accad. dei Lincei anno CCLXXXIX*, Ser. 4ª, Vol. I, Part I, 21–53 (1892). It was discussed by Maspero, *Revue Critique*, 1892, II, 357–66;

south, involving indirect traffic with the Sudan. Harkhuf was the most successful of the energetic caravan-leaders among the Assuan nobles. He made four journeys to the distant southern Nubian country of Yam and finally thence westward into unknown regions. Three of these journeys were under Mernere (§§ 332–35) and the last under Pepi II (§§ 350 ff.). His inscriptions and those of the other Assuan nobles, for the first time reveal to us the active commerce with the south conducted by these nobles residing on the southern frontier.

326. Harkhuf's full titles were:[a] "*Count (ḥᵓty-ᶜ), governor of the South,[b] wearer of the royal seal, sole companion, ritual priest, caravan-conductor.*" Besides these offices, he was also, "*chamber-attendant, attached to Nekhen, lord of Nekheb.*"

327. He first enumerates some of the less important incidents of his life, in connection with some of the qualities of his character.

328. I came today from my city, I descended from my nome, I built a house, I set up the doors. I dug a lake, and I planted trees. The king praised me. My father made a will for me, (for) I was excellent ———— [one beloved] of his father, praised of his mother,

---

translated and discussed by Erman, *Zeitschrift der Deutschen Morgenländischen Gesellschaft*, XLVI, 574–79; with text, *Zeitschrift für ägyptische Sprache*, 1892, 78–83 (journeys), and *ibid.*, 1893, 65–73 (letter). The entire tomb with plan and texts is published by de Morgan (*Catalogue des monuments*, I, 162–73), but very inaccurately. As Erman's text (in *Zeitschrift für ägyptische Sprache*) is based on indistinct photographs, no accurate text has yet been published. The accompanying translation is based upon my copy of the Berlin squeezes, photographs by Borchardt, and Erman's recent collation of the original, which he kindly placed at my disposal.

Since writing the above, the excellent text of Sethe has appeared (*Urkunden*, I, 120–31).

[a]This and the following statement of his virtues are inscribed over the door of the tomb. See also the list of titles introducing the journeys.

[b]Harkhuf must have succeeded Uni in this office, who held it under Mernere also, dying under this king; but it was now becoming merely a rank.

whom all his brothers loved. I gave bread to the hungry, clothing to the naked, I ferried him who had no boat.

329. O ye living, who are upon earth, [who shall pass by this tomb whether] going down-stream or going up-stream, who shall say: "A thousand loaves, a thousand jars of beer for the owner of this tomb;" I will ⌐—⌐ for their sakes in the nether world. I am an excellent, equipped spirit, a ritual priest, whose mouth knows.[a]

330. As for any man who shall enter into [this] tomb [as his mortuary possession, I will seize[b]] him like a wild fowl; he shall be judged for it by the great god.

331. I was one saying good things and repeating what was loved. Never did I say aught evil, to a powerful one against any people, (for) I desired that it might be well with me in the great god's presence. Never did I [judge two brothers[c]] in such a way that a son was deprived of his paternal possession.

Introduction[d]

332. [1]Count, sole companion, ritual priest, chamber-attendant, judge attached to Nekhen, lord of Nekheb, wearer of the royal seal, caravan-conductor, privy councilor of all affairs of the South (*tp-ršy*), favorite of his lord, Harkhuf (*Ḥr-ḫwf*), [2] . . . .[e] who brings the products of all the countries to his lord, who brings the tribute of the royal ornaments, governor of all countries of the South (*tp-ršy*), who sets the terror of [3]Horus[f] among the countries, who does that which his lord praises,[e] . . . . the revered by Ptah-Sokar, Harkhuf.

First Journey

333. [4]He says:

The majesty of Mernere (*Mr-n-Rꜥ*) my lord, sent me, together with my father, the sole companion, and ritual priest, Iri (*Yry*) to Yam (*Yꜣm*), in order to explore a road to this country. [5]I did it in only seven

---

[a]This is again a promise to intercede with the powers of the hereafter on behalf of the living who repeat a prayer for the sake of the deceased; as in § 252.

[b]See Seneni, § 338, l. 4.   [c]See Pepinakht, § 357, ll. 3, 4.

[d]At the right of the door in fourteen columns on the façade, before the figure of Harkhuf with staff.

[e]Some of the same titles repeated.   [f] The king.

months,[a] and I brought all (kinds of) gifts from it ⌜— —⌝. I was very greatly praised for it.

Second Journey

334. His majesty sent me a second time [6]alone; I went forth upon the Elephantine road, and I descended[b] from Irthet (*Yrṯt*), Mekher (*M ꜥ ḫr*), Tereres (*Trrs*), Irtheth (*Yrṯṯ*), being an affair of eight months. When I descended[b] [7]I brought gifts from this country in very great quantity. Never [8]before was the like brought to this land.[c] I descended from the dwelling of the chief of Sethu[d] (*Sṯw*) and Irthet (*Yrṯt*), [9]after I had explored[e] these countries. Never had[f] any companion or caravan-conductor who went forth to Yam (*Y ꜣ m*) [10]before this, done (it).[g]

Third Journey

335. His majesty now sent me a third time to Yam; [11]I went forth from ⌜—⌝ upon the Uhet (*Wḥ ꜣ ·t*)[h] road, and I found the chief of Yam [12]going to the land of Temeh (*Ṯmḥ*)[i] to smite Temeh [13]as far as the western corner of heaven. I went forth after him to the land of Temeh, [14]and I pacified him, until he praised all the gods for the king's sake.

---

[a]This is the length of the entire journey to and from his destination, including his stay there.

[b]"*Descend*" usually means "*return;*" but it is uncertain whether it has this meaning in both cases here, though it certainly does in the second.

[c]Egypt.

[d]See Maspero (*Recueil*, XV, 103 f.), who places Sethu on both sides of the river south of Keneset, which is the first district south of Assuan.

[e]*wb ꜣ*, cf. § 312, Uni, l. 22, note.　　　[f]*Gmyy* is perhaps a particle.

[g]The conclusion of this journey describes the unusual road taken to reach home, after he has already narrated the journey out, and the gifts brought back.

[h]According to the analogy of l. 6 ("*Elephantine road*"), Uhet must be the starting-point of the road. Hence Griffith's proposal to identify this word with *wḥ·t* "*oasis*," seems to me improbable (*Proceedings of the Society of Biblical Archæology*, XVI, 50). The verb *wḥ ꜣ* commonly means "*to quarry stone;*" may this not be a word for "*quarry*," and the road is then the old quarry road still used at the cataract? Harkhuf then later crosses to the west side.

[i]Same as later Temeh (*Tmḥ*) or Temehu (*Tmḥw*).

Supplement to Third Journey[a]

336. [1]————[b]t,[c] *Yam* (*Y ꜣ m*) who followed — — in order to inform the majesty of Mernere, my lord, [2]————[b] after the chief of Yam. Now when I had pacified that chief of Yam [3]———— below[d] Irthet (*Yrṯt*) and above Sethu (*Sṯw*), I found the chief of Irthet, Sethu, and Wawat [4]— — ⌈— — —⌉.

I descended with 300 asses laden with incense, ebony, heknu, grain, [5]⌈panthers, — —⌉, ivory, ⌈throw-sticks⌉, and every good product. Now when the chief of Irthet, Sethu, [6]and Wawat saw how strong and numerous was the troop of Yam, which descended with me to the court, and the soldiers who had been sent with me, (then) [7]this [chief] brought and gave to me bulls and small cattle,[e] and conducted me to the roads of the highlands of Irthet, because I was more excellent, vigilant, and — [8]than any count, companion or caravan-conductor, who had been sent to Yam before. Now, when the servant[f] there was descending to the court, one[g] sent the —, [9]sole companion, the master of the bath, Khuni (*Ḥwny*),[h] up-stream with a vessel laden with date-wine, ⌈cakes⌉, bread, and beer. [10]The count, wearer of the royal seal, sole companion, ritual priest, treasurer of the god, privy councilor of decrees, the revered, Harkhuf.

[Continued §§ 350 ff.]

———

[a]In horizontal lines from right to left, on the left side of the door (on the façade). Below it Harkhuf's son, Zemi (*Ḏmy*), offers him incense.

[b]Over one-third line. Harkhuf evidently sent a messenger to inform the Pharaoh that he had gone *"after the chief of Yam."*

[c]Either Wawat or Irthet preceded, as determinative shows.

[d]He is here giving his return route.   [f]Modest for "I."

[e]Or gazelles; not asses.   [g]The king.

[h]Or *R ꜥ -wny*, the *R ꜥ* or *ḫ*-sign is possibly a hole; one is tempted to find our old friend Uni here.

REIGN OF PEPI II

CONVEYANCE OF LAND BY IDU, CALLED ALSO SENENI[a]

337. Idu, or Seneni, was priest of Pepi I, Mernere, and Pepi II, This document recorded in his tomb constitutes a gift of land to his wife, apparently as her mortuary endowment, though it is not so called. Strangely enough, the location, size, and limits of the field are not given.

338. [1]Seneni, he saith:

[2]"As for this field, which I have conveyed ———— [3]which I have given to my beloved wife, Disnek (*Dyy· s-nk*) [[it is her]] true [[possession. As for any persons]] [4]who shall take it from this Disnek, they shall be —[b] for it by the great god, [5]lord of heaven, and I will seize them [like[c]] wild fowl. I am (now) an — and excellent spirit. I know [6]———— .... [9][I have done] this for this Disnek, because she was so greatly honored in [10]my heart; she said nothing to oppose my heart ...."

Disnek, she saith:

"I was one amiable — —, beloved of her entire city. As for any persons who shall take this land from me, I will enter into judgment with them, by[d] the great god."

SINAI INSCRIPTIONS[e]

339. There is no relief with the king's titulary, but the queen-mother is depicted with her inscription. The

---

[a]Inscription in his cliff-tomb in Kasr-es-Saiyâd; published by Lepsius, *Denkmäler*, II, 114, *a;* Sethe, *Urkunden*, I, 115–117.

[b]Some verb of condemnation is lost.

[c]See Harkhuf, § 330.   [d]We expect "before."

[e]Cut on the rocks of Wadi Maghara; text: Lepsius, *Denkmäler*, II, 116, *a*, and Brugsch, *Thesaurus*, VI, 1496, No. 25; Sethe, *Urkunden*, I, 112, 113; Morgan, *Recherches*, 236; Weill, *Sinai*, 126; see Rougé, *Recherches sur les monuments qu'on peut attribuer aux VI premières dynasties*, 130, 131.

date, the royal names and titles occupy four vertical columns, and beneath these is the inscription of the officers and officials who conducted the expedition.

Date

340. Year of the second numbering of all large and small cattle of the North and South.[a]

King's Name

Horus: Nuterkhu, Neferkere ($Ntr-\underline{h}^cw$, $Nfr-k^\jmath-R^c$), who lives forever; King of Upper and Lower Egypt, Golden Horus: Kherep; Neferkere, who lives forever, like Re.

Queen's Name

341. King's-mother, attached to[b] the pyramid: "Neferkere-Remains-Living," king's-wife, his beloved, attached to the pyramid: "Merire-Remains-Beautiful," Enekhnes-Merire, whom all the gods love.

Leader of the Expedition

342. Royal commission, sent with the treasurer of the god, Hepi ($\underline{H}py$), to the terrace, the name of which is "Malachite:"[c]

Members of the Expedition

343. Captain, Bekneptah.
Overseer of stone-work,[d] Uzai ($W\underline{d}^\jmath y$).
Chief scribe, Senezem.
Captain and } { Merire-onekh.
Caravan-conductor } { Neke-onekh ($N-k^\jmath-{}^c n\underline{h}$).

---

[a]Cf. the same fiscal date under Isesi (§ 266). It is remarkable that we find "*North*" placed first here.

[b]This is not a simple genitive $n(y)t$ belonging to the preceding as it has always been rendered, but an independent title: $n(y)t \ Nfr-k^\jmath-R^c \ mn \ {}^c n\underline{h} = $ "*One who belongs to the pyramid, etc.;*" compare the title of the princess Henetre: $n(y)t \ Wnys \ nfr \ y\check{s}wt$ (Mariette, *Mastabas*, 360). *N* masculine is employed in the same way with kings' names, as in Sabu's tomb (Mariette, *Mastabas*, 375).

[c]See duplicate under Isesi (§ 266).   [d]Read $\check{s}t$, see § 239, note.

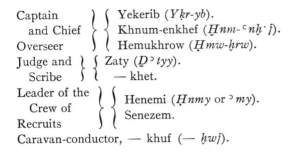

Captain and Chief Overseer	} {	Yekerib (*Yḳr-yb*). Khnum-enkhef (*Ḥnm-ᶜnḫ·f*). Hemukhrow (*Ḥmw-ḫrw*).
Judge and Scribe	} {	Zaty (*Ḏ᾽tyy*). — khet.
Leader of the Crew of Recruits	} {	Henemi (*Ḥnmy* or *᾽my*). Senezem.

Caravan-conductor, — khuf (— *ḫwf*).

STELA OF THE TWO QUEENS, ENEKHNES-MERIRE[a]

344. The history of the royal family disclosed by this stela is of great interest as well as of historical importance. Zau, the vizier and chief justice under Pepi II, and perhaps earlier, erected the monument in memory of his brothers and sisters at Abydos. He was the son of a prince, named Khui, and his mother's name was Nebet. Both his sisters married king Pepi I; one became the mother of Mernere, the other of Pepi II, so that besides being half-brothers, the two kings were on the mother's side also cousins. The family tree appears thus:

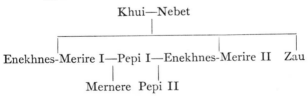

Khui—Nebet

Enekhnes-Merire I—Pepi I—Enekhnes-Merire II   Zau

Mernere   Pepi II

With both his sisters queens and likewise successively the mother of the king, we can see how Zau became vizier

---

aTablet found built into a well at Abydos by Mariette, now in Cairo, No. 1431; complete text: Mariette, *Abydos*, I, 2; Rougé, *Inscriptions hiéroglyphiques*, 153, 154; see also Mariette, *Catalogue général d'Abydos*, No. 523, and Rougé, *Recherches sur les monuments qu'on peut attribuer aux VI premières dynasties*, 129–84; I also had access to Erman's collation for the lexicon, which corrected a number of mistakes in the published texts. This collation is now published by Sethe, *Urkunden*, I, 117–19.

and chief justice under Pepi II; Pepi II's mother Enekhnes-Merire II was much honored by him, and appears with him in the dating of his Sinai inscription (§ 339).

Inscription over First Queen

345. King's-wife, (attached to)[a] the pyramid (called): "Merire-Remains-Beautiful," very amiable, very favored, ⌜great in possessions⌝, companion of Horus,[b] ⌜—⌝ of Horus,[b] king's-mother, (attached to) the pyramid (called): "Mernere-Shines-and-is-Beautiful," Enekhnes-Merire.

Inscription over Second Queen

346. King's-wife, (attached to) the pyramid (called): "Merire-Remains-Beautiful," very amiable, very favored, daughter of the god, ⌜great in possessions,⌝ companion of Horus,[b] ⌜—⌝ of Horus, king's-mother, (attached to) the pyramid (called): "Neferkere-Remains-Alive," Enekhnes-Merire.

Inscription over Man

347. Their brother, the chief justice and vizier, Zau ($D^c w$).

Below the preceding is Zau's dedicatory inscription introduced by an enumeration of his five brothers, all of whom bore the name Zau. Thus, the whole family, six brothers Zau, and two sisters Enekhnes-Merire, are all commemorated.

Dedicatory Inscription

348. Their brother, the real hereditary prince, count ($h^ɔ ty$-^{c}) and governor of the pyramid-city, chief justice and vizier, overseer of the king's records, prophet of the gods of Buto, prophet of the gods of Nekhen, chief ritual priest, sem priest and master of all wardrobes, wearer of the royal seal, judge ⌜—⌝, revered by the god, Zau.

349. I made this in Abydos of Thinis, as one in honor with the majesty of the king of Upper and Lower Egypt, Neferkere, who lives

---

[a]That the pyramid names in these titles are to be so rendered is made certain by the Wadi Maghara inscription of Pepi, I (§§ 302 ff.), where they occur also, but with $n(y)t$ preceding; see note, *ibid.*

[b]The king.

forever, with the majesty of King[a] Merire and King[a] Mernere, out of
love for the nome in which I was born by the favorite of the king,
Nebet (*Nb·t*), to my father the hereditary prince, count, (meri-nuter)
priest, honored by the great god, Khui (*Ḫwy*).   O ye living, who are
upon earth, every superior prophet, every prophet, every ⌜—⌝, of the
temple of the majesty of my lord, Osiris (*Ḫnty ymntyw*); as the king
lives for you,[b] ye shall take for me the mortuary offerings from the
income of this temple, of that which I have conveyed by a decree, and
of that which ye convey for yourselves, when ye see my offices with
the king; because I was more honored by my lord than [any] noble

————.

————

INSCRIPTIONS OF HARKHUF

[Continued from § 336]

LETTER OF PEPI II

350. Harkhuf has made a fourth voyage to Yam, and
having sent word to the king of his safe return with many
products of the south and especially a dancing dwarf, the
king writes him a letter of thanks, promising great rewards,
etc., if the dwarf is safely brought to court.   This letter,
Harkhuf had engraved on the façade of his tomb, which
was already complete, so that a further space for the letter
had to be smoothed on the extreme right of the façade,
where none of the other Assuan tombs has any inscriptions
at all.   Thus was preserved to us the only complete royal
letter of the Old Kingdom.[c]   It is as follows:

————

[a]Same as preceding title of Neferkere.   Both these kings were deceased at
this time, as they do not receive the predicate "*who lives forever.*"

[b]An oath.

[c]With the exception of the Berlin papyrus fragments (§ 325, note) and the fragmentary letters (§§ 271, 273), it is the only letter of any kind surviving from the
Old Kingdom.

Date and Introduction

351. [1]Royal seal, year 2, third month of the first season, (third month), day 15.

[2]Royal decree (to)[a] the sole companion, the ritual priest and caravan-conductor, Harkhuf (*Ḥr-ḫwf*).

Acknowledgment of Harkhuf's Letter

[3]I have noted the matter of this thy letter, which thou hast sent to the king, to the palace, in order that one[b] might know that thou hast descended [4]in safety from Yam with the army which was with thee. Thou hast said [in] this thy letter, that thou hast brought [5]all great and beautiful gifts, which Hathor, mistress of Imu (*Ym⸗w*) hath given to the ka of the [6]king of Upper and Lower Egypt Neferkere (*Nfr-k⸗-R꜄*), who liveth forever and ever. Thou hast said in this thy letter,[c] that thou hast brought a dancing dwarf[d] [7]of the god from the land of spirits, like the dwarf which [8]the treasurer of the god Burded (*B⸗-wr-dd*) brought from Punt in the time of Isesi (*Yssy*). Thou hast said to my majesty: "Never [9]before has one like him been brought by any other who has visited[e] Yam."

Harkhuf's Rewards

352. Each year ⌜—⌝ thee [10]doing that which thy lord desires and praises; thou spendest day and night ⌜with the caravan⌝ in doing that which [11]thy lord desires, praises and commands. His majesty will make [12]thy many excellent honors to be an ornament for the son of thy son forever, so that all people will say [13]when they hear what my majesty doeth for thee: "Is there anything like this[f] which was done for the sole companion, Harkhuf, [14]when he descended from Yam, because of the

---

[a]Omitted also in both the letters to Senezemib (§§ 271, 273).

[b]Circumlocution for "the king."

[c]By emending in accordance with the preceding sentence.

[d]Lit.: "*a dwarf of dances;*" cf. the same usage in Hebrew syntax. See Erman's explanation, *Zeitschrift für ägyptische Sprache*, 1893, 72, 73, and Pietschmann, *ibid.*, 73, 74.

[e]The verb is *yry* "*to make or do*" with Yam as direct object; the reading is certain. The same usage occurs in Uni (l. 41), and Khui (§ 361); see Breasted, *Proceedings of the Society of Biblical Archæology*, May, 1901, 237–39.

[f]*Nf*.

vigilance which he showed, to do that which his lord desired, praised and commanded!"

King's Instructions

353. [15]Come northward[a] to the court immediately; ⌈—⌉ [16]thou shalt bring this dwarf with thee, which thou bringest living, prosperous and healthy from the land of spirits, [17]for the dances of the god, to rejoice and ⌈gladden⌉ the heart of the king of Upper and Lower Egypt, Neferkere, who lives forever. [18]When he goes down with thee into the vessel, appoint excellent people, who shall be beside him [19]on each side of the vessel; take care lest he fall into the water. When [he] sleeps at night appoint excellent people, [20]who shall sleep beside him in his tent;[b] inspect ten times a night. [21]My majesty desires to see this dwarf more than the gifts of Sinai[c] and [22]of Punt (*Pwnt*). If thou arrivest at court this dwarf being with thee [23]alive, prosperous and healthy, my majesty will do for thee a greater thing than that which was done for the treasurer of the god, Burded (*B⸗-wr-dd*) [24]in the time of Isesi (*Yssy*), according to the heart's desire of my majesty to see this dwarf.

354. [25]Commands have been sent to the chief of the New Towns,[d] the companion, and superior prophet, to command that sustenance[e] be taken [26]from him in every store-city and every temple, without stinting therein.

————————

INSCRIPTIONS OF PEPI-NAKHT[f]

355. This nobleman of Elephantine was of high rank, and was entrusted with important commissions by King Pepi II.

————————

[a]It is not necessary to emend *dḫ·t* to *dp·t;* undoubtedly *ḫd·t*, infinitive of *ḫd* "*sail down-stream*" is meant; *ḫd* makes feminine infinitive in early texts; see Sethe, *Verbum*, I, 238.

[b]This word (*ḫn*) is certain from Merneptah's Karnak text, l. 62 (III, 589), where it also means "*tent.*"

[c]*By⸗*, the name of a mining region in Sinai; as it is sometimes used with the demonstrative (*pn*, "*this*"), I have rendered it "*mine*" in the inscriptions of the Middle Kingdom, where it is not uncommon.

[d]See § 628.

[e]*śś⸗*=lit.: "*a causing to be satisfied;*" the reference is to the provisioning of the expedition by the places passed as it returns. The king has sent orders to the proper officer in each place that he shall furnish such provision.

[f]From his cliff-tomb opposite Assuan (see § 325, note, on the excavation of this tomb); it is No. 9 in de Morgan's plan (*Catalogue des monuments*, 142). The inscription occupies the façade, seven columns on each side of the door; and

He led two campaigns in Nubia (§§ 358, 359), and a remarkable expedition to the north Red Sea for the rescue of the
body of a nobleman bound for Punt, who had been killed
by the Sand-dwellers while building his ship for the voyage
(§ 360).

356. His titles were as follows:[a]

[1]Custodian of the domain, scribe of the phyle of the pyramid
(called): "Neferkere-Remains-Alive," wearer of the royal seal, sole
companion, Hekib (*Ḥk꜄-yb*);[b] governor of the pyramid-city: "Pepi-
Remains-Beautiful," sole companion, ritual priest, caravan-conductor,
who brings the products of the countries to his lord, Pepi-nakht; [3]chief
of the phyle of the pyramid: "Mernere-Shines-and-is-Beautiful;" who
sets the terror of Horus [among] the countries, the revered Hekib,
[4]count, sole companion, chamber-attendant, judge attached to Nekhen,
lord of Nekheb, revered by the great god, Pepi-nakht.

One more title: "*Governor of foreign countries,*" is found
in column 14.

357. His narrative inscription[c] is as follows:

[1]. . . . .[d]

Pepi-nakht's Character

[2]I was one who said that which was good, and repeated that which
was loved. Never did I say anything evil to a powerful one against any
people, (for) I desired that it be well with me in [3]the great god's presence. I gave bread to the hungry, and clothing to the naked. Never

---

originally four lines of titles at the top on each side, but only two remain on the
north (right) side. The texts (with plan of tomb) are published in de Morgan,
Catalogue des monuments, 174–76, but de Morgan's copyists (see 325, note) have
failed of the correct reading in all difficult passages. The accompanying translation is based upon my copy of the Berlin squeezes; a collation of the original by
Erman and Steindorff, very kindly placed at my disposal. [Later: Sethe's
collation with the squeezes has since been published by him (*Urkunden*, I, 131–35).]

[a]Four lines at the top, south side, omitting repetitions.

[b]North side, last upper line states that this was Pepi-nakht's "*beautiful name.*"

[c]Seven columns on each side of the door; we take the right side first.

[d]Titles (next the door); numbering then passes to outside (right) and proceeds toward the door.

did I judge two brothers ⁴in such a way that a son was deprived of his paternal possession. I was one beloved of his father, praised of his mother, ⁵whom his brothers and sisters loved.

First Nubian Expedition

358. The majesty of my lord sent me, to hack up Wawat (*W'w'·t*) and Irthet (*Yrṭt*). I did ⁶so that my lord praised me. I slew a great numberᵃ there consisting of chiefs' children and excellent commanders of ⌜—⌝. I brought ⁷a great number of them to the court as living prisonersᵇ, while I was at the head of many mighty soldiers as a hero. ⁸The heart of my lord was satisfied with me in every commission with which heᶜ sent me.

Second Nubian Expedition

359. Now, the majesty of my lord sent me to pacify these countries. ⁹I did so that my lord praised me exceedingly, above everything. I brought the two chiefs of these countries to the court in safety, ¹⁰bulls and live ⌜goats⌝ which they ⌜—⌝ to the court, together with chiefs' children, and the two commanders of ⌜—⌝, who were with them. ¹¹— — that which the lords of the South do, because I was excellent in watchfulness and because I did that which my lord desired.

Expedition against Asiatics

360. Now the majesty af my lord sent me ¹²to the country of the Asiatics (*'m[w]*) to bring for him the sole companion, ⌜commander⌝ᵈ of the sailors, the caravan-conductor, Enenkhet (*'n-'nḫt*), who was building a ship there for Punt, ¹³when the Asiatics (*'mw*) belonging to the Sand-dwellersᵉ (*ḥr(y)w-š'*) slew him, together with a troop of the army which was with himᶠ ¹⁴ . . . . .ᵍ

ᵃ*ṭr* a variant of *ṭnw*.   ᵇDeterminative of men and women.

ᶜThe pronoun (*f*) is in the joint of the masonry.

ᵈSome such title must have been in the lacuna; this title and the preceding (*smr*) "*companion*" are written beside the column. The whole is totally unrecognizable in de Morgan, *Catalogue des monuments*.

ᵉThe Sand-dwellers have either pushed very far south at this time (if able to disturb the building of ships for the Punt voyage) or these ships were built in the extreme northern Red Sea. The former supposition is the more probable.

ᶠAn idiom for: "*under his command.*"

ᵍPepi-nakht's name and titles.

15————a 16————— [17]among his people. I ⌜—⌝ and I slew
people among them, (I) and the troop of the army which was with me.
. . . . . . .b

<hr />

INSCRIPTION IN THE TOMB OF KHUIc

361. One of the pillars contains the following text over
Khnemhotep, one of the officials so commonly called *ḥrp-
sḥ*, who is carrying offerings to Khui (*Ḥwy*):

The *ḥrp-sḥ*, Khnemhotep, says: "I went forth with my lord, the
count and treasurer of the god, Thethi (*Ṯṯy*) to Kush, and (my lord
the count and treasurer of the god), Khuid (*Ḥwy*), to Punt, ⌜11⌝ times.
I was brought back in safety after I had visitede these countries.

<hr />

INSCRIPTIONS OF SEBNIf

362. The adventure which Sebni engraved upon the
façade of his tomb is not merely a tale of the greatest interest,
but also very important for its religious, geographical, ad-

<hr />

aIt is probable that this fragment of four lines (of which only two are preserved)
form the conclusion of the expedition against the Asiatics. Sethe has also inserted
them here.

bPepi-nakht's name and title.

cIn the cliffs opposite Assuan; No. 9 on de Morgan's plan (*Catalogue des
monuments*, 142); texts, *ibid.*, 157, 158, but so badly that it is very difficult to use
them, and I unfortunately had no other copy (for this tomb was overlooked by
both Budge and Bouriant, see § 325, note on excavation), for my note (*Proceedings
of the Society of Biblical Archæology*, May, 1901, 238), where text is also published.
Sethe has since published the same text (*Urkunden*, I, 140, 141), and his explanation
is more probable than mine, though it does not affect the conclusions of my note.

dIt is quite incomprehensible that Khui's name should not appear here as the
lord of Khnemhotep. Hence Sethe's restoration is very probable. This Thethi's
tomb is located in the same cliff (de Morgan, *Catalogue des monuments*, 199); besides
the titles above, he bore the title: "*who brings the products of the southern countries
to the king*," which we should expect of one who voyaged to Kush.

eLit.: "*done*," as in Uni, § 322, l. 41 and Harkhuf, Letter, § 351, l. 9.

f From his tomb hewn in the cliffs on the west shore at Assuan (for the excavation see § 325, note); it bears the No. 26, and is called No. 2 on de Morgan's
plan (*Catalogue des monuments*, 14). It is the largest tomb at Assuan. It is
described by Budge with plan (*Proceedings of the Society of Biblical Archæology*,
X, 16–23) and by Bouriant (*Recueil*, X, 182–85) both of whom took squeezes and

ministrative, and historical data, coming from a period of which we know so very little. Unfortunately, we possess only the second half of the narrative, and this in a condition so fragmentary that a general outline is necessary in order to make the contents clear.

363. The first half, now no longer legible, must have contained the narrative of an expedition into Nubia by Sebni's father, Mekhu. On this expedition Mekhu in some way meets his death.[a] Here the surviving portion of the inscription begins; information of Mekhu's death is brought to his son Sebni, and he sets out with troops and 100 asses, laden with presents to rescue his father's body for embalmment; otherwise of course there would be no life hereafter for Mekhu (ll. 1-3). He sent messengers to the king to inform

---

promised (1887) soon to publish the long text. It was finally published (1893) by de Morgan (*Catalogue des monuments*, 147, 148), but his copyists have clearly spent no time on the difficult collation, and the publication is unusable; the inscription has never been translated or treated. The long text occupies nineteen columns on the right of the door; these are the continuation from the beginning on the left of the door, which has now unfortunately almost totally disappeared. The nineteen columns are crossed by six wide horizontal cracks, some of which were filled up and did not interrupt the scribe's writing, and some of which he jumped over. It is always a question whether the crack has caused a lacuna, e. g., in ll. 11-17 in the third crack from the top there are no lacunæ. Moreover, the whole text is very badly weathered, and one can sit for hours poring over one line in varying lights, without being certain of the reading. The accompanying translation is based on my copy of the Berlin squeezes, collated with Erman's collation of the original; Erman and I then spent an entire day going over the doubtful passages in the squeezes together, and it is to be hoped that the text is now fixed. Sethe has since published all our readings and his own collation of the squeeze (*Urkunden*, I, 135-40).

[a] It is certainly remarkable that of the three narrative inscriptions of Assuan, two contain accounts of the death of a nobleman on a foreign expedition and the rescue of the body: Mekhu in Nubia and Enenkhet on the northern shores of the Red Sea (§ 360). For the tomb of an Egyptian buried in Sinai, see Borchardt, *Zeitschrift für ägyptische Sprache*, 1897, 112. Another Egyptian who apparently perished in the desolate quarries of Hammamat is commemorated on the rocks as follows: "*O ye living, the ones who come to this land, who desire to return to the king, bearing their gifts to their lord; say ye, '1000 loaves, 1000 jars of beer, etc., etc., for the wearer of the royal seal, etc., Sheme (Šmꜣ).*'" Text in Golénischeff, *Hammamat*, III, No. 1.

him of his departure and the purpose of his journey (l. 3).
He reached Wawat, and pacified it and its further neighbors,
secured the body of his father and started upon the return
(ll. 3–6).   On reaching Wawat again, he sent the officer Iri
and two companions to the court with some of the native
products which his father had acquired (ll. 6, 7).   They
were evidently instructed to return with embalmers and
equipment for embalming the deceased Mekhu, for as Sebni
descended the river he met Iri returning from the court with
all the people and paraphernalia necessary for the embalmment (ll. 8–10).   Iri brought also written instructions from
the king to Sebni, containing promises of great reward for
his pious deed (ll. 10–12).   Sebni then buried his father and
proceeded to Memphis with the Nubian products which his
father had gotten (ll. 12, 13).   He was highly praised by the
king, and given very rich gifts (ll. 14–16).   Later a communication from the vizier reached him, conveying to him
a gift of land, either as a further reward for his good deed to
refund him his expenses, or as an endowment of his father's
tomb (ll. 17–19).

364. Sebni's titles are:[a] *Count, wearer of the royal seal,
governor of the South, sole companion, ritual priest, Sebni
(S⁾ bny).*

365. The long text is as follows:

Information of Mekhu's Death

1————b [⸢Then came⸣] the ship captain, Intef (*Yntf*), and the
overseer of — ⸢—⸣ — Behkesi (*Bhksy*),[c] to give information[d] that the
sole companion, and ritual priest 2Me[khu] [⸢was dead⸣].

---

[a]De Morgan, *Catalogue des monuments*, 146, omitting repetitions.
[b]One-third line.

[c]Probably the name of a Nubian; it is determined by the soldier, but bearing
an ⸢⸣ *m*-club; a similar club is before the *y* (!) which renders the reading questionable.   Of course, one thinks of *nḥsy*, but we have the wrong *s*.

[d]*r rd·t rḫ ntt.*

Departure of Sebni

366. ⌜Then I took⌝ a troop of my estate, and 100 asses with me, bearing ointment, honey, clothing, oil (*ṯḥnt*) and ⌜—⌝ of every sack,[a] in order to ⌜make presents [in]⌝ these countries ⌜⌜and I went out to⌝⌝ these countries of ³the negroes.

Sebni's Message to the King

367. ————[b] ⌜⌜Then I sent⌝⌝ people[c] who were in the Door,[d] and I made letters to give information that I had gone out to bring this my father, from Wawat (*W ᵓ w ᵓ · t*), and Utheth (*Wṯṯ*).

Expedition of Sebni

368. I pacified ⁴these countries ————[e] ⌜in⌝ the countries of ⌜—⌝ the name of which is Mether (*Mṯr*). ⌜⌜I loaded⌝⌝ the body of this sole companion upon an ass, and I had him carried by the troop of my estate. ⁵I made for him a coffin ————[f] I brought ⌜—⌝ — — — — in order to bring him out of these countries. Never did I send ⌜—⌝ or any negro-caravan ⁶————.[g] I was greatly praised on account of it.

Return of Sebni

369. I descended to Wawat and Uthek (*Wṯk*)[h] and I ⌜sent⌝ the royal attendant Iri (*Yry*) with two people of my estate as ⌜—⌝,[i] ⁷bearing incense, clothing,[j] ————,[k] 3 cubits long, one tusk, in order to give information that my ⌜best one⌝ was 6 cubits long; one ⌜hide⌝, and that I had brought this my father and all kinds of gifts from these countries.

---

aOr "*every equipment*" (*ᶜ pr*) or "*every costume*" (*ḏbᵓ*) ?

bOne-third line,

cThe determinative and plural ending are all that is visible.

dElephantine is often called the "*Door of the South;*" and it is probably meant here.

eOne-quarter line.

fOne-quarter line, followed by fragmentary words.

gOne-quarter line.

hOr "*Uthek of Wawat.*" The *ṯ* of Uthek is doubtful.

iIt is possible that this curious word contains the names of the two people.

j*imnḥ·t-nṯr.*   kOne-fifth line.

Embalmment of Mekhu

370. [8]When I descended to give information ————[a] from the bend, (*W ꜥ r · t*) behold, Iri [ᵣcameᵣ] from the court, ᵣas Iᵣ came, to embalm[b] the count, wearer of the royal seal, sole companion, ritual priest, [9]this Mekhu (*M ḫw*). He brought — — embalmers, the chief ritual priest, *ymy-w ꜥ b*, — *sḫd*,[c] the mourners and all offerings of the ᵣWhiteᵣ House. He brought festival oil from the double White House [10]and secret things from the double *w ꜥ b · t*-[d]house, — — from the *ꜥ ḥ ꜣ*-house, clothing of the double White House, and all the burial equipment which is issued from the court, like the issuance for the hereditary prince, Meru.

Sebni's Letter from the King

371. Now, when this [11]Iri arrived, he brought to me a command (also), [ᵣtoᵣ] praise me on account of it. It was said in[e] this command: "I will do for thee every excellent thing, as a reward for this great deed, because of bringing thy [father][f] ————. [12][N]ever[g] has the like happened before.

Mekhu's Burial

I buried this my father in his tomb of the necropolis; never was one of his rank[h] (so) buried [before].

Sebni's Honors at Court

372. I [went north] to Memphis[i] bearing the gifts [13]of these countries which this count[j] had brought. I deposited every gift which this my father deposited — before this my army and the negroes ᵣ— —ᵣ. [14]The servant[k] there was praised at the court, and the servant there ᵣgave praiseᵣ to the king, because the servant there was so greatly favored

---

[a]One-fifth line.   [c]Titles of funeral functionaries.
[b]Or ceremoniously to receive.   [d]The "*pure*" house.
[e]*r* as in the letter of Harkhuf, § 351, l. 7.
[f]The determinative of "*father*" is still visible.
[g]The negative *n* is not visible either on the squeeze or original.

[h]Lit.: "*his equal.*" Zau affirms the same regarding his father (§ 382); there is a remarkable resemblance between this and the inscription of Zau.
[i]Lit.: "*the wall*," a designation for Memphis, e. g., several times in Papyrus Harris.
[j]His father.   [k]Common circumlocution for "I."

by ⌜the king⌝ ¹⁵⌜—⌝. There was given to me a chest of carob wood, — containing — and containing ointment; there was given [to me] ⌜—⌝ — — — with clothing; ¹⁶there was given to me the gold of praise; there were given to me rations, meat, and fowl. Now, when ⌜—⌝ — — ⌜—⌝ — — ¹⁷by my lord.

Sebni's Reward

373. Said the servant [a]there: "There came to me a command of the chief judge — — — [lord of] Nekheb, ¹⁸the inferior prophet Ini (*Yny*) while he was ⌜—⌝ in Per[b]-Hathor-Resit (*Pr-Ḥtḥr-rśy·t*) [⌜saying: that I might bring[c]⌝] this [⌜my father⌝] immediately ¹⁹that I might bury this [⌜my father⌝] in his tomb north of Nekheb.

Sebni's Reward

374. There were given to me 30 ($+^{d}x$) stat of land in the North and Southland, in the domain[e] of the pyramid: "Neferkere-Remains-Alive," — — in order to honor the servant there.

INSCRIPTIONS OF IBI[f]

375. The nomarch, Ibi, begins the history of a new family in the twelfth nome, whose relations with the royal house are especially instructive. In all probability Ibi was the son of the powerful Zau of Abydos (§§ 344 ff.), nomarch of the Thinite nome, whose two sisters became the queens of Pepi I. Ibi was a contemporary of Pepi I, Mernere, and Pepi II during the first part of his reign. Although Mernere appointed him to the nomarchy of the Cerastes-Mountain, it

---

[a]Common circumlocution for "I."　　　[c]I see traces of *nḏ* on the squeeze.

[b]See II, 728.　　　[d]Not more than 70.

[e]Or possibly "*as custodian of the domain of the pyramid, etc.;*" meaning that he received the gift by virtue of his office.

[f]From his tomb in the southern necropolis of Der el-Gebrâwi;. published by Davies, *The Rock Tombs of Deir-el-Gebrâwi*, Pl. 23 and 7; Sethe, *Urkunden*, I, 142-5 (from Davies).

is also probable that he was appointed to it in confirmation of his title to it through his marriage to a lady named Rahenem ($R^c hnm$), in whom we may recognize the heiress to the said nome. He thus became the head, not only of his hereditary nome of Thinis, the ancient capital of Egypt, but also of the twelfth nome. To the latter for some reason he transferred his residence. It is possible that he had not at first received the Thinite nome, and that on his marriage, he went to the Cerastes-Mountain first, as his only nome, and remained there even after his appointment to the Thinite nome. But it is his office in the latter of which he is most proud.

376. The office of "*great lord*" or at least that of "*count*" ($h^3 ty$-^{c}) of a nome, was at this time evidently one of appointment by favor of Pharaoh. The royal house thus maintained control of the landed lords, who were the descendants of the local governors of the Fourth and Fifth Dynasties.

Ibi introduced a severe and effective discipline into the organization of the nome, and must have prospered greatly from its revenues. His son Zau-Shemai succeeded him in both nomes.[a] (§ 380)

377. [2]Wearer[b] of the royal seal, commander of a stronghold, sole companion, great lord of the Thinite nome, Ibi (*Yby*); he saith:

"I was a youth who bound on the gir[dle under] ⌜the majesty⌝ ⌜of⌝ the King of Upper and Lower Egypt [Merire (Pepi I)]."

["The majesty of] [3]my lord, the King of Upper and Lower Egypt, Mernere, living — ⌜— —⌝ [appointed me] as count ($h^3 ty$-^{c}), sole companion, and great lord of the nome of the Cerastes-Mountain."

378. "The majesty of my lord, the King of Upper and Lower Egypt [Neferkere (Pepi II)], appointed me governor of the South."

The real governor of the South, [4]Ibi; he saith: "As for any people who shall enter into this tomb [as] their mortuary property, [I] will

---

[a]Davies, *ibid.*, 33, 34.   [b]Over the east wall, on the left, Davies, Pl. 23.

seize [them] ⁵like wild fowl. I am an excellent, equipped soul, I know every charm and the secrets of the court, the ⌜—⌝ which is in the nether world. I was ⁶one beloved of [his] father [praise]d of his mother, honored by the king, honored by his city-god, possessed of love, Ibi."

ᵃ——— "Now, I gave [bread] to [the hungry], clothing ⁵to the naked . . . . of grain, ⁶of oxen, and of the peasants of my domain.

379. ¹. . . . . .ᵇ I have made thisᶜ from the towns of my domain as a mortuary possession, and from the royal mortuary offering which the majesty of my lord gave to me; in order to make for me ——— ²with peasants of my domain, filled with bulls, goats, and asses, as ⌜—⌝ —, except the possessions of my father, while I was commander of the stronghold of the granary: 203 stat of land [which] the majesty of my lord gave [to me], to make me rich.

———

INSCRIPTION OF ZAUᵈ

380. This nomarch of the Cerastes-Mountain was the grandson of Ibi whom Mernere had appointed to this nome. Ibi's son Zau-Shemai died early, and his son Zau succeeded him. He was a contemporary of Pepi II, under whom he held the office of "*keeper of the door of the South*," an office usually belonging to the nobles of Elephantine. At his father's death he was obliged to petition the king that he might succeed to the paternal nomarchy.ᵉ His account

———

ᵃOver the east wall, on the right; Davies, Pl. XXIII.

ᵇOn the east wall over the scenes of cattle and under women bringing offerings (Davies, Pl. VII). The omitted introduction contains only name and titles of Ibi, preceded by "*For* [*the k⌐ of*]."

ᶜThe endowment from which the offerings depicted before him are drawn. It includes eleven villages or settlements.

ᵈIn the Gebel Marâg, marked on the Fund map (Pl. IV) as "Dêr-el-Gebrâwi Tombs," north of Assiut on the east side of the river. Text copied by Sayce and published in *Recueil*, XIII, 65–67; comments by Maspero, *ibid.*, 68 ff. Corrections by Sayce, *ibid.*, XX, 170 ff.; better by Davies, *Deir-el-Gebrâwi*, II, Pl. XIII, but unfortunately the inscription suffered much in the interim between Sayce's and Davies' visits; Sethe (from Davies), *Urkunden*, I, 145–47. See also Newberry, *Egypt Exploration Fund Archæological Report*, 1892–1893, 14, 15.

ᵉSee Davies, *ibid.*, II, 35 ff.

of his construction of a common tomb for his father, and himself, is the most remarkable expression of sentiment which this remote age has bequeathed us. He seems to have been the last of his line.

Introduction

381. [1]His eldest son, his beloved, of his body; — — — [2]his favorite, his darling,[a] prince of the palace, wearer of the royal seal, commander of a stronghold, [3]real sole companion, great lord[b] of the nome of Cerastes-Mountain,"[c] Zau ($D^c w$).   I say: "I [4]was one beloved of his father, praised of his mother, [5]whom his brothers and sisters loved.

Father's Burial

382. I buried [6]my father the count, Zau, beyond the splendor, beyond the goodliness of any [ʳequalˡ] of his [7]who was in this South. I requested as an honor[d] [8]from the majesty of my lord, the king of Upper and Lower Egypt, Neferkere (Pepi II), who lives forever, that [9]there be taken[e] a coffin, clothing, and festival perfume [10]for this[f] Zau.   His majesty caused [11]that the custodian of the royal domain should bring a coffin of wood, festival perfume, [12](sft-)oil, clothing, 200 (pieces) of prime ($h^ꜣ tyw$) linen, [13]and of fine southern linen of ʳ—ˡ, taken from the double White House [14]of the court for this Zau.   Never had it been done [15]to another of his rank.

Son's Burial

383. Now, I caused that I should be buried in the same tomb [16]with this Zau, in order that I might be with him in one place; [17]not, however, because I was not in a position[g] to make a second tomb; but I did this in order that [18]I might see this Zau every day, in order that I might be with him in one place."

---

[a]Lit.: "*in his heart, belonging to the place of his heart.*"

[b]The rule that this title ($hry-ḏꜣ ḏꜣ - cꜣ$) is to be found only in the Middle Kingdom (*Bersheh*, II, 4) does not hold.   The title arose in the Sixth Dynasty.

[c]Name of the Antaeopolite nome.

[d]The same rare word $šꜣr$ "*honor*" as in Harkhuf, Letter, § 352, l. 11.

[e]$šd;$ it occurs in precisely the same connection in the Abydos inscription of $Dꜣw$, see § 349, and is the regular word for legally collecting.

[f]The demonstrative is customary in referring to the dead; cf. the deceased Mekhu in the Sebni inscription or the pyramid texts *passim.*

[g]$hr-c$; lit.: "*having the hand*" or "*power.*"

Zau's Prayer

384. The count, commander of a stronghold, sole companion, [19]Zau; I say: "O ye living, who are upon earth, servants like me; those whom the king shall love [20]and their city-god shall favor, are they who shall say: 'A thousand loaves, beer, oxen, geese, clothing for Zau, son of Zau.'"

Zau Succeeds His Father

385. I requested [21][fro]m [his majesty][a] that I might fulfil the office of count, of this Zau. His majesty caused that there be issued (lit., made) the decree appointing him[b] count, as an offering which the king gives.[c]

---

[a]Something similar must have been in the lacuna (nearly one-third line); there is not room for "*as an honor from,*" as in ll. 7, 8.

[b]The change of person is very sudden, but Zau can be referring to no other than himself, from the standpoint of the command issued.

[c]The mode of obtaining the office of *ḥꜣty-ꜥ* "*count*" at this time, points clearly to its source in the royal favor. The designation of the appointment as "*an offering which the king gives.*" the usual term for a mortuary gift of the king, certainly indicates that this term did not originally designate solely a mortuary gift, but must have at first enjoyed a wider application, which in course of time was narrowed to exclusively funerary largesses of the king. [Later: A letter from Eduard Meyer suggests that the rank of count was given to the deceased father after his death as a mortuary honor. This would explain its designation as a mortuary gift, and the pronoun "*him.*"]

REIGN OF ITY

HAMMAMAT INSCRIPTION[a]

386. This is the only inscription of King Ity known. His pyramid mentioned in the inscription has never been found[b] and the place of the king in the series of Pharaohs is uncertain. The inscription is dated in his first year, and records an expedition which was sent to procure the finer stone necessary for the king's pyramid.

387. Year of the first occurrence (of the numbering), fourth month of the first season, day 2.

— Ihy (*Yhy*); Khufu (*Ḥwf*); commander of the army — Yakhetirni (*Y꜄ḫ·t yrn(y)*).[c]

Came the ship captain, Ipi (*Ypy*), and Nekuptah (*Ptḥ-n-k꜄w*) to do the work on the pyramid (called): "Fame-of-Ity" (*Yty*); together with 200 soldiers and 200 ⌜workmen, making⌝ 200 (sic!).

---

[a]Cut on the rocks in the Wadi Hammamat; text: Lepsius, *Denkmäler*, II, 115 f.; partially Golénischeff *Hammamat*, VII; Sethe, *Urkunden*, I, 148; see Maspero, *Recueil*, 17, 56 ff.

[b]See Maspero, *ibid.*, 56 ff.

[c]These names were perhaps later inserted between the date and the following.

REIGN OF IMHOTEP

HAMMAMAT INSCRIPTION

388. This unknown king, from whom we have no other documents, sent his eldest son Zaty, who held the office of treasurer of the god, as well as that of general in the army, to the Hammamat quarries to procure a monument, possibly a statue for the king. Zaty left the following record of the enterprise:

389. [1]Commission which the eldest king's-son, the treasurer of the god, commander of the army, Zaty ($\underline{D}^{\supset}ty$), called Kenofer ($K^{\supset}\text{-}nfr$) executed.

390. [2]I was at the front of the people ($h^{\supset}m$) in the day of battle, [3]I controlled the going in the day of attack, by my counsel. [4]I was exalted above multitudes, I made this work of Imhotep[a] [5]with [6]1,000 men of the palace, 100 quarrymen, [7]1,200 ꜥsoldiersꜥ and 50 ꜥ—ꜥ. [8]His majesty sent this numerous troop [9]from the court. [10]I made this work while ꜥ—ꜥ in every ꜥ—ꜥ, while his majesty gave [11]50 oxen and 200 asses[b] every day.

Palace-overseer, Intef.

Scribe of the marine, Mereri.

---

[a]The name is in a cartouche with the determinative of a king.

[b]For the transport of the monument.

THE NINTH AND TENTH DYNASTIES

INSCRIPTIONS OF SIUT[a]

391. Of the five inscribed tombs of Siut, three[b] date from the period of the Ninth and Tenth Dynasties, and form our only contemporary source of information for that obscure epoch. They belonged to three princes of the Lycopolite nome: Tefibi (§§ 393–97), his son Kheti I (§§ 398–404), and another Kheti (II) (§§ 405–14), whose relation to the two others is not clear. These princes as nomarchs all bore the same titles: *"Hereditary prince, count, wearer of the royal seal, sole companion, superior prophet of Upwawet, lord of Siut."* They were the continual friends and supporters of the weak Heracleopolitan kings, forming a buffer state, warding off the attacks of the rebellious Theban princes, who are the ancestors of the Eleventh Dynasty.[c] Unfortunately, they do not mention any of the Thebans against whom they fought, and only one of the Heracleopolitans whom they served—Merikere.

392. The language of these texts is exceedingly obscure and difficult; these hindrances, together with the very

---

[a]In an upper row of three tombs, side by side, high up in the face of the cliffs overlooking the modern city of Assiut (or Siut). First copied by the expedition of Napoleon, they were almost wholly neglected till late in last century, having in the interim been frightfully mutilated (serving as a stone quarry!). Finally, after repeated visits, from 1886 to 1888, Mr. F. Ll. Griffith published a careful text, not only of the difficult original, but, where necessary, also of all existing earlier fragmentary copies (*The Inscriptions of Siût and Dêr Rîfeh*, London, 1889). Mr. Griffith furnished an account of his edition, and a digest of the content of the texts in the *Babylonian and Oriental Record*, III, 121–29, 164–68, 174–84, 244–52, where he also gives an exhaustive bibliography. Maspero (*Revue critique*, II (1889), 410–21) reviewed Griffith's work and gave a very free paraphrase of the texts, some of which is repeated, *Dawn*, 456–58.

[b]For the remaining two, which belong to the Twelfth Dynasty, see §§ 535 ff.

[c]See §§ 415 ff.

fragmentary state of the texts, often make translation quite impossible. The restorations make no claim to reproduce the lost words, but merely indicate the probable connection.

I. INSCRIPTION OF TEFIBI[a]

393. The conflict with the South is here clearer than anywhere else, but unfortunately the unfinished condition of the inscription (see l. 16, n., § 396) breaks all continuity. The content in outline is as follows: Tefibi adjures all passers-by to pray for him (l. 1). He sets forth the beneficence of his rule—a rule without distinction of persons, maintaining the security of all, even if abroad at night (ll. 2–12). Because of his beneficent rule his son, when a child, succeeded him without opposition (ll. 13–15). On his (Tefibi's) first campaign, the southern nomes from Elephantine to an uncertain point on the north were united against him (l. 16). He defeated them first on the west shore, driving them as far as *"the fortress of the port of the South"* (Abydos? ll. 16–18). He then crossed to the east shore, where he defeated a second army of the enemy (ll. 19–22) and also discomfited a hostile fleet (ll. 23, 24). He thus suppressed rebellion and had opportunity to promote deserving officers (ll. 25–27). The result was widespread respect for his energetic government, prosperity of the temples. and envy of the evil-minded (ll. 36–40).

Address to Passers

394. [1]O ye living! O ye who are upon earth, children who shall be born; those who shall sail down-stream, those who shall sail up-stream,

---

[a]Tomb III. The southernmost of the three tombs on the same terrace, north wall east of pillars. Published by Griffith, *Siut*, 11, 12. See above, § 391, note.

those who shall come in the following of Upwawet, lord of Siut, those who shall pass by this bend,[a] those who shall enter into this tomb, those who shall see that which is in it; as Upwawet, lord of Siut and Anubis, lord of the ⌐cave⌐, live for you, ye shall pray for the mortuary offering for the prince Tefibi.

Tefibi's Kind Rule

395. [2]The hereditary prince, count, wearer of the royal seal, sole companion, superior prophet of Upwawet, lord of Siut, Tefibi (*Tf-yby*), says: —————[b] [3]⌐—⌐. Hearken to me, ye who are to come. I was openhanded to everyone, ⌐— —⌐ —————[b] [4]⌐— —⌐, I was one of excellent plans, one useful to his city, one ⌐—⌐ of face toward a petition, —————[b] [5]⌐— — —⌐ one of open face to the widow. . . . . I was a Nile[c] —————[b] [6]for his people. . . . . [7]. . . . .[d] [10]When night came, he who slept on the road gave me praise, for he was like a man in his house; the fear of my soldier was his protection. . . . .[13]. Then[e] came my son in my place, the officials were ⌐under⌐ his ⌐authority⌐. He ruled as a child[f] of a cubit (high); the city rejoiced over him, she remembered [14]the good.[g] Because, any noble who shall do good to the people, who shall surpass the virtue of him that begot him, he shall be — [15]blessed in the hereafter, his son shall abide in his father's house, his memory shall be pleasant in the city, his statue shall be glorified and ⌐carried⌐[h] by the children of his house.

---

[a]Used alike of the cliffs or the river.   [b]About one-third line.

[c]Amenhotep IV also calls himself a Nile for his people.

[d]The omissions contain obscure phrases, chiefly referring to Tefibi's kindness to his people.

[e]See Sethe, *Zeitschrift für ägyptische Sprache,* 1893, 108.

[f]The text has "*person.*" The stature indicated, "*1 cubit,*" is that of a newborn child, as shown by Papyrus Westcar (X, 10), where the three children are each "*of one cubit*" at birth. The same statement is made of Khety II (§ 413, l. 21), where it is c⌐nfirmed by the context), and seems to be a favorite boast of such princes: in Benihasan (Tomb 13), the owner, Khnumhotep, boasts of being one "*whose place was advanced while he was a child.*" The Pharaohs make the same boast.

[g]Meaning the good his father had done, as the following shows.

[h]It shall receive the proper ceremonies and be carried in the festal processions. Cf. the contracts of Hepzefi, §§ 535 ff.

War with the South

396. [16a]The first time that my soldiers fought with the southern[b] nomes, which came together southward as far as Elephantine and northward as far as ⌜—[c] —————⌝, [⌜they smote them⌝] as far as [17]as the southern boundary.[d] ⌜—⌝ — — the west side.[e] When I came to the city,[f] I overthrew [⌜the foe⌝] —————[g] [⌜I drove him⌝] [18]— as far as the fortress of the port of the South.[h] He gave to me land, while I did not restore his town —————[g] [19]⌜— — —⌝ I reached the east side, sailing up-stream; [⌜there came⌝] another,[i] like a jackal ⌜— —⌝ —————[g]

---

[a]Lines 16–40 were never finished; the lower third was never cut (my restorations chiefly indicate the probable connection). Moreover, they were plastered over, and a new inscription containing the conventional encomium was painted on the plaster. As the content of this very portion of the text is political, this must have been the motive for effacing it. See Griffith, *Babylonian and Oriental Record*, III, 128. As the effacement was done before the inscription was finished, it would seem that there was interference from the south during the construction of the tomb.

[b]The word "*southern*" is broken and not quite certain. It exactly fits the remaining traces as well as the context. and later course of the war.

[c]Maspero reads "Gaou" (*Ḳau*), (*Revue critique*, 1889, II, 416), but wisely adds? The same name occurs at Benihasan (§ 620, note), but cannot be located.

[d]The southern boundary of the Heracleopolitan kings (?), which was then not far north of Abydos; cf. § 423. In this case there would have been an invasion of the Heracleopolitan kingdom by the Thebans, who were then driven out.

[e]A reference to his campaign on the west shore of the river; the east shore follows in l. 19.

[f]This must have been a city on the frontier between the territory of the north and south, for he has just passed "*the southern boundary*," and in the next line reaches "*the fortress of the port of the South*."

[g]About one-third line.

[h]See Erman (*Zeitschrift für ägyptische Sprache*, 1891, 120), who suggests that *tp ršy* is really the south, and *šmᶜ* middle Egypt. This distinction is apparently maintained in these Siut texts, and is clear at this point, where Tefibi drives his enemy as far as the southern (*ršy*) border of the Northern Kingdom, and then "*as far as the fortress of the port of the South* (*tp ršy*)." The northernmost point to which *tp ršy* is applied is the Thinite nome. Now, the Theban king, Intef (Horus: *Wᵓḥ ᶜnḥ*), states that he captured all of the Thinite (Abydos) nome, and "*opened all her fortresses*" (§ 423), using the very word for fortress (*ytḥ*) employed in l. 18, above. He also made the Aphroditopolite nome (just north of the Thinite nome) "*the door of the North*" (*ibid.*). Remembering that Tefibi's campaign is thus far confined to the west shore, one would suspect that Tefibi's "*port of the South*" is Intef's "*door of the North*." All the indications, therefore, point to this region as the southern extremity of Tefibi's campaign.

[i]With the determinative of a person.

²⁰with another army from his confederacy. I went out against him with one —. There was no fear ————.ᵃ ²¹He hastened to battle like the ⌜light⌝; the Lycopolite nome — like a bull going forth ————ᵃ ²²— forever. I ceased not to fight ⌜to the end [making use⌝ of the south wind] as well as the north wind, of the east wind as well as [of the west wind] ————ᵃ ²³⌜— —⌝. He fell in the water, his ships ran aground, his army were like bulls, ————ᵃ [⌜when attacked by wild beasts, and running⌝] ²⁴with tails to the front.ᵇ ⌜— —⌝ — — — fire was put ————ᵃ ²⁵⌜— — — —⌝ I drove out rebellion by —, by the plan of Upwawet, ————ᵃ ²⁶of a mighty bull. When a man did well, [I placed] him at the head of my soldiers ————ᵃ ²⁷for his lord.ᶜ . . . . ————ᵃ ³⁶Heracleopolis. The land was under the fear of my soldiers; no highland was free from fear. If he made ————ᵃ ³⁷fire in the southern nomes. He did it as an affair of his land, to equip ————ᵃ

Conclusion

397. ³⁸The temples were made to flourish, offerings were made to the gods; the wicked saw it, ————ᵃ ³⁹he put not eternity before him, he looked not to the future, he saw evil ————ᵃ ⁴⁰. . . . . .

II. INSCRIPTION OF KHETI Iᵈ

398. Kheti (called Iᵉ to distinguish him from Kheti II of the next tomb) was the son of Tefibi of the preceding tomb. He inherited the lands and titles of his father, being a nomarch by inheritance from his mother (l. 8). Besides the usual functions of the Assiut nomarchs, he was also

---

ᵃAbout one-third line.   ᵇOf the pursuer.

ᶜThe following lines, to l. 35, inclusive, are very fragmentary and obscure. In l. 28 there is reference to "*the South*" ("*Oh, speak a word to the South (tp ršy)*"). In l. 33 the goddesses "*Bast of the South*" (*Bꜣ stt nt tp-ršy*) and Hereret (*Ḥrrt*) are mentioned, and the following lines (to l. 35, inclusive) consist of epithets in the feminine, referring to one of them. In l. 35 there is reference to Middle Egypt (*šmꜥ*) and the building of "*its fortresses.*"

ᵈIn the middle tomb (IV) of the three on the same terrace, on the north wall, opposite the scene of the soldiers with large shields. Text in Griffith, *Siut*, Pls. 13, 14, 20. See also § 391.

ᵉGriffith, *Siut*, IV, 75; cf. Kheti II's title, § 410.

"military commander of the whole land." His inscription is of great importance for the inner history of the Heracleo-politan kingdom, but is unfortunately fragmentary and ob-scure. After some references to Kheti's services to the king, Merikere (ll. 1–7), and the ancient origin of Kheti's family (ll. 7–9), it is stated that he has chastised Middle Egypt for the king's sake (l. 10), a clear indication of insur-rection within the Heracleopolitan kingdom. This trouble quelled, Kheti conducts the king up-river, probably to receive the homage of the kingdom, which, including the nobles of Ehnas, was in great fear, as Kheti's enormous fleet passed up (ll. 10–15). Returning to Ehnas-Heracleopolis, the king is received with acclamation by old and young (ll. 16, 17). Kheti now returns to his home and is commissioned to restore the ancient temple of Upwawet, which, at the present day, lies somewhere beneath the modern buildings of Siut (ll. 17–31). The people lived in peace and security during the remainder of Kheti's reign (ll. 31–34).

399. Of the first seven lines only the upper portion (from a third to a half line) is preserved. The content was im-portant, but only the merest scraps are now intelligible. They show that the text is an address to the deceased Kheti, of historical import, and are as follows: [1]"———— *a stock*[a] *of ancient time* ———— . . . . [3]. . . . . *King of Upper and Lower Egypt, Merikere (Mry-k³-Rˁ)* . . . . [6]*of Heracleopolis. Thou overthrowest the rebels.* . . . . ———— [7]*lord of the two regions, beloved of the god, shade of the whole land."* These last epithets (l. 7) refer to the king; and probably Kheti's serv-ices to him in overthrowing the rebels, furnish the connection. The text now becomes more connected, though still very obscure in places.

---

[a]Referring to the ancient origin of Kheti's family; see also l. 8.

Kheti's Lineage

400. [ʳHeirˡ] [8]of a ruler, ruler of rulers,[a] son of a ruler, son of the daughter of a ruler, an ancient stock ————[b] [ʳson ofˡ] the daughte]r of a ruler, [9ʳ—ˡ] of the beginning, a noble ʳwithoutˡ an equal. . . . .
[10]. . . . .[c] for thou hast put ʳfearˡ in the land, thou hast chastised Middle Egypt for his[d] sake alone.

Services for the King

401. Thou didst convey him up-river, the [11]heaven cleared for him,[e] the whole land was with him, the counts of Middle Egypt, and the great ones of Heracleopolis, the district[f] ʳofˡ the queen[g] of the land, who came [12]to repel the evil-doer. The land trembled, Middle Egypt ʳfearedˡ, all the people were in terror, the villages in ʳpanicˡ, [13]fear entered into their limbs. The officials of Pharaoh were (a prey) to fear, the favorites to the terror of Heracleopolis. [14]The land burned in its[h] flame

---

[a]Griffith (*Babylonian and Oriental Record*, III, 164) and later Maspero (*Revue critique*, II [1889], 413) have interpreted this passage as indicating that Kheti was the descendant of five princes. It seems to me there are two convincing objections to this: (1) five princes could be written in Egyptian only by employing the usual construction with the numeral 5, not by repeating the word "*prince*" (*ḥkꜣ*) five times! (2) The usual method of indicating a line of descent is the one employed in this very passage, by repeating the paternity of the parent (*sꜣ sꜣt ḥkꜣ*); hence a male descent through five generations of princes would be written (*sꜣ ḥkꜣ*) "*son of a ruler*," repeated five times. (I have rendered the politically very unprecise title *ḥkꜣ* by the equally unprecise "*ruler;*" it is probably synonymous with nomarch in this passage.) Of the 5 *ḥkꜣ*-signs, the first is genitive after a lost noun preceding, as shown by the surviving *n;* the second is *nomen regens* of a genitive construction in which the following plural of *ḥkꜣ* (written three times as often) is *nomen rectum*. The last construction, written in the same way with four *ḥkꜣ*-signs, is found in Sirenpowet's tomb (Assuan, de Morgan, *Catalogue des monuments*, 185, l. 8), and often with other words, e. g., in the name of Amenhotep IV's queen (*nfr-nfrw* with four *nfr*-signs).

[b]About one-third line.

[c]King Merikere's benefits to Kheti are referred to.

[d]The king's sake.

[e]See Erman (*Gespräch*, 69, 70), who makes the verb transitive: "*he cleared the heavens.*"

[f]Lit.: "*(river)-bend*" (many different localities are so designated) apparently in apposition with Heracleopolis. See Erman, *Zeitschrift für ägyptische Sprache*, 1891, 120, and Griffith, *Kahun Papyri*, II, 21, and infra index.

[g]Some protecting goddess.

[h]The pronoun refers to Heracleopolis.

. . . . .¹⁵. . . . . Never was the front of a fleet brought into Sheshotep, while its rear was still at ⌜—⌉ᵃ . . . . . .¹⁶. . . . . They descended by water and landed at Heracleopolis. The city came, rejoicing over [⌜her⌉] lord, the son of her lord; women ¹⁷mingled with men, old men and children.

Old Age

402. ᵇThe ruler's (*ḥḳ²*) son, he reached his city, entering into the house of his father. He saw the ¹⁸⌜approach⌉ to their house,ᶜ his sarcophagus, his old age. When a man is in his place (his tomb), the city ⌜— —⌉ ¹⁹of eternity ⌜— —⌉.

Building the Temple

403. Thy city-god loves thee, Tefibi's son, Kheti. He hath ⌜presented⌉ thee, that he might look to the future in order to ²⁰restore his temple, in order to raise the ancient walls, the original places of offering, to ⌜—⌉ the venerable ground, ²¹⌜— — —⌉ which Ptah built with his fingers, which Thoth founded, for Upwawet, lord of Siut,ᵈ ⌜by⌉ command of the king, ²²the ruler (*ḥḳ²*) of the Two Lands, the king of Upper and Lower Egypt, Merikere, to make a monument for the souls of Anubis, the great god; that he (the king) might spend for him (the god) millions of years, that he might repeat Sed Jubilees; ²³under the leadershipᵉ of the confidant of the king, Tefibi's son, Kheti, great lord of Middle

---

ᵃThe reading of this second locality is unfortunately quite uncertain. Maspero reads "Hou" (*Revue critique*, II (1889), 418). Sheshotep is the modern Shatb (Baedeker's *Egypt*, 1902, 205), just south of Assiut, while Hou is 125 miles farther up-river. It is impossible that the fleet should have been 125 miles long. Moreover, the direction of the fleet's movement (l. 10) is up-river, so that the rear must have been at a place below Sheshotep. The return down-river is narrated in l. 16 following. [Since writing the above, I notice that Maspero (*Dawn*, 457) has changed "Hou" to "Gebel-Abufodah," which would make the fleet about 30 miles long; but this is a guess like "Hou."]

ᵇAs the preceding paragraph closes very abruptly, it is possible that the following paragraph contains the words of the rejoicing multitude to the king as he enters the city.

ᶜHis own approach to the house, meaning the tomb of his ancestors; hence his death.

ᵈThis "*by*" would of course not refer to the building by the gods, but to the proposed restoration.

ᵉMeaning that the building of the temple is to be under Kheti's leadership.

Egypt. Behold, thy[a] name shall be forever in the temple [24]of Upwawet, thy memory shall be beautiful in the colonnade. Some shall communicate it to others,[b] ⌜—⌝ the future ⌜—⌝ [25]in years, one hundred after another hundred,[c] of added life upon earth; thou shalt (still) be among them that dwell on ⌜earth.⌝ . . . . [31]. . . . . . .[d]

Peaceful Rule

404. How beautiful is that which happens in thy time, the city is satisfied with thee. That which was concealed from the people, [32]thou hast done it ⌜openly⌝, in order to make gifts to Siut, — by thy plan alone. Every ⌜official⌝ was at his post, [33]there was no one fighting, nor any shooting an arrow. The child was not smitten beside his mother, (nor) the citizen beside his wife. There was no evil-doer [34]in ⌜—⌝, nor any one doing violence against his house ⌜—⌝. Thy city-god, thy father who loveth thee, ⌜leadeth⌝ thee.

III.   INSCRIPTION OF KHETI II[e]

405. Kheti II's relation to the two preceding nomarchs is not quite certain, but the unmolested rule which he enjoyed would seem to indicate that he lived before the war with the Thebans, and hence before Tefibi. His inscription curiously inverts the order of his life, placing his youth last, but does not mention the name of his father.[f] On the death of his maternal grandfather, who was lord of the Lycopolite nome, Kheti's mother ruled until he grew up to succeed to his maternal heritage (ll. 40–25). Meantime, he was educated with the royal children by the king (ll.

---

[a]Pronoun refers to Kheti.   [b]The text has a dittography of *n kt*.

[c]See Sethe, *Zeitschrift für ägyptische Sprache*, 1893, 113.

[d]The intervening lines contain praise of Kheti as builder of the temple. The text then proceeds to the government of the nome.

[e]In tomb V, the northernmost of the three tombs on the same terrace, in a false door on the back wall (ll. 1–24) and on the south wall, inner half. Text, Griffith, *Siut*, Pl. 15. See § 391.

[f]On his mother's name, see note on l. 38.

22, 23), and was installed in his nome at an early age (l. 21). His life was peaceful and prosperous, and devoted to the development of the material resources of the nome. He dug a much-needed irrigation canal, conducting the water to land unreached by the inundation (ll. 1–8). He was rich in grain, which he dispensed to the people (ll. 9, 10). He remitted taxes (ll. 10, 11), and his herds greatly multiplied (ll. 11–14). He built in the temple, increased its offerings (ll. 14–16), was a good soldier, and, as military commander of Middle Egypt, he raised a troop (ll. 16–18); like Kheti I, he had a navy (ll. 18, 19). His people and those of Heracleopolis were pleased with his government, and recognized the instruction of a king in it (ll. 23, 24). It is possible that Kheti II became an official of the contemporary Theban king (Eleventh Dynasty) after the triumph of Thebes and the consolidation of the country (see note on l. 38).

406. The inscription opens with the usual titles of the Siut nomarchs,[a] and Kheti states that there is no falsehood in his narrative, but that all which he did was done in the face of the people (ll. 1, 2); and then proceeds:

New Canal

407. I brought a gift for this city, in which there were no families of the Northland, nor people[b] of Middle Egypt ($šm^c$); ³making a monument in ————[c] I substituted a channel of ten cubits.[d] I excavated for it upon the arable land. I equipped a gate ⌜for⌝ ⁴its ————[e] it

---

[a]See § 391.

[b]The determinative shows that people of some sort are meant, parallel with "*families.*" The remarkable statement perhaps means that no forced labor was employed on the canal, from any part of Egypt composing the Heracleopolitan kingdom, viz., the "*Northland*" (Delta) and "*Middle Egypt.*"

[c]About one-third line is lost; it doubtless contained some reference to an insufficient canal. Kheti's gift to the city, is a larger canal "*of 10 cubits,*" probably in breadth.

[d]A little over 17 feet.   [e]About one-third line.

in the ground of ⌈—⌉ in one building, free from ⌈—⌉. I was liberal as
to the monument ⌈—⌉ 5⌈—⌉ ————.ᵃ [⌈I sustained⌉] the life of the
city, I made the ⌈—⌉ᵇ with grain-food, to give water at ⌈mid⌉day, ⁶to
⌈— —⌉ ————.ᵃ [⌈I supplied water⌉] in the highland district, I
made a water-supplyᶜ for this cityᵈ of Middle Egypt in the ⌈mountain⌉,ᵉ
which had not seen water. ⁷I secured the borders — — — ⌈—⌉. I
made the elevated land a swamp. I caused the water of the Nile to
flood over the ancient ⌈landmarks⌉, ⁸I made the arable land — — water.
Every neighbor was [⌈supplied with water, and every citizen had⌉]
Nile water to his heart's desire; I gave waters to his neighbors, and
he was content with them.

Wealth and Generosity

408. ⁹I was rich in grain. When the land was in need, I maintained the city with khaᶠ and with heket.ᶠ I allowed ¹ᶜthe citizen to
carry away for himself grain; and his wife, the widow and her son.
I remitted ¹¹all imposts which I found counted by my fathers. I filled
the ⌈pastures⌉ with cattle, ¹²[⌈every⌉] man had many colors;ᵍ the cowsʰ
brought forth twofold, the folds were full of ¹³calves. I was kind to
the cow, when she said, "It is ⌈—⌉."ⁱ I was one rich in bulls ¹⁴— his
ox; — — he lived well.

ᵃAbout one-third line.

ᵇThe determinative is a man. The word itself *ḥsb* means "*to reckon.*" Maspero
says: "*Hobsou* (reading the root as *ḥbs*) est l'homme qui paie la redevance
annuelle, le contribuable" (*Revue critique*, II (1889), 413, n. 8), and hence renders
"sujet," but I cannot find any such usage elsewhere. Furthermore, the grammatical construction is not clear.

ᶜThe same word (ᶜ-*mw*) is used in enumerating the duties of the vizier (II, 698),
among which was care of the water-supply in the whole land.

ᵈThis means Siut. Maspero (*loc. cit.*, 414, n. 2) calls it Thebes. But *šm* ᶜ
in these inscriptions means Middle Egypt, not South; and "*this city*" in a nomarch's
inscription means his own city; see II, 11.

ᵉThe sign for mountain is certain, but an uncertain sign precedes it; the
parallelism with "*highland*" demands a word like "mountain."

ᶠ*Ḥ*ꜣ and *ḥḳ·t* are measures of capacity referring here to grain. See Griffith,
Proceedings of the Society of Biblical Archæology. XIV, 425.

ᵍDoubtless referring to breeds of cattle.

ʰThe text has "*bulls*" (!) misread from l. 13, where the word "*bulls*" occurs
with "*many*" before it, as in this line.

ⁱCompare the talking cows in Papyrus d'Orbigny.

Kheti's Monuments

409. I was one rich in monuments of the temple, [15]————[a] [who ⌜increased⌝] that which he found, who repeated offerings.   I was a favorite, [16]————.[b]

His Army

410. I was one strong with the bow, mighty with his sword, [17]great in fear among his neighbors.   I made a troop of soldiers ————[a] [18]as commander[c] of Middle Egypt.

His Fleet

411. I had goodly ships, — — — — a favorite of the king [19]when he sailed up-river.[d]

His Tomb

412. I was one ⌜vigilant⌝ in that which he said; with a ⌜determined⌝ heart on the evil [⌜day⌝].   I had a lofty [20]tomb with a wide stair before the chamber.

Kheti's Childhood

413. I was a favorite of the king, a confidant of his princes, his ⌜exalted ones⌝ [21]before Middle Egypt.   He caused that I should rule as a child of a cubit[e] (in height); he advanced my seat as a ⌜youth[f]⌝. [22]He had me instructed in swimming along with the royal children.   I was one correct of ⌜speech⌝, [23]free from ⌜opposition⌝ to his lord, who brought him up as a child.   Siut was satisfied with [24]my administration; Heracleopolis praised god for me.   Middle Egypt and the Northland (Delta) said: "It is the instruction of a king.[g]

---

[a]About one-half line.   [b]About two-thirds line.

[c]The title ($ḥ^ɔ$-tpy) was also borne by Kheti, son of Tefibi (§ 398), but with the addition "*of the whole land.*"

[d]From Heracleopolis to Siut.   [e]See note, § 395, l. 13.

[f]The phrase is literally "*as a hairy one,*" and the parallelism demands a word like "child" or "youth."   It is possibly a reference to the lock of childhood.

[g]The description of Kheti's childhood is now continued in the fragmentary lower ends (mostly less than half the height) of sixteen columns on the south wall (Griffith, p. 11; but on the west wall according to Pl. 15).   Originally there were twenty-four columns.   The numbering of the lines on Pl. 15 (ll. 25–40) must be reversed, but I have retained it for convenience, beginning with 40 and going back to 25.   The probable connection between the fragments is indicated as usual in brackets, but without pretense to even approximate restoration for which the basis is lost.   For the interpretation of these lines, see § 405.

Death of Kheti's Grandfather

414. ⁴⁰Saith [Kheti] ———— ^{39⌈—⌉} ———— born of ³⁸Si[t]^a —
———— night watch ³⁷———— in glorifying his^b name.

³⁶———— [⌈Then mourned⌉] the king himself, all Middle Egypt
and the Northland (Delta) ³⁵————. The king himself and the
counts were gathered together ³⁴[⌈for the burial. He was interred in
his tomb of the⌉] highlands.

Regency of Kheti's Mother

The son of his daughter made his name to live and glorified ³³[him].
———— [⌈His daughter ruled in⌉] Si]ut, the worthy stock^c of her father
³²[⌈reigned in the city⌉] ———— beloved of Upwawet, rejoicing^d in
doing good to ⌈her city⌉ ³¹———— . . . .^e ³⁰————
beloved^f of the king, his favorite.^f The city was satisfied with that
which she said. ²⁹———— [⌈She acted as⌉] lord, until her son became
strong-armed^g ²⁸. . . . . ²⁵. . . . .^h

---

^aThe Kheti who appears with an unidentified Intef offering homage to Nib-
khru-Re = Mentuhotep at Shatt er - Regâl (cf. § 425) is elsewhere an official of the
same king (§ 426), and his mother's name is Sitre. This renders it possible that
he is the same as the Siut Kheti of our text whose mother was "Si[t] —." Our
Kheti II may therefore have become an official of the Theban Mentuhotep II
after the subjugation of the North. His tomb and inscriptions would then have
been made before the union of North and South, and show no trace of it.

^bThe deceased is the grandfather of Kheti.

^cWith a feminine determinative.   ^dFeminine ending.

^eThis obscure phrase occurs also, Griffith, *Siut*, III, 7.

^fFeminine.   ^gSee Sethe, *Verbum*, § 366, 2.

^hThe remaining fragments are apparently the usual encomium, but too dis-
connected for translation.

THE ELEVENTH DYNASTY

THE ELEVENTH DYNASTY

415. The plan of these volumes does not include dynastic discussion, but a few reasons must nevertheless be offered for the order of the kings here adopted.[a] Any arrangement of the Eleventh Dynasty must proceed from the fact that the war between the Heracleopolitans and Thebans was still going on in the reign of Horus-Wahenekh-Intef. Now, a great-grandson of a Thinite official of this king erected his tombstone at Abydos in the thirty-third year of Sesostris I (§§ 529 ff.). It was therefore not less than four generations from the reign of the said Intef to the thirty-third year of Sesostris I. Allowing 40 years to the generation, this period was some 160 years in length, of which 53 years fell in the Twelfth Dynasty. The close of this Intef's reign was therefore not later than about 100 years before the accession of the Twelfth Dynasty. The war between Thebes and the North, therefore, continued perhaps as late as 100 years before the accession of the Twelfth Dynasty, and Wahenekh-Intef's accession was not later than 150 years before the end of the Eleventh Dynasty, as we know that he reigned at least 50 years (§ 423).

416. Now, the Turin Papyrus gives 160 years as the length of the Eleventh Dynasty,[b] which corresponds admirably with the above result, viz., that the Eleventh Dynasty must have succeeded the Heracleopolitans at the latest 150 years before the rise of the Twelfth Dynasty. The Turin Papyrus had

---

[a]Other indications will be found in connection with the following translations. See also my essay, "New Light on the History of the Eleventh Dynasty," *American Journal of Semitic Languages*, XXI, 163 ff.

[b]The number is 160+x, the x not being more than 9 years, of course. That this total refers to the Eleventh Dynasty is perfectly certain; it immediately precedes the heading of the Twelfth Dynasty, and does not reach back to a beginning point behind the Eleventh Dynasty, because there is a summation preceding the seven kings of the Eleventh Dynasty. See Wilkinson, fragg. 61 and 64.

seven kings in the Eleventh Dynasty, of whom Nibkhrure-
Mentuhotep, Senekhkere-Mentuhotep, and a lost name at the
end were the last three.   The last king, whose name is lost,
was, of course, one who ruled the whole country, and whose
reign shows no trace of war with the North.   Among the
remaining kings of the time the only one who clearly fulfils
these conditions is Nibtowere-Mentuhotep.   The second half
of the dynasty is thus fairly certain.   Working back from
Nibkhrure-Mentuhotep, we find that he was suzerain of a
vassal king, Intef (§ 424), giving us then an Intef and three
Mentuhoteps as the order of this group, thus:

> Intef (other names unknown),
> Nibkhrure-Mentuhotep,
> Senekhkere-Mentuhotep,
> Nibtowere-Mentuhotep.

417. The first and second of these three Mentuhoteps
reigned not less than 74 years.[a]   The third had a prosperous reign, as the inscriptions of his second year in Hammamat show; so that the above three Mentuhoteps may easily
have reigned in all 80 years, and the whole group more than
this.   Now, Horus-Wahenekh-Intef was still reigning some
100 years before the end of the dynasty.   He therefore did
not long precede the above group of four.   But he never
ruled north of Abydos, for on his tombstone in his fiftieth
year he tells of having established his northern frontier
there (§ 423), and his treasurer, Thethi, corroborates this
(§ 423D).   He must therefore have preceded Nibhotep-
Mentuhotep, who openly boasts of having gained the Two
Lands by conquest.   But as Wahenekh-Intef was succeeded
by his son, a second Intef, both these Intefs must have preceded Nibhotep-Mentuhotep, forming a group of three
which evidently immediately preceded the above group of
four.   The only other ruler of the period remaining is the

---

[a]See table on p. 197.

nomarch Intef, who of course should head the line;[a] but he was not included in the Turin Papyrus.

418. We thus obtain seven names in the dynasty, as the Turin Papyrus prescribes. As four of these are Mentuhoteps, we have another proof that there were not more than three Intefs in the Eleventh Dynasty.[b] Thus reconstructed, the dynasty is as follows:

	Years
Horus-Wahenekh-Intef I	50^c $(+x)$
Horus-Nakhtneb-Tepnefer-Intef II . .	x
Nibhotep-Mentuhotep I	x
Intef III (Shatt er-Regâl)[d]	x
Nibkhrure-Mentuhotep II	46^e $(+x)$
Senekhkere-Mentuhotep III . . .	28^f $(+x)$
Nibtowere-Mentuhotep IV	28^g $(+x)$
Total	126 $(+x)$

As the Turin Papyrus gives at least 160 years to the dynasty, we have at least 34 years to be distributed among the seven above x's.

---

[a]As in the erratic Karnak list, Lepsius, *Auswahl der wichtigsten Urkunden*, I: better in *Zwölfte Dynastie;* Prisse, *Monuments*, I; Burton, *Excerpta hieroglyphica*, I. The publications are all very inaccurate; Prisse being probably the best. I had my own copy of the original in the Bibliothèque Nationale. That there may have been a series of Theban kings preceding the list of the dynasty as given in the Turin Papyrus, is perhaps probable, in view of the Intefs and the Mentuhotep who follow the nomarch Intef in the Karnak list.

[b]Steindorff has shown that we have contemporary monuments from only three Intefs before the Twelfth Dynasty (besides the nomarch, *Zeitschrift für ägyptische Sprache*, 1895, 77–96). No one without preconceived opinions will appeal to the Karnak list to prove that the Intefs all ruled before the Twelfth Dynasty. If we are to depend on the Karnak list, then Sesostris I ruled immediately before or after the Seventeenth Dynasty! And such absurdities abound in this list. But accepting this preposterous list as usable, we find that it puts *Nb-ḫpr (w)-Re ͨ*, Intef either just before or just after the Seventeenth Dynasty. Hence Petrie's statement (*History of Egypt*, I, 5th ed., xxi) that "the ancient lists are entirely against" the above arrangement of the Intefs must be rejected. All the other evidence, moreover, is in favor of dividing the Intefs into two groups.

[c]I, 423.

[d]Eduard Meyer writes me that he would not include this vassal king in the dynasty, but would gain the seven kings demanded by the Turin Papyrus, by inserting a Mentuhotep before Intef I, as in the Karnak list. This would give us five Mentuhoteps, thus: Mentuhotep I, two Intefs and four Mentuhoteps in succession; but the value of the erratic Karnak list seems to me very dubious.

[e]Turin Stela of Meru, No. 1447, Cat. I, 117.

[f]His highest date is the year 8; his successor celebrated a Sed Jubilee in his second year, and must therefore have been appointed crown prince 30 years earlier by Mentuhotep III, who thus reigned at least 28 years.

[g]I, 435.

THE NOMARCH, INTEF

MORTUARY STELA[a]

419. The Karnak list[b] places as first of the Intefs a nomarch, without royal title.[c] He is the founder of the Theban line, and is so recognized by Sesostris I, who dedicated a statue to him in Karnak with the inscription: "*The king of Upper and Lower Egypt, Kheperkere (Sesostris I); he made it as his monument for his father, the hereditary prince (rp^c·ty), Intefo, ... born of Ikui (Ykwy).*"[d] The following mortuary stela probably belonged to him.

420. At the top is a three-line inscription, beginning with the usual mortuary formula, for the benefit of

The hereditary prince, count, great lord of the Theban nome, satisfying the king as keeper of the Door[e] of the South, great pillar of him,[f] who makes his Two Lands[f] to live, superior prophet, ... Intef.

---

[a]Limestone stela, discovered by Mariette, in Drah abu-ᵓn-Neggah, now in Cairo, Cat. 20009; also published by him in *Monuments Divers*, 50, *b*, and p. 16; also Maspero, *Guide*, pl. and p. 34; *Dawn*, 115; Petrie, *History of Egypt*, I, 126.

[b]Lepsius, *Auswahl der wichtigsten Urkunden*, I. (See § 417, note.)

[c]The family came from Hermonthis, where they were nomarchs. Inscriptions from the tomb of an Intef, one of these nomarchs, are in Copenhagen and Berlin (No 13272; see Lange, *Zeitschrift für ägyptische Sprache*, 34, 25–35, and plate).

[d]Discovered by Legrain, in March, 1899 (*Recueil*, XXII, 64). The addition of *o* (ᶜᵓ), "*great*," is not found in the royal list of Karnak with the name of the Rp^c·ty Intef; but as there is only one rp^c·ty in the Karnak list, the two must be identical.

[e]See Piehl, *Zeitschrift für ägyptische Sprache*, 1887, 35, and Brugsch, *ibid.*, 1884, 93 f. The title continued from the Sixth Dynasty, into Saite times (IV, 995).

[f]This participial epithet is usually applied to Intef, but this is impossible; for Intef, who acknowledges a king in the phrase, "*satisfying the king*," cannot speak of himself, a mere nomarch, as "*making his two lands live.*" Nor can "*two lands*," so commonly in parallelism with the title "*King of Upper and Lower Egypt*," be made to mean the two shores of the river in Intef's nome. Compare, e. g., § 441, l. 8. Š·ᶜnḫ-tᵓwy is an epithet, like š·mnḫ-sw, designating the king. It is in excellent parallelism with "*king*," and indeed serves as king Senekhkere's Horus-name. This Intef therefore ruled before the rebellion against the North, and the "*king*" referred to is an Heracleopolitan.

REIGN OF HORUS-WAHENEKH-INTEF I

ROYAL TOMB STELA[a]

421. This is the stela referred to in the remarkable passage in the Papyrus Abbott (IV, 514), where it is described as bearing a figure of the king standing with one of his dogs. The name of the dog given in the papyrus, Behka, is still preserved on the stela. It is a Berber name,[b] and the stela accompanies it with a translation into Egyptian. The king stands on the right with his five dogs; before him were seven columns of inscription, of which only the lower half is preserved. The first two lines were occupied with an account of the king's good works for the gods; among these we may discern the following:

I filled his (Amon's) temple with august vases, in order to offer libations. . . . . ———— I built their temples, wrought their stairways, restored their gates, established their divine offerings for all eternity. I ⌜found⌝ ————.

---

[a]Lower portion of a large limestone stela, now about 80 cm. high and 130 cm. wide; now in Cairo, No. 20512. It was discovered in 1860, by Mariette, in the brick pyramid of Intef II, at Drah abu-ᵓ n-Neggah (Thebes). After making an incomplete and inaccurate copy, Mariette left the stela where he found it, to be taken by a fellah, twenty years later, and broken up for use in a sâkieh. Two years later some of the fragments were rescued with much difficulty by Maspero, and installed at Bulâq (now Cairo; cf. *Guide du Visiteur*, 67, and Mariette, *Monuments divers*, Texte, 15; *Transactions of the Society of Biblical Archæology*, IV, 193, 194). Apparently no search has ever been made on the spot for the upper portion, already lacking in Mariette's time. His copy was published in *Monuments divers*, 49 (p. 15 also); another copy by E. de Rougé (*Inscriptions hiéroglyphiques*, 161, 162). I have collated these with a careful copy of the original in Schaefer's manuscript of the Cairo catalogue.

[b]On the Berber name of one of these dogs, see Maspero, *Transactions of the Society of Biblical Archæology*, V, 127, and *Etudes de mythologie et d'archéologie*, III, 331). The others also bore foreign names, and the ancient scribe has appended a translation to each. Daressy (*Recueil*, XI, 79, 80) found a fifth dog; Basset (*Sphinx*, I, 87–92) admits a second name as possibly Berber; see also Birch, *Transactions of the Society of Biblical Archæology*, IV, 172–86. Finally, Maspero explains another name as Berber (*Recueil*, XXI, 136).

422. The statement of his good works is followed by a narrative of his conquest of territory on his northern frontier. He does not state against whom he contended, but it is of course against the Heracleopolitans, defended by the princes of Siut (see § 391). It is the only distinct reference in the Eleventh Dynasty inscriptions to the geographical location of the northern enemy in the civil wars which raged between North (Heracleopolis) and South (Thebes) for at least several generations before the overthrow of the Heracleopolitans.

423. ³———— her northern boundary as far as the nome of Aphroditopolis.ᵃ I drove in the mooring-stakeᵇ in the sacred valley, I captured the entire Thinite nome, I opened all her fortresses, I made her the Door of the North.ᶜ

⁴———— like a flood, great in possessions, like a sea, splendid for the glory of Thebes (*nwˑt*), great for the ⌜— — —⌝ of this land, which I myself have bequeathed to my son,ᵈ ⌜—⌝ ⁵————. There is no lie that has come forth from my mouth, there is no word like that which I have spoken. There was no ⌜violence⌝ for one (dwelling) upon his sandy land, nor —ᵉ for one in possession of his paternal property, nor — — ⁶———— them forever and ever.

Year 50, when this stela was set up ⌜—⌝ by — Horus, Wahenekh (*Wꜣḥ-ꜥnḫ*), King of Upper and Lower Egypt, Son of Re, In[tef], the great (*Yn[tf-]ꜥꜣ*).ᶠ

ᵃRead the serpent and feather. That this is the proper reading is rendered almost certain by the connected data. King Intef is here speaking of the establishment of his northern boundary. The inscription of Intefoker (§§ 529 ff.) shows that he ruled as far north as Akhmim, which is directly across the river from the nome of Aphroditopolis, and the latter is just north of the Thinite nome.

ᵇThis simply means "*I landed*," as in § 612, l. 14; and Papyrus Ebers, 58, 9. Cf. Sethe, *Verbum*, I, 257.

ᶜThis is parallel with the phrase "*Door of the South*" applied to Elephantine. Thus the Aphroditopolite nome under this Intef occupied the same frontier position in the North as the region of the first cataract in the South (see § 396, l. 18, note). I have retained the gender of the pronouns to show this; the Thinite nome is masculine.

ᵈThis is corroborated by the treasurer Thethi (§ 423G).

ᵉPartially broken out; read *ꜥḥꜥ*; it is evidently a synonym of the first word (ꜣr with determinative of bowstring), rendered "*violence*," with which it is parallel.

ᶠThis is the proper reading of the name as shown by l. 7, where it occurs as above restored, preceded by the same Horus-name.

REIGN OF HORUS-NAKHTNEB-TEPNEFER-INTEF II

STELA OF THETHI[a]

423A. This new and important document contains the autobiography of Thethi, the chief treasurer of Intef I and II. It is the first document from the Eleventh Dynasty clearly narrating the succession of the kingship from father to son,[b] and it also places for us the Horus-name of Intef II for the first time.[c] Besides these facts it also gives us the northern and southern boundaries of Intef I's kingdom, although the southern limit given cannot be identified with certainty as yet. The northern boundary is given as Thinis, corroborating Intef I's tomb stela (§ 423); but as Thethi's stela was made after Intef I's death, it is evident that this king never reigned north of that point. The account of Thethi's appointment and duties is also of the greatest interest.

Introduction

423B. ¹⌈⌈Live⌉⌉ Horus: Wahenekh; King of Upper and Lower Egypt, Son of Re, Intef (I), fashioner of beauty, living like Re forever.

Thethi's Titles

423C. His real and favorite servant, having an advanced seat in the house of his lord, great and favorite official, knowing the private

---

[a]Stela seen by G. C. Pier in the hands of a native dealer in 1903. Mr. Pier was able to make only a hurried copy, which he published in the *American Journal of Semitic Languages and Literatures*, April, 1905, 159 ff. The text is in places, therefore, still uncertain. The following translation was also first published, *ibid.*, 163 ff.

[b]But see § 423, l. 4.

[c]In my publication of the text, I overlooked the earlier occurrence of this Intef's Horus-name on a stela at Abydos (Mariette, *Catalogue d'Abydos*, 96, No. 544).

affairs of his lord, following him at all his goings, ⌐great⌐ hearted ²—
in very truth, head of the grandees of the palace, in charge of the seal
in the privy office, one whom his lord trusted more than the grandees,
who delighted the heart of Horus (the king) with that which he desired,
favorite of his lord, his beloved, chief treasurer, in charge of ³the privy
office which his lord loved, chief treasurer, first under the king, the
revered, Thethi (*Ṯ ṱy*), says:

Career under Intef I

423D. I was one beloved of his lord, his favorite every day. I
passed a long period of years under the majesty of my lord, Horus,
Wahenekh, King of Upper and Lower Egypt, ⁴Son of Re, Intef, this
land being under his authority up-river as far as ⌐Thes⌐ and down-river
as far as Thinis; while I was his servant, his subject, his real subordinate. He made me great, he advanced my seat, he set me in his
⁵confidential office, in his palace because of ⌐— —⌐; the treasury was
put in my charge (*m ᶜ y*), under my seal-ring, as one chosen for the sake
of every good thing brought to the majesty of my lord, from South
and from North at every ⌐accounting⌐; for the sake of pleasing (the
king) with the tribute of this whole land; because of his apprehension
lest ⁶this land diminish that which was brought to the majesty of my
lord from the sheiks[a] who are in the Red Land; and because of his
apprehension lest the highlands diminish. Then he gave this (office)
to me, recognizing the excellence of my ability. Then I reported it
to him; never was anything lacking ⁷therein ⌐— —⌐,[b] because of my
great wisdom.

423E. I was one who was a real favorite of his lord, a great and
favorite official, the coolness and the warmth in the house of his lord,
[⌐to whom⌐] the arms were drooped (in respect) among the grandees,
I did not ⌐—⌐[c] behind ⁸the two ⌐—⌐, for which men are hated. I was
one loving good, and hating evil, a character beloved in the house of
his lord, attending to every procedure according to the ⌐—⌐[d] of the
desire of my lord. Now, at every procedure on account of which he
(the king) commanded me to arise ⁹. . . . .[e] I did not exceed

---

[a]Compare § 429.   [b]*Nt ḥsf.*   [c]*Wd,* "*put, place.*"

[d]If this is *ḏ ꜣ dw,* "*audience-hall,*" then *šm · t,* "going" (rendered above "*procedure*"), is literal, viz., "*every going to the audience-hall at the desire, etc.*"

[e]When the king dismissed him, the court arose as he went out. The following
dozen obscure words indicate the compliments of the court as Thethi passed out.

the number[a] which he commanded me; I did not put one thing in the place of another[b] ⌜ — — — — ¹⁰—⌝ I did not take a thing from a legacy, (but) every procedure was attended to.   Now, as for all royal food which the majesty of my lord commanded to give to him, I made for it a list of all that his ka desired; then I rendered it to him; I carried out successfully all their administration; never ¹¹was a thing lacking therein, because of my great wisdom.

Death of Intef I

423F. I made a barge[c] for the city, and a boat[d] for following my lord.[e]   I was counted with the grandees at every time of ⌜— —⌝, while I was honored and great.   I supplied ⌜myself —⌝ ¹²with my own things, which the majesty of my lord gave to me because he so greatly loved me, (even) Horus, Wahenekh, King of Upper and Lower Egypt, Son of Re, Intef (I), living like Re, forever; until he journeyed to his horizon[f] (tomb).

Career under Intef II

423G. Then, when his son assumed his place,¹³ (even) Horus, Nakht-neb-Tepnefer, King of Upper and Lower Egypt, Son of Re, Intef (II), fashioner of beauty, living like Re, forever, I followed him to all his good seats of pleasure.   Never did he ⌜— — —⌝ therein, because of my great wisdom.   He gave me the function ¹⁴which I had in the time of his father, making it to prosper under his majesty, without anything being lacking therein.   I passed all my time on earth, as first under the king, his subject; being mighty and great under his majesty. I was one fulfilling his character, whom his lord praised every day.

---

[a]In treasury business.

[b]Perhaps meaning that in the count he did not substitute less valuable for more valuable things.

[c]*Mẖ*.   [d]*Sẖy.*

[e]One for official use at Thebes, and another for use when the king was on a journey.

[f]This is the brick pyramid-tomb on the western plain of Thebes, containing his mortuary stela (§§ 421, 422), the same tomb which the Ramessid inspectors investigated a thousand years later than this and found uninjured (IV, 514).   It has now disappeared.

REIGN OF NIBHOTEP-MENTUHOTEP I

TEMPLE FRAGMENTS FROM GEBELEN[a]

423H. These scanty fragments tell a remarkable story, not yet noticed, as far as I know, in any of the histories. The first block bears the Horus-name of the king, and thus identifies him as Nibhotep-Mentuhotep[b] (I). It represents him smiting an enemy bearing the inscription: "*Chief of Tehenu and* ⌜—⌝." The second block represents the king again smiting the enemy, four in number. The king bears the inscription: "*Son of Hathor, Mistress of Dendera, Mentuhotep.*" The first enemy is without inscription, but represents an Egyptian![c] The other three are designated as: "*Nubians, Asiatics (sttyw), Libyans.*[d]" Over the whole is the inscription: "*Binding the chiefs of the Two Lands, capturing the South and Northland, the highlands and the two regions, the Nine Bows and the Two Lands*" (sic!). The king makes no distinction between his victories over foreign foes and his conquest of Egypt itself, and actually places the figure of the conquered Egyptian among those of the barbarians on the temple wall. Mentu-

---

[a]Inscribed blocks, now in Cairo, from a temple of Mentuhotep I at Gebelen, which had been rebuilt into a Ptolemaic temple wall. They have been very inaccurately published by Daressy (*Recueil*, XIV, 26, and XVI, 42); much better by Frazer (*Proceedings of the Society of Biblical Archæology*, XV, 409, Pl. XV). Fortunately, I also found Erman's copy of them among the Lexicon manuscripts.

[b]The Intef-custom of putting "*Son of Re*" within the cartouche is observable here.

[c]Overlooked by Daressy; and seemingly not identified by Frazer.

[d]Of these three, the first two are the same in appearance; the Libyan as usual wears a feather. They symbolize the foes of Egypt on south, east, and west, in harmony with the same king's inscription on the Island of Konosso (Lepsius, *Denkmäler*, II, 150, *b* = de Morgan, *Catalogue des monuments*, 73, 44) which states: "*all countries are beneath his feet.*"

hotep I therefore acquired the land of Egypt by conquest, and made no effort to conceal the source of his title by pretense to legitimacy.   It was evidently this conquest which overthrew the Heracleopolitans of the Tenth Dynasty. Hence the reign of Mentuhotep I marks the conclusion of the war with the North.   The place of his reign is clearly after Intef II, and before the last three Mentuhoteps who controlled the whole country.[a]

---

[a]Schaefer states that similar representations were found by Borchardt in the temple of Nuserre at Abusir.   The conception may therefore be more general than I have supposed above.   See also Papyrus Anastasi II, II, 7, for similar statements concerning Ramses II.

REIGNS OF INTEF III AND NIBKHRURE-MENTUHOTEP II

RELIEFS NEAR ASSUAN

424. The Intef whom we have called the third, appears in no other monuments which can be identified as his, because we do not know his other names. He can hardly be the same as the preceding Intef II, from whom he is separated by Mentuhotep I. He was obliged to give way to another member of the family, Mentuhotep II, who permitted him to reign as a vassal.

425. The most important of Mentuhotep II's monuments[a] is the relief on the rocks at Shatt er-Regâl, near Assuan,[b] where, accompanied by his mother, a lady not of royal lineage, he receives the homage of this vassal, King Intef, who is ushered into the royal presence by Mentuhotep II's chief treasurer, Kheti. This Kheti was an important officer, who appears again on the rocks near Assuan in the presence of Mentuhotep II, with the following inscription:[c]

426. Year 41,[d] under (the majesty of) Nibkhrure (Nb-$ḥrw$-R^c), came the wearer of the royal seal, sole companion, chief treasurer, Kheti, born of Sitre,[e] triumphant; and ships to Wawat ⌜— — — —⌝.

---

[a]See list, Maspero, *Dawn*, 462, n. 1.

[b]*Proceedings of the Society of Biblical Archæology*, 1881, 99, 100; Petrie, *Season in Egypt*, XVI, 489; not in de Morgan, *Catalogue des monuments*; *Dawn*, 463.

[c]Petrie, *Season in Egypt*, VIII, No. 213. I had also a photograph, kindly loaned me by Professor Petrie.

[d]His highest date, "*year 46*," is on the tablet of Meru at Turin (No. 1447, *Catalogue Turin*, I, 117).

[e]This Kheti may be the same as Kheti II at Assiut. See § 405, and § 414, l. 38, note.

This was doubtless an expedition against the Nubians of Wawat. Mentuhotep II's inscriptions are elsewhere not infrequent, but contain only a word or two, chiefly his titles. His appearance on the monuments of later generations is such as to show that he was regarded as the first great king of the Theban line.

REIGN OF SENEKHKERE-MENTUHOTEP III

HAMMAMAT INSCRIPTION OF HENU[a]

427. As the only document of Mentuhotep III, this inscription is of great historical importance. The lists of Sakkara and Abydos show him as the immediate predecessor of the Twelfth Dynasty and the successor of the powerful Mentuhotep II; but the Turin Papyrus has after his, a lost name belonging to the last king of the dynasty. Mentuhotep III's minister, Henu, drew men for this Hammamat expedition from territory between Oxyrrhyncus and Gebelen (l. 10), which shows that practically all of Egypt above the Delta was under this king's rule. The Delta was also certainly subject to Senekhkere, for Henu calls himself (l. 8) one *"who quells the Haunebu,"* the peoples of the distant north in the Mediterranean, who could only be reached in the Delta.

Introduction

428. [1]Year 8, first month of the third season (ninth month), day 3; [2]his real favorite servant, who does all that he praises every day, wearer of the royal seal, [sole] com[panion], — overseer of that which is and that which is not, overseer of the temples, overseer of the granary and White House, [3]overseer of horn and hoof, chief of the six courts of justice, high-voiced in proclaiming the name of the king on the day of warding off ⌜—⌝ who judges the prisoner according to his desert. . . . . [7]. . . . . . . [b] Satisfying the heart of the king as keeper of

---

[a]Cut on the rocks in the Wadi Hammamat. Text: Lepsius, *Denkmäler*, II, 150, *a;* better, Golénischeff, *Hammamat*, XV–XVII. For old literature, see Maspero, *Dawn*, 495, n. 1. I had also a collation of the Berlin squeeze by Mr. Alan Gardiner, which he kindly permitted me to use.

[b]The omitted lines contain similar but exaggerated epithets indicating Henu's high rank and great power; but no formal titles; omissions of similar character follow.

the Door of the South; over the [8]administration of the nomes of the South, chief treasurer . . . . who quells (*š·bdš*) the Haunebu (*Ḥᵓ-nbw*), to whom the Two Lands come bowing down, to whom every office reports; wearer of the royal seal, sole companion, [9]the steward, Henu says:

Preparation for the Expedition

429. [My lord, life, prosperity],[a] health! sent me to dispatch a ship to Punt to bring for him fresh[b] myrrh from the sheiks over the Red Land, by reason of the fear of him in the highlands. Then I went[c] forth from Koptos [10]upon the road, which his majesty commanded me. There was with me an army of the South from —[d] of the Oxyrrhyncus nome, the beginning thereof[e] as far as Gebelen; the end thereof as far as ⌐—⌐;[f] every office of the king's house, those who were in town and field, united, came after me. The army ⌐—⌐ cleared the way [11]before, overthrowing those hostile toward the king, the hunters and the children of the highlands[g] were posted as the protection of my limbs. Every official body of his majesty was placed under my authority. They reported messengers to me, as one alone commanding, to whom many hearken.

Departure and Provisions

430. I went forth with an army of 3,000 men. [12]I made the road a river, and the Red Land (desert) a stretch of field,[h] for I gave a leathern bottle, a carrying pole (*sṭs*), 2 jars[i] of water and 20 loaves to each one among them every day.[j] The asses were laden with sandals ⌐— — — —⌐.

---

[a]Restored from Hammamat inscription of Amenemhet (vizier), § 446, l. 7 Lepsius, *Denkmäler*, II, 149. *e*, l. 7.

[b]Read *wᵓḏ*.

[c]No lacuna as in Lepsius, *Denkmäler*.   [e]Read *šᵓᶜym*.

[d]See same phrase, § 442, l. 13.   [f]Read *šᵓbt*.

[g]This passage indicates a campaign before the expedition, in order to clear the country of the Troglodytes.

[h]See a similar statement by the vizier Amenemhet (§ 447, l. 10). The same rare phrase "*stretch* or *tract of field*" (ᶜᵓd) occurs also in Sinuhe (Berlin, ll. 9, 10).

[i]Read *ḏš* later *dš*.

[j]The loaves are small like the German "Brödchen." The "*every day*" doubtless applies only to the last two articles, the rest being intended for carrying the rations. At the rate of 60,000 loaves a day, this expedition (which could not have lasted less than a month) consumed 1,800,000 loaves, which they must have brought with them from Coptos. Water skins could be replenished at the quarries. See the elaborate arrangements of Ramses IV for provisioning his expedition (IV, 467).

Wells Dug

431. Now, I made 12 wells[a] in the bush, [13]and two wells in Idehet (*Yd'ḥt*), 20 ⌜square⌝ cubits[b] in one, and 31 ⌜square⌝ cubits[b] in the other. I made another in Iheteb (*Y'ḥtb*), 20 by 20 cubits on each side ⌜— — — —⌝.

Ship Built and Sent

432. Then I reached the (Red) Sea; then I made this ship, and I dispatched it[c] with everything, when I had made for it a great oblation of cattle, bulls and [14]ibexes.

Return and Quarrying at Hammamat

433. Now, after my return from the (Red) Sea, I executed the command of his majesty, and I brought for him all the gifts, which I had found in the regions of God's-Land. I returned through the ⌜valley⌝[d] of Hammamat, I brought for him august blocks for statues belonging to the temple. Never was brought down the like thereof for the king's court; never [15]was done the like of this by any king's-confidant sent out since the time of the god. I did this for the majesty of my lord because he so much loved me.............[e]

---

[a]Mr. Griffith (*Proceedings of the Society of Biblical Archæology*, XIV, 420), has read the sign before 12 as a measure of area; giving "*a well of 12 — ?*" As this would leave the word "*well*" without either determinative or feminine ending, it is improbable. The sign in question is more probably a part of the word for well (*nm*), giving *ḥnmt* as usual.

[b]See Mr. Griffith, *ibid.*

[c]Henu only equipped and dispatched the ship, but did not accompany it to Punt; he then returned to Egypt by way of Hammamat (l. 14).

[d]Possibly *W'g*, another land.

[e]Further asseverations of the king's favor follow. The same obscure phrases also Lepsius, *Denkmäler*, II, 149, *e*, l. 13 = Golénischeff, *Hammamat*, XIII l. 13.

REIGN OF NIBTOWERE-MENTUHOTEP IV

HAMMAMAT INSCRIPTIONS[a]

434. These are among the most important of the Hammamat inscriptions. Besides their unusual archæological interest, they throw great light on the reign of Nibtowere-Mentuhotep (IV), from whom we have no other inscriptional material. They show clearly that the wars with the North (Heracleopolis), had long ceased, and that the North was now united under his rule; for he had an army of 3,000 men from the Delta to transport the lid block of his sarcophagus to Egypt (§ 453, l. 21; similar indications in § 451, 3, ll. 8–10). The only place that he can have held in the series of Eleventh Dynasty kings is therefore at the end of that dynasty. The place of Mentuhotep II and III is certain from the Turin Papyrus. Our Mentuhotep cannot precede Mentuhotep II, who supplanted an Intef; nor does the Turin Papyrus permit him to follow Mentuhotep II. The only place open after the close of the war with the North is at the end of the dynasty after Mentuhotep III, where the Turin Papyrus shows a lost name.

I. THE FIRST WONDER[b]

435. A relief shows the king offering wine before Min of Coptos; behind the king are the words: *"First occurrence*

---

[a]Cut on the rock-walls of the Wadi Hammamat. Text: Lepsius, *Denkmäler*, II, 149, *c* to *g*; Golénischeff, Hammamat, X–XV; and partially in the manuscripts of Nestor l'Hôte in the Bibliothèque Nationale, Paris. I had also collations of the Berlin squeezes by Mr. Alan Gardiner, of which he very kindly gave me the use.

[b]Lepsius, *Denkmäler*, II, 149, *c* = Golénischeff, *Hammamat*, X. Copy in manuscript of Nestor l'Hôte; translated by Erman, *Zeitschrift für ägyptische Sprache*, 1891, 60.

of the Sed Jubilee; at the top the date: *Year 2,*[a] *second month of the first season (second month), day 3."*

436. Then the following:

[1]This wonder which happened to his majesty: that the beasts[b] of the [2]highlands came down to him; there came a gazelle great with young, going with her face toward the people before her, [3]while her eyes looked ⌜backward⌝; (but) she did not turn back, until she arrived at this august mountain,[4]at this block, it being still in its place, (intended) for[c] this lid of this sarcophagus. She dropped her young upon it while this army of [5]the king was looking. Then they cut off her neck ⌜before⌝[d] it (the block) and brought fire. [6]It descended in safety.[e]

437. Now, it was the majesty of this august god, [7]lord of the highlands, who gave the offering (*mꜣꜥ*) to his son, Nibtowere (*Nb-tꜣwy-Rꜥ*), Mentuhotep IV, living forever, in order that his heart might be joyful, that he might [8]live upon his throne forever and forever, that he might celebrate millions of Sed Jubilees.

438. [9]The hereditary[f] prince, count, governor of the city and vizier, chief of all nobles of judicial office, supervisor of that which heaven gives, the earth creates, and the Nile brings, supervisor of everything in this whole land, the vizier, Amenemhet.

II. THE OFFICIAL TABLET[g]

439. The above prodigy, which doubtless occurred soon after their arrival, found record twelve days before the official record of the expedition, which is as follows:

---

[a]This king was therefore nominated as crown prince 28 years before his father's death, as he celebrates his 30-years' jubilee in his second year. Thus Mentuhotep III reigned at least 28 years.

[b]Suggested by Gardiner; Erman: *"Gebirgs (arbeiter)."*

[c]Undoubtedly this explanation of Erman is correct.

[d]Read *ẖnt-ḥrf?* l'Hôte shows a *šms*-sign before *ḥr·f;* and Gardiner saw a similar sign. The soldiers sacrificed the gazelle upon the block.

[e]That is, the block reached Egypt in safety.

[f]The leader of the expedition here adds his name and titles. A double line separates them from the king's inscription above them.

[g]Lepsius, *Denkmäler,* II, 149, *d* = Golénischeff, *Hammamat,* XI.

Date

440. [1]Year 2, second month of the first season, day 15, [2](of) Nibtowere-Mentuhotep[a] (IV) living forever.

Erection of Stela

441. [3]His majesty commanded to erect[b] this stela to his father Min, lord of the highlands in this [4]august, primeval mountain, ... [5]. . . . . [6]. . . . .[c] in order that his ka may be satisfied and that the god may [—] in his desire, as [7]does a king who is upon the great throne, first in thrones; enduring in monuments, excellent god, lord of joy, [8]mighty in fear, great in love, heir of Horus in his Two Lands, whom [9]the divine Isis, Min, and Mut, the great sorceress reared for the dominion [10]of the two regions of Horus, King of Upper and Lower Egypt, Nibtowere (Mentuhotep IV), living like Re, forever; [11]he says:

Dispatch of Expedition

442. My majesty sent forth the hereditary prince, governor of the city and vizier, chief of [12]works, favorite of the king, Amenemhet, with an army of 10,000[d] men [13]from the southern nomes, Middle[e] Egypt, and the [—][f] of the Oxyrrhyncus [14]nome; to bring for me an august block of the pure costly stone which is in this mountain, [15]whose[g] excellent things[l] Min makes; for a sarcophagus, an eternal memorial, and for monuments [16]in the temples of Middle Egypt,[h] according as a king over the Two Lands sends [17]to bring for himself the desire of his heart, from the highlands of his father Min.

---

[a]Full five-name titulary.

[b]The word "*erect*" (lit., "*cause to stand*") is here loosely used from habit, although the inscription is cut on a natural wall of rock, which could not have been "erected."

[c]Eulogistic epithets of the god.

[d]Gardiner gives the sign as certain; Golénischeff also has apparently a finger (= 10,000); both give the top pointing wrong, but this is a peculiarity of the Hammamat inscriptions (cf. Henu, Lepsius, *Denkmäler*, III, 150, *a*, l. 7, thrice!) and is only one of many instances of the influence of the hieratic in these texts. This peculiarity occurs frequently also in the Assiut texts of the same period. Cf. the 8,368 men of a later expedition, IV, 466.

[e]*Šm ꜥ w*, perhaps "*South.*"

[f]*Ḥnty* written only with the nose; determinative house.

[g]Referring to "*stone*" (feminine).   [h]*Šm ꜥ w*, perhaps "*South.*"

Dedication

443. He made (it) as his monument for his father Min of Koptos, lord of the highlands, head of the Troglodytes, in order that he (the king) might celebrate very many [Sed Jubilees], living like Re, forever.[a]

III.   THE COMMANDER'S TABLET[b]

444. On the same day, Amenemhet, the commander of the expedition, engraved his own record of the achievement, as follows:

Date and Introduction

445. [1]Year 2, second month of the first season, day 15. Royal commission, executed by the hereditary prince, count, governor of the city, chief judge, favorite of the king, chief of works, distinguished in his office, great in his rank, with advanced place in [3]the house of his lord, commanding the official body, chief of the six courts of justice, judging the people ($p^{c\cdot}t$) and the inhabitants ($rḥy\cdot t$), and hearing ⌈causes⌉; to whom the great come bowing down, [4]and the whole land, prone upon the belly; whose offices his lord advanced; his favorite, as keeper of the Door of the South; conducting for him millions of the inhabitants ($rḥy\cdot t$) to do for him the desire of his heart [5]toward his monuments, enduring on earth; magnate of the King of Upper Egypt, great one of the King of Lower Egypt, conductor of the palace, ⌈— —⌉ in stretching the measuring-cord; judging without partiality, governor of the whole South, to whom is reported [6]that which is and that which is not; conducting the administration of the Lord of the Two Lands; ⌈zealous⌉ of heart upon a royal commission; commander of those that command, conductor of overseers; the vizier of the king, at his audiences, Amenemhet, [7]says:

Choice of Amenemhet

446. My lord, the king of Upper and Lower Egypt, Nibtowere ($Nb-t^{\jmath}wy-R^c$, Mentuhotep IV) living forever, sent me, as one sending, in whom are divine members; to establish his monument in [8]this land. He chose me before his city, I was preferred before his court.

---

[a]There is an appendix here of the twenty-seventh or twenty-eighth day, which is the latest date in the series; it is translated at the end (§§ 452, 453).

[b]Lepsius, *Denkmäler*, II, 149, e = Golénischeff, *Hammamat*, XII, XIII; manuscripts of Nestor l'Hôte.

Personnel of Expedition

447. Now, his majesty commanded that there go forth to this august highland ⁹an army with me, men of the choicest of the whole land: miners, artificers, quarrymen, artists, draughtsmen, stonecutters, gold-ʳworkersᴸ, ¹⁰treasurers of Pharaoh, of every department of the White House, and every office of the king's-house, united behind me. I made the highlands a river, and the upper valleys ¹¹a water-way.ᵃ

Return with Sarcophagus

448. I brought for him a sarcophagus, an eternal memorial, an everlasting reminder. Never descended its like in this highland since the time of the god. ¹²My soldiers descended without loss; not a man perished, not a troop was missing, not an ass died, not a workman was enfeebled. It happened for the majesty of my lord ¹³as a distinction, which Min wrought for him because he so much loved him, that his ka might endure upon the great throne in the kingdom of the two regions of Horus. ʳHe made (it) as something greater than it.ᴸᵇ I am his favorite servant, who does all that he praises every day.

IV.　THE SECOND WONDER ᶜ

449. Eight days after the erection of the two preceding records, a second wonder occurred, which was immediately recorded on the rocks, as follows:

Date

450. ¹King of Upper and Lower Egypt, Nibtowere (*Nb-tʾwy-Rᶜ*, Mentuhotep IV) who liveth forever, born of the king's mother, Imi (*Ymy*), second month of the first season, day 23.

ᵃReferring to the desert march. See the similar, but more explicit, statement of Henu on the same march, § 430, l. 12. According to the figures given there, this expedition consumed 200,000 loaves a day! (See note, *ibid.*)

ᵇGrammatically, the sentence is clear, but its meaning? The same phrase in Henu, l. 16.

ᶜGolénischeff, *Hammamat*, XIV = Lepsius, *Denkmäler*, II, 149 f.

Rain and a Well

451. One set[a] to work [2]in this mountain on the ⌈lid⌉ block[b] of the sarcophagus.   The wonder was repeated, rain was made, the forms of this god appeared, [3]his fame was shown to men, the highland was made a lake,[c] the water went to the ⌈margin⌉ of the stone,[d] a well was found in the midst of the valley, [4]10 cubits by 10 cubits on its every side, filled with fresh water, to its edge, undefiled, kept pure and cleansed from gazelles, concealed [6]from Troglodyte barbarians.   Soldiers of old, and kings who had lived aforetime, went out and returned by its side, no eye had seen it, the face of man had not fallen upon it, (but) to his majesty himself it was revealed. . . . . [8]. . . . . .[e]   Those who were in Egypt (*Tꜣ-mry*) heard it, [9]the people who were in Egypt (*Km·t*), South and Northland (Delta),[f] they bowed their heads to the ground, [10]they praised the goodness of his majesty forever and ever.

V.   COMPLETION OF THE WORK[g]

452. On the twenty-eighth day of the month the work was completed, and the following appendix was added to the king's official stela:

453. [19]Day 28.   The lid of this sarcophagus descended, being a block 4 cubits, by 8 cubits, by 2 cubits,[h] [20]on coming forth from the work.   Cattle were slaughtered, goats were slain, incense was put [21]on the fire.   Behold, an army of 3,000 sailors of the nomes of the Northland (Delta) followed it in safety to Egypt.

---

[a]Lit.: "*laying the hand on the work.*"   The form is an infinitive, the same construction continuing to the end of l. 5.

[b]I am not quite certain that this rendering is correct; it is lit.: "*laid or set block of the sarcophagus.*"

[c]Water in the highland was always remarkable; compare Kheti's feat (§ 407) who "*made the elevated land a swamp*" by means of a canal.

[d]Might also be "*lake.*"

[e]Obscure references to the discovery as a favor to the king.

[f]It is clear that Nibtowere governs all Egypt.

[g]Lepsius, *Denkmäler*, II, 149, *d* = Golénischeff, *Hammamat*, XI.

[h]About 6 feet, 9 inches wide, 13 feet, 9 inches long, and 3 feet, 5 inches thick.

TABLET OF SENEKH[a]

454. This tablet does not belong to the same expedition as the preceding, but it narrates the attempts to settle with people the desert stations in Hammamat, and along the road from Coptos to the Red Sea.

455. Nibtowere (Mentuhotep IV), living forever. Commander of troops in the highlands, steward in Egypt, commander of ⌜—⌝ on the river, Senekh ($S^c nḫ$), says:

456. I was commander of the troops of this entire land in this highland, equipped with water skins[b] ($šdw$), ⌜baskets,⌝ with bread, beer, and every fresh vegetable of the South. I made its valleys green, and its heights pools of water; settled with children throughout, southward to Thau ($T^{ɔc}w$) and northward to Menet-Khufu ($Mn^{c\cdot}t$-$Ḫfw$). I went forth to the sea (Red Sea), I hunted adults, I hunted cattle. I went forth to this highland with 60 people of years, and 70 young ones of the children[c] of one (woman). I did all correctly for Nibtowere (Mentuhotep IV), living forever.

STELA OF ETI[d]

457. This biography of an active official is of interest as showing the agricultural and industrial conditions in the Middle Kingdom, when the skilful administration of resources by the governing princes was necessary to prevent a famine. Eti was so successful in this respect that he even conveyed surplus grain to neighboring towns, and Thebes, sent to him for supplies.

---

[a]Cut on the rocks at Wadi Hammamat; published by Lepsius, *Denkmäler*, II, 149, *g;* and Newberry, *Beni Hasan*, II, 18 (where the translation is misleading). I had also a collation of the Berlin squeeze, kindly loaned to me by Mr. Alan H. Gardiner.

[b]Gardiner.

[c]Or: "*I went forth to this desert as a man of 60 years, and 70 little children, the offspring of one (woman);*" "*offspring*" or "*children*" ($ms\cdot w$) is of course used in sense of "descendants."

[d]Limestone stela (0.47 m. by 0.75 m.) from Gebelên, now in Cairo, *Catalogue,* 20001; also published by Daressy, *Recueil,* XIV, 21.

458. An interesting reference in ll. 7, 8, where Eti states, *"I followed my great lord, I followed my small lord,"* may possibly indicate that we are to refer this document to the early Eleventh Dynasty, when the Theban princes ruled above Thebes, but were not yet kings. The powerful Theban prince would then be Eti's *"great lord,"* and the local nomarch his *"small lord."* In accordance with this, his field of activity did not extend below Thebes.

459. [1]The assistant treasurer Eti[a] (*Yty*); he says:

"I was an excellent citizen (*nds*), achieving with his strength, the great pillar [2]in the nome of Thebes, Nehebkauf[b] in the upper country (*ḫnty·t*). I sustained (*s·ᶜnḫ*) [3]Gebelên[c] during unfruitful years, there being 400 men ⌈in distress⌉. [4]But I took not the daughter of a man, I took not his field. I made ten herds of goats, [5]with people in charge of each herd; I made two herds of cattle and a herd of asses. I raised all (kinds of) small cattle. I made 30 ships, (then) [6]30 other ships, and I brought grain (*rsy*) for Eni (*Yny*)[d] and Hefat[e] (*Ḥfꜣ·t*), after Gebelên was sustained. The nome of Thebes [7]went up-stream.[f] Never [g]did one below or above Gebelên bring to another district.[g] I followed [8]my great lord, I followed my small lord, and nothing was lost therein. I built a house ⌈—⌉, filled with every luxury. The people said: "He is innocent of violence to another."

His beloved eldest son,[h]— made it for him.

---

[a]He was also *"wearer of the royal seal, and sole companion."*

[b]An uncertain epithet, *"who controls his ka's,"* also applied to a well-known mortuary god.

[c]*Yw-mytrw.*   [d]Eni is probably Esneh (*Yny·t*).

[e]Tuphium. Same as the Ophieion of the Cornelius Gallus inscription at Philae; see Sethe, *Sitzungsberichte der Berliner Akademie,* 1896, 482; it is located on the east bank of the Nile, between Thebes and Hermonthis.

[f]Probably for supplies.

[g]Or: *"never did Gebelên send down-stream or up-stream* (⌈dy⌉ *ḫd ḫnt) to another district"* (namely, to procure supplies).

[h]The name of the son is lacking, but one surviving sign would indicate that it was also *Yty.*

THE TWELFTH DYNASTY

CHRONOLOGY OF THE TWELFTH DYNASTY

460. As the chronology of the Twelfth Dynasty is more fully and accurately known to us than that of any dynasty in or before the Empire, it has seemed necessary to insert a statement of it, with a reconstruction based on the latest data from the monuments. The contemporary monuments and the Turin Papyrus enable us to make the following table[a] of the dynasty (excluding coregencies):

Amenemhet I	20[b] years
(10 years more with his son)[c]	
Sesostris I	42[d] "
(at least 3 years more with his son)[e]	
Amenemhet II	32[f] "
(at least 3 years more with his son)[f]	
Sesostris II	19[g] "
Sesostris III	38[h] "
(coregency of uncertain length with son)	
Amenemhet III	48[i] "
(coregency of uncertain length with his son)[j]	
Amenemhet IV	9 y., 3 m., 27 d.[k]
Sebeknefrure	3 y., 10 m., 24 d.[k]

[a]See Sethe, *Zeitschrift für ägyptische Sprache*, 41, 38 ff.

[b]The stela of Intef in Cairo bears the double date: "*Year 30 of Amenemhet I, Year 10 of Sesostris I*" (Mariette, *Abydos*, II, 22 = Rougé, *Inscriptions hiéroglyphiques*, VIII = Rougé, *Album photographique*, No. 146; = Mariette, *Catalogue général d'Abydos*, 104, No. 558).

[c]Amenemhet I died in the thirtieth year of his reign. See Tale of Sinuhe (§ 491).

[d]The stela of Upwaweto at Leyden (V., 4) bears the double date: "*Year 44 of Sesostris I = Year 2 of Amenemhet II*" (Lepsius, *Auswahl der wichtigsten Urkunden*, Pl. 10; Lepsius, *Zwölfte Dynastie*, II, No. 4; also my own photograph of the original; and the Turin Papyrus gives him 45 years, so that he must have ruled 3 years with his son.

[e]On the stela of Simontu (§ 594), Sesostris I is still living in the third year of Amenemhet II.

[f]The inscription of Hapu at Assuan (§ 614).

[g]Kahun papyri of the second find, fragment transliterated by Borchardt and distributed in private copies at the Congress of Orientalists, Rome, 1899.

[h]The highest date on the monuments is year 33 (Griffith, *Kahun Papyri*, II, 85). Sethe's reconstruction of the Turin Papyrus proves that 38 is to be restored.

[i]The highest date is year 46 (*ibid*, 86); 48 is certain from Sethe's reconstruction.

[j]Lepsius, *Auswahl der wichtigsten Urkunden*, 10; Prisse, *Monuments égyptiens*, 9; its length is unknown.

[k]Turin Papyrus, see above.

461. The Turin Papyrus gives 213 years, 1 month, and 17 days, as the total length of the dynasty.

The Sothis date in the Kahun Papyri enables us to establish the date of the accession of Amenemhet I as 2000 B. C.[a]

462. We may then construct the following table:[b]

	Length	Date B. C.	Coregencies
Amenemhet I.....	30 years	2000–1970	2000–1980 alone 1980–1970 with his son
Sesostris I........	45 "	1980–1935	1980–1970 with his father 1970–1938 alone 1938–1935 with his son
Amenemhet II....	35 "	1938–1903	1938–1935 with his father 1935–1906 alone 1906–1903 with his son
Sesostris II.......	19 "	1906–1887	1906–1903 with his father 1903–1887 alone
Sesostris III......	38 "	1887–1849	Uncertain period with son
Amenemhet III...	48 "	1849–1801	Uncertain period with father[c]
Amenemhet IV[d] ..	9 "	1801–1792	
Sebeknefrure	4 "	1792–1788	

[a]Borchardt, *Zeitschrift für ägyptische Sprache*, 37, 99 ff.; Mahler, *ibid.*, 40, 83; Meyer's calculation (*Aegyptische Chronologie*, 51, 52, 57, 58) has slightly modified the date as calculated by Borchardt and Mahler, without affecting the principle employed, carrying back the beginning of the dynasty to 2000 B. C.

[b]This table differs considerably in the last four reigns from that given by Mahler (*Zeitschrift für ägyptische Sprache*, 40, 83–85, and *Orientalistische Litteraturzeitung*, June, 1902, 248 f.), as he unfortunately has overlooked the higher dates in the reigns of Sesostris III and Amenemhet III, found since the publication of Brugsch's and Meyer's tables, upon which Mahler depends.

[c]The coronation of Amenemhet III as coregent with his father was narrated on the walls of a temple probably that of Crocodilopolis in the Fayûm. Fragments of the inscription are preserved in Berlin (Nos. 15801–4), and published in *Aegyptische Inschriften aus den Königlichen Museen*, III, 138. The coronation inscription of Hatshepsut at Der el-Bahri was copied from this of Amenemhet III. I am indebted for these facts to my friend, Mr. Alan H. Gardiner, who kindly called my attention to them.

[d]The length of his coregency with his father is unknown, and hence not indicated in years.

The opposite table is as nearly correct as the astronomical data will permit, the most nearly accurate of all the Egyptian dynasties back of the Twenty-sixth, and the earliest series of absolute dates known in history, in spite of the margin of four years within which each date falls.

REIGN OF AMENEMHET I

INSCRIPTION OF KHNUMHOTEP I[a]

463. Khnumhotep I was the first of the powerful Beni-hasan nobles in the Twelfth Dynasty of whom we have any account. He was evidently of service to Amenemhet I during that king's final and successful struggle for the mastery and the crown of Egypt. The text is in such a fragmentary state that much must be read between the lines. It is, however, clear that Khnumhotep accompanied the king on an expedition in which "*20 ships of cedar*" were engaged, which resulted in expelling a certain foe from Egypt (l. 5). This foe, referred to only by the pronoun "*him*," whom it was necessary to expel from Egypt, must almost certainly have been one of Amenemhet's rivals for the crown. Then follows the submission of foreign foes, the Asiatic in the North and the Negro in the South, and of highland and lowland alike ("*the two regions,*" l. 6). This accomplished, the king rewards his faithful adherents, and Khnumhotep is made "*count of Menet-Khufu*" (l. 7) where he ruled to the complete satisfaction of the king.

464. His titles are:[b] "*Hereditary prince and count, wearer of the royal seal, sole companion, ⌜—⌝ great lord of the Oryx nome ⌜— —⌝, attached to Nekhen (judge)*." This shows that he was later intrusted with the entire principality of the Oryx, in agreement with the statements of his grandson, Khnumhotep II, whose long inscription narrates the

---

[a]Tomb No. 14 at Benihasan; first noticed and copied by Newberry and published by Newberry, *Beni Hasan*, I, Pl. XLIV; see also p. 84 and II, 7, 8. The text is painted on the west wall, and is exceedingly fragmentary.

[b]*Ibid.*, II, Pl. XLIV, l. 1.

same appointments of his grandfather and follows the history of the family (§§ 619 ff.) in this fief for several generations.

465. I came out from my city, I went to [my nome]. Never did I commit evil against a man. . . . . 4. . . . . Then appointed me [my lord] the King of Upper and Lower Egypt, ⁵Sehetepibre (*Shtp-yb-R ͨ*), Son of Re: Amenemhet (I) living forever and ever, to the ⌐office⌐ — —. I went down with his majesty to ⌐—⌐,ᵃ in twenty ships of cedar ⌐which⌐ he ⌐led⌐, coming to —. He expelled him from the two regions (Egypt). ⁶Negroes ⌐— —⌐, Asiatics, fell; he seized the lowland, the highlands, in the two regions ⌐— —⌐ with the people — remain in their positions ⌐— —⌐ — — — ⌐— —⌐ ₇————. Then his majesty appointed me as count of Menet-Khufu. My administration was excellent in the heart of his majesty, pleasant in —. Then I ⌐—⌐ my city, I benefited my people. His majesty caused to be done for me, that which my mouth uttered ⌐— — —⌐ ⁸— the — were —, the — were —, its taxpayers were —, the citizens were servants. . . . .

HAMMAMAT INSCRIPTION OF INTEFᵇ

466. This inscription records the only official expedition of Amenemhet I to Hammamat of which we know anything.ᶜ Only one block is mentioned, for which Intef spent eight days in a vain search, and only succeeded in finding it after propitiating the local gods.

ᵃThere must have been a geographical name here, which is corrupt in the original or has been imperfectly read.

ᵇCut on the rocks of Wadi Hammamat; published by Lepsius, *Denkmäler*, II, 118, d=Golénischeff, *Hammamat*, VIII=Maspero, *VIIIe Congrés International des Orientalistes, Section africaine*, 50–54. I had also a collation of the Berlin squeeze, kindly loaned me by Gardiner. It is, like all the Hammamat inscriptions, strongly influenced by the hieratic; the graver, who did not know hieratic, has then so corrupted the scribe's sketch that much of it is unintelligible.

ᶜThe other Hammamat inscription bearing his name (Golénischeff, *Hammamat*, II, 4=Maspero, *ibid.*, 156), is incomplete; it does not record an official, but a private expedition, and the introduction, containing references to the safe conduct of the expedition ("*I returned . . . . . none missing, none dead*") does not

467. Above is the full titulary of Amenemehet I, without further date. Then follow the titles of Intef:[a] *"Hereditary prince and count, wearer of the royal [seal], sole companion, royal messenger, superior prophet of Min.* After the conventional series of personal epithets (ll. 2–6), his narrative then proceeds:

468. [6]......... My lord sent me to Hammamat, to bring this august stone; never was brought its like since the time of the god. There was no hunter who knew [7]the marvel of it, none that sought it reached it. I spent 8 days searching this highland; I knew not the ⌈place⌉ wherein it was. I prostrated myself to Min, to Mut, to ⌈—⌉ Great-in-Magic, and all the gods of this highland, giving to them incense upon the fire. The land brightened at early morning,[b] I ⌈— —⌉ [8]to go forth to the mountain ⌈—⌉ Hammamat, the ⌈—⌉ being behind me, and the ⌈—⌉-people scattered upon the mountains, searching this whole [desert].[c] Then I found it, and the ⌈—⌉ were in festivity, the ⌈entire⌉[d] army was praising, it rejoiced with ⌈obeisance⌉;[e] I gave praise to Montu.[f]

---

mention the name of the leader as usual. Then follows (l. 3): *"Fourth month of the third season, day 3; came the wearer of the royal seal, sole companion, inferior prophet, privy councilor of the treasurer of the god, Idi (Ydy), (l. 4) to bring down stone for the merinuter priest, the hereditary prince, ritual priest, sole companion, superior prophet, governor of the South [superior prophet of Min]* (restored from Golénischeff, *Hammamat*, III, 3, l. 3), *Putoker (P꜂wt-ykr)* (l. 5). *I brought down for him 2 blocks, each one* (l. 6) *10 cubits* (over 17 feet) *in length, — cubits in its width."* Idi has another inscription in the vicinity (Golénischeff, *Hammamat*, III, 3 = Maspero, *ibid.*, 157) as follows: *"Year* ⌈—⌉, *third month of the third season, day* ⌈—⌉; *came the .... (titles) Idi, to bring down stone for ..... (titles) Putoker. I brought down for him a block of 12 cubits* (about 20 feet, 6 inches), *with 200 men. I brought 2 oxen, 50 asses,* ⌈—⌉ 5 ⌈—⌉". It is clear that Idi is here executing the commissions of Putoker, an official of high rank, not those of the king.

[a]According to l. 6, his name may have been Sebeknakht, and his father's name Intef.

[b]Read *dw꜂ dw꜂*, as in Sinuhe, l. 248.

[c]Suggested by Gardiner.

[d]Read *r ḏr·f?*

[e]Read *sn-t꜂?*

[f]The last line was omitted by Lepsius, and it is possible that even in Golénischeff's copy the conclusion is lacking, for the concluding phrase above is very abrupt.

INSCRIPTION OF NESSUMONTU[a]

469. The stela is dated at the top in the "*year — 4*" of Amenemhet I, and adds the titulary of Sesostris I. As Sesostris I was associated with his father in the twentieth year of the latter, we must restore the above date as "*year 24.*"

470. The stela contains the conventional mortuary texts and representations, but in the lower right-hand corner adds nine short columns of historical content:[b] showing that Nessumontu led expeditions against the Bedwin ("*Sand-dwellers*") and other Asiatics at the north end of Egypt's eastern frontier.

471. [1]Respecting [every] word of this tablet, it is truth, [2]which happened by my arm, it is that which I did in [3]reality.[c] There is no deceit, and there is no lie therein. [4]I ⌈defeated⌉ the Asiatic Troglodytes, the Sand-[5]dwellers. I overthrew the ⌈strongholds[d]⌉ of the [6]⌈nomads⌉, as if ⌈they had never⌉ been. ⌈I⌉ coursed[e] through [7]the field, I went

---

[a]Stela in Louvre (C 1); the top lines containing the date are published by Lepsius, *Auswahl der wichtigsten Urkunden*, 10, and Lepsius, *Zwölfte Dynastie*, II, 3. The entire text: Maspero in *Report of First International Congress of Orientalists at Paris*, 1873, II, 48–61, and again in Maspero, *Études de mythologie et d'archéologie*, III, 153–64; Pierret, *Inscriptions*, 2, 27; Gayet, *Stèles*, I. All these are inaccurate. A good text is given by Piehl, *Inscriptions*, I, I–II, but he unfortunately overlooked the nine lines of historical text and copied them from Maspero. Brugsch (*Thesaurus*, VI, 1467) copied them from Pierret. These nine lines alone have been carefully given by Müller (*Orientalistische Litteraturzeitung*, 1900, 47–48), who, however, does not consider his copy "einen völlig abschliessenden Text." I therefore carefully copied and collated the original (in January, 1901, for the Berlin Dictionary) under excellent light, which insured some additional readings, and it is probable that my text may be regarded as final. I have since published it, *American Journal of Semitic Languages and Literatures*, XXI, 153 ff. Müller also gives a translation, from which mine differs in several places, but is indebted to him for several suggestions.

[b]It is unfortunately only this important corner of the stela which is badly broken and weathered, seriously mutilating the text.

[c]*Yr(y)i ꞏ n ꞏ y pw m wn ꞏ m* ᵈ ᶜ.

[d]The word cannot be *ḥn*, "*tent*," as Müller suggests, for it ended in feminine *t*, while *ḥn*, "*tent*," is masculine, as shown by Harkhuf, *Letter*, l. 20. The feminine form cited by Müller from the Israel stela is not "*tent*," but "*water skin*" (*ḥn ꞏ t*). I connect our word with *ḥn ꞏ t*, "*prison.*"

[e]Read *ḥns;* see Müller, *Orientalistische Litteraturzeitung*, III, 433.

forth ⌈before those who were⌉ behind [8]their defenses, without [my] equal therein,[a] [9]by command of Montu, to him who followed the plan of —.

INSCRIPTION OF KORUSKO[b]

472. The Nubian conquests of the Twelfth Dynasty, were already begun by Amenemhet I, and the place where the following inscription was discovered, over half-way up to the second cataract, indicates that the statement in the king's "Teaching" (§ 483) is trustworthy.

473. Year 29,[c] of the King of Upper and Lower Egypt, Sehetepibre (*Shtp-yb-R[c]*, Amenemhet I), living forever. We came to overthrow Wawat — —

THE TEACHING OF AMENEMHET[d]

474. This composition purports to be the practical injunctions of the old king, Amenemhet I, to his son and coregent, Sesostris I. Maspero thinks they were posthu-

---

[a]*Nn sn˙y ym.*

[b]Cut on a rock at the entrance of the valley road leading from Korusko to Abu Hamed. It was discovered by Dr. Lüttge in 1875, and by him shown to Brugsch (*Geschichte*, 117, 118), who published it seven years later, *Zeitschrift für ägyptische Sprache*, 1882, 30; and in *Thesaurus*, V, 1213.

[c]Maspero's statement (*Dawn*, 478, n. 2) that this inscription belongs to the "XXXth year" must be an oversight.

[d]The text is preserved in seven hieratic manuscripts of the Empire, mostly incomplete, as follows:

1. Millingen Papyrus (original lost), published from copy of Peyron, by Maspero, *Recueil*, II, 70, and XVII, 64.
2. Papyrus Sallier, II, 1–3, British Museum.
3. Papyrus Sallier, I, 8, Verso (=Millingen, I, II, 1).
4. Ostracon, British Museum, 5623 (=Millingen, I, II. 6).
5. Ostracon, British Museum, 5638 (=Millingen, II, 5–11); Dümichen, *Zeitschrift für ägyptische Sprache*, 1874, 30 ff.
6. Papyrus, Berlin, 3019 (Milligen, I, 9 to II, 11).
7. Leather Manuscript Louvre, 4920, "now completely spoiled." "All these appear to be of about one period, perhaps from the end of the reign of Ramses II to the reign of Seti II" (Griffith, *Zeitschrift für ägyptische Sprache*, 34, 36; Millingen

mous,[a] but Griffith does not agree.[b] It can hardly be doubted that the composition is a work of the Twelfth Dynasty, and there is no serious reason why it should not be attributed to the old king, whose *"teaching"* the introduction distinctly states it is. Griffith regards the occasion of the work as the attempt on his life when the king determines "to announce his son's succession in a formal manner." This would date the work from the beginning of the coregency in the twentieth year of Amenemhet I. There is a reference in the document, however, which would indicate a later date. In III, 2, the king speaks of his campaign against Nubia. Now, the only campaign of Amenemhet I in Nubia known to us was in his twenty-ninth year (§ 473).[c] This reference, therefore, would date the work not long before the king's death in his thirtieth year, and is an indication that we have in it his final instructions to his son.

475. Its chief purpose was to warn the young Sesostris against any confidences or intimate associations with those about him. To enforce this warning, the old king dwells on the kindness and beneficence, the order and prosperity, of his reign; in contrast with which he bitterly depicts the treachery and ingratitude which have been his reward. There is an element of pathos in these words of the old man, which do not fail of their effect even after nearly four thousand years.

---

may be later), and are in a frightful state of corruption. The best manuscript, Millingen, is unfortunately incomplete, almost all of the third page being lost. The latest and best treatment and text, employing all the manuscripts, are by Griffith (*Zeitschrift für ägyptische Sprache*, 34, 35–49), from whom the above statement of materials is taken. An excellent translation of the clearer passages by Erman also in *Aus den Papyrus des königlichen Museums zu Berlin*, 44, 45. To both these the present version is much indebted. The older "translations" are very free paraphrases; for bibliography of them, see Maspero, *Dawn*, 467, n. 2.

[a]*Dawn*, 466.   [b]*Zeitschrift für ägyptische Sprache*, 34, 38.

[c]An earlier campaign is not impossible, but remains an assumption.

476. The composition is in poetic form, and the lines are separated as usual in the New Kingdom by a dot at the end of each line.[a]   It must have been a favorite composition, to judge from the number of manuscripts which have survived. They are all, however, so excessively corrupt that much is unintelligible, and has been omitted in the version below.

477. Whether the historical statements in the document are authentic or not, there is no reason to doubt their truth; on the contrary, all but the attempt upon the king's life are corroborated by conclusive external evidence.   These statements, in the order of their occurrence, are as follows: (1) the attempt on the king's life (I, 11—II, 4); (2) Sesostris I's coregency (II, 5, 6); (3) the king's reorganization of Egypt (II, 10, 11); (4) the agricultural prosperity (II, 11—III, 1); (5) foreign conquests in Nubia and among the Bedwin (III, 2, 3); (6) building of a palace (III, 2–6).   There seems to be no chronological order in this enumeration, for the reorganization of the country took place in the first years, long before the coregency.   It is fair to conclude, however, that the attempt on the king's life was the cause of the association of Sesostris on the throne.

478. I. [b]1Beginning with the teaching, which the majesty of the King of Upper and Lower Egypt; Sehetepibre, Son of Re: Amenemhet (I) triumphant, composed.

He saith, 2while distinguishing truth,
For his son, the All-Lord;
He saith: "Shine as a god!
Hearken to that which I say to thee,
That thou mayest be king of the earth,
That thou mayest be ruler of 3the lands,

---

[a]The paragraph division, retained in the accompanying translation, is also indicated by rubrics.

[b]Numbering of pages (Roman numerals) and lines (Arabic numerals) from Papyrus Millingen, after Griffith.

That thou mayest increase good.

479. ⌜Harden⌝ thyself against all subordinates.

The people give heed [4]to him who terrorizes them;[a]

Approach them not alone.

Fill not thy heart with a brother,

Know not a friend,

Nor make [5]for thyself intimates,

Wherein there is no end.

When thou sleepest, guard for thyself thine own heart;

For a man has no people,

In the [6]day of evil.

I gave to the beggar, I nourished the orphan;

I admitted the insignificant as well as him who [7]was great of account.[b]

(But) he who ate my food made insurrection,

He, to whom I gave my hand, aroused fear therein;

They who put [8]on my fine linen looked upon me as ⌜—⌝.

They who anointed themselves with my myrrh, ⌜defiled [9]me⌝ ⌜—⌝

. . . . [10]. . . . . [11]. . . . .

480. It was after the evening meal, night had come.

I took [12]an hour of heart's ease.

Lying upon my couch, I relaxed;

II [1]My heart began to follow slumber.

⌜Behold, weapons were flourished⌝,

⌜Council was held against me,⌝

⌜While I was like a serpent of [2]the desert.⌝

I awoke to fight, utterly alone.

. . . . [3]. . . . . .

As I quickly grasped the weapons in my hand,

I hurled back the wretches . . . . . .

[4]. . . . .

. . . .

. . . .

---

[a]But see Gardiner's careful grammatical analysis of this line (*Proceedings of the Society of Biblical Archæology*, 24, 353 f.). He renders: "That cometh to pass, to whose terrors no thought has been given." This is grammatically better than the above rendering, although it does not fit either the preceding or following context.

[b]Lit.: "*him who was not, as well as him who was.*" Compare the saying of the unjust official: "*The name of a poor man is mentioned, by reason of his lord*" (*Eloquent Peasant*, Berlin, 3023, l. 20).

481. [5]Behold, the abomination occurred, while I was without thee,
While the court had not (yet) heard that I had delivered to thee (the kingdom).
While I had not yet sat with thee.
[6]Let me adjust thy administration;
For I do not terrify them, I do not think of them,
My heart does not endure the slackness of servants.
[7]. . . . . [9]. . . . . . . [a]

482. [10]I sent to Elephantine,
I reached the Delta,
I stood on the borders of the land,
[11]I inspected its interior,
I carried forward the boundaries of valor by my bravery, by my deeds.

483. I was one who cultivated [12]grain, and loved the harvest-god;[b]
The Nile greeted me in every ⌜valley⌝;
None was hungry in my years, none thirsted (III) ⌜then⌝;
One dwelt (in peace) through that which I did; conversing concerning me.
All that I commanded was correct.
I ⌜captured⌝ [2]lions, I took crocodiles,
I ⌜seized⌝ the people of Wawat,
I captured the people of Mazoi.
[3]I caused the Bedwin to go like hounds.[c]
I made a ⌜palace⌝ decked [4]with gold,
Whose ceilings were of lazuli, ⌜and the walls therein⌝.
The floors ⌜— —⌝,
[5]The doors were of copper,
The bolts were of bronze,
[6]Made for everlastingness,
At which eternity fears.[d]

---

[a]The general sense is: the conspiracy was formed in the palace.

[b]Bebi, in whose inscription Brugsch thought to find references to Joseph's famine (*Geschichte*, 246), uses verbatim the same words (Brugsch, *Thesaurus*, VI, 1527, l. 11) regarding himself.

[c]This line is slightly doubtful, but compare similar phrase, *Piankhi*, l. 3.

[d]Not being able to destroy it. The remainder of p. III, for which Papyrus Millingen is wanting, is too corrupt for translation.

DEDICATION INSCRIPTION[a]

484. A relic of Amenemhet I's building activity at Karnak, is preserved in this dedication, found on the base of a shrine from the Karnak temple of Amon, whence it had been taken to the Ptah-temple:

Amenemhet I; he made it as his monument for his father Amon-Re, lord of Thebes (*Ns·wt-t'wy*), making for him a shrine of pink granite, that he may thereby be given life forever.

485. Another dedication[b] at Bubastis runs as follows:

Amenemhet I; he made it as his monument for his mother Bast, making for her[c] a gate —————.

———————

THE TALE OF SINUHE[d]

486. The tale of Sinuhe is a highly artificial piece of "fine writing" in poetical form,[e] most of which is lost to our modern taste. It is, however, so rational and sober throughout, and breathes such an air of reality, that it is not to be disregarded as a historical source.

———————

[a]*Annales*, III, 102.   [b]Naville, *Bubastis* I, Pl. 33A.

[c]An *s* has been omitted, either in the publication or by the ancient scribe.

[d]The bulk of this tale (311 lines) is preserved in a hieratic papyrus of the Middle Kingdom, now in Berlin (P. 3022), published by Lepsius, *Denkmäler*, VI, 104–7. The beginning, lacking in the Berlin Papyrus, is preserved in a hieratic ostracon (a large flake of limestone) discovered in a Twentieth Dynasty tomb by Maspero (now in Cairo, No. 27149), and published by him in *Mémoires de l'Institut égyptien*, II, 1–23, and Pls. I, II, 1886. This fragment, excessively corrupt, is supplemented by eleven lines from the Amherst Papyrus (Newberry, *Amherst Papyri*, Pl. I), which have been incorporated with the Cairo ostracon and published in transcription by Griffith (*Proceedings of the Society of Biblical Archæology*, XIV, 453, 454). The whole has been translated by Erman in *Aus den Papyrus des königlichen Museums zu Berlin*, 14–29. My materials were: all the above publications except Maspero's (which was not accessible), the Berlin original, and especially a transcription of the Cairo ostracon, made by Erman from the original, which he kindly placed at my disposal.

[e]The Cairo ostracon containing the beginning separates the lines by red dots, and divides into stanzas. The above translation preserves these lines and stanzas as far as the ostracon goes, after which the division is uncertain.

487. The hero, Sinuhe, a noble of high rank, is with the young coregent, Prince Sesostris I, in the western Delta, on a campaign against the Libyans, when the message announcing the death of the old king, Amenemhet I, reaches the camp. Sesostris I does not allow the news to be made public, but secretly returns to the royal residence, in order firmly to establish himself as king before any pretender can precede him. Sinuhe accidentally overhears the message, and, evidently for political reasons, immediately flees the country, making Palestine his goal. Here he spends many years, experiencing manifold adventures, until in old age, after becoming rich and powerful, he is pardoned by Sesostris I, and permitted to return to Egypt.

488. The date of Amenemhet's death, given in the tale as in the thirtieth year of his reign, is corroborated by the monuments, where his highest date is also the thirtieth year;[a] hence the introductory narrative may probably be accepted as essentially historical. Moreover, the style of the writing in the Berlin papyrus shows that the document could not have been written very much later than the reign of Sesostris I, when the historical facts were still well known.

489. The geography of the flight[b] is correct as far as traceable, but the error of Upper Tenu for Upper Retenu, the Empire term for Palestine, shows unfamiliarity with one of the most important, and later the most frequent, designations in the Egyptian's geography of Asia.[c] But it is the earliest occurrence of the name; for the tale offers us

[a]The stela of Intef bears the joint date: "*Year 30 of Amenemhet I, year 10 of Sesostris I*" (Cairo, Mariette, *Abydos*, II, 22 = Rougé, *Inscriptions hiéroglyphiques*, VIII = Rougé, *Album photographique*, No. 146; Mariette, *Catalogue général d'Abydos*, 104, No. 558).

[b]See especially Müller, *Asien und Europa*, 38-47.

[c]Retenu was, however, known in the Middle Kingdom, and is mentioned in a Sinai inscription (see Weill, *Sinai*).

the oldest account of pre-Israelitish Palestine from any source. This account appears to be essentially true to the facts, and shows us how superior was the Egyptian of this time, to the Bedwin of Palestine.

490. Hereditary prince, count,
Wearer of the royal seal, sole companion,
Judge, local governor,
King [ᴿamongᴸ] the Bedwin,
Real confidant of the king, his beloved,
The attendant, Sinuhe, saith:
   I was one who follows his lord,
A servant of the royal ᴿharemᴸ of the queen,
Rich in praise,

. . . .
. . . .
. . . . .ᵃ

   491. In year 30, second month of the first season, on the 7th day,
Departed the god into his horizon,
The king of Upper and Lower Egypt, Sehetepibre.
He ascended [to] heaven, joined with the sun;
The divine limbs were mingled with him that begat him.
In the court, silence ᴿ — — — —ᴸ.
The great double doors were closed,
The court sat (in mourning),
The people ᴿbowed down inᴸ silence.
   492. Behold, his majesty had sent out
A numerous army to the land of the Libyans;
The eldest son was commander thereof,
The Good Godᶜ Sesostris.
Now, just as he was returning, having taken
Living captives of the Libyans,
And all cattle, without limit;
The companions of the court,
They sent to the west side,ᵇ

ᵃThese three lines are totally corrupt; the names of Amenemhet and Sesostris, and the pyramid-city, Kenofer (*K* ᵓ-*nfr*) are mentioned.
   ᵇToward Libya.

In order to inform the king[a]
Of their plan, conceived in the cabinet chamber.
The messengers found him on the way,
They reached him at the time of evening.
. . . .

The hawk,[b] he flew, together with his following,
Without letting his army know ⸢it⸣.
Then sent the royal children,
Who followed this army;
No one had called ᶜ⸢to⸣ one of them.[d]
Behold, I stood; I heard his voice
[2]As he spoke, while I ⸢— —⸣,
My heart cleaved, [3]my arms opened,
While trembling fell on all my members.
I stole away [4]⸢— —⸣ —,
To seek for myself a place of concealment.
I placed [5]myself between two bushes,
To ⸢avoid⸣ the way which they went.
I [6]proceeded up-stream,
[7]Not intending (however) to reach the court;
I thought there was fighting (there).
. . . .

493. [8]I reached ⸢—⸣ in the region of Sycomore,
[9]I arrived at the Isle of Snefru.[e]
I tarried in a stretch [10]of field,[f]
It grew light, I went on, when it was day.
I came upon a man, standing [11]in ⸢—⸣ the way;
He saluted me, and was afraid.
[12]When the time of the evening meal[g] drew on,
I reached the city of [13]the Ox ($Ng^{\jmath}w$).
I ferried over, in a vessel without a rudder,

---

[a]Sesostris I.

[b]Poetical designation of the prince, Sesostris, who now secretly leaves the camp and hastens to the royal residence, to be crowned.

[c]The Berlin papyrus begins here; the line numbers refer to that manuscript.

[d]To inquire after the absent Sesostris.

[e]See § 312, l. 21, note.   [f]See § 430, l. 12, note.

[g]Compare the same meal in § 480.

[14][By means of] a wind of the west.[a]
I passed by on the east of the quarry,
[15]Past the highland goddess, mistress of the Red Mountain.[b]
As I gave [16]the way to my feet, [going northward],[c]
I came to [17]the Walls of the Ruler,
Made to repulse the Bedwin,
[And to smite the sand-rangers][d]
I bowed [18]down in the bushes,
For fear the sentinels [19]on the fort,
Who belonged to its day (-watch), should see me.
I went on [20]at time of evening,
As the earth brightened, I arrived at Peten (*Ptn*).[e]
[21]When I had reached the lake of Kemwer (*Km-wr*),[f]
I fell down for thirst, [22]fast came ⌜my⌝ breath,
My throat was hot,
[23]I said: This is the taste of death.
I upheld my heart, I [24]drew my limbs together,
As I heard the sound of the lowing of [25]cattle,
I beheld the Bedwin.
[26]That chief among them, who had been in Egypt, recognized me.
[27]He gave me water, he cooked for me milk.[g]
I went [28]with him to his tribe,
Good was that which they did (for me).
One land sent me on to [29]another,
I loosed[h] for Suan (*Swn*),[i]

---

[a]This shows clearly the eastward direction of his flight.

[b]This is the mountain of red conglomerate just northeast of modern Cairo. It is still called the Red Mountain (Gebel el-Aḥmar), and is still used as a quarry. See Baedeker, 74, and Murray, 418.

[c]Only in Empire text.

[d]Found only in the Empire text.   [e]Unknown land.

[f]Lit.: "*the great black*," the earlier northern extension of the Gulf of Suez. See Maspero, *Dawn*, 351, n. 3, and 471, n. 3, who renders "the *very* (*wr·t*) black," although the writing is always *wr* (="*great*," without *t*); and Müller, *Asien und Europa*, 39–43.

[g]Here the Cairo ostracon stops, and the verse division is from here on uncertain.

[h]Perhaps a nautical term.

[i]From "*swn*," "*to trade*," evidently a trading-post on the Asiatic frontier, like *Swn* (Assuan) on that of Nubia.

I arrived at Kedem[a] (Ḳdm);
I spent [30]a year and a half there.

494. Emuienshi, that sheik [31]of Upper Tenu,[b] brought me forth
Saying to me: "Happy art thou with me,
(For) thou hearest the speech [32]of Egypt."
He said this, (for) he knew my character,
He had heard of [33]my wisdom;
The Egyptians [34]who were there with him, bare witness of me.

495. Emuienshi now questions Sinuhe as to the reason
of his flight, and the latter responds evasively, merging
his reply into a long hymn in praise of the king (ll.
34–77). Whereupon Emuienshi replies:

496. [78]"Behold, thou shalt now abide with me;
Good is that which I shall do for thee."
He put me at the head of his children,
He married me [79]to his eldest daughter,
He made me select for myself of his land,
[80]Of the choicest of that which he had,
On his boundary with [81]another land.
It was a goodly land, named Yaa (Y⸣⸣);[c]
There were figs [82]in it and vines,
More plentiful than water was its wine,
Copious was [83]its honey, plenteous its oil;
All fruits were upon its trees.
[84]Barley was there, and spelt,
Without end all [85]cattle.
Moreover, great was that which came to me,
Which came for love [86]of me,
When he appointed me sheik of the tribe,

---

[a]Long misread "Edom;" first corrected by Erman, in 1885, *Aegypten*,
495. The region was east of Jordan and the Dead Sea, and receives the same
name in the Old Testament.

[b]This is the first occurrence of Upper [Re]tenu, the usual designation, in the
Empire for the higher portions of Palestine. That the text has omitted an *r* is
almost certain. See Müller, *Asien und Europa*, 47.

[c]An unknown district in Palestine; it is written as if it were the name of
some plant.

From the choicest of [87]his land.
I portioned the daily bread,
And wine [88]for every day,
Cooked flesh, and fowl [89]in roast;
Besides the wild goats of the hills,
Which were trapped [90]for me, and ⌈brought⌉ to me;
Besides that which my dogs captured for me.
[91]There was much — made for me,
And milk in [92]every sort of cooked dish.
I spent many years,
My children [93]became strong,
Each the mighty man of [94]his tribe.
The messenger going north,
Or passing southward to the court,[a]
[95]He turned in to me.
For I had all men turn in (to me).

497. The tale now proceeds with examples of the personal prowess of Sinuhe, but the remainder of over 200 lines contains nothing of historical importance.[b]

---

[a]The court of Egypt is meant.

[b]The remainder of the story can be read in the latest and far the best translation by Erman, *Aus den Papyrus des königlichen Museums zu Berlin*, 20–29 (German), or a very free paraphrase by Maspero, *Contes populaires*, or an English version after Maspero, by Petrie, *Egyptian Tales*.

REIGN OF SESOSTRIS I

THE BUILDING INSCRIPTION OF THE TEMPLE OF HELIOPOLIS[a]

498. This building inscription in its present form has a very interesting history. It is not preserved to us upon a great stela, to which such inscriptions were usually intrusted, but has reached us on more fragile material—a roll of leather. This had been used by a scribe in the third year of Amenhotep II[b] for scratching down various data, either for the sake of practice or for temporary preservation; for they were often washed off and replaced by others. At present we can read, although half washed out, part of the legal proceedings of a sculptor against his own son, and notes regarding the receipt and issue of lumber.[c] To one of these notes he has fortunately fixed the date, as given above. On the other side of the leather our scribe copied the beginning of the dedicatory building inscription of Sesostris I, placed by him on a great stone stela[d] in his temple at Heliopolis. In the time of our scribe the stela had already been standing five hundred years. It has since utterly perished, with the temple in which it stood, and thus the great king's building inscription has survived only in the accidental copy of a humble scribe.

---

[a]A hieratic manuscript, written in two columns on one side of a piece of leather; bought in Thebes by Brugsch, 1858 (*Geschichte*, 123); first published by Stern, *Zeitschrift für ägyptische Sprache*, 1874, 85 ff.; then by Birch, *Egyptian Texts*, 49–58. It has been translated by Stern, *Records of the Past*, XII, and by Erman, *Aus den Papyrus des königlichen Museums zu Berlin*, 59–63. My materials were the original now in Berlin (P. 3029) and a transcription by Erman. The above translation depends, with a few exceptions, upon his version in *loc. cit.*

[b]Not Amenhotep IV, as read by Stern.

[c]See Erman, *Aus den Papyrus des königlichen Museums zu Berlin*, 87, 88.

[d]See § 501, l. 5.

499. In form the inscription was a poem, and its lines have been separated by the scribe by red dots, as usual in the Empire. The content is obscured by elaborate phraseology, but its drift is nevertheless evident. In his third year Sesostris I called together his court, and announced his purpose of erecting a temple to the sun-god at Heliopolis (§§ 501–3). The court responds with the conventional encomium (§ 504), and the king then deputes the treasurer to undertake the building (§ 505). An interval of time having elapsed of which there is no indication in the narrative, the ground plan of the building is laid out with the customary ceremony (§ 506). As usual in such inscriptions, there must have followed some description of the construction, material, and furniture of the temple, but the scribe unfortunately copied no farther.

500. This was of course not the first temple at Heliopolis, but an extension of the old, undoubtedly on a much larger scale. A fragment of a building inscription[a] from the same temple perhaps belonged to Sesostris I. It shows that he, or one of his name, built throughout Egypt. It reads:

¹(For) ———— a *mšn·t*-stone necklace, a necklace (*mny·t*), many great seals ⌜—⌝ ———— ²———— many great — ⌜—⌝ —. (For) Anuket: a *mšn·t*-stone necklace, a seal — a silver vase,[b] a golden vase, a bronze vase, two copper vases, an ebony censer, a silver censer. (For) First of the Westerners, Lord of Abydos (Osiris): ———— ³———— a bronze vase, two copper vases, an ebony censer. (For) Onouris: in Thinis: a silver vase, a golden vase, a bronze vase, two copper vases, an ebony censer, a silver[c] censer. (For) Min (*Ypw*): a silver vase, a golden vase, a bronze vase, two copper vases, an ebony censer, a silver

---

[a]Engraved on two sides of a piece of a red grit-stone door-post, now in a native house by the Mosque of el-Azhar in Cairo. Published by Daressy, from a copy by Ahmed bey Kamal, in *Annales* IV.

[b]*Ḥs;* all the vases herein recorded are of this form.

[c]The published text is evidently to be so corrected.

[censer] ———— 4————. (For) ———— a necklace. (I) built a
temple for Satet, for Anuket and Khnum, lord of the cataract, of ⌈sculp-
tured⌉[3a] stone.   (I) built a temple for Horus of Nubia (T°-$pd\cdot t$) in the
(nome of) Apollinopolis Magna ($W\underline{t}s$-$\underline{H}r$)[b] ———— 5————.   He
[made] (it) as his monument for Atum, lord of Heliopolis: silver vessels
————6[c] ———— a golden $dwd\cdot t$, a silver ———— 7———— a
royal statue of —[d] for Sais. Buto, mistress of Pe and Dep, was fashioned,
a copper bowl ⌈—⌉. A royal statue of Sesostris (⌈III⌉) for Pe ⌈—
— —⌉ Nephthys ———— 8————. (For) the Nine Gods in Kher-
eha ($\underline{H}r$-$^{c}h^{\circ}$): a copper bowl; Hapi was fashioned.   (I) sailed up-
stream to Elephantine, offering-tables were given to the southern gods.
(For) Hathor, mistress of Dendera: a golden ———— 9———— a
$hm^{\circ}g\cdot t$-stone necklace, — — a — stone necklace — —.   (For) Hathor,
mistress of Cusae: a $hm^{\circ}g\cdot t$-stone necklace, a $m\acute{s}n\cdot t$-stone necklace
————.

This list of the king's good works for the gods doubtless
comes from the Heliopolis temple, the building of which
is recorded in our leather roll, as follows:

501. [1]Year 3
Third month of the first season, day —, under
The majesty of the King of Upper and Lower Egypt, Kheperkere,
Son of Re, Sesostris (I), triumphant.[e]
Living forever and ever.
[2]When the king appeared in the double crown,
Occurred the sitting in the audience-hall,[f]
One took counsel with his suite,
The companions of [3]the court,

---

[a]$S^{c}h^{c}$, see IV, 231, ll. 6, 8, and 11; possibly we should render $S^{c}h^{c}$ here with
its usual meaning, "*erect*," and regard the following sign (the builder), as the
determinative, and render "*I erected.*"

[b]Second nome of Upper Egypt.

[c]The inscription here passes around the corner of the block; it is uncertain
whether the two faces should be connected as above.

[d]Remains of a cartouche.   [e]Inserted by the Empire scribe.

[f]This hall ($\underline{d}^{\circ}dw$) is mentioned also in the reign of Sahure (see § 239), where
it was part of a house called: "*Sahure-Shines-or-Appears-With-Crowns.*" The
name also occurs in the Fourth Dynasty in the same connection (Sethe, *Urkunden*,
I, 22, l. 14), and must be an audience-hall.

The princes at the place of ⌜—⌝.
Oneᵃ commanded, while they heard,
One took counsel, while ⁴making them reveal:
"Behold, my majesty is exacting a work,
And taking thought in an excellent matter.
For ⁵the future I will make a monument,
And set up an abiding stela for Harakhte.

502. He begat me ⁶to do that which he did,
To execute that which he commanded to do.
He appointed me shepherd of this land.
He recognized ⌜him who should defend⌝ ⁷it,
He hath given to me that which he protects,
And that which the eye,ᵇ that is in him, illuminates.
⌜Doing throughout⌝ᶜ as he desires.
I have ⌜rendered⌝ ⁸that which he exacted ⌜—⌝.ᵈ
I am a king of his character,
A sovereign, to whom he ⌜—⌝ not.
I conquered as ⁹a lad,
I was mighty in the egg.
. . . . ᵉ
He appointed me lord of the two halves,ᶠ
As a child, ¹⁰before the swaddling-clothes were loosed for me,
He appointed me lord of mankind,
⌜—⌝ ¹¹in the presence of the people.
He perfected me to be occupant of the palace,
As a youth, before my two ⌜—⌝ came forth.
He gave his length and his breadth [to me].
Who have been brought up ¹²in his character, which he took.
To whom was given the land; I am its lord.
My fameᵍ has reached ¹³the height of heaven,
My excellence ⌜————⌝.

. . . .

ᵃThe king.
ᵇThe sun; that which the eye illuminates is, of course, the earth.
ᶜIt is all obedient to him?
ᵈA very uncertain line.   ᶠUpper and Lower Egypt.
ᵉA mutilated line.   ᵍLit.: "Fame for me . . . . . ."

¹⁴He has commanded me to conquer that which he conquered,
⌐—⌐ — Horus, who have[a] numbered ⌐his limbs.⌐

503. I have established the offerings of ¹⁵the gods,
I will make a work, namely, a great house,
For my father Atum.
He[b] will make it broad, according as he has caused me to conquer.
¹⁶I will victual his altars on earth,
I will build my house in the ⌐—⌐.[c]
My beauty shall be remembered ¹⁷in his house,
My name is the pyramidion, and my name is the lake,[d]
Eternity is that excellent thing which ⌐I⌐ have made;
The king ¹⁸dies not, who is mentioned by reason of his achievements.
. . . .
It is my name ⌐—⌐ which is mentioned ¹⁹in reality,
Which passes not away because of eternal things.
That which I make is that which shall be,
That which I seek is ²⁰the excellent things.
Excellent food is ⌐—⌐.
It is vigilance in eternal things."

504. II. ¹Then spake these companions of the king,
And they answered before their god:[e]
"Hu is [in] thy mouth, and Esye[f] ²is behind thee.
O sovereign, it is thy plans which are realized,
O king, who shinest as Favorite of the Two Goddesses,
To ³⌐—⌐ in thy temple.
It is excellent to look to the morrow,
And with excellent things, to (coming) time.

---

[a]First person.

[b]We expect "I," viz., "I will make it broad according as he has made my kingdom broad."

[c]$S\,{}^{\flat}\underline{h}$, which occurs also as the place where a temple is built, in II, 890, l. 24.

[d]Meaning that these accessories of the temple will be memorials of his name. By a curious accident, the only witness to the king's building surviving on the spot is his solitary obelisk (at Maṭarîyeh-Heliopolis), surmounted as usual by the "*pyramidion.*"

[e]The king.

[f] Hu and Esye are the deities of taste and wisdom.

The multitude completes nothing [4]without thee,[a]
For thy majesty is the two eyes of all people.
Thou art great that thou mayest make thy monument,
[5]In Heliopolis, the dwelling of the gods.
Before thy father, the lord of the great house,
Atum, the bull of the gods.
Let thy house arise, [6]that it may offer to the oblation-tablet;
That it may do the service for its favorite statue,
For thy figure in all [7]eternity.

    505. The king himself said
To the wearer of the royal seal, the sole companion,
The overseer ⌜of⌝ the double [8]White House,
The privy councilor of ⌜—⌝:
It is thy counsel, which shall cause the work to be done.
Of which my majesty desires, [9]that it should be;
Thou art the commander belonging to it,
Who shall do, according to that which is in my heart,
. . . . [10]vigilance,
That it may come to pass without laxity,
That all the work . . . . [11]. . . . . .
. . . . [12]. . . . . .b
[13]I have commanded those who work,
To do according as thou shalt exact.

    506. The king was crowned with the diadem,
[14]All the people were following him,
The chief ritual priest and scribe of the sacred book stretched [15]the cord,
. . . . the ⌜stake⌝ in the earth,[c]
[16]— was done in this temple,
His majesty had [17]a royal scribe go ⌜before⌝ the people,
[18]Who were gathered [in] one place, south and north,
[19]. . . . .

---

[a]Text has *nb* for *k*—a mistake which could have been made only from the hieroglyphic, thus showing that the scribe certainly had the stone original before him.

[b]Four verses are omitted.

[c]This is a description of the usual measuring and staking out of the ground plan of the temple, which was a sacred ceremony conducted by the king in person.

INSCRIPTION OF MERI[a]

507. The usual texts of the Middle Kingdom mortuary stelæ are here preceded by seven lines referring to the building of Sesostris I's pyramid-chapel, which was intrusted to Meri. The mention of columns and gates may indicate that only the chapel, and not the pyramid entire, is meant.[b] If the date at the top is, as we may suppose, that of Meri's death, then Sesostris I had completed his mortuary chapel, and perhaps his pyramid at Lisht, by his ninth year.

508. [1]Year 9, second month of the first season, day 20, [2]under the majesty of Sesostris I,[c] living like Re, forever. [3]His real servant, his favorite, who does all that which he praises every day, [4]the revered assistant treasurer, Meri (*Mry*), born of Menkhet (*Mnḫ·t*), says:

509. I was a zealous servant, great in character, amiable in love. [5]My lord sent me with a commission, because I was so very zealous, to execute for him an eternal dwelling,[d] greater in name than Rosta, and more excellent[e] in appointments [6]than any place, the excellent district[f] of the gods. Its columns[g] pierced heaven; the lake which was dug, it reached[h] the river; the gates,[i] towering [7]heavenward, were of limestone of Troja. Osiris, First of the Westerners, rejoiced over all the monuments of my lord; I myself rejoiced, and my heart was glad at that which I had executed.

---

[a]Mortuary stela in the Louvre (C 3), published by Pierret, *Inscriptions*, II, 104, 105; Gayet, *Stèles*, IV, V; Maspero, *Mélanges d'archéologie égyptienne*, II, 221 f.; again Maspero, *Études de mythologie et d'archéologie*, III, 208 f.; and Piehl, *Inscriptions*, I, II–IV. Of these, the only careful copy is Piehl's. He also offers an excellent translation (*ibid.*, 3–5).

[b]This chapel and pyramid at Lisht were excavated by J. E. Gautier (*Mémoire sur les fouilles de Licht* par J. E. Gautier et G. Jéquier [Cairo, 1902], 3–43; in *Mémoires de l'Institut*, VI, fasc. 1).

[c]Full titulary.   [d]The pyramid; it is lit., "*an eternal seat.*"

[e]Lit.: "*More advanced.*"

[f]Read *wᶜr·t*, originally a bend in the cliffs or river. Maspero reads *whm·t*, "repeating, reproducing the excellences of the gods." Compare Piehl, *Inscriptions*, I, 4.

[g]Piehl's text has "*walls.*"

[h]This may be figurative, viz., "*reached,*" in the sense of "*equaled,*" which suits the context.

[i]Belonging to the chapel on the east side.

WADI HALFA INSCRIPTION OF MENTUHOTEP[a]

510. This carries the Nubian wars of Sesostris I to their southernmost point.[b] It was set up in the eighteenth year, by the general, Mentuhotep.[c]

At the top is a relief showing Sesostris I standing, facing *"Montu, Lord of Thebes,"* who says: *"I have brought for thee all countries which are in Nubia (Tᵓ-pd·t), beneath thy feet, Good God."* Suiting these words, the god leads and presents to the king a line of bound captives, symbolizing Nubian towns. The head and shoulders of each captive surmount an oval, containing the name of the town represented. There were originally ten of these towns (of which four have disappeared),[d] as follows: (1) *kᵓ š*, (2) *y ⌐—⌐*,

---

[a] A sandstone stela found in the sanctuary of the northernmost of the two temples on the west shore opposite Wadi Halfa village. First noticed by Ricci, it was taken out by Champollion and Rosellini in 1829, who failed to notice that they had left the lower portion in situ under the sand. This upper portion has been in Florence for many years (No. 1542). Some sixty years later, (1893) Captain Lyons took out the lower portion, and it is now in Florence; only one intermediate line has been lost, for the two parts fit together, at one corner. The upper portion has often been published, but with no approach to accuracy: Rosellini, *Monumenti Storici*, XXV, 4; Champollion, *Monuments*, I, 1; Champollion, *Notices descriptives*, I, 34–36; II, 692; Schiaparelli, *Catalogue*, I, 243–46; Berend, *Monuments du Musée égyptien de Florence*, 51, 52; Brugsch, *Thesaurus*, 1444 f.; a photograph in Petrie's *Italian Photographs*, No. 46. The lower portion was published by Pellegrini in *Bessarione*, Anno V, Vol. IX, Nos. 59, 60. I photographed and copied both portions (the readings from my copy were incorporated in Pellegrini's publication), repeatedly collated the original, and the Berlin squeeze (A 1375) of the upper portion, as well as the old publications for signs now lost, and published the whole in *Proceedings of the Society of Biblical Archæology*, May, 1901, 231–35, and three plates.

[b] Another expedition under Sesostris I, which extended an uncertain distance southward, was accompanied by the nomarch of Elephantine, Sirenpowet. It is recorded in his Assuan tomb (de Morgan, *Catalogue des monuments*, 183), but is so fragmentary and so badly published, that very little can be made of it. The following is discernible: *"His majesty [⌐sent me or came⌐] to overthrow K[ush]* ——— *the vile . . . . His majesty ⌐came⌐ bringing . . . ."* Before the latter phrase an elephant is mentioned, to which there is probably reference in the last line: *"Four men brought him ———."*

[c] The date and name of the officer are furnished by the newly discovered lower portion (§ 512).

[d] All ten were still partially readable in Champollion's time, and he gives the complete list (*Notices descriptives*, II, 693); the later publications all give only six, and do not add Champollion's material.

(3) *prww*, (4) *ym ꜣw*, (5) *ḥꜥ—ꜣ*, (6) *w ꜣw*,[a] (7) *yḫrkyn*,
(8) *šꜣ ꜥ · t*, (9) *ḥšꜣy*, (10) *šmyk*. The Kummeh temple of
Thutmose III was built of "*good white stone of šꜣ ꜥ · t*,"[b] the
eighth district in this list, which must therefore have been
in the vicinity of Kummeh, some thirty-seven miles above
Wadi Halfa where our monument was set up. It is safe
to conclude that none of the others, although little known,
was far south of Kummeh. Thus the conquests of
Sesostris I had already reached the southern limit, later
marked, and fortified by Sesostris III (§§ 651–60).

511. Below the relief were two inscriptions; the first belonging to the king—the second to Mentuhotep. Of the
king's inscription only fragments of six lines survive, showing the titulary of Sesostris I, followed by the epithet,
"*Horus who seizes in an instant*" (l. 1).[c] Other phrases
discernible are: [2]"[ꜥ*Light*ꜥ] *of the eyes, star*[d] *of the South,
illuminating the Two Lands, white Bull, trampling the Troglodytes*" (l. 2); and in l. 4 is a reference to "*smiting Nubia.*"
On the lower, more recently recovered portion, two more,
fragmentary lines, continue similar epithets of the king.[e]

512. Mentuhotep's inscription begins with his titles, as
follows:

[8]Hereditary prince, count, wearer of the royal seal, sole companion,
favorite of the king ————[f] [9]local governor, attached to Dep, lord

---

[a]According to Champollion, *Notices descriptives*, but the original shows the
goose as the last sign, and not *w; w ꜣ* with *w* and eagle is also suspicious.

[b]Lepsius, *Denkmäler*, III, 67, *b;* Brugsch, *Thesaurus*, 1444.

[c]Preserved completely in Champollion, *Monuments*, but misplaced at the
beginning of l. 1, although it belongs at the end after the royal name.

[d]See Thutmose III's Hymn of Victory (II, 658, l. 15).

[e]The king's inscription is in horizontal lines, and the following inscription of
Mentuhotep is in vertical lines.

[f]The numbering of lines is continued from the inscription of the king on this
fragment. There is an uncertain amount lost at the end of each line, and even
the portions above the final break are very fragmentary.

of Pe. . . . . .¹¹. . . . . .^a commander of recruits, commander of the army, ——— ¹²Sesostris I made me ———. ¹³Year 18, first (month) of the second season, day 8, the day of ——— ¹⁴broad in stride, the King of Upper and Lower Egypt, [Kheper]ke[re] (Sesostris I). ¹⁶Their life is finished,^b slain, ——— ¹⁷fire in the tents^c ———. ¹⁸Her grain cast to the Nile,^d ——— ¹⁹zealous, not trangressing [the command of the palace] ——— ²⁰a man in the strength of his ka, in ——— ²¹forever, the Son of Re, Sesostris (I) ——— ²²I myself swear, this happened in^e ²³very truth; I, the general of the army, ²⁴Amu's son, (ʿmw) Mentuhotep.

513. It is clear that ll. 12 and 13, and probably two lines before, contained important historical statements, of which the merest fragments are now discernible. The description is similar to the one on the second Semneh stela of Sesostris III (§§ 655–60).

514. Below at the left was the figure of Mentuhotep, of which only the top of the head is preserved. This is not the only place where his figure appeared on the stela. In the upper relief behind the king is the figure of a hawk-headed deity, very rudely done and not of the same workmanship as the other figures. A close examination reveals hieroglyphics under this figure. Over its head is a fan, the handle of which cuts across the head and shoulders of the figure.^f It is clear, then, that this hawk-headed figure is not original, but was cut in later to displace the figure of

---

^aConventional epithets.

^bThis phrase is common in the Twentieth Dynasty; hence the reading here with *km*-sign inverted is certain.

^cThe determinative is lost; it may be that we have Yam (Yꜣm).

^dThis phrase (ḫꜣ m n ytr) occurs also in Papyrus Westcar (IV, 10), where the unfaithful wife is burned and "*cast to the Nile*," and on the Mentuhotep stela (§ 748), l. 19.

^eI read *m wn m*ʿꜣ; there is no loss at the end of l. 17; for it is like ll. 18 and 19, which are stopped by Mentuhotep's head, the top of which can barely be seen under the lines, the rest of the head and figure being lost.

^fNone of this appears in any of the old publications.

a fan-bearer, who could have been no one else but Mentu-hotep.   He must have fallen into disfavor, and for some reason have been displaced from his position of honor behind the king.

_____

INSCRIPTION OF AMENEMHET[a] (AMENI)

515. Amenemhet was one of the most powerful of the Benihasan[b] princes.   He succeeded his father (I, 465, ll. 7–8) Khnumhotep I, the founder of the Benihasan family, in the eighteenth year of Sesostris I, and ruled twenty-five years.   He records three royal expeditions, the first of which he accompanied as commander of the military contingent from his nome, in a war against Nubia.   It cannot be certainly identified with any of the Nubian expeditions of Sesostris I recorded in other sources.

516. The second and third expeditions were both for the purpose of bringing gold; the destination of the third was the mines back of Coptos,[c] and that of the second, although not stated, was probably the same.

517. The inscription concludes with an interesting and important description of Amenemhet's administration of his principality.

518. [1]Year 43 under the majesty of [2]Sesostris I,[d] living forever and ever; [3]corresponding to year 25[e] in the Oryx nome with the heredi-

_____

[a]Carved on the jambs of the doorway of his cliff-tomb in Benihasan (No. 2), copied by Champollion in 1828 and published (*Monuments*, 395, 399; *Notices descriptives*, II, 427–30); copied by Hay in 1828 (British Museum, *Add.* Manuscript No. 29813, 84, 85); by Wilkinson in 1834 (*Manuscripts*, II, 22–26); by Lepsius in 1842, published (*Denkmäler*, II, 122); from Lepsius by Birch, *Egyptian Texts*, 7–11; and Bunsen, *Egypt's Place*, 2d ed., V., 724 f.; finally by Newberry (*Beni Hasan*, I, Pl. VIII; see his bibliography, 24).

[b]On the Benihasan princes and Amenemhet's place therein, see §§ 620 ff.

[c]For the mines of Wadi Foakhir, on the Coptos road, see Erman, *Life in Ancient Egypt*, 463, and Wilkinson-Birch, II, 238.

[d]Full titulary.

[e]This fixes the accession of Amenemhet in the Oryx nome, in the eighteenth year of Sesostris I.

tary prince, count, ⌜—⌝ Amen[emhet],ᵃ triumphant. ⁴Year 43, second
month of the first season, day 15. O ye who love life and hate ⁵death,
say ye, 1,000 loaves and beer, 1,000 oxen and geese ⁶for the ka of
the hereditary prince, count, ⌜—⌝, great lord of the Oryx nome, ⌜—⌝,
attached to Nekhen, lord of Nekhbet, chief of prophets, Ameni,
triumphant.

First Expedition

519. I followed my lord when ⁷he sailed southward to overthrow
his enemies among the fourᵇ barbarians. I sailed southward, as the
son of a count, wearer of the royal seal, and commander in chief of
the troops of ⁸the Oryx nome, as a man represents his old father,ᶜ
according to [his] favor in the palace and his love in the court. I passed
Kush, ⁹sailing southward, I advanced the boundary of the land, I
brought all gifts; my praise, it reached heaven. Then ¹⁰his majesty
returned in safety, having overthrown his enemies in Kush the vile. I
returned, following him, with ready face.ᵈ ¹¹There was no loss among
my soldiers.

Second Expedition

520. I sailed southward, to bring gold ore for the majesty of the
King of Upper and Lower Egypt, Kheperkere (Sesostris I), living forever and ever. ¹²I sailed southward together with the hereditary prince,
count, oldest son of the king, of his body, Ameni.ᵉ I sailed southward, with a number, 400 of all the choicest of ¹³my troops, who returned
in safety, having suffered no loss. I brought the gold exacted of me;
I was praised for it in the palace;ᶠ ¹⁴the king's-son praised god for me.

ᵃThe full form of this nomarch's name is Amenemhet (Ymn-m-$ḥ$ᵓ·t = "$Amon is$
$in front$"). In place of this, another form of name is frequently used in these
inscriptions, viz., Ameni ($Ymny$ = "$Belonging to Amon$"), sometimes defectively
written "$Amen$."

ᵇCompare the "$four eastern countries$," § 675, l. 9.

ᶜThis shows that he must have succeeded his father in the Oryx nome.
Although his father's name is lacking here, it must have been Khnumhotep (I),
the first of the Benihasan family (see § 627, l. 56).

ᵈOrders were always given "$in the face of$" an officer; an officer prepared
for efficient service is therefore "$ready of face$" in the Egyptian idiom.

ᵉThis is the crown prince, who afterward became King Amenemhet II; his
name, like that of our nomarch Amenemhet often, is here in the form Ameni.

ᶠThe inscription here proceeds to the left (north) door jamb.

Third Expedition

521. Then I sailed southward to bring ore, to the city of Coptos, together with the hereditary prince, count, governor of the city and vizier, Sesostris. I sailed southward with a number, 600 [15]of all the bravest of the Oryx nome. I returned in safety, my soldiers uninjured; having done all that had been told me.

Ameni's Able Administration

522. I was amiable, and greatly loved, a ruler beloved of his city. Now, I passed years [16]as ruler in the Oryx nome. All the imposts of the king's house passed through my hand. The gang-overseers of the crown possessions of the shepherds of the Oryx nome gave to me[a] 3,000 bulls in their yokes. I was [17]praised on account of it in the palace each year of the loan-herds. I carried all their dues[b] to the king's house; there were no arrears against me in any office of his. The entire Oryx nome labored[c] for me [18]in ⌜— —⌝.[d]

Ameni's Impartiality and Benevolence

523. There was no citizen's daughter whom I misused, there was no widow whom I oppressed, there was no ⌜peasant⌝ whom I repulsed,[e] there was no shepherd whom I repelled, [19]there was no overseer of serf-laborers whose people I took for (unpaid) imposts, there was none wretched in my community, there was none hungry in my time. When years of famine came [20]I plowed all the fields of the Oryx nome, as far as its southern and northern boundary, preserving its people alive

---

[a]This means that Amenemhet received a herd of 3,000 cattle from the royal herds, to be maintained by him on shares. He kept them so well that he was praised for it each year when his payments fell due. The cattle of the king on the estate of Thuthotep (*Bersheh*, I, Pl. XII) are also clearly distinguished from his own; thus: "*. . . . . . great numbers of his cattle from the king, and his cattle of the estate in the districts of the Hare nome;*" his own cattle being those of "*the estate.*"

[b]The dues for the herds which he had received. On this entire transaction, see Müller, *Zeitschrift für ägyptische Sprache*, 1885, 85, 86.

[c]To labor or work for a king or nobleman is to pay him an impost from the results or products of one's labor. It is used of entire countries in the Empire.

[d]"*In extended goings,*" probably meaning in widely extended activity.

[e]Read ḥsf(w)·n·y = relative form.

and furnishing its food so that there was none hungry therein. I gave to the widow as (to) her who had a husband; [21]I did not exalt the great above the small in all that I gave. Then came great Niles,[a] possessors of grain[b] and all things, (but) I did not collect the arrears of the field.[c]

STELA OF IKUDIDI[d]

524. This stela was erected at Abydos on the occasion of Ikudidi's visit there, while on an expedition to the oases which lie in the desert behind Abydos. It is the mention by him of the occasion of his visit which makes his stela of importance; for this is the earliest expedition to these peoples of which we know anything.

The inscription is very crude and difficult, and contains many hieratic signs which the artist could not put into hieroglyphic.

Date

525. [1]Year 34 under the majesty of the king of Upper and Lower Egypt, Kheperkere, the Good God, Lord of the Two Lands, Lord of [2]Offering, Beloved of All Gods, Son of Re, Sesostris (I), living forever and ever.

Prayer

526. [3]An offering which the king gives, etc., ... [4]. . . .[e] for the revered one [5]before the great god, the lord of heaven, the steward, Ikudidi (*Ykw-dydy*).

---

[a]Inundations.

[b]Meaning that the inundations brought these things; two kinds of grain were apparently mentioned.

[c]Meaning that he did not collect the balance due after the short payments of taxes during the unfruitful years.

[d]Stela from Abydos in the Berlin Museum, No. 1199, *Ausführliches Verzeichniss des Berliner Museums*, 89. I used a copy kindly furnished me by Schaefer.

[e]The usual mortuary prayer in the name of Osiris.

Expedition

527. I came from Thebes, as a king's-confidant, [6]doing all his pleasure, in command of the youth of the recruits, to visit the ⌜—⌝ of the land of the Oasis-[7]dwellers, as an excellent official, whom his lord knows, effective in plan, [8]whom the officials of the palace exalt.[a]

Tomb

528. I have made this tomb at the stairway of the great god, in order that I may be among [9]his followers, while the soldiers who follow his majesty give to my ka of his bread [10]and his ⌜provision⌝, just as the king's-messenger does, who comes inspecting the boundaries of his majesty.

INSCRIPTION OF INTEFYOKER[b]

529. In striking corroboration of the stela of Intef I is that of Intefyoker. Above is the date: "*Year 33 under the majesty of Kheperkere* (Sesostris I), *living forever.*" The usual mortuary offering is then invoked:

"For the revered, scribe of ⌜—⌝,[c] supervisor of fields in the Thinite, nome of the South (*tp rśy*),[d] Imsu (*Ymsw*), southward as far as the Crocodile nome,[e] northward as far as the Panopolite nome.[e] The

---

[a]Or: "*who exalts the officials of the palace,*" their position being subject to him.

[b]Mortuary stela, in Leyden Museum (V, 3; Leemans, *Description raisonnée des monuments égyptiens à Leide*, 264–66). The historical portion was first published by de Rougé, *Revue archéologique*, 1st ser., VI, 560; then completely by Piehl, *Inscriptions*, III, XXI–XXII. I had also an excellent copy from the original by Sethe, which he kindly loaned me.

[c]Brugsch (*Geographical Inscriptions*, I, 211) states that this is the "Hinterland" of the Thinite nome.

[d]See § 396, l. 18, note.

[e]In the list of Ramses II at Abydos (Mariette, *Abydos*, I, 11, *a*) and in the oldest of all the lists, discovered February, 1900 (MS. Borchardt's *Tagebuch*) by Borchardt at Abusir, the Crocodile nome occupies the sixth place from Elephantine, and the order is Thebes, Coptos, Crocodile (end of Abusir list), Diospolis parva, Abydos, Akhmim. Hence the ancient Thinite (Abydos) nome was bounded on the north by the Panopolite (Akhmim) nome, and on the south by the Crocodile nome; the nome of Diospolis parva being a later division.

father's father of my father[a] was field-scribe in the waters of Abydos of the Thinite nome, since the time of Horus: Wahenekh $(W^{\jmath} h\text{-}{}^c nh)$, King of Upper and Lower Egypt: Son of Re, Intef (I)."[b]

INSCRIPTIONS OF MENTUHOTEP[c]

530. The inscriptions of Mentuhotep contain little of historical importance, but were regarded as so excellent in style and content that they were partially copied[d] on the mortuary stela of Sehetepibre, a nobleman living under Sesostris III and Amenemhet III. Their favor continued even into the Empire, when a nobleman under Queen Ahhotep also copied them on his stela.[e] The text on the front, beginning with the names of Sesostris I, proceeds as follows:

531. Hereditary prince, vizier and chief judge, attached to Nekhen, prophet of Mat (goddess of Truth), giver of laws, advancer of offices, confirming[f] the boundary records, separating a land-owner from his neighbor, pilot of the people, satisfying the whole land, a man of truth before the Two Lands, ⸢accustomed⸣ to justice like Thoth, his like in satisfying the Two Lands, hereditary prince in judging the Two Lands,

---

[a]Imsu's great-grandfather was therefore a contemporary of King Intef I. Allowing 40 years for a generation, this Intef was still living over 100 years before Amenemhet I. Cf. § 415 and Steindorff, *Zeitschrift für ägyptische Sprache*, 1895, 90, 91, and Birch, *Transactions of the Society of Biblical Archæology*, IV.

[b]The king's name is not inclosed in a cartouche.

[c]On his mortuary stela found at Abydos, now in Cairo (No. 20539); published by Mariette, *Abydos*, II, 23 (very inaccurate; *Catalogue général d'Abydos*, 144, No. 617) = Rougé, *Inscriptions hiéroglyphiques*, 303, 304; Daressy has added the verso, *Recueil*, X, 144–49. I had also a copy of the original by Schaefer, which he kindly loaned me.

[d]The form of the representations in the arch of the stela was also adopted. See Daressy, *Recueil*, X, 144.

[e]The text on the verso was the one copied. It is much mutilated. Daressy has published all three in a parallel arrangement.

[f]Or: "*recording*."

supreme head in judgment, putting matters in order, wearer of the royal seal, chief treasurer, Mentuhotep.

Hereditary prince, count, chief of all works of the king, making the offerings of the gods to flourish, setting this land ⌐— — —⌐ according to the command of the god. ⌐————————⌐, sending forth two brothers satisfied with the utterances of his mouth, upon whose tongue is the writing of Thoth, more accurate than the weight, likeness of the balances, fellow of the king in counseling ⌐— —⌐, giving attention to hear words, like a god in his hour, excellent in heart, skilled in his fingers, exercising an office like him who holds it, favorite of the king before the Two Lands, his beloved among the companions, powerful among the officials, having an advanced seat to approach the throne of the king, a man of confidences to whom the heart opens.

532. Hereditary prince over the ⌐—⌐ of the (royal) castle (*wsḫ·t*), finding the speech of the palace, knowing that which is in every body (heart), putting a man into his real place, finding matters in which there is irregularity, giving the lie to him that speaks it, and the truth to him that brings it, giving attention, without an equal, good at listening, profitable in speaking, an official loosening the (difficult) knot, whom the king (lit., god) exalts above millions, as an excellent man, whose name he knew, true likeness of love, free from doing deceit, whose steps the court heeds, overthrowing him that rebels against the king, hearing the house of the council of thirty, who puts his ⌐terror⌐ among the barbarians (*ḥᵓš·tyw*), when he has silenced the Sand-dwellers, pacifying the rebels because of their deeds, whose actions prevail in the two regions, lord of the Black Land and the Red Land, giving commands to the South, counting the ⌐number⌐ of the ⌐—⌐ of the Northland, in whose brilliance all men move, pilot of the people, giver of food, advancing offices, lord of designs, great in love, associate of the king in the great castle (*wsḫ·t*), hereditary prince, count, chief treasurer, Mentuhotep, he says:

533. "I am a companion beloved of his lord, doing that which pleases his god daily, prince, count, sem priest, master of every wardrobe of Horus, prophet of Anubis of ⌐— —⌐, the *ḥry ydb*, Mentuhotep, prince in the seats of 'Splendor,'[a] at whose voice they (are permitted to) speak in the king's-house, in charge of the silencing of the courtiers, unique one of the king, without his like, who sends up the truth to the

---

[a]Name of a building.

palace, great herald of good things, alone great, sustaining alive the people.   One to whom the great come in obeisance at the double gate of the king's-house; attached to Nekhen, prophet of Mat, pillar ⌜before⌝ the Red Land, overseer of the western highlands, leader of the magnates of South and North, ⌜advocate of the people, — —⌝, merinuter priest, prophet of Horus, master of secret things of the house of sacred writings, ⌜— —⌝, governor of the (royal) castle, prophet of Harkefti, great lord of the royal wardrobe, who approaches the limbs of the king, ⌜————⌝, overseer of the double granary, overseer of the double silver-house, overseer of the double gold-house, master of the king's writings of the (royal) presence, wearer of the royal seal, sole companion, master of secret things of the 'divine words' (hieroglyphics), chief treasurer, Mentuhotep." He says: . . . .

534. Here follows a mortuary prayer, after which the concluding lines (22, 23) refer specifically to his building commissions at Abydos, as follows: "*I conducted the work in the temple, built his*ᵃ *house (pr), and dug the lake; I masoned the well, by command of the majesty of Horus.*" The backᵇ also contains references to buildings at Abydos:

I conducted the work in the temple, built of stone of Ayan. . . . . I conducted the work on the sacred barque (*nšm·t*), I fashioned its colors. . . . . ———— offering-tables of lapis lazuli, of bronze, of electrum, and silver; copper was plentiful without end, bronze without limit, collars of real malachite, ornaments (*mn-nfr·t*) of every kind of costly stone. — — — of the choicest of everything, which are given to a god at his processions, by virtue of my office of master of secret things.

ᵃThis must refer to the king or the god.

ᵇThe text of the back as copied very copiously by Sehetepibre, has been translated only once, to save space (see §§ 746 ff.).   Only the references to building are translated here.   The back begins with a royal decree, commanding that there be built for Mentuhotep "*a tomb at the stairway of the great god, lord of Abydos, recording all thy offices and all the pleasing things which thou didst.*" It was to be furnished with statues and endowments; but the conclusion is illegible.

THE CONTRACTS OF HEPZEFI[a]

535. Legal documents from civil, as distinguished from criminal, processes of early Egypt are so rare, and the contracts of Hepzefi also throw so much light on both political and social conditions in the Middle Kingdom, that it seemed necessary to include them in these historical translations. They offer nothing in the political history of the family of the Siut nobles, and it is not possible to connect the nomarch, Hepzefi, in any way with the earlier generations, known to us at Siut in the Tenth and Eleventh Dynasties (§ 391). He doubtless marks a new family installed here by the powerful Twelfth Dynasty, in preference to the earlier family, which had been friendly to the northern dynasty.

The ten contracts were made solely to secure to Hepzefi, after his death, certain ceremonies and offerings from the priesthoods of Siut. Similar contracts were customarily made with the priests of Abydos. Mentuhotep and Sehetepibre, nobles of the same time, say on their Abydos tombstones: *"I gave contracts for the remuneration of the prophets of Abydos"*[b] (§ 746). The kings did the same (§ 765).

536. The form of the contracts is sufficiently clear; but the language is very involved, and burdened with an excess of relative clauses. Space will not permit the full commentary which they need in many places;[c] but attention

---

[a]Engraved upon the east wall of the great hall in Hepzefi's cliff-tomb at Assiut (see § 391 and note). The only complete copy is that published by Mr. Griffith (F. L. Griffith, *The Inscriptions of Siût and Dêr Rîfeh*, London, 1889), which is a model of care and accuracy. It is unnecessary to refer to the earlier publications, as Mr. Griffith has collated them all. The first adequate treatment was that of Erman, written, unfortunately, before the appearance of Mr. Griffith's text (*Zeitschrift für ägyptische Sprache*, 1882, 159–84), which fact necessitated leaving some obscure passages unrendered. Cf. also Maspero, *Etudes de mythologie et d'archéologie*, I, 62–74.

[b]Reverse of the well-known Mentuhotep stela, *Recueil*, X, 146.

[c]The general reader should refer to Erman, *Life in Ancient Egypt*, 145–47, 497, 498.

should at least be called to the sixth contract which Hepzefi as count made with himself as superior prophet of Upwawet.

Two facts in the socio-political organization of the time are brought out by these contracts: (1) The property of the prince was held under two different titles, viz., (a) by inheritance from his father, the property being called the "*paternal estate*" (*nw-pr-yt*), which he could bequeath at will; and (b) by virtue of his appointment[a] as "*count*" (*ḥꜣ ty-ꜥ*) by the king, the property being called the "*count's estate*" (*pr-ḥꜣ ty-ꜥ*), which he could not legally bequeath. The distinction between these two estates is clearly maintained throughout, and whenever Hepzefi bequeathes anything from his "*count's estate*" he concedes that such a title can endure only so long as his successors are willing to recognize it, and by appeal to the common feeling in such matters, he urges his successors to recognize it (e. g., § 547, ll. 280, 281) (2) There are in the contracts four classes of society: the "*count*" (*ḥꜥ ty-ꜥ*), or nomarch; the official (*śr*); the "*citizen*" (*nḏs*, lit., "*the small*"), and the "*peasant*" (*yꜥ ḥty*), lit., "*belonging to the field*," enumerated in descending scale. The interrelations of the four are not wholly discernible. The "*citizen*," like the count, gives to the temple from fields called "*his field*," which he therefore either owned or held in rental.   The peasant is called "*his* (the citizen's) *peasant*," and may therefore have been his serf or slave.   He cultivated the field for the citizen, and carried the harvest offering to the temple for him (cf. ll. 280, 281).   The "*official*" (*śr*) may have been of the same social class as the "*citizen.*"

The importance of these contracts in a study of the mortuary customs and beliefs is evident, but a discussion of

---

[a]On such appointment by the king, see § 385.

these questions does not fall within the scope of the present translations.[a]

537. There is a title above (l. 260):[b] *"The command, which the hereditary prince and count, etc., Hepzefi, made,"* which belongs to an introduction, giving instructions to Hepzefi's mortuary priest, as follows:

538. [269]The hereditary prince and count, the superior prophet, Hepzefi; he says to his mortuary priest:[c] "Behold, all these things, which I have secured by contract from these priests, are under thy charge. For, behold, it is the mortuary priest of a man, who should maintain his possessions and maintain his offering.

[270]Behold, I have informed thee; (as for) these things, which I have given to these (*w⁽c⁾b-*) priests, as compensation for these things, which they have given to me, take heed lest anything among them be lacking. (As for) every word of my lists, which I have given to them, let thy son hear it, thy heir, [271]who shall act as my mortuary priest. Behold, I have endowed thee with fields, with people, with cattle, with gardens (and) with everything, as every count of Siut (does), in order that thou mayest make offerings to me with contented heart. Thou standest over all my possessions, which I have put [272]under thy hand. Behold, they are before thee in writing.[d] These things shall belong to thy particular son, whom thou lovest, who shall act as my mortuary priest, before thy (other) children, as food which I have ⌜bequeathed⌝ to him; not permitting that he divide them to his children, (but) according to this word which I have commanded thee."

I. FIRST CONTRACT

Title

539. [273]Contract which the count, the superior prophet, Hepzefi, triumphant, made, with the lay priests of the temple of Upwawet, lord of Siut, to-wit:

---

[a]See Erman's treatment, *Zeitschrift für ägyptische Sprache*, 1882, 163–65.

[b]The numbering of lines follows Griffith's edition.

[c]Lit., "*servant of his ka*" (*k⌜?⌝*), indicating his office very clearly as a mortuary one; hence the above rendering.

[d]Referring either to these inscriptions or papyrus originals in possession of the mortuary priest.

What Hepzefi Receives

540. There shall be given[a] to him: A white loaf per individual (*w*c*b*-) priest, for his statue, which is in the temple of Anubis, [274]lord of Rekreret (*Rḳrrt*) on the first of the 5 intercalary days, when Upwawet, lord of Siut, proceeds to this temple.

What He Pays

541. He hath given[a] to them for it his share in the bull offered to Upwawet, lord of Siut, in this temple, when [275]he proceeds to it, consisting of his quarter, due to the count.

Source of Payment

542. Lo, he spake to them, saying: "Behold ye, I have given to you this quarter due to me from this temple, in order that this white bread may be endowed, [276]which ye give to me." Lo, they had given to him the inherited portion of the bull, for his statue, (which is) in charge of his mortuary priest, before he gave to them of this quarter.

Conclusion

543. Lo, they were satisfied with it.

II.   SECOND CONTRACT

Title

544. [277]Contract, which the count, the superior prophet, Hepzefi, triumphant, made with the lay priests of the temple of Upwawet, lord of Siut, to-wit:

What Hepzefi Receives

545. There shall be given to him:

(*a*) White bread by each one among them, for his statue, (which is) in charge of his mortuary priest, in the first month of the first season on the first day, [278]New Year's Day, when the house makes gifts to its lord, when the fire is kindled in the temple.

---

[a]The verbal forms are regularly in the first clause an infinitive (lit., "*concerning giving to him*") and in the second a relative form ("*what he hath given*").

(*b*) And they shall[a] go forth following his mortuary priest, at his glorification, until they reach the northern corner of the temple, as they do, when they glorify their own noble ones,[b] [279]on the day of kindling the fire.

What He Pays

546. He hath given to them for it a heket of grain from every field of the estate (*pr-dt*), from the first of the harvest of the count's estate; as every citizen of Siut does, from the first of his harvest. Now, behold, he begins [280]with having his every peasant give it into this temple, from the first of his field.

Injunction to Future Nomarchs

547. Lo, he said: "Behold, ye know that, as for anything which any official (*šr*) or any citizen gives into the temple, from the first of his harvest, it is not agreeable to him, that there should be lack [281]therein. Therefore shall no future count diminish to future priests, that which is secured by contract of another count. This grain shall belong to the lay priests, each by himself; [282]no priest, who shall give to me this white bread, shall divide (it) to his colleagues; because they give this white bread, each by himself."

Conclusion

548. Lo, they were satisfied with it.

III. THIRD CONTRACT

Title

549. [283]Contract which the count, the superior prophet, Hepzefi, triumphant, made, with the official body of the temple, to-wit:

What Hepzefi Receives

550. There shall be given to him bread and beer in the first month of the first season, on the eighteenth day, the day of the Wag-feast. List of that which shall be given:

---

[a]An infinitive construction continued from the first clause (lit., "*besides the going forth on their part*").

[b]The dead.

[284]Register of Names	(Ḳby-) Jars of Beer	Flat Loaves	White Loaves
Superior prophet.	4	400	10
Announcer.	2	200	5
Master of secret things.	2	200	5
⌈Keeper of the wardrobe⌉	2	200	5
Overseer of the storehouse.	2	200	5
Keeper of the wide hall.	2	200	5
Overseer of the house of the ka	2	200	5
Scribe of the temple.	2	200	5
Scribe of the altar.	2	200	5
Ritual priest.	2	200	5

What He Pays

551. He hath given to them for it, 22 temple-days, from his property of his paternal estate, but not from the property of the count's estate: [285]4 days to the superior prophet, and 2 days to each one among them.

Definition of "Temple-Day"

552. Lo, he hath said to them: "Behold, as for a temple-day, it is 1/360 [286]of a year. When ye therefore divide everything that comes into this temple, consisting of bread, of beer, and of meat for each day, that which makes [287]1/360 of the bread, of the beer, and of everything, which comes into this temple, is the unit [b]in these temple-days which I have given to you. [288]Behold, it is my property of my paternal estate, but it is not the property of the count's estate; for I am a priest's (w^{c}b) son, like each one of you. Behold, [289]these days shall belong to every future official staff of the temple, since they deliver to me this bread and beer, which they give to me."

Conclusion

553. Lo, they were satisfied with it.

IV. FOURTH CONTRACT

Title

554. [290]Contract which the count, the superior prophet, Hepzefi, triumphant, made with the lay priests of Upwawet, lord of Siut, to wit:

---

[a]I do not understand the ḫnt inserted here.

[b]Lit., "the per unum" (ḥr w^c), as we use per centum; ḥr is here the distributive preposition as in all the passages, indicating the individual priest.

What Hepzefi Receives

555. There shall be given to him:

(*a*) A white loaf per each individual among them, for his statue, which is in the temple, in the first month of the first season, on the eighteenth day, [291]the day of the Wag-feast.

(*b*) And they shall go forth, following his mortuary priest, at his glorification, when the fire is kindled for him, as they do when they glorify their own noble ones, on the day of kindling the fire in the temple. Now, [292]this white bread shall be under the charge of my mortuary priest.

What He Pays

556. He hath given to them for it:

(*a*) A khar[a] (*ḫᶜr*) of fuel for every bull, and an uhet[a] (*wḥꜣ·t*) of fuel for every goat, which they give into the storehouse of the count, when each bull and each goat is offered to the temple, [293]as ancient[b] (dues) which they give into the storehouse of the count. Lo, he hath remitted it to them, not collecting it from them.

(*b*) And hath given to them 22 jars (*ḳby*) of beer and 2,200 flat loaves which the official body of the temple give to him in the first month of the first season, on the eighteenth day, [294]as compensation, for their giving white bread per each individual among them, from that which is due to them from the temple, and (as compensation for) his glorification.

Further Specification

557. Lo, he spake to them, saying: "If this fuel be reckoned against you[c] by a future [295]count; behold, this bread and beer shall not be diminished, which the official body of the temple deliver to me, which I have given to you. Behold, I have secured it by contract from them."

---

[a]Measures of bulk. The meaning of this clause is obscure; but probably it means that each bull or goat due the prince (of those offered to the temple) is given him by the priests together with fuel. This latter he now remits as part payment for the white bread.

[b]Or: "*as recompense for that which they give, etc.*"

[c]Lit., "*reckoned from you*," probably meaning: "as due from you." The fuel, etc., could not be legally conveyed by the count, because they belonged to the count's and not to the paternal estate. If payment of the fuel, etc., should be ultimately exacted, the lay priests would still have the bread and beer which the prince has secured by contract from the "*official body*" of the Upwawet temple (see third contract).

Conclusion

558. Lo, they were satisfied with it.

V.   FIFTH CONTRACT

Title

559. ²⁹⁶Contract, which the count, the superior prophet, Hepzefi, triumphant, made with the ⌐keeper of the wardrobe⌐ of the temple, concerning:

What Hepzefi Receives

560. Three ⌐wicks⌐ with which the fire is kindled for the god.

What He Pays

561. While he (the count) has given to him (the keeper) for it: 3 temple-days. Now, these 3 temple-days shall be due to every future ⌐keeper of the wardrobe⌐, because ²⁹⁷these 3 ⌐wicks⌐ are due to him (the count).

Disposition of Wicks

562. 1. Lo, he spake to him, saying: "One of them shall be given to my mortuary priest, when he goes forth, kindling the fire with it for the god, on the fifth of the 5 intercalary days, New Year's[a] night, by the ⌐keeper of the wardrobe⌐. He shall ⌐deliver⌐ it ²⁹⁸to my mortuary priest after he does that which he does with it in the temple."

563. 2. "He shall give another on New Year's Day, in the morning, when the house makes gifts to its lord, when the lay priests of the temple give to me this white bread, which they give to me per individual priest (*wᶜb*), on New Year's Day. It shall be due ²⁹⁹from my mortuary priest at my glorification."

564. 3. "He shall give another in the first month of the first season on the eighteenth day, the day of the Wag-feast, at the same time with the white bread, which they give to me per individual priest (*wᶜb*). This ⌐wick⌐ shall be due from my mortuary priest when glorifying me, together with the lay priests."

Lo, he said to him:

---

[a]Really the evening before New Year's Day.

Definition of "Temple-Day"

565. [300]"Behold, as for a temple-day, it is 1/360 of a year.[a] When ye[b] therefore divide everything that comes into the temple, consisting of bread, beer, and everything for each day, that which makes 1/360 of the bread, of the beer, and of everything which comes into this temple, is the unit in these temple-days which I have given [301]to thee. Behold, it is my property, of my paternal estate, but not of the count's estate."

Future Validity of Agreement

566. "Now, these 3 temple-days shall belong to every future ⌜keeper of the wardrobe,⌝ because these 3 ⌜wicks⌝ are due to him, which thou hast given to me for these 3 temple-days, which I have given to thee."

Conclusion

567. Lo, he was satisfied with it.

VI.   SIXTH CONTRACT

Title

568. [302]Contract which the count, the superior prophet, Hepzefi, triumphant, made with the superior prophet of Upwawet,[c] concerning:

What Hepzefi Receives

569. The roast of meat which is due upon the altar, which is placed upon the oblation-table, for every bull which is slaughtered in the temple.

And one (st°-) jar for (every) (ds-) jar of beer every day [303]of a procession; which shall be due to every future superior prophet.

What He Pays

570. He (the count) hath given him (the superior prophet) for it, 2 temple-days from his property, of his paternal estate, but not from the property of the count's estate.

---

[a]See the same computation in the second contract.

[b]Although speaking to the keeper of the wardrobe, as the conclusion (l. 301) shows.

[c]That is, with himself! In his capacity as count he makes a contract with himself in his capacity as superior prophet of Upwawet.

Disposition of Meat

571. Lo, the count Hepzefi spake, saying: "When [304]this roast of meat and this (*st*ʾ-) jar of beer come for every day of a procession, they are due to my statue, (which is) in charge of my mortuary priest."

Conclusion

Lo, he was satisfied therewith, in the presence of the official body of the temple.

VII.   SEVENTH CONTRACT

Title

572. [305]Contract which the count, the superior prophet, Hepzefi, triumphant, made, with the great (*w*ᶜ*b*-) priest of Anubis, concerning:

What Hepzefi Receives

573. Three ⌜wicks⌝ due to him, with which the fire is kindled in the temple of Anubis:

One on the fifth of the 5 intercalary days, the New Year's night.

Another on New Year's Day.

Another [306]in the first month of the first season, on the seventeenth day, the night of the Wag-feast.

What He Pays

574. He hath given to him for it: 1,000 (*h*ʾ·*t*)-measures of land in ⌜— —⌝,ᵃ from the fields of his father, as compensation for these 3 ⌜wicks⌝, which he gives to my mortuary priest, in order to kindle the light for me therewith.

Conclusion

575. Lo, he was satisfied therewith.

VIII.   EIGHTH CONTRACT

Title

576. [307]Contract which the count, the superior prophet, Hepzefi, triumphant, made, with the lay priests of the temple of Anubis; to-wit:

ᵃ*Sm*ʾ*-ršy* = "*the southern union*," a designation of some locality in Hepzefi's estate.

What Hepzefi Receives

577. There shall be given to him:

(*a*) A white loaf per each individual among them, for his statue, in the first month of the first season, on the seventeenth day, the night of the Wag-feast.

(*b*) And that they shall go forth, following his mortuary priest, and kindle for him (the count), the fire at [308]his glorification, until they reach the lower steps of his tomb, just as they glorify their noble ones, on the day of kindling the fire.

(*c*) And that the priest belonging in each month shall give ⌐—⌐ of bread (*p* ˀ *ḳ*) and a jar of beer for his statue, which is on the lower steps of his tomb, when he comes forth from offering in [309]the temple[a] every day.

What He Pays

578. He hath given to them for it: grain from the first of the harvest of every field of the count's estate, as every citizen of Siut does from the first of his harvest. Now, behold, he begins with having his every peasant give it from the first of his field into the temple of [310]Anubis.

Injunction to Future Nomarchs

579. Lo, the count, Hepzefi, said: "Behold, ye know, that, as for every official (*šr*) and every citizen, who gives the first of his harvest into the temple, it is not agreeable to him, that there should be lack therein. Therefore shall no future count diminish to future priests that which is secured by contract of another count."

Individual Payment and Remuneration

580. [311]This grain shall belong to the lay priests, per each individual[b] priest, who shall give to me this white bread. He shall not divide it to his colleagues, because they give this white bread, each by himself.

---

[a]This would imply that the temple of Anubis was close to the necropolis and Hepzefi's tomb; a similar indication is seen in the fact that the officials of the necropolis receive the wicks from the "*great priest*" of Anubis to be carried to the mortuary priest. The temple of Upwawet was, on the contrary, in the town. See Erman, *Zeitschrift für ägyptische Sprache*, 1882, 165.

[b]Heretofore this idea has been expressed by the distributive preposition *ḥr*, "*per;*" but in this passage a remarkable idiom appears, lit., "*by the mouth of the head of each priest.*"

Conclusion

581. Lo, they were satisfied therewith.

IX.　NINTH CONTRACT

Title

582. [312]Contract which the count, the superior prophet, Hepzefi, triumphant, made, with the overseer of the necropolis, and with the mountaineers,[a] to-wit:

What Hepzefi Receives

583. There shall be given:[b]

(*a*) That they go to the house of Anubis, on the fifth of the 5 intercalary days, (being) New Year's night, and on New Year's Day, to receive 2 ⌜wicks⌝, which the great priest ($w^c b$) of Anubis gives to the count, Hepzefi.

(*b*) And that they go, at his glorification, until they reach [313]his tomb.

(*c*) And that they give this one ⌜wick⌝ to his mortuary priest, after they glorify him, just as they glorify their noble ones.

What He Pays

584. He hath given to them for it:

(*a*) 2,200 ($h^{\flat} \cdot t$-) measures of land in the ⌜—⌝,[c] from his property of the paternal estate, but not of the count's estate:

[314]Register of Names	($H^{\flat} \cdot t$-) Measures
Overseer of the Necropolis	400
Chief of the Highland	200
Eight mountaineers	1,600

(*b*) Besides giving to them the foot of the leg of every bull, that shall be slaughtered upon this highland, in every temple.

---

[a]Lit., *"those who are upon the mountain"* (*tpyw-ḏw*); they must also be connected with the necropolis, and receive their name from its location in the mountainous cliffs.

[b]The usual *"to him"* is omitted.

[c]$W^{\flat} b \cdot t.$

What Hepzefi Further Receives

585. They have given to him:[a]

The Overseer of the Necropolis, 2 (ds-) jars of beer; 100 flat loaves; 10 white loaves.

The Chief of the Highland, 1 (ds-) jar of beer; 50 flat loaves; 5 white loaves.

[315]Eight mountaineers, 8 (ds-) jars of beer; 400 flat loaves; 40 white loaves.

For his statue, (which is) in charge of his mortuary priest, in the first month of the first season, on the first day, (being) New Year's Day, when they glorify him.

Future Validity of Contract

586. Lo, he said to them: "Behold, these ($h^{\text{>}} \cdot t$-) measures of land, which I have given to ⌈you⌉,[b] shall belong to [316]every overseer of the necropolis, to every chief of the highland, and to every mountaineer who shall come (hereafter), because they shall deliver to me this bread and beer."

Additional Stipulation

587. [317]"And ye shall be behind [my] statue which is in my garden, following it when ————,[c] [318]at every feast of the beginning of a season, which is celebrated in this temple."

Conclusion

588. Lo, they were satisfied therewith.

X.   TENTH CONTRACT

Title

589. [319]Contract which the count, the superior prophet, Hepzefi, made, with the overseer of the highland, to-wit:

---

[a]The addition of a second stipulation of payments to the count is in violation of the usual form.

[b]Mr. Griffith saw traces of *f* ("*him*") in this place, which is broken, but the context demands "you."

[c]From l. 316 on, the lines are shorter, so that not more than five or six words are lost here.

What Hepzefi Receives

590. There shall be given to him 1 (*hbn· t-*) jar of beer, [320]1 large (— *rrt-*) loaf, 500 flat loaves, and 10 white loaves, for his statue, (which is) in charge of his mortuary priest, in the first month of the first season, on the seventeenth day, the night of the Wag-feast.

What He Pays

591. [321]He hath given to him for it:

(*a*) 1,000 (*ḥꜣ·t-*) measures of land in ⌜—⌝,[a] from his property of his paternal estate, but not from the property of the count's estate.

(*b*) And [322]a quarter of every bull that is slaughtered on this high-land in every temple.

Future Validity of Contract

592. Lo, he said to the overseer of the highland: [323]"Behold, these (*ḥꜣ·t-*) measures of land shall belong to every future overseer of the highland, because he delivers to me this [324]bread and beer."

Conclusion

593. Lo, he was satisfied therewith.

---

[a]*W ꜣ b· t.*

REIGN OF AMENEMHET II

INSCRIPTION OF SIMONTU[a]

594. Besides determining the succession of the first three kings of the Twelfth Dynasty, this stela is also important because it shows that Sesostris I was living in the third year of his son, Amenemhet II's reign. They were therefore coregent at least that long.

Date

595. [1]Year 3 [2]under the majesty of the King of Upper and Lower Egypt, Nubkure (*Nb-k⸢ɔ⸣w-R⸤c⸥*, Amenemhet II), living like Re.

Simontu's Titles

596. [3]Hereditary prince, count, wearer of the royal seal, sole companion, favorite of Horus, lord of the palace, who does that which his lord praises [4]every day, royal scribe, Simontu (*S⸢ɔ⸣-Mnṯw*), the revered; he saith:

Simontu's Birth and Childhood

597. I was born[5] in the time of the majesty of the King of Upper and Lower Egypt, Sehetepibre (Amenemhet I) triumphant. I was a child who fastened on the girdle[b] under his majesty (Amenemhet I), [6]when he departed in peace.[c]

---

[a]On a stela in the British Museum (No. 828, also called "Anastasi 17"); published by Champollion, *Notices descriptives*, II, 697; Sharpe, *Egyptian Inscriptions*, I, 83; from Sharpe by Bunsen, *Egypt's Place*, 2d ed., V, 724 f.; Brugsch, *Thesaurus*, VI, 1250; Maspero, *Etudes de mythologie et d'archéologie*, I, 39, 40; Piehl, *Sphinx*, II, 131-36 after Brugsch. None of these texts is without considerable divergence from the rest. A collation of the Berlin squeeze (No. 1083), and later of the original in London, shows that no copy is without error.

[b]See the same phrase § 294, l. 1.

[c]Piehl has shown from the well-known parallel examples of the Old Kingdom (*Sphinx*, II, 135) that the words here: "*proceeded, departed, or passed on in peace,*" mean "died." This is undoubtedly correct, but the question is: Whose death is referred to? It cannot be the death of Sesostris I, who is called "*living forever,*"

Career under Sesostris I

598. The king of Upper and Lower Egypt, Kheperkere (Sesostris I), living forever; his majesty appointed me scribe ⁷of the harem ⌐— —⌐;ᵃ he praised me on account of it very greatly.

His majesty appointed me scribe ⁸of ⌐—⌐; his majesty praised me on account of it very greatly.ᵇ

His majesty made me grain-registrar ⁹in South and North; his majesty praised me on account of it very greatly.

His majesty appointed me scribe of the great harem; ¹⁰his majesty praised me on account of it very greatly.

His majesty appointed me royal scribe and chief of works ¹¹in the entire land; his majesty praised me because I was silent,ᶜ he loved me, because I repelled the ⌐inflamed⌐,ᵈ I never repeated any evil word.

The revered royal scribe, Simontu.

INSCRIPTION OF SIHATHORᵉ

599. Sihathor's sole title is that of "*assistant treasurer*," an office which he really administered, and one which called him to varied enterprises of historical importance, the chief of which were his expeditions to Nubia and Sinai. After the usual mortuary formularies follow the biographical remarks.

---

and was therefore still living when the inscription was made. Grammatically, it is also impossible to accept Sesostris as subject of the verb, when verb and adverbial phrase precede the subject. Hence the verb must be a pseudo-participle, in a temporal clause, belonging to the preceding sentence. This leaves Sesostris without a verb, so that it must be an anticipatory subject, in apposition with "*his majesty*," of l. 6.

ᵃIs this the official called *sḏm* in the Empire?

ᵇ"*Greatly*," omitted in all the copies, is clear on the squeeze.

ᶜ*Gr*, as shown by the squeeze against all the copies, which have *ḫr* (except Sharpe).

ᵈSee the clever explanation of Piehl, *Sphinx*, II, 135 f.

ᵉMortuary stela from Abydos, now in the British Museum (No. 569), published by Sharpe, *Inscriptions*, II, 74; Birch, *Zeitschrift für ägyptische Sprache*, 1874, 112 f., and *Egyptian Texts*, 21–24. These texts are so bad that it is difficult to use them at all. The translation is made from my own copy of the original. See also Brugsch, *Geschichte*, 136 ff.

Sihathor's Many Commissions

600. I was real "beloved of his lord," the king of Upper and Lower Egypt, Nubkure (*Nb-kꜣw-Rᶜ* Amenemhet II), living forever. He commanded, he sent me many times on every excellent commission, the things which his majesty desired should be done according to the desire of the heart of his majesty.

Pyramid Statues

601. His majesty commanded that I should be brought to the pyramid: Amenu-kherep (*Ymnw-ḫrp*),[a] living forever, to superintend the work on his 16[b] statues of hard stone of millions of years, which happened ⌈within⌉[c] a day of two months. Never happened the like with any superintendent ⌈——⌉.

Expeditions to Sinai and Nubia

602. I visited[d] the Mine-land (Sinai) as a youth, and I forced the (Nubian) chiefs to wash gold. I brought malachite,[e] I reached Nubia (*tꜣ-pd·t*) of the negroes. I went, ⌈overthrowing⌉,[f] by the fear of the Lord of the Two Lands; I came [⌈to⌉] He (*Ḥꜣ*),[g] I went around its islands, I brought away its produce.

603. The real beloved of his lord, his favorite, saying the good and repeating that which is loved, doing that which the Lord of the Two Lands praises, communicating his design, not ⌈knowing⌉ the ⌈—⌉ hearted, free from blemish, defending his boundary, watching his possessions, watchful without laxity, the assistant treasurer Sihathor, triumphant.

---

[a]This is the pyramid of Amenemhet II. A similar reference to him, with name Ameni for Amenemhet, occurs at Benihasan (§ 520). (See Griffith, *Proceedings of the Society of Biblical Archæology*, XIV, 39 f.) The name of the pyramid is also written Ameni-kherep on the Stela No. 839 in the British Museum.

[b]So the original; the publications all have 15. [c]*Ḫm n.*

[d]On the verb *yry* ("*make*") in the sense of "*visit*," see § 351, l. 9, note. The Mine-land (*Byꜣ*) is here written with feminine *t;* it is elsewhere masculine, so that it is possible that we should render it merely "*mine.*"

[e]*Fꜣkꜣ·t* is of course to be read *mfꜣkꜣ·t* as in the Pyramid Texts, see the same writing § 266. This is equivalent to saying "*I visited Sinai,*" and this gives us a second antithetic parallelism with Sinai and Nubia; that is, north and south, as the extremes.

[f]Read *ḥr šḫr·t?*

[g]Birch's and Brugsch's reading "*Ḥeḥa*" is impossible, otherwise one would identify the place with Heh (*Ḥḥ*) = Semneh. It is near Abu Simbel; see III, 496.

INSCRIPTION OF KHENTKHETWER[a]

604. The tablet is of particular importance, having been found on the Red Sea at Wadi Gasus, of which it furnishes the Egyptian name, "*Sewew*" (*š⁾ww*), to which place an expedition led by Khentkhetwer returned from Punt, in the twenty-eighth year of Amenemhet II.

605. Above is Amenemhet II offering a libation to Min of Coptos; below is the figure of Khentkhetwer with arms uplifted in worship, accompanied by the following inscription:

[1]Giving divine praise and laudation to Horus ⌜—⌝, to Min of Coptos, [2]by the hereditary prince, count, wearer of the royal seal, the master of the judgment-hall [3]Khentkhetwer (*Ḥnt-ḫt-wr*) after his arrival in [4]safety from Punt; his army being [5]with him, prosperous and healthy; and his ships having landed [6]at Sewew (*Š⁾ww*). [7]Year 28.

SINAI INSCRIPTION[b]

606. The inscription records the opening of a new mine in the twenty-fourth year of Amenemhet II.

Year 24, under the majesty of the King of Upper and Lower Egypt, Amenemhet II.

Mine-chamber which the real king's-confidant . . . .[c] the captain of sailors,[d] Men, born of Mut, triumphant and revered, excavated.[e]

---

[a]On a stela discovered by Burton (Wilkinson, *General View*, 364) in the Wadi Gasus on the coast of the Red Sea opposite Coptos; now in the Museum of Alnwick Castle (No. 1935); published first by Erman from a squeeze, in *Zeitschrift für ägyptische Sprache*, 1882, 204, 205; then by Birch, *Catalogue Alnwick Castle*, pl. III, 268 ff. Cf. Brugsch, *Völkertafel*, 54, 55, and 68; Schweinfurth, *Wadi Gasûs*, 11, n. 2.

[b]Cut on the rocks near the great reservoir in the Sarbût el-Khadem; published from British Museum squeeze, No. 99, by Weill, *Sinai*, 158.

[c]Conventional epithets, but the text is unsafe.   [d]*Mr-⁽ prw.*

[e]Verb of the relative clause; a similar record under the same king, but without the year, is in the vicinity (Weill, *Sinai*, 159).

STELA OF KHENTEMSEMETI[a]

607. This stela is chiefly occupied with a pompous recitation of honors, such as is characteristic of the time. Many of the noble's functions in connection with the royal person—he had charge of the king's wardrobe—are entirely unintelligible. The interest and importance of the monument lie in Khentemsemeti's meager record of a journey of inspection among the temples of Egypt, undertaken by command of the king. He went up the river as far as Elephantine, and on his return stopped at Abydos, where he improved the opportunity of his official visit, as so many other functionaries did, to erect a memorial stela at the sanctuary of the great god of the dead. This is the stela with which we are dealing.

Introduction

608. [1]Amenemhet II, beloved of Osiris, First of the Westerners; given life. [2]His real favorite servant, master of secret things of the king's wardrobe, Khentemsemeti (*Ḥnt-m-smy·ty*); he says:

His Honors

609. "His majesty set me [3]at his feet in youth, my name was mentioned before my equals. His majesty greeted [4]me, he ⌈—⌉ a daily marvel, and I was verily ⌈— —⌉; I was praised [5]today more than yesterday. I became real king's-confidant, and his majesty received my approaches. When the officials were placed in their stations,[b] [6]I ⌈held⌉ office before them ⌈— — — — —⌉; priest of the Southern Crown, (of) the Northern Crown, [7](of) Khnum; servant of the royal toilet, adjusting (the crown called) "Great-in-Magic," supporting the White Crown in the "Great House" (*Pr-wr*). Great lord of Nekheb (El Kab), servant [8]of Neit in the northern palace, to whom (the goddess)

---

[a]From Abydos; now in British Museum, No. 574; published by Sharpe, *Inscriptions*, I, 79; Piehl, *Inscriptions*, III, XV, XVI. I had my own copy of the original.

[b]At royal audiences.

Rekhet gives the hand, one whose approach is avoided, when adjusting the Red Crown, when ⁹bringing forth in splendor, Horus, lord of the palace. Nurse of the god (Pharaoh) in the private chamber ⌜————⌝. Chief of Sais, ¹⁰in the administration of private affairs, lord of fear in the houses of Neit, great companion in the gold-house, at the birth of the god in the morning.

His Appointment to Inspect Temples

610. ¹¹I came at the front in the presence of his majesty, he had me inspect the divine fathers,ᵃ to expel evil and to prosper the fashion ¹²of their work, in eternal affairs.ᵇ I commanded to fashionᶜ their offering-tables (*wḏḥ*), the electrum was under ¹³my seal.

Arrival at Elephantine

611. I reached Elephantine according to this command; I kissed the earth before the lord of the cataract (Khnum).

Return to Abydos

612. I returned by ⌜the way⌝ over which I had passed.   ¹⁴I drove in the mooring-stakeᵈ at Abydos.

Erection of Stela

613. I fixed my name ¹⁵at the place where is the god Osiris, First of the Westerners, lord of eternity, ruler of the West, (the place) ¹⁶to which all that is, flees, for the sake of the benefit therein, in the midst of ¹⁷the followers of the lord of life, that I might eat his loaf, and come forth by day; that my spirit might enjoy ¹⁸the ceremonies of people, kind in heart toward my tomb, and in hand ¹⁹toward my stela. For I have not done ⌜——⌝; that the god may ⌜be favorable⌝ to me in ²⁰judgment, when I am "there;"ᵉ that I may labor, being a spirit in the necropolis-cliff, ²¹the ruler of eternity; that I may operate the rudder, that I may descend into the sacred barque (*nšm·t*); that I may smell ²²the earth before Upwawet. Khentemsemeti, triumphant, lord of reverence.

ᵃPriests.   ᵇTemple matters.

ᶜ*Nb*, the verb used especially of metal-work; the determinative is probably a man with a blow-pipe.

ᵈMeaning "I landed," as in § 423.

ᵉA designation of the abode of the dead.

REIGN OF SESOSTRIS II

INSCRIPTION OF HAPU[a]

614. The following inscription contains a double date, showing that Sesostris II was associated as coregent with his father in the latter's thirty-second year, the coregency continuing at least three years. It also shows that the forts in Nubia were subject from time to time to inspection by officers especially sent thither for the purpose; but, unfortunately, not all have recorded their mission on the rocks as did the officer Hapu.

615. On the right is the name of Amenemhet II, "*beloved of Satet, mistress of Elephantine;*" on the left is the name of Sesostris II, "*beloved of Khnum, lord of the cataract region;*" between them is the following inscription:

616. Made in the year 3, under the majesty of Horus: Seshmutowe (*Sšmw-t꜒wy*=Horus-name of Sesostris II), corresponding to the year 35[b] under the majesty of Horus: Hekenemmat (*Ḥkn-m-m꜓t*=Amenemhet II). The ⌜—⌝,[c] Hapu (*Ḥ꜒pw*) came, in order to make an inspection in the fortresses of Wawat.[d]

---

[a]Cut on the rocks near Assuan; published by Young, *Hieroglyphics*, Pl. 61 (very bad); Lepsius, *Auswahl der wichtigsten Urkunden*, 10 (copied from Young); Lepsius, *Zwölfte Dynastie*, II; Lepsius, *Denkmäler*, II, 123, *e* (good), and de Morgan, *Catalogue des monuments*, 25, No. 178 (date wrong). I also had Lepsius' squeeze (No. 360, *a*) which I collated with all the publications; the text of de Morgan, *ibid.*, is almost as bad as Young's.

[b]So all the texts except de Morgan's (*Catalogue des monuments*, 25), which has 36! As we have a double date here, this would increase the reign of Amenemhet II by an entire year, if correct. The squeeze is quite clearly 35; this was also the opinion of Sethe, who examined the squeeze with me.

[c]An uncertain title (⌜—⌝-*kf꜒-yb*), which occurs also with Hapu's figure below the inscription; see Bergmann, *Recueil*, VII, 187.

[d]The original has the mountain-determinative against de Morgan's hill-country.

INSCRIPTION OF THE TREASURER KHNUMHOTEP[a]

617. Above stands Sesostris II, before the god Soped, from whom he receives the symbol of life. Below stands Khnumhotep, accompanied by the following inscription:

618. [1]Year 1, his monument in God's-Land was executed. [2]The treasurer[b] of the god, real king's-confidant, his beloved, his favorite, the darling of his lord, [3]knowing the law, discreet in executing (it); [4]zealous for him[c] who favors him; [5]not trespassing against the injunction of the palace, the command of the court; [6]favorite of the crown, being in the palace, praiser of [7]Horus, Lord of the Two Lands; presenting the court to the king, [8]truly accurate like Thoth, master of the double cabinet, Khnumhotep.

INSCRIPTION OF KHNUMHOTEP II[d]

619. The inscription of Khnumhotep II is our fullest and most important source for a study of the relations between the powerful nomarchs, the local counts or barons of the Twelfth Dynasty, and their contemporary kings. Like the nobles of El Kab at the rise of the Eighteenth Dynasty, the princes of Benihasan were a mainstay of the royal house in the early Twelfth. Their domain was the principality of

---

[a]Stela found at Wadi Gasus on the Red Sea, opposite Coptos; now in the collection of Alnwick Castle (No. 1935); first published by Erman from a squeeze, *Zeitschrift für ägyptische Sprache*, 1882, 204, 205; then by Birch, *Catalogue Alnwick Castle*, Pl. IV, 268–70. Cf. Brugsch, *Völkertafel*, 54, 58, and 68; Schweinfurth, *Wadi Gasûs*, 11, n. 2; Wilkinson, *General View*, 364.

[b]This title is at the left of the second line (first vertical line), and appears only in Birch's text.

[c]The king.

[d]Cut on the walls of the superb chapel chamber in his tomb at Benihasan; published by Burton (*Excerpta Hieroglyphica*, 33, 34); by Champollion (*Notices descriptives*, II, 418–22); by Lepsius (*Denkmäler*, II, 124, 125); by Brugsch (*Monuments de l'Egypte*, 15–17; and *Thesaurus*, VI, 1513–25); and by Newberry (*Beni Hasan*, I, Pls. XXV, XXVI). The last, the publication of the Archæological Survey of the Egypt Exploration Fund, contains in two volumes the entire Benihasan necropolis. Its text of the great inscription of Khnumhotep II

the Oryx (the sixteenth nome of Upper Egypt), which included both banks of the river between the Hare nome on the south and the Jackal nome on the north. The desert cliffs are not far from the river on the east shore, and the narrow strip thus inclosed was sometimes detached from the Oryx nome, as a separate principality, known as *"Horizon of Horus,"* designated usually by its chief town, Menet-Khufu, the birthplace of the great Fourth Dynasty king, Khufu. The sole witnesses to the ancient power and prosperity of this principality are its tombs, those of the Middle Kingdom being located at Benihasan, 169 miles above Cairo.

620. The first of the family in this principality, Khnum-hotep II's grandfather, Khnumhotep I, was appointed by Amenemhet I; at first as count only of Menet-Khufu, and finally of the entire Oryx nome (§§ 625, 626). The narrative of the appointment refers significantly to Amenemhet I's personal visit to the principality, establishing the boundary lines, *"when he cast out evil,"* meaning of course rebellion, or at least of unjust aggression, the last expiring struggles of other ambitious noblemen in their opposition to the new dynasty,[a] marking the close of the long obscure period of such wars, between the Old and the Middle Kingdom. As

---

is much the best. The texts of Maspero (*Recueil*, I, 169–81) and Krebs (*De Chnemothis nomarchi inscriptione aegyptiaca commentatio*, Berlin, 1890) are taken from the publications. The original text contains many patent blunders of the scribe, which render certain parts unintelligible; Mr. Griffith furnishes some useful emendations of such passages (*Proceedings of the Society of Biblical Archæology*, 1890, 263–68), and some others I have added, which will be evident from the notes. The lines of the original are so short, that the translation could not be so often divided, and only every fifth line is there numbered. It has not been practicable to cut up the inscription, and assign each portion to the reign which it concerns; hence the whole has been put in the reign from which it dates.

[a] The reference is not so clear as those in the inscription of Ahmose of El Kab, who narrates three rebellions against King Ahmose I at the rise of the Eighteenth Dynasty (II, 11, 15, 16).

a special favor of the king, Sesostris I, Khnumhotep I's sons received the same domain; Nakht being appointed to Menet-Khufu (§ 627), and Amenemhet[a] receiving the Oryx nome, in the king's eighteenth year (§§ 518, ll. 1–3, and 627). At the same time, the sister of these two princes, Khnumhotep I's daughter Beket, married a powerful official at the court, the vizier and governor of the royal residence city Nehri, who was also probably prince of the neighboring Hare nome (§ 628). Of this union was born Khnumhotep II, who received Menet-Khufu as his just claim through his mother, on the death of his predecessor, his uncle, Nakht,[b] in the nineteenth year of Amenemhet II. He ruled with great prosperity until at least the sixth year of Sesostris II,[c] in which year a party of thirty-seven Bedwin visited him, bringing gifts and probably desiring traffic.[d] Khnumhotep II greatly strengthened his family by marrying Kheti, the eldest daughter of the prince of the Jackal nome. His eldest son, Nakht, was therefore appointed to the princedom of the Jackal nome as his inheritance from his mother,[e] while his next son, Khnumhotep (III), after honors at

---

[a]Amenemhet (Ameni) is not mentioned by Khnumhotep II's great inscription. See note, l. 56.

[b]Nakht had held the principality, therefore, 43 years.

[c]This is the latest date in the tomb (Newberry, *Beni Hasan*, I, Pl. XXXVIII), so that Khnumhotep II ruled at least nineteen years. If born not long after his uncle Nakht's accession, he would have been not less than forty years of age at his own accession, and nearly sixty years old at the above latest date in his tomb.

[d]This is the subject of the famous scene in his tomb, naïvely identified by early Egyptologists with Abraham's visit to Egypt, with which, it is needless to say, it had nothing to do. The accompanying inscription is as follows: "*The arrival, bringing eye-paint, which 37 Asiatics bring to him*" (Newberry, *Beni Hasan*, I, Pl. XXX). Their leader is called: "*Sheik of the highlands, Ibshe (Yb-š⸗)*," a good Hebrew name. The report handed in by Khnumhotep's secretary dates the event in the sixth year of Sesostris II, and calls them "*Asiatics of the desert*" (ꜥꜣ mw n šw, ibid., Pl. XXXVIII).

[e]For a similar inheritance through the mother, of the grandfather's office at Siut, see §§ 413 ff.

court, was appointed to his father's countship of Menet-Khufu.[a]

621. We are thus able to trace the history of the family through four generations in this great inscription, but the Benihasan tombs do not carry the career of these princes farther, and, perhaps because of increasing power and centralization on the part of the kings, these tombs cease abruptly at this point in the middle of the Twelfth Dynasty.

Introduction

622. [1]The hereditary prince, count, king's-confidant, whom his god loves, governor of the eastern highlands, Nehri's (*Nḥry*) son, Khnumhotep, triumphant; born of a count's (*ḥᵓty-ᶜ*) daughter, the matron, Beket (*Bᵓ ḳ·t*), triumphant.

The Tomb, its Paintings and Inscriptions

623. He made (it)[b] as his monument; his first virtue was in adorning [5]his city, that he might perpetuate his name forever, and that he might establish it for eternity in his tomb of the necropolis; that he might perpetuate the name of his official staff, establishing (them) according to their offices: the excellent ones, who were in [10]his household, whom he raised over [11]his peasant-slaves (*mr·t*); every office that he sustained; all artificers according to their kind.[c]

His Appointment as Count of Menet-Khufu

624. His mouth saith: [14]"The majesty of . . . .[d] Amenemhet (II), who is given life, stability, satisfaction, like Re, for-

---

[a]This is not stated in the great inscription, but is referred to in a hunting scene (Newberry, *Beni Hasan*, I, Pl. XXXII): "*to whom was given the rule (ḥḳᵓ· t) of Khnumhotep (II) triumphant, in Menet-Khufu, when his son was appointed to the rule of ⌜—⌝.*" To whom the last son refers is not clear, and the name of the princedom is unknown. It occurs also at Siut (§ 396, l. 16), as the northern limit from which the troops of the south were mustered against Siut, and must therefore be south of Siut, and not near Benihasan.

[b]The tomb in which the inscription is found.

[c]All his favorite servants and officials of his estate are represented in the superb tomb paintings, engaged in their various duties, with their names added; it is this "*perpetuation*" which is meant in ll. 7–12.

[d]Full fivefold titulary.

ever, appointed me to be hereditary prince, count, governor of the eastern highlands, priest of Horus, and [priest] of Pakht; to the inheritance of my mother's father in ²⁰Menet-Khufu (*Mn ᶜ·t-Ḥwfw*).ᵃ He established for me the southern landmark;ᵇ he perpetuated the northern, like the heavens. He divided the great river along its middle, as was done for the father ²⁵of my mother, by command which came forth from the mouth of the majesty of . . . . .ᶜ Amenemhet I, who is given life, stability, satisfaction, like Re, forever.

His Grandfather Appointed Count of Menet-Khufu

625. ³⁰He appointed him to be hereditary prince, count, governor of the eastern highlands in Menet-Khufu. He established the southern landmark, perpetuating the northern, like the heavens; he divided the great river along its middle; its eastern side ³⁵of the "Horizon of Horus,"ᵈ was as far as the eastern highland; at the coming of his majesty, when he cast out evil, shining like Atum himself, when he restored that which he found ruined; that which a city had taken ⁴⁰from its neighbor; while he caused city to know its boundary with city, establishing their landmarks like the heavens, distinguishing their waters according to that which was in the writings, investigating according to ⁴⁵that which was of old, because he so greatly loved justice.

His Grandfather Appointed Prince of Oryx Nome

626. Lo, he appointed him to be hereditary prince, count, ⌜—⌝, great lord of the Oryx nome. He established the landmarks: the southern on his boundary as far as ⁵⁰the Hare nome; his northern as far as the Jackal nome. He divided the great river along its middle: its water, its fields, its trees, its sand as far as the western highlands.ᵉ

Khnumhotep II's Uncle, Nakht, Made Count of Menet-Khufu

627. He (the king) appointed his (Khnumhotep I's) eldest son, Nakht (I) ⁵⁵triumphant, revered, to the rule (*ḥḳ ᵓ*) of his inheritance in

---

ᵃThe chief town of the countship. It means "*Nurse of Khufu*," and was located in the region of Benihasan. See note, § 625.

ᵇLit.: "*tablet*."   ᶜFull fivefold titulary.

ᵈThe "county" or principality of which Menet-Khufu was the chief town (see note on ll. 19, 20, § 624). It occupied the east side of the valley to the cliffs.

ᵉThe principality, or nome, therefore occupied the western side of the valley to the cliffs.

Menet-Khufu[a] as a great favor of the king, by the command which issued [from] the mouth of the majesty of king . . . .[b] [61]Sesostris I, who is given life, stability, satisfaction, like Re, forever.

Khnumhotep II's Birth

628. This my chief nobility is my birth, my mother having gone to be hereditary [65]princess, and countess, as the daughter of the ruler ($ḥḳ$) of the Oryx nome, to Hat-Sehetepibre[c] . . . . to be the wife of the hereditary prince, count, ruler ($ḥḳ$) of the "New Towns," the ⌈—⌉[d] of the king of Upper Egypt, the ⌈—⌉[d] [70]of the king of Lower Egypt, ⌈in⌉ his rank of governor of the residence city, Nehri ($Nḥry$), triumphant, revered.

His Appointment as Count of Menet-Khufu

629. The King of Upper and Lower Egypt, Nubkure (Amenemhet II), who is given life, stability, satisfaction, like Re, forever, brought me, being the son of a count ($ḥ゚ty-ᶜ$), into the inheritance of the rule ($ḥḳ゚·t$) of my mother's father, because [75]he so greatly loved justice. He is Atum himself, Nubkure (Amenemhet II), who is given life, stability, satisfaction, gladness of his heart, like Re, forever. He appointed me to be count ($ḥ゚ty-ᶜ$) in the year 19, in Menet-Khufu.

His Buildings and Piety

630. Then I adorned [80]it, and its treasures[e] grew in all things. I perpetuated the name of my father; I adorned the houses of the ka's

---

[a]Although the fact remains for some reason not mentioned here, it is clear that the Oryx nome, that is, the bulk of the principality, goes to Amenemhet, who began his rule in the eighteenth year of Sesostris I (§ 518, ll. 1–3), for the Oryx nome here remains unaccounted for, during the life of Nakht I.

[b]Fivefold titulary,

[c]The name of the city where Nehri lived; it means: "*House of Amenemhet I*," and is followed by the usual royal salutations. As Nehri was "*governor of the residence city*," this must be the name of the city where the king lived. The residence city of Amenemhet I was Ithtowe ($Y_t-t゚wy$) between Medum and Memphis, and probably that of Sesostris I, also. Griffith thinks therefore that Hat-Sehetepibre is simply another name for Ithtowe (Griffith, *Kahun Papyri*, II, 88), a very plausible conclusion.

[d]Both unknown titles, here parallel.

[e]As emended by Griffith (*Proceedings of the Society of Biblical Archæology*, 1890, 263).

and the dwelling thereof; I followed my statues[a] to the temple; I devoted for them [85]their offerings: the bread, beer, water, wine, incense, and joints of beef credited to the mortuary priest. I endowed him with fields and peasants; I commanded the mortuary offering of bread, beer, oxen, and geese, at every feast [90]of the necropolis: at the feast of the first of the year, of New Year's Day, of the great year, of the little year, of the last of the year, the great feast, at the great Rekeh, at the little Rekeh,[b] at the feast of the 5 intercalary days, at ⌜— —⌝, [95]at the 12 monthly feasts, at the 12 mid-monthly feasts; every feast of the happy living, and of the dead.[c] Now, as for the mortuary priest, or any person, who shall disturb them, he shall not survive, his son shall not survive in his place.

Khnumhotep II's Honors at Court

631. Greater [100]was my praise at the court than (that of) any sole companion. He (the king) exalted me above his nobles, I was placed[d] before those who had been before me. ⌜—[e] [105]the official body of the palace, giving praise according to my appointment, according to (my) favor which came to pass in the (royal) presence, the command of the king [110]himself. Never happened the like to servants ⌜————⌝. He knew the manner of my tongue, the ⌜moderation⌝ of my character. [115]I was an honored one with the king; my praise was with his court, my popularity was before his "companions." The hereditary prince, count, [120]Nehri's son, Khnumhotep, revered.

Appointment of K. II's Son, Nakht, as Prince of Jackal Nome

632. Another honor accorded me (was): my eldest son, Nakht, born of Kheti[f] was appointed to the rule (ḥḳꜣ) of the Jackal nome, to the inheritance of his mother's father; [125]made sole companion; appointed to be forefront of Middle Egypt.[g] There were given to him

---

[a]He means the statues of his ancestors.

[b]Rekeh (Rkh) means "heat."

[c]Lit., "every feast of the happy one in the (valley-) plain, and of the one on the mountain;" those who are on the plain still live, but those on the mountain are the dead in the cliff-tombs.

[d]Read dy.   [f]One of Khnumhotep II's two wives.

[e]The verb.   [g]Or possibly: "the South."

all ranks of nobility by the majesty of[a] . . . . . [130]. . . Sesostris II, who is given life, stability, satisfaction, like Re, forever.   He (the king) made his monuments in the Jackal nome, restoring that which he found obliterated, that which a city had taken from its neighbor; causing him to know [135]his boundary according to the ˹record˺, investigating according to that which was of old, putting a landmark at his southern boundary, perpetuating the northern like the heavens, establishing on the fields [140]of the low ground,[b] a total amounting to 15 landmarks;[c] establishing upon its northern fields its boundary as far as Oxyrrhyncus. He divided the great river along its middle, [145]its western side (going) to the Jackal nome as far as the western highlands; when the hereditary prince, count, Khnumhotep's son, Nakht, triumphant, revered, petitioned, saying: "My waters know not the great favor of [150]the king's[d] presence."

Honors of Khnumhotep II's Second Son, Khnumhotep

633. Another prince (*wr*) is counselor, sole companion, great ˹among˺ the sole companions, of numerous gifts to the palace,[e] sole companion.   [155]There is not one possessed of his virtues; to whom the (*sḏm· w-*) officers hearken, the unique mouth,[f] closing (other) mouths, bringing advantage to its[g] possessor, keeper of the door of the highlands,

---

[a]Full fivefold titulary.

[b]Rendered by Krebs *campus hostium*, and treated as a proper name. The determinative of *ḫrw* is not that of the enemy as in Krebs' text, but merely a falling man, as might be expected after the root *ḫr*.   It has a second determinative of land, and the word is not unknown as "*low land*," the best, most fertile land, next the river.

[c]The passage was rendered with essential correctness thirty years ago by Maspero (*Recueil*, I, 166) giving "quinze stèles-frontières" and "Ouob" = Oxyrrhyncus.   It is therefore an oversight as now rendered in his history (*Dawn*, 524), recording the gift to Khnumhotep of fifteen nomes extending "from Aphroditopolis to Thebes," thus making one nomarch ruler of three-fourths of Upper Egypt.   The careful establishment of the northern boundary by erecting 15 landmarks was natural, as Oxyrrhyncus is in the vicinity of the home of the hostile northern families, the descendants of the Ninth and Tenth Dynasties who fought the rising Thebans of the Middle Kingdom (see §§ 391 ff.).

[d]Meaning the king had not yet determined the limits in this nome, and the settling of the limits just mentioned was a result of this request.

[e]Lit., "*numerous of gifts of the palace;*" the word "*gifts*" indicating "that which is brought;" cf. the Arabic *hâdîyyătŭn*.

[f]Meaning "*unique counselor.*"

[g]"*Its*" refers to "*advantage*," not to "*mouth.*"

Khnumhotep, son of Khnumhotep, son of Nehri, [160]who was born of the matron, Kheti.

His Restoration of Ancestors' Tombs

634. I kept alive the name of my fathers, which I found obliterated upon the doorways,[a] (making them) legible[b] in ⌜form⌝; accurate in reading, not [165]putting one in the place of another.[c]   Behold, it is an excellent son, who restores the name of the ancestors; Nehri's son, Khnumhotep, triumphant, revered.

His Father's Mortuary Buildings

635. [170]My chief nobility was: I executed a cliff-tomb, (for) a man should imitate that which his father does.[d]   My father made for himself a house of the ka in the town of Mernofret, of [175]good stone of Ayan, in order to perpetuate his name forever and establish it eternally; that his name might live in the mouth of the people and abide in the mouth of the living, [180]upon his tomb of the necropolis, in his excellent house of eternity, his seat of everlastingness; according to the favor of the king's presence, his love in the court.

His Father's Excellent Administration

636. He ruled his city as a babe, [185]before he was loosed from swaddling-clothes;[e] he executed a royal commission, and his two[f] plumes danced, as a child not yet circumcised; ⌜for⌝ the king knew[g]

---

[a]The doorways of the tombs, where it was customary to engrave the name and titles; for similar restorations by posterity, see §§ 688, 689.

[b]*Rḥ* in the negative is used in the sense of "*undiscernible, illegible*" on a stela, of Sabako, in the British Museum (No. 135), see Breasted, *Zeitschrift für Aegyptische Sprache*, 39, Pls. I, II, l. 2.

[c]He means he was careful and accurate in reading the names, not introducing confusion among them, by restoring a name in the wrong place.

[d]He begins to tell of the construction of his own tomb, but is diverted by the reference to his father, whose tomb and early favor at court he recounts, before he again reverts to his own tomb and other buildings (l. 192).

[e]There is no doubt that this is the same word used in the description of Sesostris I's youth (§ 502, ll. 9, 10), although much corrupted.

[f]His plumes of office.

[g]Read *rḥ štny*, as shown by Griffith (*Proceedings of the Society of Biblical Archæology*, 1890, 267).

the manner of his tongue, the ᴿmoderationᴸ of his character, [190]Sebek-enekh's son, Nehri, triumphant, revered, whom he exalted before his nobles to be ruler (ḥḳᵓ) of his city.

His Own Buildings

637. The achievements of the count, Khnumhotep: I made a monument in the midst of my city; I built a colonnaded hall which I found [195]in ᴿruinᴸ;[a] I erected it with columns anew, inscribed with my own name. I perpetuated the name of my father upon them.[b] I [ᴿrecordedᴸ] my deeds upon [200]every monument.

I made a door of 7 cubits, of cedar wood without ᴿ—ᴸ for the first doorway of the tomb; double doors for[c] an opening of 5 cubits, 2 palms, for the shrine of the august chamber, which is in this tomb.[d] A prayer [205]for offerings, the mortuary oblations of bread, beer, oxen, geese, was upon every monument, which I made. I . . . .[e] greater in monuments ᴿinᴸ this city than the fathers; [210]a child of this city, more excellent in monuments of its burial place than the ancestors, ᴿin the buildingsᴸ made before me.[f]

---

[a]This stands in place of the usual *m wš* "*in ruin,*" and probably means something similar. (See Loret, *Revue égyptologique*, X, 87–94.) What this building in the city was, it is impossible to say; all city buildings having perished. Compare also the work of Kheti another member of the family, as recorded thus: "*Prince and count, sole companion,* ᴿ—ᴸ *great lord of the Oryx nome, who made eternal monuments in the temple (ḥt-ntr) of Khnum, lord of Herur (Ḥr-wr)*" (Champollion, *Notices descriptives*, II, 354).

[b]*N* and plural strokes are lost in the lacuna; the feminine *s* could not have stood alone, for the building is masculine.

[c]Lit., "*of.*"

[d]"*The first doorway*" is, as we should expect, the main entrance to the tomb chapel. A comparison of the height of the "*door*" given above (7 cubits) with the surviving doorway shows that the door was enough higher than the doorway to lap slightly at top and bottom. The second doorway was for double doors; the only double doors in the tomb of Khnumhotep are those of the shrine containing his statue, in the back wall of the chapel chamber. A comparison of the height of this doorway, given by the inscription, with the surviving doorway itself, shows exact correspondence. On the whole passage, see Breasted, *Proceedings of the Society of Biblical Archæology*, XXII, 88–90.

[e]These lines are unintelligible.

[f]The syntax of both these comparisons is doubtful in several places; it is clear in both that he is comparing his own building activity with that of his ancestors; the first comparison referring to his works in the city, and the second to those in the highland of the necropolis.

Crafts Encouraged

638. I was munificent in monuments; I taught every craft [215]which had been ⌜neglected⌝ in this city, in order that my name might be excellent upon every monument which I ⌜made⌝, ...[a]

Conclusion

639. [220]The hereditary prince, count, Nehri's son, Khnumhotep, born of Beket, triumphant, revered.

[22] Foreman of the tomb, the chief treasurer, Beket.[b]

---

[a]Unintelligible.

[b]This is the architect's "fecit," the signature of the official who conducted the work.

REIGN OF SESOSTRIS III

THE CONQUEST OF NUBIA

640. Sesostris III completed the conquest of Nubia, begun by his predecessors nearly one hundred years before, and was known in the Empire as the real conqueror of the region between the first and second cataracts. He conducted not less than four campaigns in this district, and probably more; and by his canalization of the cataract passages, and the erection of fortresses at strategic points, he made this country a permanent possession of the Pharaohs, which was never lost except for a time during the Hyksos period, until the dissolution of the Empire. Important material documents, like the fortresses of Kummeh and Semneh, are graphic witnesses of the character and permanence of this conquest.[a]

641. The documentary materials for Sesostris III's operations in Nubia are as follows:

I. The Canal Inscriptions (§§ 642–48).

II. The Elephantine Inscription (§§ 649, 650).

III. The First Semneh Stela (§§ 651–52).

IV. The Second Semneh Stela (§§ 653–60).

V. Inscription of Ikhernofret (§§ 661–70).

VI. Inscription of Sisatet (§§ 671, 672; see also §§ 676 ff., and 687).

I. THE CANAL INSCRIPTIONS

642. In order to establish unbroken water communication with the country above the first cataract, Sesostris III

---

[a]A further reference to one of these Nubian campaigns of Sesostris III is found in the life of Sebekkhu (§§ 676 ff.).

cleared a channel[a] which permitted the passage of his war fleets, and later doubtless of much commerce also. Although this enterprise had been begun in the Sixth Dynasty, it was now over five hundred years since Uni's attempts to pierce the cataract (§ 324). Sesostris III's achievement was recorded in the two following inscriptions, cut on the rocks of the Island of Sehel. The first, recording the *"making"* of the canal, is undated, but as the second states, he repaired (*"made anew"*)[b] the canal in the eighth year, it must have been made before this date, and probably in anticipation of the campaign of that year.

First Inscription[c]

643. A scene above, represents the king, Sesostris III, standing before the goddess Anuket, exactly as below (§ 646) before Satet; below them is the inscription:

644. He made (it) as his monument for Anuket, mistress of Nubia ($T^{,}$-$pd\cdot t$) — — —, making for her a canal, whose name is: "Beautiful-Are-the-Ways-of-Khekure" (Sesostris III), that he may live forever.

645. In the eighth year the channel was already in need of repair, and had to be cleared for the passage of the expedition of that year. This is recorded in the

---

[a]Mr. Wilbour and Mr. Somers Clarke found a rock-cut canal south of Sehel, but its dimensions do not coincide with those given in the inscription (see *Zeitschrift für ägyptische Sprache*, 1894, 63, 64).

[b]But it should be remembered that *"anew"* may possibly mean " for the first time" as it later sometimes does.

[c]Text published by Lepsius, *Denkmäler*, II, 136, b = de Morgan, *Catalogue des monuments*, 87, No. 39. This inscription was known fifty years before Mr. Wilbour's discovery below, but the name of the canal was misunderstood as that of a city (e. g., Wiedemann, *Aegyptische Geschichte*, 252). The inscription did not become clear until the publication of Mr. Wilbour's discovery (cf. quotation of Erman's letter, *Recueil*, XIII, 203). The old misunderstanding still survives, and the canal appears as "an emporium" bearing the name "Ways of Khâkerî" in some publications.

Second Inscription[a]

646. In a scene at the top stands the king, Sesostris III, wearing the crowns of Upper and Lower Egypt, and bearing the (*wꜣs-*) scepter and (*ḫrp-*) baton. The goddess "*Satet, mistress of Elephantine*," stands before him, presenting him with life; while behind him is the "*chief treasurer . . . . . chief of works.*"[b] Below is the following inscription:

647. Year 8 under the majesty of the King of Upper and Lower Egypt: Khekure (*Ḫꜥ-kꜣw-Rꜥ*, Sesostris III), living forever. His majesty commanded to make the canal anew,[c] the name of this canal being: "Beautiful-Are-the-Ways-of-Khekure-[Living]-Forever," when his majesty proceeded up-river to overthrow Kush, the wretched.

Length of this canal, 150 cubits; width, 20; depth, 15.

648. The canal was still in use in the New Kingdom, and was cleared again by Thutmose I and III (II, 75, 76, 649, 650).

II.   ELEPHANTINE INSCRIPTION[d]

649. In addition to the great works on the canal, Sesostris III also gave some attention to the fortress[e] of Elephantine as he passed southward on the campaign of the eighth year. The work was recorded there by Ameni, the officer commissioned to do it, in the following inscription:

---

[a]Discovered by Mr. Charles Wilbour, and published by him in *Recueil*, XIII, 202–4; later by de Morgan, *Catalogue des monuments*, 86, No. 20.

[b]He has been omitted by Wilbour, and his name is lacking in de Morgan, *Catalogue des monuments.*

[c]Or possibly: "*for the first time.*"

[d]From a small stela now in the British Museum (No. 852); it was published by Birch (*Zeitschrift für ägyptische Sprache*, 1875, 50), and again, *Egyptian Texts*, 12, 13. I used my own copy of the original, as that of Birch contains a number of inaccuracies.

[e]The fortress is supposed by Maspero (*Recueil*, XIII, 204) to be the wall connecting Assuan and Philæ, of which there are considerable remains at the present day.

650. Year 9,[a] third month of the third season under the majesty of the King of Upper and Lower Egypt, Khekure (Sesostris III) beloved of Satet, mistress of Elephantine, living forever. Command of his majesty to the Magnate of the South, Ameni, [rto maker] a doorway in the fortress of Elephantine, to make a r—r (a building) for the crown-possessions[b] of the South — — the — people in the region of Elephantine; when [my lord, life! prosperity! he]alth! journeyed to overthrow the wretched Kush.

III.   THE FIRST SEMNEH STELA[c]

651. Sesostris III, having, in his eighth year, pushed his southern advance above the second cataract, to a point about thirty-seven miles south of Wadi Halfa, set up his landmark, the stone marking the southern boundary of his realm. His great-grandfather, Sesostris I, had already conquered to this point (§§ 510 ff.), but Sesostris III was now prepared to maintain the conquest.

652. [1]Southern[d] boundary, made in the year 8, under the majesty of the King of Upper and Lower Egypt, Khekure (Sesostris III), who is given life forever [2]and ever; in order to prevent that any Negro should cross it, by water or [3]by land, with a ship, (or) any herds of [4]the Negroes; except a Negro who shall come to do trading in Iken[e] (*Yḳn*), [5]or with

---

[a]Birch has 8, but the original has 9: the last unit on the left is very faint, and was therefore overlooked. This is doubtless the date on which the work was finished, the order having been given as the king passed, a year previously. It is hardly probable that there was another campaign in the ninth year after that of the eighth.

[b]Cf. § 522, l. 16.

[c]A red granite stela discovered by Lepsius at Semneh on the west bank of the Nile. It is now in Berlin (No. 14753); published by Lepsius, *Denkmäler*, II, 136, *i*, and (copied therefrom) Lemm, *Lesestücke*, 62.   On its strange history, see § 653, note, p. 294.

[d]At the top of the stela is the single word "*West*," indicating on which side of the river it belonged. There must have been another on the other side, but it has never been found.

[e]Unknown place.

a commission. Every good thing[a] shall be done with them, but without allowing [6]a ship of the Negroes to pass by Heh[b] (*Ḥḥ*), going downstream, forever.

IV.   THE SECOND SEMNEH STELA[c]

653. After the campaign of the eighth year, it was again necessary in the twelfth year to chastise the Nubians. Of this expedition only the meagerest record has reached us in an inscription[d] on the rocks at Assuan, of which, beside the date and the name of Sesostris III, we can read only the following: "*His majesty journeyed to overthrow Kush.*"

654. Already in the sixteenth year further disturbances in Kush again called the king thither, and this expedition is twice recorded: on the second Semneh stela; and on a duplicate found on the island of Uronarti, just below Semneh.[e] The duplicate contains in the first line, after the

---

[a]Read *yḫ · t*, "*thing*," the hieratic for which was mistaken by the copyist for *tw* (Erman).

[b]Modern Semneh (see Baedeker's *Egypt*, 1902, 379), on the west side of the river, about thirty-seven miles above Wadi Halfa. Here and at Kummeh, on the eastern side, Sesostris III erected two fortresses for enforcing the blockade above decreed.

[c]Red granite stela set up on the west shore at Semneh in the temple in the fortress of Sesostris III (see § 640). It has had a remarkable history since its discovery by Lepsius in July, 1844. Broken into two pieces, the upper portion after packing, was forgotten by Lepsius' workmen, and with the "First Semneh Stela" (§§ 651 f.) was left in Semneh, so that only the lower portion of the "Second Stela" reached Berlin. Some forty years later (1886) the forgotten pieces were found by Insinger on the banks of the river, still in Lepsius' boxes. They were taken to Cairo, where they remained in the Gizeh (Bulak) collection for many years, but were at last secured by the Berlin Museum, and the two portions of the "Second Semneh Stela" were rejoined in 1899, after a separation of over fifty years (Berlin, No. 1157). Published by Lepsius (*Denkmäler*, II, 136, *h*); I also had a copy from the original, kindly loaned me by Professor Erman.

[d]Petrie, *Season in Egypt*, XIII, 340. It has been omitted in de Morgan's *Catalogue des monuments*.

[e]It was discovered by Steindorff, Borchardt, and Schaefer in March, 1900. It is not yet published, and I collate the variants from a copy by Borchardt, cited in the note as U. An account of it, with a copy of the title, is given by Steindorff in *Berichte der philologisch-historischen Classe der Königlichen Sächsischen Gesellschaft der Wissenschaften zu Leipzig*, Juni, 1900, p. 233.

king's name, a variant of great historical importance, as follows: *"Stela made in the year 16, third month of the second season, when the fortress: 'Repulse-of-the-Troglodytes'*[a] *was built."*

655. It was on this campaign, therefore, that the Uronarti fortress was built. The temple in the Semneh fortress was already built for a feast, likewise called *"Repulse-of-the-Troglodytes,"*[b] doubtless in commemoration of this victory, which was celebrated in it on the twenty-first of Pharmuthi, a month later. This feast continued to be celebrated in the Empire, and the enactments for offerings upon it, and the other feasts of this temple, were reinstituted by Thutmose III (see II, 167 ff.).

656. The "Second Semneh Stela" is as follows:[c]

Introduction

[1]Live the King of Upper and Lower Egypt, [2]Sesostris III,[d] who is given life, stability, satisfaction forever.

Boundary Established

657. [3]Year 16, third month of the second season,[e] (occurred) his majesty's making the southern boundary as far as Heh[e] (*Ḥḥ*). [4]I

---

[a]This is certainly the name of the fortress on Uronarti; we could render: *"the fortress which repulses the T.,"* for which we have the parallel: *"the walls of the prince, made to repulse the Bedwin"* (§ 493); but the fact that a feast of Sesostris III, probably celebrating this victory, was also called *"Repulse-of-the-Troglodytes"* (II, 171), is clear evidence that we have here a name for the fortress. Moreover, another fortress of Sesostris III is mentioned in the same way in the inscription (Lepsius, *Denkmäler*, 151, *c*) of an officer of one of the first Sebekhoteps, cut on the neighboring rocks to record the height of the Nile (§§ 751, 752).

[b]There was another feast celebrating a similar victory in this temple, called *"Binding-of-the-Barbarians"* (see II, 171, l. 12), at which offerings were made to the queen, *"great king's-wife Merseger."*

[c]The variants in the duplicate are chiefly of grammatical importance, but where they clear up the meaning, I have adduced them in the notes.

[d]Text has full titulary.

[e]This phrase is lacking in U; and in its place appears the statement above (§ 654) regarding the fortress.

have made my boundary beyond[a] (that) of my fathers; I have [5]increased that which was bequeathed to me.[b]   I am a king who speaks and executes; that which my heart conceives [6]is that which comes to pass by my hand; (one who is) eager to possess, and ⌐powerful⌐ to [7]⌐—⌐; not allowing[c] a matter to sleep in his heart . . . . [8]. . . . . ⌐attacking him who attacks⌐, silent in a matter,[d] or [9]answering a matter according to that which is in it; since, if one is silent after attack, it strengthens [10]the heart of the enemy.   Valiance is eagerness, cowardice is to slink back; he is truly a craven [11]who is repelled upon his border; since the Negro hearkens ⌐to⌐ the ⌐—⌐ of the mouth; [12]it is answering him which drives him back; when one is eager against him, he turns his back; when one slinks back, he begins to be eager.   [13]But they are not a people of might, they are poor and broken[e] in heart.   [14]My majesty has seen them; it is not an untruth.

Plundering of Nubia

658. I captured their women, I carried off[15] their subjects, went forth to their wells, smote their bulls; I reaped[f] their grain, and [16]set fire thereto.   (I swear) as my father lives for me, I speak[g] in truth, without a lie[h] therein, [17]coming out of my mouth.

Future Maintenance of Boundary

659. Now, as for every son of mine who shall maintain this boundary, [18]which my majesty has made, he is my son, he is born to my

---

[a]Lit., "*in front of*," which is to an Egyptian the same as "southward of."

[b]At this point the narrative is interrupted by a encomium on himself by the king, which is in poetic parallelism, and in parts is unintelligible.   It merges into satire on the Negroes, and continues to l. 14, where the narrative is resumed.

[c]U has *tm ssḏr*, lit., "*not causing a matter to sleep*."

[d]U has *gr mdt*.

[e]U has *sd·w* "*broken, pierced*," heretofore known only in connection with a wall, an egg, or the like; it has nothing to do with "tails," as rendered, Petrie, *History of Egypt*, I, 180.

[f]This word does not mean "destroy," as so often rendered, but is used of gathering the harvest, the vintage, or even getting stone from a quarry, e. g., inscription of Uni (§ 323, l. 43).   U has the finite form: *wḥ ꜣ·ny*, "*I reaped*."

[g]U has "*I have spoken*" (*ḏd-ny*).

[h]U has: *ḥn ym n ꜥbꜥ*, in which we are to read *ḥn n ꜥbꜥ* together like *ḥn-n-mdwt*; *ḥn n* is a pleonastic phrase before nouns indicating speech (see Erman, *Glossar, s. v.*).

majesty, the likeness of a son who is the champion of his father, [19]who maintains the boundary of him that begat him, Now, as for him who shall relax it, and shall not fight [20]for it; he is not my son, he is not born to me.

Royal Statue at Boundary

660. Now, behold, my majesty caused a statue[a] [21]of my majesty to be made upon this boundary, which my majesty made; in[b] order that ye might prosper because of it, and in order that ye might fight for it.[c]

V.   INSCRIPTION OF IKHERNOFRET[d]

661. The following commission of Ikhernofret to Abydos, of great interest and importance in many respects, is inserted here especially for its bearing on the Nubian wars of Sesostris III.   It is not dated, but we are able to date it from another source with considerable probability.   Ikhernofret was accompanied to Abydos by one of his officials, Sisatet;[e] each of the two men erected a stela there on this occasion, and that of Sisatet states that the visit was made "*when . . . . Sesostris III journeyed to overthrow the wretched Kush, in the year 19.*"   The gold taken from Kush (ll. 3, 4) was therefore probably captured in the campaign of the sixteenth year (§ 657).   We have nowhere else any record of the campaign of the nineteenth year.

662. Ikhernofret narrates how he executed the king's commission, and adds a statement of the functions which

---

[a]No trace of this statue has ever been found.

[b]U has the proper genitive *n*.   [c]Or: "*upon it,*" the boundary.

[d]On his memorial tablet erected at Abydos; now in Berlin (No. 1204, *Ausführliches Verzeichniss des Berliner Museums*, 90, 91); published by Lepsius, *Denkmäler*, II, 135, *h*. It is in bad condition, and full of gaps. I had a copy made from the original, which Schaefer kindly placed at my disposal; it filled nearly all of the gaps in Lepsius' *Denkmäler*. Schaefer has since published it, with full translation and commentary, in Sethe's *Untersuchungen*, IV, but I have not yet seen it.

[e]§§ 671 ff.

he fulfilled at the feasts of Osiris and the celebration of the sacred drama, re-enacting incidents from the myth of the god. Among these duties, there is one of the greatest interest, viz., the conduct of Osiris "*to his tomb before Peker.*" This is, of course, none other than the tomb of the hoary old King Zer, which already at this time was misunderstood as the tomb of Osiris.

Introduction

663. ¹Live the King of Upper and Lower Egypt, Khekure (Sesostris III),ᵃ who is given life forever and ever.

Royal Letter; Introduction

664. ²Royal command to the hereditary prince, count, —, wearer of the royal seal, sole companion, lord of the double gold-house, lord of the double silver-house, chief treasurer, Ikhernofret (*yy-ḫr-nfr·t*), revered:

Commission to Abydos

665. ³"My majesty commands that thou shalt be sent up-river to Abydos,ᵇ to make monuments for my father Osiris, First of the Westerners, to adorn his secret place with the gold, ⁴which heᶜ caused my majesty to bring from Upper Nubia in victory and in triumph. Lo, thou shalt do this in ⁵— — for offering, in satisfying my father Osiris, since my majesty sendeth thee, my heart being certain of thy doing everything ⁶according to the desire of my majesty; since thou hast been brought up in the teaching of my majesty; thou hast been in the training of my majesty, ⁷and the sole teaching of my palace. My

---

ᵃFull fivefold titulary.

ᵇThe reference shows the royal residence was down-river, that is, northward from Abydos. An inscription of the king's sixth year, hitherto unnoticed, furnishes further indication of his interest in the Abydos temple. The mortuary stela of a certain Sebekhotep (British Museum, No. 257) after the usual prayer, states: "*His majesty commanded to dispatch the servant (the deceased) to the crown possessions of Thinis of the South (tp rśy), to cleanse the temples. He did them; ⌐cleansed⌐ that they might be pure for the monthly feast, and clean for the half-monthly feast.*" At the top is the date.

ᶜProbably Osiris.

majesty appointed thee —, while thou wast a young man (*ḥwn*) of 26 years. My majesty hath done this, [8](because) I have seen thee to be one excellent in character (*sḫr*), ready of tongue on coming forth from the body, and sufficient in speech. My majesty [sendeth][a] thee [9]to do this, (since) my [majesty] has recognized that no one doing it possesses thy good qualities. Quickly go thou, and do thou according to all that my majesty has commanded."

Execution of the Commission

666. [10]I did according to all that his majesty commanded, by adorning all that my lord commanded for his father, Osiris, First of the Westerners, lord of Abydos, great, mighty one residing in Thinis.

Temple Monuments and Utensils

667. [11]I acted as "Son, Whom He Loves," for Osiris, First of the Westerners, I adorned the great — forever and ever. I made for him [12]a portable shrine,[b] the "Bearer-of-Beauty" of the "First-of-the-Westerners," of gold, silver, lazuli, fragrant woods, carob wood, and meru wood. (I) fashioned the gods [13]belonging to his divine ennead, (I) made their shrines anew.

Priestly Duties

668. I caused the lay priests to [⌜know how⌝] to do their duties, (I) caused them to know [14]the stipulation of every day, the feasts of the beginnings of the seasons. I superintended the work on the sacred barque (*nšm[· t]*), I fashioned (its) chapel.[c] [15]I decked (*sḥkr*) the body of the lord of Abydos with lazuli and malachite, electrum, and every costly stone, among [16]the ornaments of the limbs of a god. I dressed (*db ꜣ*) the god in his regalia (*ḥ ꜥ w*) by virtue of my office as master of secret things, and of my duty as (⌜*wtb*⌝-) priest. [17]I was pure-handed in decking the god, a (*sm-*) priest of clean fingers.

---

[a]Only the determinative of a verb of going or motion is preserved.

[b]*Ḳnyw.*

[c]This word (*snṯyy*, perhaps *sny· t*, as on the Piankhi stela,) has a determinative exactly like the chapel or cabin in the determinative of *nšm· t*.

Osirian Festival Drama

669. I celebrated the (feast of) "Going Forth" of Upwawet, when he proceeded to champion his father. [18]I repelled the foe from the sacred barque (*nšm· t*), I overthrew the enemies of Osiris. I celebrated the "Great-Going-Forth,"[a] following the god at his going. [19]I sailed the divine boat (*dp· t*) of Thoth upon — —. I equipped the barque (called): "Shining-in-Truth" of the lord of Abydos, with a chapel. [20](I) put on his regalia when he went forth to — Peker; I led the way of the god to his tomb[b] before Peker; I [21]championed Wennofer at "That Day of the Great Conflict;" I slew all the enemies upon the ⌈flats⌉[c] of Nedyt (*Ndy· t*). I conveyed him [22]into the barque (called): "The Great," when it bore his beauty; I gladdened the heart of the eastern highlands; I —ed the rejoicing in the western highlands [23]When they saw the beauty of the sacred barge, as it landed at Abydos, they brought [Osiris, First of the Westerners, lord] of Abydos to his palace, and I followed the god into his house, [24]to attend to his —, when he ⌈resumed⌉ his seat. I loosed the knot in the midst of — — — — — his ⌈attendants⌉, among his courtiers.

670. Below appear five of Ikhernofret's relatives, among them Sisatet, whose stela follows herein (§§ 671–73), Sitameni, the mother, is also mentioned, as she is likewise on the stela of Sisatet. [d]

VI. INSCRIPTION OF SISATET[e]

671. After a prayer for the benefit of Sisatet's father, Ameni, follows a long list of his near relatives, beginning

---

[a]This is the designation of a funeral procession *"going forth"* to the necropolis, as is evident from the description in Bergmann, *Hieroglyphische Inschriften*, VI, l. 12. It refers above to the funeral procession of Osiris in the drama.

[b]This is unquestionably the tomb of Zer, already in the Twelfth Dynasty mistaken for the tomb of Osiris.

[c]This is the word (*ṯsw*) used in Uni (§ 323, l. 45; see note) for *"flats"* or the like.

[d]Ikhernofret's mortuary stela, erected at Abydos on his death, is now in Cairo (Catalogue No. 20310). It contains nothing of historical importance.

[e]On his family mortuary stela, from Abydos, now in the Museum of Geneva; published by Maspero in *Mélanges d'archéologie égyptienne*, II, 217–19, and again, Maspero, *Etudes de mythologie et d'archéologie*, III, 211–15. I had also my own copy of the original.

with his mother, Sitameni. The inscription of Sisatet then follows, giving the occasion of his visit to Abydos, during which, of course, he erected this stela to secure for his family the favors of Osiris in the next world. It is as follows:

672. Master of the double cabinet,[a] Sisatet; he saith: "I came to Abydos, together with the chief treasurer, Ikhernofret, to carve (a statue of) Osiris, lord of Abydos, when the King of Upper and Lower Egypt, Khekure (Sesostris III), living forever, journeyed, while over-throwing the wretched Kush, in the year 19."

673. Some nineteen years later, perhaps at Sisatet's death, his own memorial stela[b] was erected at Abydos. The inscription above begins:

"Year 1, under the majesty of the King of Upper and Lower Egypt, Nematre (N-$m^{\supset c}$-t-R^c, Amenemhet IIi), living forever and ever. Stela which the master of the double cabinet of the office of the chief treasurer, Sisatet, made, in order that his name might endure at the stairway of the great god.

HAMMAMAT INSCRIPTION[c]

674. The principal interest attaching to this inscription arises from the destination of the stone taken out, which is stated to be Ehnas Heracleopolis. The text is so barbarously cut that much is unintelligible:

675. [1]Year 14, fourth month of the first season, day 16, under the majesty of ...... [2] ..... the King of Upper and Lower Egypt, Khekure (Sesostris III), living forever and ever, [3]beloved of Min-Hor of Coptos. Behold, his majesty commanded to dispatch me to

---

[a]His title on his own mortuary stela is: "*Master of the double cabinet of the office of the chief treasurer.*"

[b]Now in the Louvre (C 5); published by Gayet (*Stèles*, VIII-IX, very inaccurate).

[c]Engraved on the rocks in the Wadi Hammamat; published by Lepsius, *Denkmäler*, II, 136, *a*.

4Hammamat, to bring a monument, which his majesty commanded to make 5for Harsaphes (*Ḥr-š·f*), lord of Heracleopolis, for the sake of the life of 6the King of Upper and Lower Egypt, Khekure, living forever and ever; being a beautiful block of 7black basalt.[a] He sent me as foreman of the work, because I was valuable in the opinion of his majesty, a true leader ⌐— —¬ for his lord, smiting for him the four eastern countries,[b] bringing for him the good products of Tehenu, by the greatness of his majesty's fame; saying good things, and reporting pleasing things, at the utterances of whose mouth there is satisfaction; knowing the place of his —, free from lying, kind-hearted, void of ⌐—¬, excellent in speech, — hearted, reporting to the king; one whose foot is firm, real king's-confidant, his beloved, his favorite, steward of the storehouse of the leader of works, Khui (*Ḥ ᶜwy*) born of Hapi (*Ḥᵓpy*)."

STELA OF SEBEK-KHU, CALLED ZAA[c]

676. This stela, as furnishing the only mention of an invasion of Syria by any Pharaoh of the Middle Kingdom, is of great importance. Sebek-khu, who states at the top of the stela that his other or *"beautiful name"* was Zaa (*dᵓᵓ*), gives a brief outline of his career on this mortuary stela which he erected at Abydos. He was born in the twenty-seventh year of Amenemhet II (l. 11), at whose death he was therefore five years old.

677. Of his life during the nineteen years' reign of Sesostris II he says nothing, but with the accession of Sesostris III, Sebek-khu, who was now twenty-four years old, was

---

[a]This stone (*bḫn*) is the same as the two obelisks in the British Museum (*Description*, V, 21, 22), which are stated by the inscription to be *bḫn*. An examination, kindly made by Mr. Gardiner, shows that the obelisks are of the black basaltic rock of Hammamat.

[b]Compare the four countries in the inscription of Ameni, § 519, l. 7.

[c]A small limestone stela discovered at Abydos (Arábah) by Mr. John Garstang, and published by him (*El Arábah*, Quaritch, London, 1901, Pls. IV, V), with a translation by Newberry (*ibid.*, 32, 33); see also Müller, *Orientalistische Litteratur-zeitung*, VI, 448, 449.

made an attendant of the king (l. 13), with six men under him (l. 14). He was presently promoted among the personal troops of the king as "*attendant* (lit., *follower*) *of the ruler*" (l. 14), and commanded sixty men on an expedition of the same king into Nubia. Which one of Sesostris III's Nubian campaigns (§§ 640–73) this was, it is impossible to say, but Sebek-khu's gallantry won him a promotion as a "*commander*" (*šḥḏ*) of the king's personal troops, with one hundred men under him.

678. His next expedition was against a region called Sekmem (*Skmm*) in Retenu, or Syria.[a] We are unfortunately unable to locate this Sekmem with certainty, but it could hardly have been very far northward.[b] A battle occurred here (l. 2), during which Sebek-khu commanded the reserves (l. 3). When finally his men mingled in the fight (l. 3) he personally captured a prisoner (l. 4), whom he delivers to two of his men, to be disarmed. Continuing the battle (l. 4), he is finally rewarded by the king with a rich gift of arms, as well as the weapons of his prisoner.[c] There is no evidence that this, the only Syrian campaign known under the Twelfth Dynasty, gained anything more than plunder for Sesostris III, or that any attempt was made to hold the territory of the conquered Sekmem.[d]

679. Sebek-khu now became "⌜*commandant*⌝ (*wᶜrtw*) *of the* (*residence*) *city*," the office which he held when he

---

[a]This campaign was so important in Sebek-khu's life that he places it at the beginning of his autobiography, though it chronologically belongs toward the end.

[b]Müller (*l. c.*) suggests Shechem, and would explain the second *m* as the plural ending of a nisbe, which is of course exceedingly doubtful.

[c]Compare the same gifts to brave officers of the Eighteenth Dynasty kings; this is the earliest example of the custom.

[d]This Syrian expedition is not likely to have been the only one made by this dynasty. The language of Sinuhe, exiled in Syria, just before Sebek-khu's time, shows that the power of the Pharaoh was known and feared there, this implies similar expeditions thither under the first kings of the dynasty.

erected this stela (ll. 7 and 10), some time before the death of Sesostris III. He doubtless, like so many officials visiting Abydos, erected the stela himself, hence it does not contain the end of his career. A number of years later, in the ninth year of Amenemhet III, when Sebek-khu could not have been less than sixty-six years old, he appears superintending the king's observations of the height of the inundation at the second cataract.[a] He then held the rank of "˹commandant˺ of the ruler," but of the end of his career we know nothing.

Asiatic Campaign

680. [1]His majesty proceeded northward, to overthrow the Asiatics (*Mntyw-Stt*). His majesty arrived at a district, Sekmem (*Śkmm*)[b] was its name. [2]His majesty led the good way[c] in proceeding to the palace[d] of "Life, Prosperity, and Health," when Sekmem had fallen,[e] together with Retenu (*Rtnw*) the wretched, [3]while I was acting as rearguard.

Sebek-khu's Valor

681. Then the citizens[f] (*ᶜnḥw*) of the army mixed in, to fight with the Asiatics (*ᶜᵓmw*). Then [4]I captured an Asiatic (*ᶜᵓm*), and had his weapons seized by two citizens (*ᶜnḥw*) of the army, (for) one did not

---

[a]Lepsius, *Denkmäler*, II, 136, *b*.

[b]Possibly *Śkmkm*.

[c]This idiom (*dyˑ f tpˑf nfr*) is parallel with the similar one common in the Empire (*śsp tp wᵓˑt nfrˑt*). It has no connection with *tp-nfr* "*good conduct*," an inseparable compound, into which *f* could not be inserted.

[d]The successful outcome of the adventure and the return home are indicated at the beginning, as is common in oriental narrative. Moreover, the following battle may have occurred on the return march.

[e]Lit., "*Sekmem, it had fallen.*"

[f]These men (*ᶜnḥ-w*) are of the class to which belong the men under Sebek-khu (who with the bodyguard is in the rear), as is shown by l. 4, where two of them are under his command. They now rush forward into action. (See also wild-cattle hunt of Amenhotep III, II, 864, and especially Decree of Harmhab, III, 51, 57, 59); they are always spoken of as "*of the army.*"

turn back from the fight, (but) my face was to the front, and I gave not my back to the Asiatic ($^{c\, \circ}m$).[a]

His Rewards

682. As Sesostris lives, [5]I have spoken in truth. Then he gave to me a staff of electrum into my hand, a bow, and a dagger wrought with electrum, together with his[b] weapons.

His Titles

683. [6]The hereditary prince, count, firm of sandal, satisfied in going, treading the path of him that favors him, [7]whose plenty the Lord of the Two Lands has furnished, whose seat his love has advanced, the great ⌜commandant⌝[c] of the (residence) city, Zaa ($\underline{D}^{\,\circ\circ}$).

His Tomb

684. [8]He says: "I have made for myself this splendid tomb; its place is inserted at the stairway of [9]the great god, lord of life, presider over Abydos, at the bend: 'Lord-of-Offerings,' and at the bend: 'Mistress-of-Life;'[d] ⌜that I may⌝ smell the incense [10]that comes forth from this — as the odor of the god."

His Career; Birth

685. The chief attendant of the (residence) city, Zaa; [11]he says: "I was born [in] the year 27 under the majesty of the King of Upper and Lower Egypt, Nebkure (Amenemhet II), triumphant.

Commander of Six

686. [12]The majesty of the King of Upper and Lower Egypt, Khekure (Sesostris III), triumphant, appeared with the double diadem upon the

---

[a]He means that as the fight kept on he was unable to disarm his prisoner, and therefore turned him over to two privátes, while he himself continued fighting. There is also a touch of boasting in it, as it took two men to manage the prisoner he had captured alone.

[b]Those of the Asiatic whom he had captured.

[c]$W^{c}rtw$. This uncertain title is shown to be, here at least, that of the officers of the king's personal troops; but the frequent defining additions show that it was a title of general meaning, like "chief," or "leader," (see Müller's useful note Recueil, IX, 173, 1).

[d]Evidently two promontories of the desert margin in the cemetery of Abydos.

Horus-throne of the living.   [13]His majesty caused that I should render service as a warrior, behind and beside his majesty, with six men of [14]the court.

Campaign in Nubia

687. Then I made ready at his side, (and) his majesty caused that I be appointed to be an 'attendant of the ruler.' [15]I furnished[a] sixty men when his majesty proceeded southward to overthrow the [16]Troglodytes of Nubia.   Then I captured a Negro in —[b] alongside my city.[c]   [17]Then I proceeded   northward, following with six[d] of the court;   then he appointed (me) commander of the attendants, and gave to me 100 men[e] as a reward."

INSCRIPTIONS OF THUTHOTEP[f]

688. Thuthotep and his line were nomarchs of the Hare nome, the chief city of which was Khmunu (Hermopolis, Eshmunen) nearly opposite el-Bersheh, where the tombs of the family are located.   Their immediate neighbors on the north were the princes of the Oryx nome, with whom they were probably related.   Thuthotep's family was an ancient

---

[a]Or. "*commanded sixty men* (lit., *heads*)."

[b]Geographical, as shown by the determinative.

[c]It is inconceivable that Zaa's city should have been in Nubia. He probably means the city where he held command temporarily in Nubia.

[d]The original six of his command, the sixty during the Nubian campaign being a temporary command.

[e]Lit.: "*heads*."

[f]From his tomb at el-Bersheh. The scene of the transport of the colossus early drew attention to this tomb (discovered by English travelers in 1817), but beyond this scene very little in the el-Bersheh group was copied. After many years of neglect, during which they suffered lamentable mutilation, the tombs were exhaustively copied and surveyed by the Archæological Survey of the Egypt Exploration Fund in 1891–92, and published in two volumes: *Bersheh*, I (Newberry and Fraser), *Bersheh*, II (Griffith, Newberry, and Fraser), London. This work has consulted and collated all the earlier publications. The scene of the transport will also be found: Rosellini, *Monumenti civili*, II, 48, 1; Wilkinson Birch, *Manners*, II, 305; Lepsius, *Denkmäler*, II, 134, 135; Chabas, *Mélanges égyptologiques*, III, Pl. V (long inscription only); and often in the later histories. See full account of literature and existing manuscripts in *Bersheh*, I ——.

one, and regarded the hoary Sixth Dynasty princes, who were buried in the neighboring tombs of Shekh Sa ͨ îd, as their ancestors. Their interest in these remote predecessors of theirs was such that at least two of them repaired their ancestors' fallen tombs at Shekh Sa ͨ îd, and recorded the pious deed in the following words:[a]

689. He made (it) as his monument for his fathers, who are in the necropolis, the lords of this promontory; restoring what was found in ruin and renewing what was found decayed, the ancestors, who were before, not having done it. By the count, ˹marshal of the two thrones˺, superior prophet, overseer of the king's-house, governor of the South, great lord of the Hare nome, great in his office, great in his rank, of advanced position in the king's-house, Thutnakht, born of Teti.

690. It is, however, very difficult to trace back the earlier family.[b] The neighboring alabaster quarry of Hatnub contains a number of inscriptions (hieratic graffiti) recording the incessant activity of the family there, in which the princes frequently boast of their wealth and power. These records also show that the princes of the Hare nome were not merely provincial nobles, but that they sometimes held high offices under the king. Only one royal date, however (thirty-first year of Sesostris I), occurs in these quarry inscriptions; otherwise they are dated according to the year of the nomarchy, which is a striking indication of the inde-

---

[a]This inscription occurs four times in the tombs of Shekh Sa ͨ îd; three times with the name of Thutnakht (Lepsius, *Denkmäler*, II, 112, *e*, and 113, *b*, *c*); and once with the name of Ihe (*Yḥ ͻ*) (*Bersheh*, II, 10), both of whom were themselves buried at el-Bersheh. See also Davies, *Shekh Said*, Pl. XXX, and cf. *ibid.*, Pl. XXIX. The same inscription occurred at least once at el-Bersheh also (*ibid.*, 11), showing the restoration of pre-Middle Kingdom tombs there also. At Kasr-es-Sayâd there are also records of the restoration of Sixth Dynasty tombs by Twelfth Dynasty nobles (Baedeker's *Egypt*, 1902, 216).

[b]The material from the tombs of el - Bersheh and the quarry of Hatnub has been carefully sifted in an interesting reconstruction of the family tree by Griffith *Bersheh*, II, 4–14. The following data have been taken thence.

pendence of these princes at some time, probably before the Twelfth Dynasty. Probably at least four generations lived during the Eleventh Dynasty. Two of these earlier princes say: "*I rescued my city in the day of violence from the* ⌜—⌝ *terrors of the royal house,*"[a] which may be a reference to the aggression of the Eleventh Dynasty as it pushed northward.

691. The tomb of Thuthotep is the only one at el-Bersheh, in which royal names have been preserved. It contains the names of Amenemhet II and Sesostris II and III, under whom Thuthotep lived. His appointment as prince of the Hare nome, in which he succeeded his grandfather, is referred to in the tomb as follows:[b]

692. His utterance before his father, that he might [establish] the name of him from whom he came forth. Are not these praises very great before my father and before my god, in that he appoints me chief of his city and great lord of the Hare nome, as successor of him who begat him? He was the staff of the old age of this[c] his father, and he hath appointed me as chief of his city.

693. His father calls upon the people to rejoice, and adds:

See this! which my lord has done for me; hear[d] this! which my

---

[a]Graffiti Nos. I and VIII. Blackden and Fraser, *Hatnub*, transliterated by Griffith, *Bersheh*, II, Pl. XXII.

[b]Inscription of the shrine, *Bersheh*, I, Pl. XXXIII (=Lepsius, *Denkmäler*, II, 134), accompanying Thuthotep and his father Key, who stand facing each other; essentially Mr. Griffith's rendering (*ibid.*, II, 13).

[c]"*This his father*" is of course Key's father; the use of "*this*" implying that he was now deceased. His name was Nehri. Thus Nehri lived to a very advanced age, and Key was so old at his father's (Nehri's) death that he immediately resigned the succession to his own son. This would explain the succession from grandfather to grandson, in which Key seems to have the appointing power. The references to the father and son (Key and Thuthotep) as together deserving the praise of the people (§§ 700–704) are thus explained by the fact that Key survived his son Thuthotep's accession.

[d]*Sdm*, not *hsb* "*reckon*" (as in the Survey notes).

god has done for me, in that he hath appointed my son as chief of his city, great lord of the Hare nome, as successor of him that begat me.[a]

694. The well-known scene of the transport of the colossus has made the tomb famous. The only other inscriptions of historical importance are those connected with this scene. They throw much light upon the power and organization of the government in a Middle Kingdom nomarchy, and, of course, the whole scene is of unusual archæological interest.

695. The quarries from which the great block for the statue was cut are located ten miles from the river in the desert back of el-Amarna.[b] The difficult road from the quarries over the desert, down the cliffs, and across the plain to the river at the modern village of Hagg-Kandîl, had been in use since the days of Khufu, and Uni had transported stone upon it (§ 323). Along this road the block was transported to the river,[c] and then floated down-stream to Hermopolis-Eshmunen, where the statue was sculptured.

---

[a] "Him that begat me" is the grandfather Nehri. He may be the same Nehri who was the father of Khnumhotep II.

[b] They were first seen by Mr. Newberry, who was taken there by natives in 1891. Excellent map by Petrie (Amarna, XXXIV) and very useful description (ibid., 3, 4); also by Fraser (Proceedings of the Society of Biblical Archæology, XVI, 73 ff.). They contain numerous graffiti published by Blackden and Fraser (Collection of Hieratic Graffiti from the Alabaster Quarries of Hatnub).

[c] That the statue would be sculptured in the desert quarry, nearly a day's journey from water and supplies, then to run the risk of the long and dangerous transportation to Eshmunen, as is usually supposed, is a priori exceedingly improbable. The inscription is also clearly against this supposition. The scene depicts the arrival of the statue at its destination, and naturally the inscription begins with that event, which it describes in six lines. Then (l. 6) it reverts to the work of getting the stone from the quarry, and says distinctly that on leaving the quarry the statue was "a squared block." After this the ships for the river transport are referred to, and then Thuthotep mentions his arrival "in the district of this city" (doubtless Eshmunen). Similarly the statue of Amenhotep III, now lying unfinished at the Assuan quarry, was merely roughed out to reduce its weight for transportation (de Morgan, Catalogue des monuments, 62 f.).

It was then conveyed to its destination, some building[a] in the city where it was permanently deposited. This event is depicted with great detail in the famous scene of the transportation. Behind the statue march the *"foremen of the work on this statue"* and other officials, who are followed by Thuthotep himself; accompanied by the following inscription:

696. [1]Following a statue of 13 cubits,[b] of stone of Hatnub. Lo, the way, upon which it came, was very difficult, beyond anything. Lo, [2]the dragging of the great things upon it was difficult for the heart of the people, because of the difficult stone of the ground,[c] being hard stone.

697. I caused [3]the youth, the young men of the recruits to come, in order to make for it (the statue) a road, together with shifts of necropolis-miners and of quarrymen, the foremen and the wise. The people of strength said: "We come to bring it;"[d] while my heart was glad; the city was gathered together rejoicing; very good it was to see [5]beyond everything. The old man among them, he leaned upon the child; the strong-armed together with the tremblers, their courage rose. [6]Their arms grew strong; one of them put forth the strength of 1,000 men.

698. Behold, this statue, being a squared block on coming forth from the great mountain,[e] was [7]more valuable than anything. Vessels were equipped, filled with supplies, ⌈in advance⌉ of my army of recruits, the youth [8]bore ⌈— in advance of⌉ it. Their words were laudation, and my praises from the king. My children [9]— adorned were behind me.

---

[a]Perhaps the *"house of the ka"* ($ḥ·t-k$ʾ), which appears as part of the temple at Siut and at Benihasan. See also the contracts of Hepzefi (§ 535 ff.) for the services and ceremonies due to such statues.

[b]Over 22 feet, indicating the height. It would weigh toward 60 tons, and is the largest alabaster statue known. The immense alabaster statue of Amon found in 1899 by Legrain at Karnak may have been nearly as large.

[c]The stony ground through which the road passed; such stone would be alabaster at the quarry, and limestone afterward. *Rwd·t* (*"hard stone"*) is applied to the stone of Hatnub also in Uni (§ 323, l. 42); it is later *"sandstone."*

[d]Another possible rendering is: *". . . . the foremen and the wise; saying: 'O people of strength, come to me to bring it.'"*

[e]This is a reference to the crude block which was brought from the quarry.

My nome shouted praise. I arrived in the district of this city, [10]the people were gathered together, praising; very good it was to see, beyond everything. The counts who were of old; the judge and local governor who were appointed for [11]— in this city, and established for the ⌜—⌝ upon the river, their hearts had not thought of this which I had done, ⌜in that I made⌝ for myself [12]— established for eternity, after that this my tomb was complete[a] in its everlasting work.

699. The statue is drawn by 172 men in four double rows,[b] manning four ropes. The middle two rows consist of the priests and the soldiers; the outside two, of the youths from the two banks of the river.[c] Each row is accompanied by an inscription as follows:

First Row

700. The[d] youths of the west of the Hare nome come in peace. Utterance: "The west is in festivity, their hearts are glad, when they see the monuments of their lords, the heir who comes in their midst, his house and the house of his father when he was a child. — — —."

Second Row

701. The youths of the warriors of the Hare nome arrive in peace. Utterance of the recruits of the youths whom their lord mustered, the heir who prospers in the favor of the king, the lord: "Let us come, let us prosper his children after him! Our hearts are glad at the favor of the king who abides permanently."

---

[a]The text is poetic and has, lit., "*had rested from its everlasting work.*" Thuthotep means that after the work on his tomb was complete, he had the great statue made for it, and that his ancestors had never conceived such a great enterprise.

[b]A man, standing on the knees of the statue, beats time for the men at the ropes. He has the inscription: "*Beating time for the soldiers by the* ⌜*foreman*⌝ [*of*] *Thuthotep, beloved of the king.*" Before him is a man offering incense, whom the inscription calls the artist of this tomb. Beneath are men of the "*estate*" "*carrying water,*" and with them workmen "*carrying planks for the dragging.*" For further details, see the Archæological Survey volumes.

[c]On the social relations of these men, see Griffith, *Kahun Papyri*, II, 24, 25.

[d]From above.

Third Row

702. The courses of the priests of the Hare nome come in peace. Utterance: "He whom Thoth loves, Thuthotep, beloved of the king, he whom his city loves, whom all its gods praise; the temples are in festivity; their hearts are glad, when they see thy favor with the king."

Fourth Row

703. The youths of the east of the Hare nome come in peace. Utterance: "My lord hath proceeded to Thereti (*Trty*), the god rejoices over him; his fathers are in festivity, their hearts are glad, rejoicing over his beautiful monuments."

704. Over the men at the ropes are platoons of youths bearing (palm?) branches; inscription:

The Hare nome is in festivity, its heart is glad; its old men are children, its youths are refreshed, its children jubilate; their heart is in festivity, when they see their lord, the son of their lord as a favor of the king, making his monument.

705. In advance of all these, oxen are being slaughtered, and rows of servants approach laden with offerings; inscription:

Bringing forward the chief offerings which the districts that are in the Hare nome have brought, for this statue of the count, Thuthotep.[a]

706. A doorway appears behind these people, which is intended to be the entrance of the building for which the statue is destined. It bears the name and titles of Thuthotep and the name of the building itself: "*The love of Thuthotep abides in the Hare nome.*"[b]

---

[a]This inscription clearly settles whose the statue is, and there is no ground for the supposition that it was a statue of the king.

[b]In the doorway at one side appears the figure of Thuthotep standing with staff. This is the usual figure, cut on the thickness of the doorway, which is here swung out, as it were, like a door, that it may be seen.

HAMMAMAT INSCRIPTIONS[a]

707. Already in his second year Amenemhet III carried on work at Hammamat, under an officer named Amenemhet. His inscription[b] is dated: *Year 2, third month of the first season, day 1*, and is followed by ten lines of self-praise, in which we find the only phrases of historical value: *"smiting the Negro, opening the land of the Asiatic"* (l. 7). His titles occupy two lines (ll. 11, 12): *"commander of troops (mnfy·t), commander (shd) of followers, Amenemhet, son of Ibeb (Ybb), triumphant; his father was Aabu (ᶜᵓᵓbw)."* At the end there is only the following meager record of one line: *"I came to this highland in safety with my army by the power of Min, lord of the highlands."* Exactly a year and two days later four officers recorded the date and their names.[c] The chief expedition was in the nineteenth year, of which we have three records. The material taken out was intended for a place or building called Enekh-Amenemhet, *"Life of Amenemhet."* We naturally think of his pyramid-temple at Hawara. The first record,[d] is as follows:

708. [1]Year 19, first month of the second season, [day] 15; [2]the Good God, Lord of the Two Lands, Lord of Offering, King of Upper and Lower Egypt, Nematre (Amenemhet III), who is given life, stability, satisfaction, like Re, forever.

709. [3]His majesty sent to bring for him(self) monuments from [4]the valley of Hammamat, of beautiful black (basaltic) stone[e] as [5]far as "Enekh-Amenemhet,"[f] living forever and ever; at [6]the house of Sebek, of Crocodilopolis:[g] 10 statues of 5 cubits,[h] upon a throne,

---

[a]Besides the publications I had also for these inscriptions a collation of the Berlin squeezes, kindly furnished by Mr. Alan Gardiner.

[b]Cut on the rocks in Wadi Hammamat; published by Lepsius, *Denkmäler*, II, 138, *a*.

[c]Lepsius, *Denkmäler*, II, 138, *b*.   [e]See § 675, note.

[d]Lepsius, *Denkmäler*, II, 138, *e*.   [f]See above, § 707.

[g]An adjective (*nisbe*) belonging to Sebek; it does not necessarily show that the temple was in Crocodilopolis.

[h]Five cubits high (8½ feet) when seated.

⁷quarried in this year by the real "beloved of his lord" . . . . .ᵃ
the overseer of the ⌜—⌝ (gs) of the miners, Sesostris.

710. Another official ᵇ has left a record ᶜ of the same expedition, in which he also refers to the "*10 statues of 5 (cubits).*" ᵈ He also adds the numbers of the men in the expedition: "*His soldiers of the necropolis, 20; quarrymen, 30; sailors, 30; a numerous army, 2,000.*" ᵉ

711. Still another officer ᶠ dates an inscription ᵍ in the nineteenth year of Amenemhet III, which doubtless refers to the same expedition. The date occupies one line, the usual phrases in eulogy of self thirteen lines, and the following record is in the last line: "*He came to this inaccessible highland of Hammamat, on a commission of Horus, lord of the palace (the king), to bring a monument for his majesty.*"

712. The latest and only other record ʰ is dated: *Year 20, third month of the first season, day 13.*

INSCRIPTIONS IN SINAI

I.   WADI MAGHARA

713. The earliest inscription of Amenemhet III in the peninsula of Sinai, is that of Khenemsu ⁱ in the Wadi Maghara.   It is as follows:

ᵃThe usual encomium of self, made up of obscure phrases.

ᵇHis name is uncertain, but may have been "*Meri's son, Hu (Ḥwꜣ)*" according to l. 8.

ᶜLepsius, *Denkmäler*, II, 138, c = Golénischeff, *Hammamat*, IX, No. 1.   It is very obscure and uncertain, but seems to refer to difficulties in getting out the blocks for the ten statues.

ᵈHe omits the word "*cubits,*" l. 13.   ᵉLines 14, 15.

ᶠHis name is likewise uncertain (it is at the beginning of l. 14).

ᵍLepsius, *Denkmäler*, II, 138, d = Golénischeff, *Hammamat*, IX, No. 2.

ʰLepsius, *Denkmäler*, II, 138 f.

ⁱCut on the rocks in the Wadi Maghara; published by Champollion, *Notices descriptives*, II, 689 = Burton, *Excerpta hieroglyphica*, XII = Lepsius, *Denkmäler*, II, 137, c = Brugsch, *Thesaurus*, VI, 1492 = Laval, *Voyage dans la Péninsule Arabique*,

Inscriptions of Khenemsu

Year 2 under the majesty of the King of Upper and Lower Egypt, Nematre (N-$m^{\circ c \cdot}t$-R^c), Son of Re, Amenemhet (III), living forever and ever.   The treasurer of the god, master of the double cabinet, chief of the treasury, Khentkhetihotep-Khenemsu was dispatched, in order to bring malachite and copper.   List of his soldiers: 734.

714. Below stands the king before Thoth and Hathor, and three petty officers have appended a mortuary prayer at the bottom.

715. Khenemsu's expedition (§§ 713, 714) also operated in Sarbût el-Khadem in the same year,[a] and his officers have left their names on the rocks, surmounted by the date and a relief showing Amenemhet III before "*Hathor, mistress of the malachite country.*"[b]

716. Below[c] are the figures of four officers accompanied by their names:

1. Treasurer of the god, master of the double cabinet, chief of the treasury, Khenemsu.

2. Deputy of the chief treasurer, Ameniseneb.

3. —seneb, son of Stira (*Sty-r$^{\circ}$*) ———.

4. Master of the double cabinet of the treasury, Sebeko, son of Metenu.

Inscription of Harnakht

717. The following inscription[d] of Harnakht, a subordinate treasury official, evidently connected with the preceding

---

Pl. 5, No. 2 = Weill, *Sinai*, 129; see last for British Museum squeeze and manuscript sources.   An official of the same expedition named Sesostris-Seneb dates a prayer on the rocks in the year 2 (Brugsch, *Thesaurus*, VI, 1487); Weill, *Sinai*, 131, 132.   Below is a list of his workmen (*l. c.*).

[a]Another inscription at Sarbût el-Khadem, of the year 20, shows only the date (Lepsius, *Denkmäler,* II, 137).

[b]Lepsius, *Denkmäler*, II, 137, *a.*

[c]Back of the king stood the chief treasurer, but his figure is now gone, and only a portion of his titles is still visible.

[d]Wadi Maghara; published by Brugsch, *Thesaurus*, VI, 1488; better by Spiegelberg, after squeeze by Euringer, *Recueil*, 21, 51; and Weill, *Sinai*, 134.

expedition, is of especial interest as showing that the journey to Wadi Maghara was made by water.   Even if the customary point of departure was at the extreme north end of the Gulf of Suez, a wearisome desert journey in Sinai was thus avoided.

718. Year 2 under the majesty of the king of Upper and Lower Egypt, Nematre (Amenemhet III), living forever.   The chosen before his subjects, who treads the path of his benefactor, (says): "I crossed over the sea, bearing luxuries[a] (*špšš*), by commission of Horus, lord of the palace (Pharaoh)."   Official of the treasury (*yry-ᶜt-n-pr-ḥḏ*), chief fowler,[b] Harnakht (*Ḥr-nḫt*); his beautiful name, Harnetamehu (*Ḥr-n-tᵓ-mḥw*).

Inscription of Sebekdidi

719. An inscription of the year 41[c] records an expedition in the Wadi Maghara, which was conducted by a palace official named Sebekdidi-Ranefseneb.   It reads:

Year 41 under the majesty of the King of Upper and Lower Egypt, Lord of the Two Lands, Nematre (*N-mᵓᶜ·t-Rᶜ*, Amenemhet III), given life, like Re, forever.

720. The real king's-confidant, his beloved, his favorite, conductor of the palace, Sebekdidi-Ranefseneb.   May Ptah-South-of-His-Wall, and Hathor,[d] mistress of the malachite country, love him who shall say: "An offering which the king gives for the ka of the treasurer, the assistant of the chief treasurer, Sesostris —— (*S[n]-Wsr·t* ————).

Below is a short list of subordinate officers.

-----

[a]The connection would indicate that these were offerings from the Pharaoh to be presented to the local Hathor; although *špšš·w* are frequently the costly stones of Sinai.

[b]This not uncommon title (*ḥb-ᶜᵓ*, with determinative of a goose), has been strangely misunderstood in the last two editions of the text.

[c]Lepsius, *Denkmäler*, II, 137 f. = *Ordnance Survey*, III, Pl. 3 = Burton, *Excerpta hieroglyphica* XII; Weill, *Sinai*, 137, 138.   A short inscription of the year 30 is in Weill, *Sinai*, 135; it is without historical content beyond the statement of the official: "*I worked (yry·ny) the gmy and the malachite therein.*"

[d]Misread by Weill.

Inscription of Ameni

721. In the year 42 there was evidently an important expedition in the Wadi Maghara, for which the following meager record is our only source:[a]

Year 42, under the majesty of the king, Lord of the Two Lands, Nematre (Amenemhet III), living forever, [beloved][b] of Hathor, mistress of the malachite country.

722. The master of the double cabinet, chief of the White House (*wr pr ḥḏ*), Ameni, triumphant, beloved of Hathor, mistress of the malachite country.

The treasurer,[c] assistant of the chief treasurer, Sesostris—seneb-Sebekkhi, favorite of Hathor, mistress of the malachite country, of Soped, lord of the east, of Snefru,[d] lord of the highlands, and of the gods and goddesses who are in this land.

723. There were made for Hathor, all beautiful (mine)-chambers.

May he be beloved and arrive in safety who shall say: "An offering which the king gives for the ka of the treasurer, the assistant of the chief treasurer, Sebekhotep, beloved of Hathor, mistress of the malachite country; the storeroom-keeper, Yatu (*y*ꜣ-*tw*); —— —— —— mmu (— *mmw*); the chief of the house of Pharaoh, Senebtefi; and 20[e] (+*x*) quarrymen ————.

Another expedition left a short inscription in the year 43.[f]

---

[a]Champollion, *Notices descriptives*, II, 690 = Burton, *Excerpta hieroglyphica*, XII = Lepsius, *Denkmäler*, II, 137, *g* = *Ordnance Survey*, III, Pl. 3 = Brugsch, *Thesaurus*, VI, 1490 (inaccurate) = Weill, *Sinai*, 140, with full literature. There is another inscription of the same year at this place, but only the date, king's name, and epitheta, with two signs at the top of each of three lost vertical lines, are preserved.

[b]Omitted by the scribe; see Lepsius, *Denkmäler*, II, 137, *h*.

[c]It is clear that this official, who has attached the longest blessing to his name, was the personal leader of the expedition.

[d]Snefru as a god of Sinai. His name is here in a cartouche (with Horus-hawk as determinative); he appears in the same way with Soped, and Hathor in an inscription of Amenemhet III's sixth year (Brugsch, *Thesaurus*, VI, 1491, No. 9).

[e]Not more than thirty; a list of subordinate workmen followed, but it is now broken off.

[f]Lepsius, *Denkmäler*, II, 137, *i* = Weill, *Sinai*, 142.

II. SARBÛT EL-KHADEM

724. Amenemhet III began work here as early as the year 2,[a] and dated inscriptions of the years 20,[b] 30,[b] and 38[c] indicate its continuance, although they are without historical content, and show only the date and the king's name.

Inscription of Sebek-hir-hab

725. In the year 44, however, the king opened a new mine, and Sebek-hir-hab, the official in command, has left a record of the event there, which he had engraved in the form of a stela,[d] on the walls of the reservoir furnishing the water-supply of the expedition. The place of the stela indicates some connection between the expedition of Sebek-hir-hab and the completion of the reservoir.

Opening of the mining chamber[e] successfully; "Flourish-its-Army-Which-Delivers-That-Which-is-in-it," is its name.

Year 44 under the majesty of the King of Upper and Lower Egypt, ... Amenemhet III, beloved of Hathor, mistress of malachite, given life, like Re, forever.   O ye who live upon earth, who shall come to this Mine-land! As your king has established you, as your gods favor you, that ye may arrive (at home) in safety, so say ye: "A thousand loaves, jars of beer, cattle, fowl, incense, ointment, and everything on which the gods live, for the ka of the master of the double cabinet of

---

[a]List of his officials in that year (perhaps the same expedition recorded in Wadi Maghara in that year, § 713), in Weill, *Sinai*, 163.

[b]Weill, *Sinai*, 164.   [c]*Ibid.*, 165.

[d]Copied by Ricci, and from his copy, by Champollion, as published in *Notices descriptives*, II, 691.   Birch says of it: "Tablet engraved on the rock inside of the large reservoir, which is one mile due south of the Sarbût el Khadem" (*Ordnance Survey*, I, 183, 184).   Published much better, from British Museum squeezes, by Weill, *Sinai*, 166.

[e]The word used (*ḥt·t*) is the usual one for a quarrying or mining excavation; but as the inscription is cut on the wall of an excavated reservoir, it might be the reservoir which is here meant.   Against this is the name of the excavation, which refers to its valuable content.   Hence some new mine in the vicinity is probably meant.

the treasury, Sebek-hir-hab (*Sbk-ḥr-ḥb*), living again happily, repeating a happy life (*whm ⁶ nḥ nfr*), born of the matron Henut (*Ḥnwt*), triumphant."

726. Master of the double cabinet, Sebek-hir-hab; he says: "I excavated a mine-chamber for my lord, and my youths returned[a] in full quota, all of them. There was none that fell among them."

This official, he says: "O ye king's-grandees, companions of the palace! Give praise to the king, exalt [his] fame, laud the king, and watch that which belongs to him. The mountains bring forth what is in them ———— and the hills bear their wealth.[b] His father Keb,[c] he gives it, because of —."

727. Sebek-hir-hab then closes with an account of his offerings to Hathor:

I brought for her offering-tables of mesnet stone, linen (*pḳ⁾·t*) ———— I presented to her divine offerings, bulls, ⌜fowl⌝ ————. She ⌜led⌝ me ⌜in⌝ by her gracious going ⌜—⌝ ———— to the — terrace, which I made for her. I swear, I have spoken in truth.

Inscription of Ptahwer

728. The last dated inscription[d] of Amenemhet III at the Sarbût el-Khadem is of the year 45, and it reads as follows:

Year 45 under the majesty of the Good God, Lord of the Two Lands, Nematre (Amenemhet III), given life forever, beloved of Hathor.

[⌜I was one sent⌝] to bring plentiful — from the land of —,[e] ready in his reports to his lord, [delivering] Asia (*Stt*) to him who is in the palace (the Pharaoh), bringing Sinai (*Mntw*) at his heels, traversing inaccessible valleys, bringing unknown extremities (of the world), the master of the double cabinet, chief of the treasury, Ptahwer, triumphant, born of Yata (*Y⁾-t⁾*).

---

[a]Lit., "*came.*"

[b]Similar phrases, Weill, *Sinai*, 178, and again, 179.

[c]The earth-god. A similar idea is found in the Kubbân Stela (III, 288, ll 17, 18).

[d]Weill, *Sinai*, 168.   [e]Lost name ending in *kwy*.

729. An undated inscription[a] of this reign records the opening of a mine called *"Vision-of-the-Beauty-of-Hathor;"* and another[b] contained a memorandum of a month's supplies delivered: *"1 measure of grain, 23 large and small cattle, 2 wꜣ d̠-fowl, 30 mnyˁt-geese,"* followed by a list of six petty officials.

Inscription of Amenemhet[c]

730. The king who dispatched this officer to the Sarbût el-Khadem, where his inscription is engraved, is not mentioned, but as the officer's name is Amenemhet, he certainly belongs under a Twelfth Dynasty Pharaoh. The reference to Snefru is of interest, and, besides this, it is evident that Amenemhet worked somewhere else, evidently Maghara, before going to Sarbût el - Khadem. This conclusion is corroborated by the same thing observable in the expedition of Harurre (§§ 733–38).

Work in Wadi Maghara (?)

731. This god dispatched the treasurer of the god, the master of the double cabinet, leader of recruits, companion of the palace, Amenemhet, to bring splendid, costly stone for his majesty. This treasurer of the god says: "I came to the mine of Ka[d] (K꜄); I exacted the impost (*bkw*), I attended to the levying of the impost of malachite, being ⌜—⌝[e] for ⌜every⌝ 5[f] men every day correctly ⌜— — —⌝. Never had the like been done since the time of the King of Upper and Lower Egypt, Snefru, triumphant.

---

[a]Weill, *Sinai*, 169.

[b]*Ibid.*, 170.

[c]Niebuhr, *Reisen nach Arabien*, I, Tab. XLV; Lepsius, *Denkmäler*, II, 144, *q* =Laval, Pl. IV, 5; mentioned by Birch, *Ordnance Survey*, I, 185, but is not among the photographs of the Survey.

[d]The name of the man in charge, who was evidently responsible for a fixed amount each season.

[e]Here was evidently the amount exacted from each gang of men daily.

[f]Or possibly 15.

Work in Sarbût el-Khadem

732. Then I arrived at this land,[a] and I completed the work successfully. The might of the king ————. It is a ⌜command⌝ of his majesty ————.

Inscription of Harurre[b]

733. This interesting stela is unfortunately not dated, but it is unquestionably of the Middle Kingdom, and is here provisionally placed in the reign of Amenemhet III. It is of importance because it shows that expeditions were not customarily sent to Sinai in summer. Harurre, treasurer of the god, in the service of an unknown king, erected our stela to inform future generations, who might come in the same unfavorable time of year, that he had survived the heat, when "*the mountains brand the skin*," and had brought more than the amount of ore exacted of him. He arrived at Maghara in the seventh month; then later transferring his force to Sarbût el-Khadem,[c] he completed the work in the ninth month. These two months of the civil calendar fell in summer, thus corroborating the place of the calendar furnished by the Kahun Sothis date.

734. The language of the monument is in a number of places very obscure and difficult, chiefly in the speeches, so that the general sense of the whole document is fortunately not in doubt. The remarkable use of the word *ynm* "*skin*," which appears four times—three times with a meaning

---

[a]That is Sarbût el-Khadem; the malachite mine was therefore in another locality, which he had first visited.

[b]Stela in Sarbût el-Khadem (Niebuhr, *Reisen nach Arabien* [4to, Kopenhagen, 1778], Tab. XLV; Laval, IX, 2; *Ordnance Survey*, III, 10 [photograph]; Weill, *Sinai*, 174, after manuscript copy by Burton, and squeeze in British Museum). I had also a photograph by Borchardt, which gives more in the last line than Weill.

[c]The sudden statement that he "*arrived in this land*" (Sarbût) long after the account of his arrival in Sinai, can be explained in this way only. The same thing is observable in the inscription of Amenemhet (§§ 730–32).

evidently quite unusual—is noteworthy. What its meaning may be is not evident. I have not burdened the translation with conjectures in any of the questionable passages.

Work in Maghara (?)

735. ¹The majesty of this god dispatched the treasurer of the god, master of the double cabinet ⌜—⌝, Harurre (*Ḥr-ʿwr-Rᶜ⌝*) ²to this Mine-land (*Byᵓ*); I arrived in this land in the third month of the second season (*pr·t*), although it was not the season for going ³to this Mine-land.

736. This treasurer of the god saith to the officials who shall come to this Mine-land at this season:ᵃ ⁴"Let not your faces flinch on that account;ᵇ behold, Hathor will turn it ⁵to profit. I looked to myself, and I dealtᶜ with myself; when I came from Egypt, ⁶my face flinched, and it was hard for me ⌜—ᵈ — —⌝. The highlands are hot ⁷in summer, and the mountains brand the skin ⌜—⌝. When morning dawns, ⁸a man is ⌜— — —⌝. I addressed the workmen concerning it: ⁹'How favored is he who is in this Mine-land!' They said: 'There is malachite ¹⁰in this eternal mountain; it is ⌜—⌝ᵈ to seek (it) at this season.ᵉ ¹¹One like us hears the like of (such) marvels,ᶠ coming at this season. It is ⌜—⌝ᵈ ¹²to ⌜—⌝ for it in this evil summer-season.'"

Work in Sarbût el - Khadem

737. Now, when ¹³I was dispatched to this Mine-land; the souls of the king put it in my heart. ¹⁴Then I arrived in this land, and I began the work prosperously. ¹⁵My army arrived in full quota, all of it, there was none that fell among them. My face flinched not ¹⁶before the work.

ᵃViz., the hot season.

ᵇViz., because they have come in the wrong season.

ᶜLit., *"did something with myself,"* probably meaning: "I struggled with myself."

ᵈ*Ynm* (with the sign of a skin); but it evidently is here a folk-etymology for something quite different from "*skin*," the usual meaning of the word.

ᵉSummer time.

ᶠOr: *"Our hearing is like a marvel, etc."*

738. I succeeded in mining the good sort,[a] and I finished in the first month [17]of the third season ($šmw$). I brought genuine costly stone for the luxuries, more than [18]any one who came (hither), and (more than) all the exactions ⌜— — — [19]— — — —⌝. It was better than the accustomed seasons thereof. Offer ye, [20]offer ye to the mistress of heaven, appease ye Hathor; if ye do it, it will be profitable [21]for you. If ye increase to her, it shall be well among you. [22]I led my army very kindly, and I was not loud-voiced [23]toward the workmen. I acted before all the army and the recruits, [24]and they rejoiced in me, — official [25]————.[b]

TURRA INSCRIPTION[c]

739. At the top is the date: "*Year 43*,[d]" beneath which, with accompanying names of Ptah, Anubis, and Hathor, is the name of the king: "*Son of Re, Amenemhet;*" this must be the third, for no other Amenemhet ruled so long.

740. [1]Quarry-chambers were opened anew,[e] to quarry[2] fine limestone of Ayan ($^c yn$), for the temples of ⌜this prophet,⌝[1f] of millions [3]of years. Executed under the hand of the hereditary prince, count, wearer of the royal [seal], sole companion [4]————[g] [5]————.

---

[a]The same statement is found in two other inscriptions at Sarbût el-Khadem (Weill, *Sinai*, 179 and 180).

[b]Possibly one more line lost.

[c]Cut in the walls of the quarry at Turra; published by Vyse (*Operations*, III, opp. p. 94) and Lepsius (*Denkmäler*, II, 143, *i*).

[d]Omitted by Lepsius, *Denkmäler*.

[e]The *n* after *m - w ·t* is an error for the book-roll; cf. Lepsius, *Denkmäler*, III, 3, *a*.

[f]This remarkable phrase (quite clear in both texts) designates the king, for in the Turra inscription of Ahmose (II, 26 ff.) we have "*his* (the king's) *temples*" as a parallel; but this is so unusual that an error in the text is more probable, possibly for "this god?"

[g]The name of the official is lost. Cf. the similar inscription of Ahmose (II, 26 ff.) at the beginning of the Eighteenth Dynasty. They are so similar that one cannot imagine the usually accepted lapse of one thousand years between them.

EL KAB STELA[a]

741. If the *"Wall of Seshmu-towe"* is a designation of the stronghold of El Kab, then its famous wall is the work of Sesostris II, whose Horus-name is Seshmu-towe. This stela was found at El Kab. The only place there which could conceivably contain a temple inclosure is the town within the wall. This document, therefore, shows that Sesostris II should be regarded as the builder of the famous wall of El Kab.

Above are the Horus- and throne-names of Amenemhet III, *"beloved of Nekhbet, mistress of heaven;"* and below is the following inscription:

742. Year 44, under the majesty of this god. He made (it) as his monument; his majesty commanding to build the inclosure wall, which is in *"Wall of Seshmu-towe,"*[b] triumphant ———.

INSCRIPTION OF SEHETEPIBRE[c]

743. Besides a meager record of works, which he executed for Amenemhet III at Abydos, Sehetepibre also placed upon his mortuary stela a very interesting poem containing

[a]Found at El Kab by Rev. H. Stobart in 1854–55; it has since disappeared; published in *Egyptian Antiquities Collected on a Voyage Made in Upper Egypt, etc.*, by Rev. H. Stobart, M.A. (Paris and Berlin, 1855), Pl. I, and from Stobart by Legrain, *Proceedings of the Society of Biblical Archæology*, March, 1905.

[b]In cartouche; it is a designation of the king, meaning *"Leader or administrator of the Two Lands,"* the Horus-name of Sesostris II. There is nothing unique in the use of the Horus-name in a cartouche. M. Legrain's recent explanation of the name as "Samou" (reading *"two lands"* as *m*, *Proceedings of the Society of Biblical Archæology*, March, 1905, 106 ff.) is impossible, as the horizontal *m* does not occur until long after the Twelfth Dynasty.

[c]Mortuary stela discovered by Mariette at Abydos, now in Cairo (No. 20538); published very inaccurately by him, *Abydos*, II, 25 (=*Catalogue général d'Abydos*, No. 670). It is accurately published by Piehl, *Inscriptions*, III, Pls. IV–VII. I was also able to use a collation of the Berlin squeeze by Sethe, and afterward a copy of the original by Schaefer.

instructions to his children regarding the proper plan of life. It consists simply in serving the king faithfully and cultivating his favor. With the exception of this instruction, a large portion of the inscriptions was copied from the stela of Mentuhotep,[a] a powerful official under Sesostris I.

744. Above[b] is the Horus-name of Amenemhet III, surmounted by the Horus receiving life from Osiris; below is the following inscription, which is a good example of the exaggerated titular epithets conventionally applied to the Middle Kingdom noble of power and favor at court.

Titles and Honors

745. [1]The hereditary prince, count, wearer of the royal seal, sole companion in love, magnate of the King of Upper Egypt, great one of the King of Lower Egypt, prince at [2]the head of the people, overseer of horn, hoof, and feather,[c] [ʳoverseerˀ] of the two pleasure-marshes,[d] whose coming is heeded by the court, [3]to whom the bodies tell their affairs, whose excellence the Lord of the Two Lands sees, whom he hath exalted before the two regions, possessed [4]of silver and gold, mighty in costly stones,[e] a man of truth before the Two Lands, a truthful witness [5]like Thoth, master of secret things[f] in the temples, chief of all works of the king's-house, more accurate than the weight, [6]the likeness of the balances, taking thought,[g] excellent in counsel, speaking that which is good, repeating that which is loved, [7]taking thought, without his like, good at listening, excellent in speaking, a prince who

---

[a]See §§ 530 ff.; compare Daressy (*Recueil*, X, 144–49), who arranges both parallel. He unfortunately uses Mariette's inaccurate text of Sehetepibre without revision.

[b]Recto.   [c]The live-stock of the royal estate.

[d]These are the "preserves" of fish, wild fowl, etc. There were officially two, in deference to the conventional fiction, one for Upper and one for Lower Egypt.

[e]Lit., "*Belonging to silver, etc;*" these and the epithets in l. 2 are poetical references to his office.

[f]This has no reference to esoteric teachings, for Sehetepibre was not a priest, but refers simply to the secret chambers of the temples, containing costly images, etc.

[g]Lit., "*putting the heart*" (exactly parallel with the Hebrew שִׂים לֵב) I find it used in parallelism with *sḫ* ꜣ = "*remember*" (e. g., Lepsius, *Denkmäler*, II, 149, *e*, l. 10).

looses the knot,[a] whom his lord exalts [8]before millions, real image of love, free from acting deceit, favorite of the heart of the king, to whom is assigned (the office of) "Pillar of the South" [9]in[b] the king's-house, who follows his lord at his goings, entering into his heart before the court; belonging behind his lord, being the favorite of the Horus, [10]excellent in the palace; the real favorite of his lord; to whom secret matters are told, who finds the word of counsel, [11]sweetening misfortune, doing things by good rule, the wearer of the royal seal, overseer of royal property, deputy of the chief treasurer, Sehetepibre; he saith:[c] . . . .

Abydos Tomb

746. [1d]Now, I made this excellent tomb, [2]and beautified its place. I gave contracts for the remuneration of the prophets [3]of Abydos. I acted as "Son-Whom-He-Loves" in the conduct of the house of gold, in the secrets of the lord of Abydos. [4]I conducted the work on the sacred barque, I fashioned its colors, I acted as Hakro ($H^{\circ}k\text{-}r^{\circ}$) [5]of his Lord (at) every procession of Upwawet, making for him all the festal offerings, which the prophet read. I clothed the god at his processions by virtue of my office as master of secret things, and my duty as ⌜— 7 —⌝. I was one whose two hands were ⌜—⌝ in adorning the god, a (sm-) priest with pure fingers.[e] May I be a follower of the god, [8]in order that I may be glorious and mighty at the stairway of the lord of Abydos.

The Instruction

747. The beginning of[f] the teaching which he composed before his children. [9]I speak great things, I cause you to hear, I cause you to know the eternal manner, the true manner of [10]life[g]—the passing of life in peace.

---

[a]Referring to difficult matters; compare our "knotty problem."

[b]Mentuhotep has: "*of the king's-house.*"

[c]A mortuary prayer follows.

[d]This new numbering begins on the verso.

[e]The reference is to the festal processions in which the god appeared in public. The festal decoration of the figure was the work of Sehetepibre, and for this duty he possessed the requisite ceremonial purity.

[f]Lit., "*The beginning with the teaching,*" the usual introduction of such compositions.

[g]$N\text{-}m^{\circ c}w\text{-}R^{c}$, a pun on the following name of the king, $N\text{-}m^{\circ c}\text{-}t\text{-}R^{c}$; but its meaning is not certain.

Adore the king, Nematre (Amenemhet III), living forever, in the
midst [11]of your bodies;
Enthrone his majesty in your hearts.
He is Esye[a] (Sy᾽) in the hearts;
His two eyes, they search [12]every body.
He is the Sun, seeing with his rays;[b]
He illuminates the Two Lands more than the sun-disk.
He makes the Two Lands green [13]more than a great Nile;
He hath filled the Two Lands with strength.
(He is) life, cooling the nostrils;
When he begins [14]to rage,[c] he is satisfied to ⌜—⌝.
The treasures[d] which he gives are food for those who are in his
following;
He feeds those who tread [15]his path.
The king is food (k᾽),
His mouth is increase.
He is the one creating that which is;
He is the Khnum[e] of [16]all limbs;
The Begetter, who causes the people to be.
He is Bast protecting the Two Lands.
He who adores [17]him shall ⌜escape⌝ his arm,
He is Sekhmet[f] toward him who transgresses his command.
He is ⌜gentle⌝ toward him who has ⌜—⌝.
748. Fight for his name,
[18]Purify yourselves by his oath.
And ye shall be free from trouble.
The beloved of the king shall be [19]blessed;
There is no tomb for one hostile to his majesty;
But his body shall be thrown[g] to the waters.
Do ye this, and your limbs shall be sound;
Ye shall be glorious ⌜—⌝ forever.[h]

---

[a]God of wisdom and knowledge. The argument is: honor the king in your
innermost hearts, for he knows your hearts.

[b]Or: *"by whose rays there is seeing"* (passive participle).

[c]Or: *"He is far from raging, he is satisfied, etc."*

[d]Read ᶜ h ᶜ w *"heaps;"* but it possibly belongs to preceding.

[e]One of the gods, who created man.   [g]Ḳm᾽ n, see § 512, l. 18.

[f]Goddess of war and terror.   [h]Another mortuary prayer follows.

REIGN OF AMENEMHET IV

KUMMEH INSCRIPTION[a]

749. All of the few dated records of Amenemhet IV are beyond the borders of Egypt. The earliest is the rock inscription of Kummeh, recording the height of the Nile there.

Height (r^3) of the Nile of the year 5, under the majesty of the King of Upper and Lower Egypt, Makhrure (M^{3c}-ḥrw-R^c, Amenemhet IV), living forever and ever.

SINAI INSCRIPTIONS

750. Amenemhet IV continued the exploitation of the Sinaitic mines at least as late as his sixth year. At Wadi Maghara his officials have left two records, the first[b] containing only the date and the leader's titles, as follows:

Year 6 under the majesty of the King of Upper and Lower Egypt, Makhrure (Amenemhet IV), given life forever, — beloved of Soped, [lord of the East] and Hathor, mistress of malachite.

————————[c] desire, treading the way of him (the king) who favors him; whom the soldiers love, ┌—┐ his designs, giving attention, ┌— — — —┐, storeroom-keeper of the palace, Kheye ($Ḫ^{c3}y$), [born of] Henut ($Ḥnw[t]$).

A further inscription[d] also bears the same date, but contains only a mortuary prayer.

At Sarbût el-Khadem two inscriptions[e] contain only the Pharaoh's name.

---

[a]Engraved on the rocks above the river at Kummeh; Lepsius, *Denkmäler*, II, 152 f.

[b]Lepsius, *Denkmäler*, II, 137, *d;* Weill, *Sinai*, 145.
[c]Titles of the official.   [d]Weill, *Sinai*, 148.
[e]Lepsius, *Denkmäler*, II, 140, *o. p.;* Weill, *Sinai*, 171, 172.

FROM THE THIRTEENTH DYNASTY TO
THE HYKSOS

REIGN OF SEKHEMRE-KHUTOWE

RECORDS OF NILE-LEVELS[a]

751. These four inscriptions are the latest of the well-known records on the rocks at Semneh, above the second cataract, which mark the maximum level of the river. They begin under Amenemhet III, and continue into the reign of Sekhemre-Khutowe, when they abruptly cease with these four, here discussed, which thus possess a certain importance. These Nile records are indeed our only historical inscriptions from the reign of this obscure king,[b] and the first ray of light after the fall of the Twelfth Dynasty. They continue uninterruptedly from the year 1 to the year 4, inclusive, but only that of the year 3[c] contains more than the words, *"Height of the Nile of the year —;"* it is as follows:

752. Height of the Nile of the year 3, under the majesty of King Sekhemre-Khutowe ($Sḥm-R^c-ḫw-t^{\jmath}wy$), living forever; when the wearer of the royal seal, the commander of the army, Renseneb ($Rn šnb$), was commanding in the fortress: "Mighty-is-Khekure" (Sesostris III).[d]

---

[a]Inscribed on the rocks above Semneh; published by Lepsius, *Denkmäler*, II, 151, *a–d*.

[b]Administrative documents from his first, and probably also his second and fifth years, are found in the Kahun Papyri (Griffith, *Kahun Papyri*, Pl. X, ll. 1, 3; and Pl. IX, l. 9; see Griffith's remarks, p. 86). Blocks bearing his name were found also at Bubastis. There is no evidence connecting this king with the name Sebekhotep.

[c]Lepsius, *Denkmäler*, II, 151, *c*.

[d]This is evidently either the fortress of Semneh or that of Kummeh opposite.

REIGN OF NEFERHOTEP

GREAT ABYDOS STELA[a]

753. As the only considerable document of this king, containing more than his name or those of his family, this inscription is of great importance; but, besides this, its unique content renders it of especial interest. Neferhotep was the son of a priest, "*the divine father, Ha-enkhef (ḥ ʾ-ᶜnḫf)*" and "*the royal mother, Kemi (Kmy),*"[b] through whom he possibly inherited royal blood, although he is more likely to have usurped the throne, thus giving his mother her title. Like the ephemeral Khenzer, he gave special attention to the maintenance of the Abydos temple, and this stela, erected to testify to his zeal, tells how he investigated the ancient records at Heliopolis to ascertain exactly what was due to Osiris, particularly the proper form for the divine statue, as it was at the beginning of the world.

754. In order to carry out what he had found in the records, he proceeded in person to Abydos, sending a mes-

---

[a]A sandstone stela, nearly 6 feet high and over 3 feet wide, set up on the wall of the road leading to the Middle Kingdom Osiris-temple. It was in such bad condition that Mariette left it in situ; but, after years of exposure to weather and vandalism, it has now been brought to the Cairo Museum. It was evidently exceedingly indistinct and difficult to copy, and the two copies of Mariette and Devéria, from which the text is published (Mariette, *Abydos*, II, 28–30; *Catalogue général d'Abydos*, 233, 234, No. 766) contained many errors, only a portion of which it is possible to correct. These and the frequent lacunæ render a complete translation impossible, but enough has been given to make the essential progress of the narrative clear. A better text is now hardly a possibility.

[b]Family list cut on the rocks at Assuan (Petrie, *Season in Egypt*, XIII, No. 337 = Lepsius, *Denkmäler*, II, 151, e = *Text*, IV, 126) and on Sehel at the first cataract (Mariette, *Monuments divers*, 70, 3); also on several scarabs (Petrie, *Scarabs*, Nos. 293–98.

senger thither before him, to bring forth the statue of the god to meet him. The divine image was carried in festal procession to the sacred barge, which sailed out on the canal, probably to the Nile, seven miles away, where the king was met and accompanied back to the temple amid a celebration in which the incidents of the Osiris-myth were dramatically enacted by the priests. On his arrival the king personally carried out all that he had discovered in the records of Atum. He then admonished the priests to vigilance and pronounced a curse on those who should disregard his established offerings.

Introduction

755. ¹Year 2, under the majesty of King Neferhotep,ª born of the royal mother, Kemi (*Kmy*), who is given life, stability, satisfaction, like Re, forever. ²His majesty appearedᵇ upon the throne of Horus in the palace, "⌈Structure⌉-of-Beauty."ᶜ His majesty spake to the nobles, and companions, who were in his suite, the real scribes of the hieroglyphs, the masters of all secrets:

King's Speech

756. "My heart hath desired to see the ancient writings of Atum;ᵈ open ye for me for a great investigation; let the god know concerning his creation, and the gods concerning their fashioning, their offerings and ⌈their⌉ oblations . . . . (let) me know the god ⁴in his form, that I may fashion him as he was formerly, when they made the ⌈statues⌉ in their council, in order to establish their monuments upon earth.ᵉ They have given to me the inheritance ⌈of Re as far as⌉ the

---

ªFull fivefold titulary.

ᵇRead *ḫꜥ·t*, lit., "*the appearance of his majesty . . . .*"

ᶜOr: "*Bearer (wṯs)-of-beauty*," which must be the name of the palace.

ᵈThe sanctuary of Atum was at Heliopolis, and his writings would be there; this explains why the messenger of the king journeys southward to Abydos (l. 14), whereas he would have gone northward from the royal residence in Thebes.

ᵉThe reference is apparently to a council of the gods in which the form of the god's statue was determined once for all. This the king expects to find in the ancient writings.

circuit of the sun ⁵ . . . . I will increase that which I shall have investigated,ᵃ and they shall ⌜increase⌝ love for me — to ⁶do according to that which they command."

Reply of Court

757. These companions said: "That which thy ka hath ⌜commanded⌝ᵇ is that which happens, O sovereign and lord. Let thy majesty proceed to the libraries,ᶜ and let thy majesty see every hieroglyph."

Examination of Ancient Rolls

758. His majesty proceeded ⁷to the library. His majesty opened the rolls together with these companions. Lo, his majesty found the rolls of the House of Osiris, First of the Westerners, lord of Abydos.

King's Purpose

759. His majesty said to these companions: "My majesty ⁸hails my father Osiris, First of the Westerners, lord of Abydos. I will fashion ⌜him, his limbs — his face, his fingers⌝ according to that which my majesty has seen in the rolls ⌜— —⌝ his ⌜form⌝ as King of Upper and Lower Egypt, at his coming forth from the body of Nut.ᵈ ⁹. . . . . . ¹². . . . .ᵉ

Messenger Sent to Abydos

760. His majesty had the king's-confidant, who was in his majesty's suite, called to him; his majesty said [to] him: ¹³"Betake thyself southward — — [⌜together with⌝] troops⌝ and marines. Sleep not night nor day until thou arrivest at Abydos; cause the First of the Westerners

---

ᵃOr: "*that which is assigned to me.*" He means he will increase what his investigation shows is demanded in the ancient writings.

ᵇThe emendation is almost certain. Cf. the similar statement in the instruction to the priests of Abydos (II, 91, l. 5).

ᶜLit., "*houses of writings or rolls.*"

ᵈHe means he has found in the writings the original form of the god as king at his birth.

ᵉThe remainder of the king's speech contains only conventional phrases, in the course of which, reference is again made to "*making the monuments of Osiris and perpetuating the name of Wennofer*" (l. 10). The answer of the courtiers is very short (occupying the first half of l. 12) and very fragmentary.

(Osiris) to proceed (forth).[a]   May I make his monuments according to
[14]the beginning."[b]

Reply of Court

761. These companions said: "⌜That which thou commandest
[is that which happens, O sovereign]⌝[c] and lord; thou doest all — in
Abydos for thy father, First of the Westerners."

Messenger Departs

762. This official betook himself southward[d] [to do] [15]that which
his majesty commanded him. He arrived at [Abydos] ⌜—⌝ — —.
The majesty of this god came to the sacred barge of the lord of eternity ⌜— —⌝ the banks of the river were flooded [⌜with his fragrance and
with⌝] [16]the odors of Punt.[e] [The majesty of this god] arrived in the
midst — — —.   One came to inform his majesty, saying: "This god
has proceeded in peace."

King Goes to Abydos

763. His majesty proceeded [⌜in⌝] [17]the sacred ship . . . .[f]
together with this god, causing that sacred offerings be presented to
his father, the First of the Westerners: myrrh — [18]and sacred things
for Osiris, First of the Westerners, in all his names . . . .[g]
those hostile to the sacred barge were overthrown.   Lo, the majesty
of this god appeared in procession,[h] his ennead united [⌜with him⌝].
[19]Upwawet was before him, he opened the ways[i] . . . .

---

[a]In order to meet the king at his coming to Abydos, as the conclusion shows.

[b]The original form as at the beginning of the world, which he learned from
the rolls.

[c]Restored from l. 6.

[d]Because the royal party is at Heliopolis (see note, l. 3) there is no reason
here to suppose that the royal residence is in the north.

[e]There is no trace of an expedition to Punt here, as frequently stated; the
description is the usual one accompanying the bodily approach of a god; see that
of Amon, II § 196.

[f]Evidently the meeting of the king and the god occurred at this point; there is
a reference to the "*head of the canal,*" probably the canal on which the god voyaged in his barge to meet the king. See Great Abydos Inscription of Ramses II,
l. 29.

[g]A series of incidents in the myth of the god are now dramatically enacted by
the priests as the procession of the king and the god moves toward Abydos.

[h]He leaves the barge, to return in procession to the temple.

[i]The name of the god Upwawet (*Wp-wꜣwt*) means: "*Opener of the ways.*"
One of the priests, wearing a jackal mask, acts the part of Upwawet.

King Executes Temple W

764. Lo, ⌈his majesty caused that this god sho⌉
that he should rest [on] his throne in the house of gold; in order to
fashion the beauty of his majesty[a] and his ennead, his oblation-tables
— — — of [20]every splendid, costly stone of God's-Land.   Behold, [the
king] himself led the work on them — gold, (for) his majesty was pure
with the purity of a god . . . .[b]

King's Concluding Speech

765. [33]. . . . . Be ye vigilant for the temple, look to the
monuments [34]which I have made.   I put the eternal plan before me,
I sought that which was useful for the future by putting this example
in your hearts, which is about to occur in this place, which the god made,
because of my desire [35]to establish my monuments in his temple, to
perpetuate my contracts[c] in his house.   His majesty loves that which
I have done for him, he rejoices over that which I have decreed to do,
(⌈for⌉) triumph ⌈has been given⌉ to him.   [36]I am his son, his protector,
he giveth to me the inheritance of the earth.[d]   [I] am the king, great
in strength, excellent in commandment.   He shall not live who is hostile
to me; he shall not breathe [37]the air who revolts against me; his name
shall not be among the living; his ka shall be seized before the officials; he shall be cast out for this god, [⌈together with⌉] him who shall
disregard the command of my majesty and those who shall not [38]do
according to this command of my majesty, who shall not exalt me to
this august god, who shall not honor that which I have done concerning his offerings [who shall not] give to me praise [39]at every feast of this
temple, of the entire [lay priesthood][e] of the sanctuary of this temple,
and every office of Abydos.   Behold, my majesty has made these monu-

---

[a]The god; he is taken to the workshop of the goldsmith, that a new statue
may be made.

[b]The further execution of the work is narrated in a few very fragmentary
sentences, in which is the interesting statement: "*No scribe who was in the suite
of his majesty had ever found it*" (l. 21), referring doubtless to the king's discovery
in the rolls.   The continuation merges (l. 22) into a long speech of the king,
addressed to the god; at l. 27 begins a prayer of the king, which merges at l. 32 into
an address to the court.

[c]See § 535.   [d]"*The estate of the earth,*" literally.

[e]Restored from Rougé, *Inscriptions hiéroglyphiques*, XXI, l. **15**.